Praise for *The Professional Soldier*

"He knew us better than we knew ourselves. In his brilliant, time-less classic *The Professional Soldier*, Morris Janowitz brought a superb sociologist's perception, candor, and yes, sympathy, to his consideration of the U.S. military officer corps. As a World War II veteran himself, he had every reason to question what made American officers tick. This classic book is the result. If you've read it before, re-read it. If you are opening *The Professional Soldier* for the first time, you are about to embark on a trip very much worth taking, guided by one of our country's finest scholars, the late and rightly renowned Morris Janowitz."

—Lieutenant General (ret.) Daniel P. Bolger, AM, PhD

"*The Professional Soldier* is as valuable as ever, both for those who serve under oath to the Republic and for those who do not. Its hypotheses still frame basic issues that military leaders must constantly address: What does it mean to be a military professional? and Why does it matter that soldiers are military professionals, not simply cogs in a big government bureaucracy? An absolute must read for military professionals and civilians alike."

—Don M. Snider, PhD, professor emeritus at West Point

"*The Professional Soldier* is a comprehensive and critical portrait of the officer's role. A must-read, it tells how professional soldiers adapt to the changing demands of war, to protect and sustain the values of liberal democratic societies."

—James Burk, professor at Texas A&M University
and president of the Inter-University Seminar
on Armed Forces and Society

MORRIS JANOWITZ

The Professional Soldier

A SOCIAL AND POLITICAL PORTRAIT

FREE PRESS

NEW YORK   LONDON   TORONTO   SYDNEY   NEW DELHI

To My Parents
on the occasion of their golden anniversary

Free Press
An imprint of Simon & Schuster, Inc.
1230 Avenue of the Americas
New York, NY 10020

This Free Press trade paperback edition July 2017

FREE PRESS and colophon are trademarks of Simon & Schuster, Inc.

For information about special discounts for bulk purchases,
please contact Simon & Schuster Special Sales at 1-866-506-1949
or business@simonandschuster.com.

The Simon & Schuster Speakers Bureau can bring authors to your live event.
For more information or to book an event, contact the Simon & Schuster Speakers
Bureau at 1-866-248-3049 or visit our website at www.simonspeakers.com.

Manufactured in the United States of America

10 9 8 7 6 5 4 3 2 1

Library of Congress Cataloging-in-Publication Data is available.

ISBN 978-0-02-916170-8
ISBN 978-1-5011-7932-7 (pbk)

Contents

IV. The Military Community: The Persistence of Manners

V. Identity and Ideology: The Public Service Tradition

VI. Political Behavior: Pragmatic versus Absolutist

VII. Political Technique: Pressure Group Tactics

VIII. Epilogue: Toward the Constabulary Concept

Prologue: The Decline of the Mass Armed Force

WHEN the original edition of *The Professional Soldier: A Social and Political Portrait*, appeared in 1960, social research on the military profession in the United States was only beginning to emerge as a subject for academic investigation. The purpose of that particular research effort was to describe the developments of the preceding half century, during which the U.S. military had emerged as a mammoth institution based on a professional cadre and a system of conscription. It had, in fact, evolved into a mass armed force parallel to the military establishments of Western Europe and the Soviet Union, since it was designed to engage in "total war."

The first years of the twentieth century, when Elihu Root established the general staff and refashioned the Army, can be considered as the period when the modern mass military originated in the United States. However, 1960 can, in retrospect, be viewed as a rather arbitrary date in the history of the contemporary military establishment. In the ensuing decade, 1960–1970, the armed forces, together with the rest of American society, experienced the agonies of prolonged hostilities. Vietnam contributed to the crisis in legitimacy of U.S. political institutions that had its roots in the tensions of social change in an advanced industrial society. Vietnam produced high levels of civilian hostility toward the military as well as pervasive dilemmas and a weakening of authority within the military. The same decade also produced the continuation of the nuclear arms race, the search for a new perspective in foreign policy incorporating the element of détente, and the emergence of President Richard Nixon's appeal for "no more Vietnams."

The mass armed force rests on the principle that the military plans for and is able to execute a vast mobilization of manpower to fight a conventional war. It uses conscription to recruit its manpower. But, since 1945, the strategy of deterrence has required a greater reliance on a force "in being"—one composed of highly trained specialists, the bulk of whom are in place. If the establishment of the mass armed force in the United States can be linked to the administration of Elihu Root, then there is every reason to believe that with the termination of conscription on June 30, 1973, the end of an epoch was signalled. On the occasion of the reprinting of *The Professional Soldier* it is appropriate to seek to extend the original hypotheses to cover the full seventy-five years from the turn of the century to the end of conscription to encompass the rise and transformation of the mass armed force.

Under the impact of nuclear weapons, the changing environment of international relations, and the persistent personal opposition to military service, the United States, like other parliamentary political systems, accepted the decline of the "citizen army" and moved toward an all-volunteer–all-"professional" force in being. Such a manpower system was recommended as appropriate for the strategy of deterrence. The movement toward an all-volunteer force was also advocated in the 1968 elections by elements of both the Republican and Democratic Congressional leadership as appropriate for the sociopolitical system of the United States. In the original edition of *The Professional Soldier*, the conception of the constabulary was offered as a construct to anticipate and explain this transformation in military organization.

To speak of the trend of the military from a mass armed force based on conscription to an all-volunteer force "in being" is not to assess the issues of adequate civilian control and organizational effectiveness for a strategy of deterrence. The introduction of the all-volunteer force in the United States was accompanied by sharp public criticism of its political implications and of the feasibility of creating an effective and responsible all-volunteer force in terms of social composition, quality, and integration in the larger society.

The basic hypotheses presented in the original edition of *The Professional Soldier* concerning the rise of the mass armed force highlighted the increased convergence of military and civilian institutions and the greater interpretation of the military and the civilian sectors of society. The shift to an all-volunteer force requires an examination of the limitations in this trend, and of the possibility of selective reversals—of a separation of the civilian and the military sectors, especially as the military struggles to maintain its organizational identity and its professional jurisdiction. Under the mass armed force, with its immense allocation of national resources and its profound impact on international relations, patterns of civil–military and civilian control have been strained. However, there is no reason to anticipate that the all-volunteer military will automatically reduce these strains on civilian control; instead, it is necessary to examine those trends which are likely to maintain political controversies concerning the position and the role of the military in American society.

Contemporary History and Military Institutions

POLITICAL scientists and sociologists who deal with contemporary military institutions must make use of an appropriate historical perspective. The second Indochina war had a profound impact on American society and on the military professional. On university campuses, opposition to the war generated a pervasive political debate and became the focal point of violent disruption. University personnel, both faculty and students, produced a vast flow of polemical literature on the military-industrial complex and an ex-tensive stream of documentation and analysis on the enormous destructive consequences of military operations. The involvement of universities in war-related research erupted into an issue of deep passion and conviction and produced physical violence, including bombings. Considerable attention was devoted to the role of the academic in the Vietnam war and to the issues of the position and responsibilities of intellectuals in contemporary American society.

The Spanish Civil War in the 1930's shook the academic community and divided it into competing political factions. The Vietnam hostilities produced even deeper political fissures, and for the moment, the very academic enterprise was threatened. Social scientists were at the center of the debate and agitation. Conditions did not appear particularly suitable for the scholarly study of military institutions and civil-military relations. There were distortions and temporary excesses in the academic enterprise. On the one hand, a handful of scholars pursued research on politico-military aspects of the war in Vietnam by means of their access to secret information and became the object of extensive attack. On the other hand, political criticism of the war in Vietnam led not only to attacks on government-sponsored social science research but to pressure on persons who were continuing their academic interests in such subjects. Nevertheless, during this decade of intense unrest in universities for the first time in American intellectual history, an initially small but enlarging group of independent academic persons were completing penetrating research on the military profession and military institutions in the United States and on a comparative basis.

The contributions of these independent scholars, including the social scientists affiliated with the Inter-University Seminar on Armed Forces and Society, helped to supply a broader context in which to observe the trends in the military profession associated with the impact of nuclear weapons and the end of conscription.* It is possible, in fact, to assert that U.S. military intervention in Vietnam represents, historically, an extension of military elements of World War II—elements of total war. This intervention can be described as a throwback in the transformation of the mass armed force rather than as a reflection of emerging trends. In effect, the impact of long-term trends in technology and international relations becomes fused with the specific consequences of Vietnam. Even without the impact of the second Indochina war, the trend away from conscription was in process. Thus it is possible to ask the questions: In what ways has the military profession in the United States undergone long-term and fundamental change since 1945? What new elements of change are emerging as a result of the end of conscription in 1973? What has happened to the basic organizational trends described in *The Professional Soldier?* In accounting for change, how relevant are the concepts offered in the original edition?

Shifts in strategic perspectives among the professional officers are of central importance. In *The Professional Soldier* a distinction was made between the "absolutists"—men who thought in terms of traditional conceptions of military victory—and the "pragmatists" —men concerned with the measured application of military force and its political consequences.** Does this distinction continue to have validity? Has there been a strengthening of the absolutist elements under the frustration of "no war, no peace" and the impact of Vietnam?

Fundamental changes in a profession and a bureaucracy as vast and as complex as the military do not take place suddenly. During the first half of the twentieth century, the long-term trend in military organization was toward the emergence and dominance of the "mass army," or, more precisely, the "mass armed force." The military in the United States, paralleling the military establishments of other major industrialized nations, underwent a continuous and consistent transformation, accelerated during World War I and World

---

* Selected bibliography of the Inter-University Seminar on Armed Forces and Society is presented on p. 467 of this volume.
** See pp. 264–267 of this volume.

War II and arrested to varying degrees during peacetime. The introduction of modern technology and large-scale managerial techniques produced the mass armed force and led to the concept and reality of total war.

Total war is a prenuclear notion. It refers to the development of mobilization plans during peacetime, to comprehensive conversion of the civilian population in support of mass armies during war, and to the military use of air power. The distinction between the military forces and the civilian population is weakened; both become the subjects of military organization and the objects of attack, propaganda, and political warfare.[1]

The transformation of the military profession during the world wars was based on existing trends in invention, organization, and firepower. The outcome was a convergence of military and civilian organization: the interpenetration of the civilian and the military is required as more and more of the resources of the nation-state are used in preparing for and making war. It became appropriate to speak of the "civilianization" of the military profession and of the parallel penetration of military forms into civilian social structure.

The transformation of the mass armed force in the Western parliamentary nations, including the United States, is obviously not linked to a single historical event, although clearly the application of nuclear theory to military enterprise is crucial. It is not possible to fix a terminal date for the historical period of the mass armed force, since the end of its dominance is a long-term and gradual process. However, the main outlines of the new directions in military organization were first manifest after the end of World War II. In varying degrees, in most industrialized nations—especially those with nuclear weapons or in alliance with nuclear powers—the new trend was toward smaller, fully professional, and more fully alerted and self-contained military forces; the direction was to move away from a mobilization force to a military force "in being."[2]

The development of nuclear weapons and their use against Japan in 1945 marked both the end of World War II and the introduction of the technology from which the new trend would develop. The Korean war was fought as a continuation of the World War II format. However, in 1952, with President Eisenhower's assumption of power, the promulgation of the doctrine of "massive retaliation" may well be taken by historians as a crucial point in the movement away from the dominance of the mass armed force. Nevertheless, the Eisenhower administration continued the draft system in order to maintain and extend the system of international alliance v·hich required important elements of the mass armed force.

The implication of nuclear weapons and "wars of national liberation" had become progressively pressing difficulties in the consciousness of U.S. political and military leaders. In 1960, the Kennedy administration came into office with the intention of reassessing U.S. foreign power and military policy. The combined strategy of "flexible response," plus the use of ground and air formations on a relatively large scale in Vietnam, required a continuation of the mass army and total warfare. The deep involvements of rank-and-file professional officers in politico-military assignments in Vietnam, such as intelligence, propaganda, military assistance, and nation-building, became increasingly important adjuncts to a military definition of their mission.[3]

Outside Vietnam, officers came to spend most of their energies on assignments connected with a strategy of deterrence of global nuclear war and on an increasing number and variety of tasks labeled "stability operations." At home in the United States, for a number of years after 1967, federal military forces became more involved in domestic law enforcement, particularly in racial conflict: tasks that were accepted with considerable reluctance. As the extent and intensity of racial conflict declined at the end of the 1960's, these involvements contracted sharply. However, the military, particularly the U.S. Army, were assigned duties related to domestic intelligence surveillance, of both doubtful constitutionality and effectiveness, giving rise to persistent opposition within and without the military establishment. There were objections to token educational programs such as Project 100,000, designed to offer remedial assistance to recruits as part of routine training functions. This opposition, plus the pressure of Vietnam, led the military leaders to define their roles in specific military terms.

Throughout the years of the second Indochina war, the intensity of the military campaign reduced pressure to restructure the military in accordance with the realities of nuclear weapons and the role of nationalism in the emerging nations. Thus, to examine trends in military organization, we must probe deeper than the impact of Vietnam, even though the operations there had a pervasive influence on professional self-conceptions and self-esteem. Again and again, the assertion—the general hypothesis—that the introduction of an all-volunteer force slows the trends toward civilianization becomes a focal point for examining civil–military relations. This is not to suggest a return to earlier forms of a highly self-contained and socially distinct military force; the requirements of technology of education and of political support make that impossible. Moreover, the outcome of the all-volunteer force is hardly predetermined; it involves the consequences of political policy and administrative leadership.

Sheer size operates as a crucial parameter: The all-volunteer force is a smaller establishment. At the height of the Vietnam war, the armed force reached a manpower total of 3.6 million. In 1970, President Nixon's Commission on an All-Volunteer Armed Force estimated that a force of 2.5 million would be attained.[4] By 1973, the Department of Defense reported that the total force level had dropped to 2.2 million; and Congress took fiscal steps in 1974 to reduce the number to approximately 2.1 million. Projections for the period after 1980 ranged from 2.0 million down to 1.75 million, as a result of both fiscal constraint and the difficulties of recruiting qualified personnel.[5]

Limits of Civilianization

THE MILITARY profession consists of a mixture of heroic leaders, military managers, and technical specialists; and one officer can come to embody various mixtures of these elements. As a result, even during the period of most intensive civilianization—World War II—the military could not be transformed into a large-scale civilian organization. With the approach of the end of the period of the mass armed force, it becomes necessary to examine and to probe the limits and countertrends in the military profession toward civilianization. First, with the end of World War II, the military establishment, like any other institution, has struggled to defend its boundaries against external intrusion and to maintain its distinctive character. Although the military has had to respond selectively to civilian influence after World War II, it has consciously sought to limit civilianization by defending prerogatives which it believed were crucial. Above all else, all three services have sought to increase the number and proportion of officers trained at the service academies and to maintain a strong emphasis on the importance of academy training as a route to elite positions. Before the Air Force Academy was established in 1955, enrollment at the two service academies numbered less than 6,200. With the establishment of the Air Force Academy and the expansion of West Point and Annapolis, the number of military cadets in the academies rose to approximately 13,000 by 1970.

The academy system is based on the notion that an early decision to become a career officer, plus four years of military academy education, will produce strong commitments to the military establishment. Since the end of World War II, college-bound youngsters graduating from high school find it more and more difficult to make an early career decision. In certain universities, as many as one-third change their academic specialization or professional goals, and a comparable uncertainty was operating in the military academies. With the end of conscription, the numbers of cadets resigning while studying at the academies, especially at the Air Force Academy, grew to such an extent as to attract attention; in 1972, more than one-third of the entering class terminated their work. This reflects the general trend of shifting undergraduate choices plus the special concerns about a military career.

Moreover, although between 20 and 25 per cent of academy graduates leave the service after their obligated tour of duty, those who remain have the strongest commitments to the autonomy of the profession and to the values of military honor. They have, in fact, risen to dominate the general and flag-officer ranks. The concentration of academy graduates among general and flag officers decreased somewhat during the early 1960's, as high-caliber personnel who had entered the officer corps directly from civilian life during World War II and had stayed in the service after the war were promoted into those ranks. But at no time was the overall dominance of academy officers threatened. This dominance manifested itself even in the Air Force, the service branch with the most open system of promotion: in 1968, all of its thirteen generals and 41 per cent of its lieutenant generals were graduates of a service academy. In the Army that same year, all fourteen generals and 79 per cent of the forty-three lieutenant generals were academy graduates. All of the forty-three admirals and vice-admirals in the Navy were graduates. In addition, 40 per cent of the one hundred eighty-six rear admirals were in this category. As the total size of the armed force is reduced, the increasingly large numbers of new academy graduates will have an even more decisive effect.

Second, the self-conceptions and professional ideology of the military officer have served as a powerful counterforce to civilianization. The activities subsumed under the term "military" are immense and, in fact, are mainly logistical and administrative. Nevertheless, the notion of combat—preparation for battle and actual battle—has remained a central military value. It is, of course, the case that an outstanding characteristic of the military is the vastly increased proportion of its personnel and resources engaged in technical, logistical, and administrative overhead which, in effect, creates an organization remotely connected with military life. Only a small minority is directly involved in combat operations. Moreover, the armed forces have incorporated many operations which could be performed by civilian agencies and which decrease the effectiveness of military units.

There has also been a long-term percentage decline in the statistics of deaths during wartime. Gilbert W. Beebe and Michael DeBakey present their analysis of the long-term decline in mortality from all causes in the U.S. Army on the basis of deaths per 1,000 men per year. From the high of 122.3 in the Mexican War, the figure declined to 12.9 in World War II.[6] On the basis of the same calculations, the rate continued to decline during the Korean hostilities but the downward trend did not continue in Vietnam.[7]

However, neither the weight of the logistical and technical services nor the decline in battle casualties reflects the "definition of the situation" as experienced by the professional soldier. In particular, the professional soldier does not consider risk to life as accidental, as the result of some malfunctioning or temporary breakdown in the system. Casualties are an expected outcome of military operations. Every casualty on civilian airlines is an accident, although its statistical frequency can be estimated and anticipated. But, in the mind of the officer, every military operation carries inherent risk and uncertainty that are "normal."

Military operations include training and, for the military, casualties are inherent in these military preparations. Even when the military are engaged in essentially defensive, protective, and constabulary types of activities, the element of risk and uncertainty is viewed as part of the standard operating procedure. This calculus is a powerful stimulant to the belief that military institutions are inherently different from the civilian.

Career officers have accepted the idea of deterrence as a strategy. Many have even accepted the belief that major wars are not inevitable, and they recognize the wide range of politico–military assignments they are likely to have. They emphasize that deterrence is effective because some men are prepared to fight. In this fighter spirit, there is very little of a "gung ho" sentiment except among some junior officers; it is more of a patterned response. The idea of a constabulary force, the notion that a soldier may have an effective career without ever fighting, has come to enjoy a widespread but superficial acceptance. But only a small minority fully realize the implications of such a professional outlook. These are the innovative nucleus of officers who are convinced that it is possible to incorporate in a single military man and a particular military institution the potentials both of combat and of arms control and peace-keeping.

Officers who aspire to high command believe that at least some combat experience is required in the development of an effective professional soldier. To aspire openly to a world without war is still thought to be irresponsible and professionally self-destructive. Vietnam and the Arab-Israeli conflicts have strengthened this outlook but, even without these realities, the combat spirit would have remained dominant.

Third, the boundaries of the military as a social organization are more than the mental definitions that its members create. The realities of military strategy, the admixture of weapons systems and the politico-military rules for employing them, have served gradually since 1945 (and more decisively since 1960) to limit the trend toward civilianization. A national defense strategy which relies on nuclear weapons produces a military force with increasingly distinct boundaries.

At the upper end of the destructive continuum, nuclear weapons of mass destruction must be manned by a force in being. The Air Force and the Army have become more and more a force in being, similar in this aspect to the Navy. The key training periods are extended, although there remains a significant number of tasks which can be filled by short-term recruits. A man is either in the nuclear deterrent or he is not. In this respect, the dividing line is more distinct than during the period of conventional weapons and mass civilian mobilization. Those who manage weapons of mass destruction are exposed to grave risks. The need to deal with the unexpected is not a matter of actual battle but an ongoing concern; a military atmosphere becomes pervasive. In short, nuclear weapons are fundamentally different from nonnuclear weapons in that their military character derives from their mere existence, without their ever being used. The incorporation of nuclear weapons creates an organizational climate which is military and distinct from nonmilitary institutions.

At the lower end of the continuum of destructive capacity, under a nuclear strategy, are conventional war units which tend to be converted (although very slowly) more and more to forces in being—that is, into smaller segments, more self-contained and readily alerted. The withdrawal of the ground forces from Vietnam accelerated this trend. Mobilization plans are deemphasized and the role of the reserves, except for those units actually in the effective ready reserves, becomes more circumscribed. Every deployment of conventional forces becomes part of the logic of strategic deterrence and the need to avoid nuclear confrontation. These forces do not have a strategy of their own, since their operations derive from the larger goal of preventing the outbreak of nuclear war. The scope of conventional military action becomes highly delimited, and, to be effective, the conventional forces must be fully trained and prepared for immediate action—again, a force in being.

The day-to-day requirements of military management of the all-volunteer force lead to a range of specific internal adaptations, since military organizations cannot be "drastically" overhauled. If the frustration and pressure of Vietnam served to retard innovative professional perspectives about the strategic role of the military, the transition to an all-volunteer force required and produced a range of specific and piecemeal adaptations of cumulative impact. By reexamining the basic propositions presented in *The Professional Soldier*, the pattern of organizational stability and change is highlighted:

1. *Changing Organizational Authority.* In the military profession, issues of authority are paramount, explicitly debated at great length, and elaborately reduced to formal regulations. Officers seek to impose a pattern of order on an intractable environment. A striking aspect of the military system is the constant effort to make these regulations more precise and detailed, carefully defining jurisdictions and command channels. The grave responsibilities of men who think of themselves as "managers of violence" make this preoccupation with authority a peculiarly military phenomenon. The emergence of a worldwide establishment with an array of weapons from nuclear warheads to darts equipped with botulinum has required a highly elaborate system of operational control called "command and control."

The older term "command" has had to be modernized, that is, given more symbolic content and made to reflect the complex tasks of maintaining military force under effective restraint. At the core of the decision-making function, a vast communications and electronic data-processing system operates. The military establishment has rapidly incorporated the mechanics of computer management, not only for logistical and personnel allocations, but also for the detailed oversight of military operations. Computer control systems have come to be used in the full range of military activities, from the worldwide employment of nuclear weapons to the establishment of data banks for combat intelligence of small units in Vietnam.

This apparatus contributes to the imagery both of centralized authority and of an organizational climate of detached and rational decision-making. Moreover, the procedures of cost-accounting, cost-benefit analysis, and other statistical devices pressed by civilian officials in the Department of Defense, especially Robert McNamara, have served to publicize the emergence of "managerial authority." Although stubbornly resistant to such statistical and accounting procedures, military planning and operations are, at any given moment, deeply imbedded in quantitative and "scientific" authority. Command and control systems often function with an important time lag behind immediate realities. Moreover, complex and vast data banks have been constructed for politico-military operations in Vietnam without regard for the quality and accuracy of the information. In preparing for domestic disorder assignments, the Army launched a computerized surveillance system of doubtful effectiveness involving over 1,000 agents which, because it exceeded the traditional role of the military, had to be curtailed in the face of widespread public criticism.

Elaborate plans and preparations are repeatedly scrapped for direct, on-the-spot intervention. It almost appears as if the more serious the crisis, the less applicable are programmed patterns of communication and response. During the Cuban missile crisis, the entire command, including the communications system, was pushed aside by the direct intervention of President Kennedy and his immediate staff. Again, in planning and supervising the military incursion in Cambodia in 1970, President Nixon created a completely ad hoc personal military staff.

The magnitude, complexity, and destructiveness of military operations in the second Indochina war have called into question the logic and effectiveness of elements of the command and control system. Each command and control system required accurate and meaningful information, yet, information on "body counts" and air raid destruction was, at crucial points, neither accurate nor meaningful. Military operations developed their own momentum which operated without effective control—or even resisted control. The specific case of the "unauthorized" bombings by General John D. Lavelle indicates that command and control systems can be distorted to permit wide deviation from political control or can be used to allow political leaders to pursue purposefully ambiguous policies.

However, the military establishment, by its own inner logic and requirements, has no alternative but to continue its preoccupation with command and control. The very notion of strategic direction of a nuclear deterrent rests in the mechanics of command and control. The initials WWMCCS stand for Worldwide Military Command and Control, a complex of men and computerized communications channels unequalled in expense and complexity by any civilian enterprise. This is an indispensable facility for preventing nuclear disaster, though its reliability is as yet unproved.

In routine operations, the military establishment, as any large-scale organization, functions with a powerful gap between formal authority and day-to-day operational requirements. All efforts at writing regulations fail to eliminate this gap. At each point, from the very top to the lowest operational unit, the elaborate chain of command and complex information-handling systems are paralleled by informal communication linkages—personal inspections, oral briefings, command conferences, and face-to-face discussions—that infuse a basic ingredient of vitality into the massive organization. In the language of the Pentagon staff officer, to "grease the skids" means to make the formal system work by means of the informal network of personal trust which binds the armed forces into a social organization. In actuality, military authority is a strange mixture of official regulations, scientific expertise, and mutual trust, plus a strong component of personal authority.

During World War I and World War II, the pressure of combat and the intervention of civilian leadership, combined with the infusion of a mass of civilian recruits, required professional officers to adjust traditional forms of authority to immediate tasks. The sheer complexity of the technology of war reinforced these external pressures. *The Professional Soldier* offered the hypothesis that there had been a change in the basis of authority and discipline in the military establishment, a shift from authoritative domination to greater reliance on explanation, expertise, and group consensus.

At the end of World War II, a reversion to the traditional discipline and authority patterns of the interwar years was a real possibility. However, the increased complexity of military technology and the continuous pressure of worldwide military operations ruled out a reemergence of old-fashioned garrison life. In addition, the changing social structure and the new moral values of civilian society meant that new generations of recruits and officers entering the armed forces held different standards of personal behavior. The clash of generations in civilian society has been strongly reflected in the military, since many regular officers felt that the armed forces, even more than civilian institutions, should enforce what they believed to be desirable norms and values.

But the military have had to separate their professional ideology from their actual practices. The need to fight a difficult war in Vietnam and the advent of an all-volunteer armed force have continued to supply powerful incentives to limit traditionalism, rigidity and ceremonialism. It is, of course, well known that the elaborate regulations and procedures of the military are attenuated during operational assignments, especially in combat. Under such conditions, authority is based less on formal rank and legal authority and more on personal leadership and the ability to create primary group solidarity and small unit effectiveness. In actual combat, there is a strong expression of consensual authority.

Strains on authority vary from service to service but the ground forces have suffered the greatest difficulties. For career officers who have been on active duty since the end of World War II, the transformation has been dramatic and immense. At the core there have been modifications in the system of military justice which have made wide areas of military life subject to review by civilian courts. Also of central importance has been the redefinition of the work day in garrison life to an eight-to-five assignment, which thereby limits the "total institution" character of the military community. The military have emphasized a variety of leadership and management training and procedures designed to reduce authoritarian and arbitrary procedures. Special seminars have been introduced on human relations, race relations, and deviant behavior. A sizable minority of military officers and noncommissioned officers have become convinced that these shifts have been excessive and represent undue civilianization.

In the Vietnam war, military authorities had to face hostile public opinion in the United States and extensive disaffection with military service among young people. The mass media highlighted dramatic antiwar incidents both in and around military bases. For the first time, the armed forces had to deal with a persistent and politically organized antiwar movement within their own ranks, and this movement, regardless of its limited size, attracted considerable attention. Antiwar petitions, underground newspapers, and the activities of a core of dedicated radicals on active duty became routine features of military life.

Indifferent and hostile mass public opinion and a weakened sense of legitimacy about the war in Vietnam have been central problems in the exercise of military authority. For the first time in contemporary history, the military forces came to believe they are not being "supported" by the population at large. The war in Vietnam placed the professional soldier in a position at variance with an important segment of the civilian population, as World War II and Korea never did. Also, in contrast to World War II, as the war in Vietnam continued, public estimation of the legitimacy of military operations in Vietnam decreased. Using an index of public opinion based on national survey data, Robert Smith found that opposition to participation in World War II fell from 34 per cent in the year prior to Pearl Harbor, 1941, to about 8 per cent in 1944.[8] However, public opposition to the war in Vietnam rose from 24 per cent in July, 1965, to 57 per cent in January, 1970.

For young men, negative attitudes to Selective Service also rose as the Vietnam war continued and reached higher levels than during World War II. For example, voluntary appeals from Selective Service classification went from 4 per 10,000 registrants in 1965 to 102 per 10,000 in 1969. In 1968, 8 per 10,000 registrants were classified as conscientious objectors, as compared with 4 per 10,000 during World War II. However, the desertion rate was lower for Vietnam than for World War II. During World War II, the rate reached 63 per 10,000, whereas for Vietnam it rose from 14.7 per 10,000 in 1966 to 29.1 per 10,000 in 1969. Young men opposed to the Vietnam war found it easier to avoid service.

Although morale problems were most serious in the ground forces, both because of their reliance on draftees and because of the character of their operational missions, the military command was not faced with a lack of initiative on the part of the Army and Marine troops in Vietnam up and through the period of the Tet offensive in Vietnam during February, 1968. Soldiers fought because of their vague perception of a military mission and the effective leadership of their junior and noncommissioned officers, who succeeded in developing high levels of primary group solidarity, a basic ingredient of military morale. Operational forces were supplied with extensive air and artillery cover, which strengthened infantry morale but made strategic objectives more difficult to attain by causing excessive civilian casualties and disruption. The rotation system, which limited a tour of duty to about eleven months, was also crucial for the exercise of military authority in the field. Morale was raised by the fact that the ordinary soldier had finite goals, but, in turn, the rotation limited the effectiveness of combat units. There is no reason to believe that powerful or extensive political convictions or ideology permeated the forces in the field. Charles Moskos, on the basis of his field studies in Vietnam, speaks of a "latent" ideology, based on generalized patriotism and a vague and stubborn anti-Communist sentiment.[9]

The impact of the Tet offensive, the decision of President Johnson not to seek reelection, and the strategy of withdrawal pursued by President Nixon presented commanders, especially junior officers in the field, with the most difficult problem of authority the military had faced since the Civil War. When it was decided to intervene in Cambodia, troop effectiveness was adequate: specific, attainable objectives are a basis of short-term high morale. Nevertheless, after 1968, a marked tendency to limit casualties and avoid combat developed. This tendency has been supported and encouraged at all levels, from the office of the President down to small unit commanders. Such a response was to be expected when the senior officers in Vietnam, including General Westmoreland, concluded that a "traditional military victory" in the field was unattainable.

The automatic application of sanctions declined and giving explicit orders yielded at points to bargaining between higher and lower-level commanders. As in any organization under stress, a small minority of key personnel continued to supply the essential initiatives. Future historians will document the various forms of personal withdrawal and overt resistance to command in the field, including physical attacks on officers. Most publicized was the increased use of drugs, which by January, 1971, was officially acknowledged to constitute a military problem and which may in retrospect be judged as much a mode of accommodation to continued involvement as a form of resistance.[10]

As a result, the transition to an all-volunteer manpower system had to be instituted during a period of immense organizational strain and turbulence. The strategy of Congressional and Executive leadership to achieve the all-volunteer force rested mainly on increased pay to make the military competitive with civilian employment. However, the character and quality of military life, especially its forms of authority and visible purpose, were crucial elements in the recruitment and retention of personnel.

It was anticipated and it emerged that the closer the conditions of day-to-day existence—training and routine operations—were to its presumed military function, the more feasible would be the transition. Thus, the Air Force, which had a strong emphasis on volunteer recruitment, experienced the least difficulty, because the ongoing tasks of the Air Force—flying, manning the nuclear deterrence, and related maintenance functions—supplied an effective basis for operational morale. The Navy had a strong volunteer tradition and it functioned as a force in being as a result of its routine flying and "sailing" responsibilities as well as its nuclear deterrence role. It was expected that the Navy would experience some difficulties in the transition, because of its extensive disruption of family life and the Navy man's long separation from home.

However, it was the ground force that faced the greatest difficulties in volunteer recruitment, especially in its combat units. This was the case not only because of the lower prestige and the less desirable quality of life in the Army, but also because of the wide gap between training and day-to-day garrison life and the expected realities of its military function. However, as a result of special bonus payments and the opportunity to enlist in a unit of one's choice the ground forces were able to meet their manpower requirement during the fiscal year 1974. The ground forces recruitment efforts also include a highly successful two-year enlistment oriented to college-bound men who were prepared to serve for this time period and who saw in the financial benefit a means of earning an important portion of their college expenses. The Marine Corps presented a special case. Its top officers believe that because of its volunteer tradition and because of its "stern" authority it would be attractive to a small faction of the U.S. youth sufficient in number to meet its manpower requirements. By mid-1974, however, it had experienced noteworthy deficits in new volunteers and was launching more intensive recruitment campaigns.

In the implementation of the all-volunteer force, the basic issue that had to be faced was the legitimate scope of military authority over the personal behavior of its members, since elaborate constraining practices had been justified as effective training necessary to prepare men to accept military discipline and to face combat. The control of personal behavior involves hazing and harsh treatment in basic training, and trivial "mickey mouse" inspections and duties in garrison life. Admiral Elmo R. Zumwalt has defined "mickey mouse" as "demeaning or abrasive regulations," thereby officially criticizing what had been accepted as traditional and indispensable.

The military elite justified such control of personal behavior because of the absence of an effective military tradition among civilians and as a device essential to maintain military effectiveness. However, the trend has been toward a gradual elimination of brutal induction procedures and excessive inspections. In training, the objective is to expose men to realistic problems and to avoid degrading experiences. In particular, the U.S. Navy, under Admiral Zumwalt, undertook extensive steps to deal with the issues of personal autonomy. As was to be expected, the reforms were viewed as overreaching, especially in matters dealing with personal appearance, and after a period of experimentation in the Navy a new equilibrium was established which is viewed as more compatible with the needs of highly technological services.

Nevertheless, surveys demonstrate that enlisted personnel, especially in the ground forces, reveal an excessive interference with personal autonomy and personal dignity as the most frequent reasons for their failure to reenlist. Military leaders have therefore instituted programs to promote some privacy in military barracks, to eliminate "make work" assignments, needless inspections, and personal harassment, but the implementation of such changes encounters pervasive organizational rigidities. At the officer level, the basic issue was not personal dignity but, rather, professional responsibility. With the end of conscription, an important segment found themselves deeply involved in operational assignments or in staff tasks under great pressure; but another segment, especially junior and middle-level officers, suffered a sense of frustration because of underemployment in meaningful tasks and excessive ritualism.[11] In part, the decrease in the size of the armed forces after Vietnam produced a short-term oversupply of officers. But the strains in adapting military organization to a format appropriate for an all-volunteer force "in being" were more fundamental.

Thus, it is possible to extend and refine the original hypothesis on the long-term transformation of authority in the military establishment. Although there was powerful ideological and institutional resistance to change in the military, the shift from authoritative domination continued throughout the years of the Vietnam war, and especially during the transition to the all-volunteer force. In specific areas, such as the contractual basis of military service, continued civilianization can be expected. However, with the actual implementation of the all-volunteer force and the elimination of "reluctant draftees," there has been clear evidence that the limits on change had been reached for this period, and in specific sectors of military life a reaction could be noted. The debate within the military concerning those elements of discipline which are essential has produced powerful ideological and organizational pressures to resist additional change that is considered weakening to military authority. The outcome of this debate depended not only on the internal balance within the military profession but on the orientation and interest of civilian political leadership as well.

2. *Narrowing Skill Differential Between Military and Civilian Elites.* One of the more precise indicators of the interpenetration of military institutions and civilian society has been the long-term increase in the transferability of skills from the military to the

civilian sector. During the period 1960–1970, the limits of this trend were reached.

For enlisted personnel, Harold Wool's comprehensive study, *The Military Specialist*, documents post-World II changes in skill structure.[12] During 1945–1957, the trend in the Army toward a greater proportion of technical specialists with direct counterparts in the civilian economy increased but then leveled out in succeeding years. Thus, the proportion of Army enlisted personnel whose primary specialty was ground combat fell from 39.9 per cent in 1945 to 28.1 per cent in 1960; by 1963, the figure remained at 28.8 per cent. A similar pattern was seen in the Marine Corps.[13]

Wool also points to another aspect which limited the trend of convergence of civilian and military skills. Enlisted personnel engage in a variety of generalized assignments, such as guard duty and housekeeping, regardless of occupational specialty and rank. The practice of having civilians employed, directly or by contract, to perform logistical and supply assignments means a greater tendency to assign uniformed personnel to purely military or combat functions.

The trend toward convergence of skills between military and civilian sectors, however, has greater consequence for commissioned officers, particularly those at the level of the military elite. The experiences of retired officers furnish a revealing index. Popular attention has focused on military officers employed in defense and defense-related industries. In 1969, Congressional investigations by Senator William Proxmire revealed that 2,000 officers—8.8 per cent of retired upper rank officers—were employed by the one hundred largest defense contractors. A few officers, of course, held top managerial posts in these industries, but a measure of the position officers typically occupied can be inferred from their salaries. In 1960, of those who had retired as three- or four-star officers, almost half were paid $15,000 or less, and more than one-fourth, $10,000, or less. By 1968, the comparable average figure had risen to $18,000. If defense-related employment were defined to include persons supplying goods or services to a predominantly military clientele—insurance and automobile salesmen, real estate agents, and employees of local establishments dependent on the military—the number of retired officers so employed would be greater, but their income level would not be raised.

Research studies demonstrate the wide variety of employment pursued by retired officers and clearly indicate residues of active-duty experience. For example, a careful sample survey of retired

officers made in 1966 revealed that employment in financial posts
was the most frequent post-service affiliation: 23 per cent were
employed as insurance or real estate salesmen or worked in banks
and other financial institutions. Government, particularly the federal
government, was the next most frequent employer (18 per cent),
while 17 per cent were engaged in manufacturing. There was also
a strong involvement in education (10 per cent).[14] These data do not
adequately assess the prestige attached to the various jobs held by
retired military personnel, but it does appear that as many as one-
quarter suffer a decline in income upon retirement, despite retirement pay.

The extent to which high-ranking retired personnel have obtained key executive and administrative posts in the federal government is a particularly significant indicator. There were noteworthy
examples immediately after World War II; these were much fewer
in the 1960s. The supply of officers with prominent public reputations has diminished, and normal sources of recruitment are more
frequently used for such high-level appointments. Popular disapproval of the practice of employing military men in such posts
has also served to limit convergence of the military and civilian
sectors of society.

To assist transition to civilian employment, the armed forces
encourage additional education in a variety of programs. At a
minimum, a bachelor's degree is considered essential for a career
officer, and a master's degree has become a desirable objective.
The increase in educational level while on active duty has been
particularly marked. An important minority of officers receive advanced schooling in civilian institutions, not only for military purposes but also to acquire skills and degrees they expect to be important to them in retirement. However, a subtle tension has
developed between the prestige structure within the military and
employability in civilian society. Particularly at the middle level,
officers with technical skills are believed to have the highest degree
of civilian employability, while they enjoy less prestige and more
limited career opportunities in the military. In contrast, combat
arms and operations officers and noncommissioned officers, the
men at the core of the military and its prestige hierarchy, are
thought to have (and often do have) fewer opportunities for
careers in civilian life and greater difficulties in making the transition. This represents a disarticulation between the prestige struc-
tures of the military and of civilian society and serves as another
limitation to the convergence of the military and civilian.

3. *Shift of Officer Recruitment.* From 1910 to 1960, the data

support the hypothesis that the military elites were shifting their recruitment from a narrow base of relatively high social status, to a broader base, more representative of the population as a whole. Although there were strong selective factors fostering a military elite drawn from "an old family, Anglo-Saxon Protestant, rural upper-middle professional background," there was little tendency for a self-perpetuating "caste" to develop. This pattern of social recruitment contributed to the civilianization of the military profession.

Since 1945, and especially since 1960, new trends in social recruitment have developed, particularly for academy cadets. First, the military profession has continued to be an avenue of social mobility for the working class. Thus, 17.6 per cent of the class of 1971 at the U.S. Military Academy were from the working class, mainly the sons of skilled workers. This figure was a continuation of post-World War II patterns, and is markedly higher than figures at civilian universities of comparable quality. Even at the U.S. Naval Academy, 20.1 per cent of cadets in the same class described their background as blue collar.[15]

Second, the armed forces have lost their last direct linkage with sons of the upper class. Such recruits, especially those who rose to the highest ranks, had been steadily declining, more rapidly in the Army and Air Force than in the Navy. In 1970, a high-ranking naval officer pointed out that only a few sons of the "best" families were in the entering class at the Naval Academy. Upper-class interest in nautical affairs could no longer overcome resistance to the modest prestige and the realities of a naval career.

The military prefers to describe its social background in diffuse middle-class terms with a strong implication of professional and upper-middle-class origin. The annual report on cadets from the U.S. Military Academy in 1969 described the typical cadet: "his father had some college education, is a business or professional person."[16] However, there has actually been a decline in sons from upper-middle-class business and professional backgrounds and a strong emphasis on lower-middle-class sources of recruitment. The number of cadets from families in high-status professions such as medicine, law, and even teaching is limited (about 3 per cent, which is fewer than in comparable civilian institutions). The modest background of cadets can be inferred from the incomes of their families. Families of more than 30 per cent of the cadets in the class of 1973 earned less than $10,000 a year, and only 6.8 per cent represented the "solid" upper-middle-class with incomes of $25,000 or more. Cadets at the Naval Academy are from a somewhat higher social background, but the same broadening trends have been at work; in the class of 1971, 8.7 per cent had fathers in the professions.[17]

The naval officer quoted above described succinctly the social transformation that has been wrought. "Of course, we want a cross-section, and we are happy to get these young men from modest families, but it is very different from when I entered the Naval Academy. We really need boys from good professional families and even the few from the really good families. They help set the tone and the outlook. It is harder to train these young officers these days in what it means to be a professional." Men from such modest backgrounds must rely more heavily on their education to develop broad cosmopolitan perspectives. This trend has also been reflected in changing religious affiliations. In the class of 1973 at West Point, only 20 per cent were affiliated with high-status Protestant denominations (Presbyterian, Episcopal, or Congregational), whereas more than twice as many belonged to the more typical Protestant denominations (Baptist, Methodist). Moreover, the proportion of Roman Catholics had risen to 35 per cent.

Third, self-recruitment has increased sharply in all three services since 1945. In the 1960's, more than one-quarter of entering cadets at the service academies came from career military families. They had fathers who either were on full-time career duty or had completed twenty years of service. If one were to include uncles and close relatives who were career military men, the percentage would, of course, greatly increase. Although precise data are not available, there has been a marked increase in the number of sons of noncommissioned officers at service academies. For these young men, entrance into the officer corps, especially as academy graduates, is a sign of social mobility and personal achievement. Among military offspring, linkages with civilian society tend to be attenuated, and a sense of social isolation is an often present potential.

During the 1960's, the supply of sons of military fathers, both officers and noncommissioned officers, increased because of the post-1945 vast expansion of the active duty military. Demographic analysis indicates that, given the size of the military establishment during the 1950's and 1960's and the high birth rate among military families, a strong supply of military sons will continue through the 1970's. The extent of their interest in the military is a problematic issue, but the number of opportunities to serve will be diminished, so that comparable levels of self-recruitment could well continue.

The three services have emphasized ROTC as the major source of short-term officers, since in any given year only 3 or 4 per cent of new officers have been academy graduates. Changes were made in the ROTC curriculum and two-year courses were introduced.[18] Nevertheless, the number of students enrolled dropped sharply; ROTC cadets fell from 264,000 in 1966 to 156,000 in 1970 and to 75,000 in 1973.

Only the Marine Corps placed strong reliance on a short officer candidate course (OCS). The services viewed ROTC procedures as an effective screening device, and they believed that ROTC units on campus raised the prestige of the military. ROTC programs insure that officers will have college degrees, whereas OCS programs involve men with fewer than four years of higher education. The armed services assume that a college degree earned before entering the military is a highly desirable qualification for an officer recruit. The ROTC program has had scholarship components, and to meet the decline in enrollments the services have pressed for their expansion.

As a result of external attack and internal reorganization, the geographical distribution of ROTC units has altered. The so-called prestige liberal arts institutions of the East and Midwest are declining as ROTC campuses, whereas the number of Southern and less prestigious hinterland institutions with ROTC units are increasing.

All three services have been increasingly sensitive to the neea for recruiting and retaining officers from minority backgrounds: blacks, Spanish-speaking Americans, and American Indians. In 1969, the ratio of black to white officers was approximately 1 to 30 in the Army, 1 to 60 in the Air Force, 1 to 90 in the Marines, and 1 to 150 in the Navy. In 1966, active recruiting programs were instituted both for service academies and for ROTC units. The results were noteworthy increases: for example, in 1969–1970 the student body of the Air Force Academy included sixty-four blacks, twenty-six Asians, thirty-one American Indians, and twenty-six Spanish-Americans.

The full sociological meaning of the new recruitment of officers comes into sharper focus when occupational background is linked to geographical and regional affiliation. As American society has become progressively urbanized and industrialized, military officers have continued to be disproportionately drawn from the hinterland. "Hinterland" does not imply rural areas but, rather, smaller population centers. Although the trend in the military toward increased geographical dispersion has continued, strong Southern (and recently Southwestern) links measured by birth, marriage, and residence during long periods of service, have persisted. The limitations on the trends toward increased social representativeness derive mainly from the marked increase in self-recruitment from military families; and the introduction of the all-volunteer force increased this element. Only in recruitment through ROTC from the metropolitan areas or by means of specialized programs involving minorities are there important countertrends. Since most of such recruitment is via ROTC they are not likely to enter the top leadership ranks. The military elite—both current and future cadres —needs to be compared with the higher echelons of the federal executive, and especially the personnel of the foreign service, who are typically drawn from urban, upper-middle-class, professional families with strong links to the New England states.[19]

It would be rewarding if these measures of the social profile could be augmented by ones reflecting the social personality of the professional soldier, especially of the entering cadet to the military academy. From repeated observations by participant-observers and from the admittedly limited data collected by annual official questionnaires, the cadets who entered the academies during the period of the Vietnam buildup did not hold attitudes markedly different from those of most comparable college freshmen. They displayed similar restlessness about their personal privileges and even about their dress and hair style. They were more likely than their civilian counterparts, however, to accept the authority of their teachers and the validity of the existing curriculum.

There is no simple and clear-cut relationship between social background and political participation in any professional group; in the contemporary period, education and career experiences weigh heavy in this regard. But the social recruitment of the military in the past—and even more so under the conditions of the selective recruitment of the all-volunteer force—contribute to the conservative cast of the military. The military, with its important element of self-recruitment, with its strong component from the hinterland of the South and Southwest, more currently augmented from "big city" Catholic universities lower-middle and upper-working class status groups—tends to "lean to the right." Nevertheless, the extent of this political orientation remained limited as of the beginning of the 1970's.

For example, the class of 1973 at the U.S. Military Academy, of course, contained no radical segment, and their political attitudes were on the conservative side of the continuum. However, 20.4 per cent reported that they were "liberal," while 33.8 per cent claimed to be "moderately conservative." No more than 5.4 per cent described themselves as "strongly conservative," and only 0.9 per cent designated themselves as "left."[20] These responses were very similar to those reported by a national sample of male freshmen entering technical institutes. The main difference from a comparable sample of freshmen entering private universities was that 5.6 per cent called themselves left and 20.1 per cent conservative. They were no more conservative, and perhaps less, than middle-ranking officers sampled in 1954.[21] When, in the early 1960's, the views of the military cadets were compared with those of the student body at Dartmouth, the cadets were found to be more "hawkish," but their views were hardly outside the political mainstream of American society. Special characteristics were their extensive involvement in high school sports and leadership posts. An overwhelming number had also had some sort of paid work experience. They had more interest in public affairs than their civilian counterparts and were more likely to acknowledge strong, if diffuse, ambitions both in self-assessment inventories and in direct conversations.

Moreover, comprehensive studies of the socialization of cadets at West Point and at Annapolis do not indicate that powerful and extensive changes in attitudes are produced at these academies.[22] The academy curriculum supplies the elements of a basic and technical education, and the cadet learns enough about the military profession to help him select his military specialty. Equally important are the friendships and commitments he develops there. Professional socialization is a gradual process that works mainly by self-selection out of those who do not fit in or are uninterested in a military career, and only to a much lesser extent by the positive molding of attitudes and perspectives. This process starts in the military academy and continues throughout each step in the military career. As in the case of studies of the military academies, empirical research on the impact of ROTC programs revealed little fundamental change in the attitude of the students. Self-selection emerges as more important.[23]

These observations about the consequences of initial officer education do not necessarily apply to the extensive programs of post-college education at civilian universities that are sponsored by the armed forces. Superior officers who have had extensive and varied military assignments appear to make effective use of these opportunities to broaden their perspective and establish linkages with civilian society. While the issues of a representative officer corps remain paramount under an all-volunteer force, education, career experience, and contacts with civilian society emerge as more and more crucial in determining whether the officer corps will become "ideologically" and "professionally" separated from the larger society.

With the advent of the all-volunteer armed force, the issue of social representation arose most drastically for enlisted personnel. For the enlisted ranks, during the mid- and late 1960's, the Selective Service System, with its medical and mental screening, under-selected the very poorest, while educational deferments exempted many middle-class youths. As a result, the cadres in Vietnam were heavily drawn from the solid core of the working class. Within the armed forces, blacks tended to concentrate in the ground forces, especially in the combat areas. The transition to the all-volunteer force presents the likelihood of a marked increase in the concentration of blacks, although the President's Commission on the All-Volunteer Armed Force predicted a maximum of 15 per cent.

By 1970, blacks in the enlisted ranks as a whole had risen to 11 per cent from 9.2 per cent in 1962. For the Army, the figure stood at 13.5 per cent as the upward trend set in. By June, 1972, the percentage of enlisted blacks in the ground forces was 15.1, and it was close to 20 per cent by 1973. Initial black enlistment for the Army was close to 30 per cent in 1974 and, with a continued higher rate of reenlistment, the trend toward a marked overconcentration of blacks had set in. This issue was deeply troublesome to the professional officer corps not only because of the problems of racial tension and organizational management, but also because of the legitimacy of an ever-increasing black enlisted structure for a democratic society. Thus, given the difficulties and high costs in manpower recruitment, the officer corps faced, for the first time since 1940, the reality that the quantity of manpower had emerged as a powerful limiting factor in military and foreign policy. Moreover, while the long-term outlook for the social composition of the military will depend on national policy, it is abundantly clear that the advent of the all-volunteer force has resulted in limitation on the trend toward social representation in the composition of the military.

4. *Significance of Career Patterns.* The advent of nuclear weapons and the burdens of prolonged conflict in South Vietnam have not altered the notion of the content of the prescribed career—the accepted career ladder into the military elite. With the introduction of the all-volunteer force in 1973, in each service, there persisted a discernible series of steps which alternate between command and staff assignments plus successful course completion at service schools, and these have changed only very slightly. On the contrary, faced with the prospect of a declining military force in the 1970's, officers strove intensely to pass through the prescribed stages of career training as they searched for es-

sential command assignments. Career management has been described by the professionals themselves as "having your ticket punched." The higher schools emphasize existing command and staff procedures and offer considerable content on public affairs and current international events. However, they are not centers for fundamental self-criticism or reformulation of doctrine, but forums for transmitting existing policy. Laurence I. Radway, long-time student of higher military education, emphasizes "the frequent testimony of many graduates that 'what you learn there is less important than the friends you make there.' "[24]

The prescribed career has been broadened to include some involvement in politico-military assignments and "stability operations," but most of these operations are carried out by specialists who frequently do not rise into the military elite. Command of troops, vessels, aircraft, or missiles remains central, and excessive involvement in politico-military assignments is thought to thwart career advancement. A retired Army colonel, who completed a Ph.D. in political science while on active duty and who has been a careful observer of career trends in the military, stressed that in the 1960's some involvement in politico-military assignments had become part of the prescribed career. Particularly, during his period of four to five years as a lieutenant-colonel, assignments had changed from the previous decade. Combat (in the form of a tour in Vietnam) plus an assignment at the Pentagon had been augmented by a politico-military tour. He pointed out that the "best" career also required a graduate degree.

But what of the hypothesis, offered in *The Professional Soldier*, that in contrast to a prescribed career, entrance into the small elite nucleus—where innovating perspectives, discretionary responsibility, and political skills are required—is given to persons with unconventional and adaptive careers? The number of officers who enter the elite nucleus via an unconventional career varies. It was high during and immediately after World War II. However, in the decade from 1960 to 1970, the route to the very top became narrower and these posts were more often filled by men pursuing conventional careers.

There were reasons for this. First, many assignments and skills that formerly marked an adaptive career have become routinized and hence have developed into career specialties. This has occurred, for example, with language skills and staff service in joint and international commands. Likewise, in the past, especially between World War I and World War II, the adaptive and unconventional career was reflected in a personal decision to become associated with new and experimental weapons such as the submarine, the tank, and the airplane. However, that type of innovative career has been closed, as weapons development has become an institutionalized process. In fact, the innovators now are the men who resist needless and marginal differentiation in weapons systems. But negative contributions like these are seldom recognized as innovative or generously rewarded. If an adaptive career is indeed a reflection of self-motivation, initiative, and risk-taking, then the scope has narrowed and the signs are more difficult to determine.

Second, while ambitious men make careers for themselves and contribute to the changing military by pursuing innovative assignments, the military circumstances must be appropriate. The war in Vietnam meant that the men who sought to innovate—mainly in the field of counterguerrilla warfare—failed. Brig. General William P. Yarborough, a strong advocate of "unconventional warfare," was a conspicuous example of a group of aspirants who failed both because of the inherent impossibility of their task and because command decisions after 1964 meant that conventional forces and leaders with prescribed careers had come into dominance.

Career success in the military has continued to be linked to the system of personal sponsorship. Proficiency ratings and selection boards emphasize universal standards for promotion. The search for talent is probably even more widespread in the armed forces than in industrial enterprise. Yet more than one candidate is available for any important post at any level in the hierarchy. A candidate's ability to rise farther depends on the particular assignment which will permit him to display his talents and make a visible contribution. High-ranking officers are able to influence the careers of particular young men by requesting their assignment to their own staffs and recommending them for appropriate posts.

Military Communities and Social Change

THE ISSUES OF national strategy, international relations, and career assignments continuously intrude on the consciousness of the professional officer, but day-to-day realities of family and military community are essential ingredients of his professional world, since his personal life is organized by the military to assist him to face routine pressures, emergencies, and disruptions. In the old armed forces, between World War I and World War II, peacetime military life had its protocol and etiquette and prescribed sociability, punctuated at designated times by exercises in the field or at sea in an atmosphere of routine. Military installations were self-contained and relatively isolated, with limited but stable social connections to the larger civilian society.

Since Pearl Harbor, the career forces have been engaged in constant operations and submerged by an immense number of short-term personnel. The system of continual rotation came to be a main ingredient of family and military community life. There can be no doubt that the military officer and his family became more a part of the larger society; but the relationship is hardly so much a pattern of integration as that of segmented linkages. Superficially, the military officer has developed a variegated network of civilian contacts. A majority of officers live off-base, their children attend civilian schools, and at different points in their careers they have assignments that expose them to the larger society. In varying degrees, the military services operate with a computerized personnel system which makes possible worldwide and frequent changes of station. Operational requirements for Vietnam increased the speed of rotation. Surveys indicate that between 40 and 50 per cent of military families have moved each year from the county in which they were living.

To adjust to the disruptions of rotation and to the increased hostility (or at least indifference) of neighbors, the military family lives mainly within its own world. Greater stability is required for meaningful participation in the local community, although the speed with which military families put down roots and extend their contacts with the outside community is striking.[25] In the Navy, there is more effort to maintain the notion of a home base where a family tries to acquire a house and civilian friends.

The services are sensitive to the needs of their families and are aware that the unhappiness of wives constitutes a major cause of resignation. They have developed an effective "welfare state" with family, medical, and social services, unparalleled by most civilian communities. Military personnel resist recognizing that they are members of a highly collectivist community. Even the base newspaper serves to strengthen the military society's sense of solidarity. To the extent that resources are available, the armed forces seek to handle the disruption of rotation by creating a more self-contained system of communities. On-base housing, medical, school, and recreational facilities, a specialist staff of dependent aides, plus volunteer assistance, tend to replicate elements of the older military community. As the size of the force is reduced, this trend is certain to intensify, and it represents another powerful counterforce to civilianization.

The military family has not demonstrated a consuming desire to isolate itself from the larger society. It recognizes the advantages that the military installation offers and the benefits to family living that come from collective action. But at the same time, it has a strong impulse to participate in the larger society. In fact, the style of life in the military—its material and cultural content—reflects the values and aspirations of civilian society. The desire for post housing, schools, and medical facilities represents a desire to be part of the larger society by having everything it offers.

But the issue runs deeper. As one careful observer of military life stated, "I would suggest that many military wives, particularly in the Navy, object to living in military communities which are characterized by long absences of most of the male members of the family. I would venture to say that a number of military families would prefer integration within the civilian community rather than to live in isolated military communities."

Human needs and desires are variegated and ambivalent; the military family seeks what support it can derive from close proximity to other military families, yet at the same time it wants to be integrated into the larger society. The outlook of the military in this regard is similar to that of an ethnic group—concerned with its solidarity and cohesion, but sensitive to any sign of exclusion from the larger society.

The military community recognizes that it cannot detach itself from the tensions of social and political change in the larger society. Its members are avid consumers of mass media and their strong interest in public affairs renders them more broadly informed than comparable civilian families. In particular, the tensions of both race and youth have penetrated the military base and placed its ordered style of life under strain.

In civilian society, the bulk of the white population has in its daily existence only occasional or partial contacts with blacks. In the armed forces, personal contact is ubiquitous, for blacks are much more in the mainstream of military life. After the Korean war, the military officially accepted the goals of racial integration and progressively higher commands pressed harder than did comparable forces in civilian society. Integration was assisted by authoritative sanctions and also by the performance of blacks in combat in Vietnam. Most officers believe that the armed forces performed an important public service when they demonstrated that racial segregation could be eliminated.

Although progress at the officer level was painfully slow, the success of blacks as enlisted personnel and noncommissioned officers was indeed striking compared with their progress in civilian industry. In the Army and Marine Corps, as Charles Moskos has demonstrated, intelligence, measured by AFQT (Armed Forces "Intelligence" Test) scores, rather than racial characteristics, accounts for assignment and advancement.[26]

In fact, by the mid-1960's, the "definition of the situation" had been reversed: blacks in the larger society and in the military were displaying a new sense of "race pride." The sudden rise of black self-consciousness in the military created resentment precisely because white personnel had come to believe that integration was the correct solution. Military solidarity and morale were such that signs of racial identity, as distinct from religious identity, were viewed as disruptive. The first indications of racial self-consciousness were shown by black draftees during the Vietnam buildup and had overtones of opposition to the war. These feelings were expressed initially and most intensely in off-duty recreation and were abated by the persistence of racial prejudice. Black noncommissioned officers with many years of service resisted these new sentiments fiercely, but their opposition served only to strengthen militant feelings, which intruded into duty assignments and on occasion erupted in outbursts of resistance and hostility. Commanders took a very lenient posture toward those involved in racial incidents, including the 250 blacks who rioted in the summer of 1968 at Long Binh stockade and the forty-three black soldiers at Fort Hood, Texas, who refused to participate in guard duty at the Democratic National Convention in Chicago. In the fall of 1970, field reports from West Germany described incidents in which black soldiers limited their responses to orders from white noncommissioned officers or gave the "black power" salute to their officers. Such incidents reflected new levels of tension and discontent.

Officers at all levels struggled for new modes of accommodation. They gradually came to acknowledge the existence of an Afro-American culture by permitting Afro haircuts and the like, by encouraging open and frank discussion of race relations, and by energetically investigating complaints of discrimination and sources of tension. Efforts to enlist blacks in white radical coalitions and the appeals of the National Liberation Front essentially failed. The basic commitment of the black soldier to the military (no doubt in part because of lesser opportunities outside) could be seen in black reenlistment rates which have remained consistently higher than white rates.

At the officer level, the norms of the profession inhibited any development of black self-consciousness. But the tense race relations in urban centers and the discontent of black enlisted personnel had their effect. The more outspoken black junior officers found themselves at odds with their older and higher-ranking counterparts. A degree of self-ghettoization in social and private matters was accompanied by strong support for the more acceptable demands of black enlisted personnel.

All three services continued a nationwide search for qualified black officer candidates, in response to civilian pressure and because of the realization that solving the problems of black enlisted personnel required more black officers. If black enlisted personnel were prone to push black consciousness aggressively, black junior officers often turned within themselves to avoid cross-pressures. As opportunities for college-trained black personnel expanded, the services experienced greater difficulties in attracting black officers and retaining them beyond their obligated tour of duty. By 1970, there were more black majors and lieutenant-colonels in the Army than first and second lieutenants. Despite the existence of black self-consciousness, however, the military is a social institution with extensive integration. With the introduction of the all-volunteer force, the most race-conscious blacks were less likely to volunteer. However, the race relations in the military under the all-volunteer system have come to focus more and more on the increasing overconcentration of black enlisted personnel, and in the persistence of race tension in particular areas, as for example, among ground force units in Western Germany.

Paralleling racial tension has been intergenerational conflict, including tension within the military community and family. The military community has been able to accommodate itself to the highjinks of its young people, but many military communities discovered that their sons and daughters joined the peace movement during the Vietnam war. The extent of such "defection" is difficult to measure, but it has been very limited and tends to be overestimated. It is one thing when a son or daughter goes to college and voices dissent quietly and discreetly; on occasion, such youngsters were the vehicle for expressing their parents' doubts. But there are the conspicuous and vocal youngsters, including children of important officers, whose opposition to Vietnam or whose hippie-like behavior received attention in the mass media. However, family ties are strong, and most officers have accepted the dissenters with a minimum of fuss or breast-beating.

But a modulated response should not hide the depth of feelings and meanings that such dissent generates among military families. Of course, the professional officer as father shares common concerns with his civilian counterparts about the social and political behavior of his children. But such a formulation omits much. Professional officers think of themselves as bearers of the positive values of American society and as subject to higher standards of behavior than civilians. They consider themselves professionals under constraint in expressing private opinions. Since the responsibilities of their assignments are thought to be overriding, the behavior of their children is not exempt from these considerations. Some service families are concerned with their lineage and want at least one son to enter the services. Most officers consider the behavior of their children part of their professional performance.

If they are to be considered good officers, their children must be sensitive to the requirements of their jobs. Public opposition to the war in Vietnam was understandable, but dissent within the military community by the younger generation was a matter of deep concern because of professional self-conceptions. With the withdrawal of U.S. troops from Vietnam and the end of conscription, campus agitations declined rapidly and political dissent among military families likewise declined. The long-term implication was to dampen interest in a military career among considerable numbers of military youngsters.

Self-Conceptions and Professional Perspectives

THE DECADE 1960–1970 was one of frustration and even profound shock to the self-esteem of the officer corps. The logic of the professional officer is that he is supposed to perform his assignment, request a transfer, or resign from service in a matter-of-fact fashion, on the basis of his skills, aptitudes, and basic beliefs, without undue display of personal mood or sentiment. When Lieutenant George W. Petrie, a Green Beret officer, told the press, after the failure of the Sontay raid into North Vietnam to free United States prisoners of war in November, 1970, that the men who participated in the raid experienced a "tremendous letdown" and "total dejection," he was violating professional norms. When he added that he and his men during training were motivated by the prospect that President Nixon would go on television on Thanksgiving Day and dramatically announce to the American people that the prisoners had been rescued, he confirmed the view of many regulars that the Green Berets were excessively theatrical. Self-conceptions and professional perspectives, nevertheless, are the subjective side of military strategy and tactics.

Officers are also concerned, like men in any profession, with their prestige. The categories of the research sociologists are revealing even if much too gross. In 1947, a national sample survey of the National Opinion Research Center placed the Army captain thirty-first in rank order of prestige among occupational groups in the United States. By 1963, he had moved up to twenty-first, roughly equivalent to public school teacher.[27] The military regarded this as low, considering their responsibilities. Clearly, such a ranking system failed to reflect subtle issues of the legitimacy and worth of the profession, which emerged as deep concerns under the impact of Vietnam.

Most officers recognize that the public image of the armed forces has suffered. They had been allocated vast human and material resources, and officers became aware that wide segments of the American public felt that its soldiers, although not defeated, had become bogged down in the field. The cease-fire meant the acceptance of a stalemate. In public opinion, the war came less and less to be characterized as a heroic effort and more and more as a vast expenditure of destructive firepower. The armed forces had to face accusations of atrocities, of overoptimistic estimates of military operations, of costly overruns in procuring weapons, and of financial scandals among officers and key noncommissioned personnel.

Public attitudes toward the military in contemporary society are strongly conditioned by the extensive and detailed reportage in the mass media. Since the Civil War, when the war correspondent and the war photographer were first permitted to accompany troops, the mass media have increased their ability to penetrate into the internal life of the military, including coverage of the violence of combat. Until the war in Vietnam, the U.S. military assumed that, by revealing its inner life to the public, it would develop closer rapport with the civilian citizenry and gain their support. But the details of front-line operations as shown on television have given civilian society a firsthand persistent view of the grim realities of the "killing business." Rapid, up-to-the-moment pictorial reporting of an infantry fire fight and the resulting human carnage served to depress enthusiasm for United States policies in Vietnam and to engender in many viewers powerful feelings of guilt, social distance, and loss of esteem for the military.

The reality and image of war have come to be body counts

of both civilians and soldiers (which the mass media labeled inaccurate or irrelevant to the basic issues of the war), extensive defoliation of the countryside, mass movement of civilian refugees, and the documentation of atrocities against civilians, with the basic question of extent and responsibility left unanswered.[28] The reports about the increasing demoralization of the troops and about incidents of outright resistance to authority, plus the widespread use of drugs, served to undermine traditional respect for the military.

Men respond to the images others hold of them. The public criticism of the military has evoked a prolonged debate within the officer corps about the legitimacy of strategic objectives and specific military tactics. The distinction offered in the original edition of *The Professional Soldier* between the absolutists (those who thought more in terms of conventional definitions of victory) and the pragmatists (those who thought in terms of changed realities of nuclear weapons and national liberation movements) has remained relevant, although at points the differences have narrowed or blurred.*

In each service, men who hold similar strategic conceptions tend to form loose alliances of friends and professional colleagues, based on common attendance at a military school, association with particular weapons, or service in a specific theater or on the same staff. During the quarter-century since 1945, a vastly expanded military has brought about many such sociometric networks, such as the key men of the Strategic Air Command and the advocates of aircraft carriers in the Navy; these are the spokesmen for specific weapons systems. But even more pervasive and important were the personal alliances which had their origin in the experiences of World War II and were linked to the dominant personalities and strategic posture of George C. Marshall vis-à-vis Douglas MacArthur. The followers of General Marshall and the men who dominated the European theater of operation developed a military style which has been called pragmatic because of its concern with the measured application of violence and its political consequences, in contrast to the more absolutist doctrine of those who served in the Far East under General MacArthur. The line of descent from General Marshall can be directly traced through a group of disciples which included Matthew Ridgway and finally Maxwell Taylor.[29] The leaders of these informal and almost tacit

* See pp. 264–277 of this volume.

coalitions and their key subordinates influenced top-level personnel assignments and played key roles in the execution of United States military policy.

The ultimate role of the office of the President has remained crucial, since internal differences in the military had made it possible for the chief executive to select officers with different sets of politico–military perspectives. This occurred, for example, when President Eisenhower broke the line of succession of Marshall's men and selected Admiral Arthur Radford, who had had extensive Far Eastern experience, as chairman of the Joint Chiefs of Staff, in order to implement the massive retaliation strategy. Admiral Radford's outlook epitomized an "absolutist" doctrine. Nevertheless, when the French government requested large-scale United States intervention in Vietnam, possibly including nuclear weapons, Eisenhower overrode Radford and followed the negative advice of Ridgway and other men of the pragmatic school.

With the passage of time, old networks become attenuated and strategic perspectives change. Nevertheless, after Korea and after the Geneva conference of July, 1954, which ended French military involvement in Indochina, there was widespread opposition among U.S. military leaders of both groups to a new commitment of ground troops to Southeast Asia. No doubt Ridgway and his associates were the most articulate and outspoken critics of such involvement. It remains for future historians to trace the process by which the civilian advisors of President Kennedy, especially W. W. Rostow, were able to reverse and override United States military doctrine and assist him in accepting a series of policies which led to large-scale involvement. The majority of U.S. officers knew that, after the Korean war, military planners were reluctant to deploy ground forces again on the mainland of Asia. They saw the decision to intervene in Indochina in 1961 as mainly a civilian decision made by the President and his personal staff with the support of key Senatorial and Congressional leaders.

General Maxwell Taylor was one who participated in the presidential planning. Although a "pragmatist" who had served under Marshall and a close associate of Ridgway, Taylor worked with Rostow in preparing a basic policy paper in 1961. This paper, which set forth guidelines for the gradual expansion of United States forces in Vietnam, contained an appendix which, at that early date, advocated strategic air bombardment of North Vietnam. Although President Kennedy accepted the study but not the appendix, it foretold the direction of United States strategy in Vietnam. The limitation of strategic air power was a lesson learned

in World War II and in Korea. It could be assumed that the
limitation would be very great against a peasant society like that
of Vietnam. But "victory through strategic air bombardment" is a
deeply ingrained conception in the United States military establishment. The pragmatic faction was more critical and doubtful
about the impact of strategic air warfare in the Vietnam setting.

The basis for the shift in Maxwell Taylor's attitude toward
commitment of ground troops remains unclear. Although many
officers were dubious about the move, only a few officially voiced
strenuous opposition. The absolutists as a group were more prone
to accept and vigorously pursue the new direction. In fact, most
ranking military personnel accepted the decision even though there
was no immediate prospect of receiving the manpower—more than
one million ground troops—they deemed essential. (In fact, they
never did receive them.) In the end, not a single chief of staff or
high-ranking officer dissented (by the acceptable procedure of
resigning) in order to establish a historical record. Among younger
military officers who fought in Vietnam, there has been little clarity
about the origins of U.S. involvement in Vietnam. By their participation, officers have increasingly come to think of it as if the
decision were their own.

Out of the military operations in South Vietnam, General William C. Westmoreland emerged as the dominant figure both as field
commander and subsequently as chief of staff of the United States
Army. In 1963, when the pace of combat in Vietnam accelerated
and President Johnson began his search for a new commander, three
names headed the list. The three had been classmates at the U.S.
Military Academy in the class of 1936: Creighton W. Abrams, Bruce
Palmer, Jr., and William C. Westmoreland. At that time, General
Maxwell Taylor was chairman of the Joint Chiefs of Staff and
strongly recommended Westmoreland. Johnson selected Westmoreland because of Taylor's recommendation and Westmoreland's
military record; but, as pointed out by Westmoreland's official
biographer, Ernest B. Ferguson, "one of the things he found most
likable was Westmoreland's lingering Southern accent."[30]

Despite the political overtones of this appointment, Westmoreland represented a "national coalition" general. He had worked
closely with Ridgway and Taylor, men trained in the tradition
of measured application of violence, and he was considered to be
sensitive to the political dimensions of war. However, he was an
admirer of General MacArthur and of associated ideological overtones. He was preoccupied with the Far East because of
his experiences in Korea. The military environment of expanded

hostilities engulfed Westmoreland as he prosecuted the war by an admixture of a conventional strategy and a variety of politico-military techniques which were applied without organizational or political effectiveness. The impact of the Tet offensive, President Johnson's refusal to send additional ground forces, and then Johnson's decision not to seek election ended the "forward" strategy in Vietnam.

The achievement of a "cease-fire" and temporary stalemate involved both military and, more pointedly, political means. In accounting for the cease-fire, the U.S. military emphasized the buildup of the South Vietnamese forces. In addition, the conditions required for a "cease-fire" were enhanced by U.S. political initiative toward regularizing the relations with Communist China. In the spring of 1972 the North Vietnamese launched a major offensive which failed to capture a single provincial capital. Even more important, under assistance and advice from the Soviet Union, in the spring of 1972, the North Vietnamese shifted their military tactics to a conventional tank assault and thereby, as a result of U.S. and South Vietnamese tactical air power, suffered their most extensive defeat of the second Indochina war. The conditions leading to the "cease-fire" were also linked to the impact of the bombing of North Vietnam during the fall of 1972. There is reason to believe that the more effective bombing techniques—optical, electronic, and laser bomb sighting—were able to inflict more serious damage than previous efforts. It is doubtful that this bombing was decisive, but it appears to have been a definite factor in the decision and terms of the cease-fire.

In assessing the outcome of the war in Vietnam, most officers have come to criticize various aspects of the United States intervention in Vietnam. Most believed that United States military tactics were inappropriate both during the period of military advisors and during the phase of large-scale intervention. A prominent theme is that the United States did not use the full force of its strategic air warfare units. The same officers knew that early military planning after 1961 postulated a frontal attack by North Vietnam across the seventeenth parallel in a fashion similar to the outbreak of hostilities in Korea. They questioned the extensive use of free-fire zones and "reconnaissance by fire" for dealing with North Vietnamese main force units. They were doubtful about "search and destroy" tactics in a counterguerrilla campaign. They had an endless series of questions about the appropriateness and adequacy of particular antiguerrilla measures.

Both combat against main force units and against guerrillas

were closely directed from higher command downward. Yet, at each phase in the expansion of United States involvement, United States advisors and local commanders sought to introduce an element of flexibility and realism into the military tasks to be performed. The Marine Corps rejected outright the doctrine of "search and destroy" and created its own local security system with mixed American and Vietnamese platoons. Individual commanders searched for new solutions and often tried to copy enemy tactics. For example, as late as August 14, 1970, approximately five thousand South Vietnamese were employed in a successful attack for which Lieutenant-Colonel M. G. Stafford was the senior military advisor. The attack involved eighty small, coordinated efforts by raiding parties of five to fifteen, without advance artillery preparation and with no airborne transport. For the moment, the standard United States formula had been completely reversed.

In the course of the Vietnam campaign, professional military opinion apparently shifted gradually toward the absolutist interpretation of events, although there are no systematic surveys or interview data to support this hypothesis. Men with strong pragmatist orientations opted out by accepting early retirement or resigning under honorable circumstances. Once removed from the strain of combat, professionals often assume a more detached and self-critical outlook. Younger officers, regardless of their personal military experience, are, of course, more prone to be introspective. At the higher military schools, a debate has begun on the strength and weakness of military operations in Vietnam that will last for many career generations.

The trauma of Vietnam plus President Nixon's declaration of "no more Vietnams" produced no basic change in planning future strategy but, rather, a slow and gradual adaptation to projected manpower reduction. Military managers think in terms of force levels. Will the downward trend from a high of 3,600,000 men level off at 2,200,000, as officially projected, or will it continue on to a figure of 2,000,000? Will increased costs of manpower and weapons result in a force of less than 2,000,000? Each service struggles for its missions under the general rubrics of "strategic deterrence" or "stability operations." Year by year, the projected manpower estimates have not been matched in the actual force levels.

In developing military strategy for the post-Vietnam period, all services accept nuclear weapons and their political implications as the central issue. From 1945 to 1970, the prospects of nuclear war were very remote indeed. Most military officers tended to emphasize the technological basis of deterrence. Only a minority were attuned to the political assumptions and initiatives making that possible, namely, that the Soviet bloc operated on the assumption that the political leaders in the United States firmly controlled their military establishment and that the United States had ruled out a preemptive nuclear attack on the Soviet Union. As a result, in military circles there has been very limited concern with the political initiatives required for the emerging decades.

Official doctrine in each service came to hold that meaningful arms control treaties were in the interest of the United States and the world community. Moreover, as the educational level of the professional soldier rose and as he was exposed to in-service instruction in international relations, a general commitment to arms control emerged as part of his professional ideology. For example, a survey of 211 middle-level Army officers at the Command and General Staff College in 1965–1966 demonstrated that only about 20 per cent could be classified as "hard liners"—opposed to inspected test ban treaties—or disagreeing with the proposition that "arms control agreements hold hope for peace."[31]

The gap between professional ideology and actual performance is a real one in any area of the military enterprise, and especially in that of arms control. The services see their role as reacting to civilian proposals and as pointing out weaknesses and defects. Professional caution, vested interest, and sheer inertia are clearly at work. Few junior officers are rewarded for a deep and innovative interest in arms control. Much of the energy of the military focuses on limited issues, such as the Navy's opposition to banning the transport of nuclear weapons through the Panama Canal by the creation of a nuclear free zone treaty for Latin America. A few high-ranking officers have been assigned to arms control missions and have pursued their tasks with energy. The services are committed to some measure of superiority in nuclear capability and only reluctantly attune themselves to the financial and political costs of the nuclear arms race. They have accepted the political realities of détente but were not imaginative sources of new management required for effective détente. To the contrary, organizational inertia at times served to compound the difficulties of searching for effective and viable arrangements for arms control.

In the arena of conventional weapons, strategic issues continued to be defined primarily in terms of prized weapons—the instruments which give men their heroic qualities. After Vietnam, the military elite anticipated a national policy of a slow, long-term reduction in overseas forces and bases. Naval planners were projecting a need for aircraft carriers, since ships remain the core element for the naval officer. Aircraft carriers were required to balance the buildup of missile-carrying submarines; it was argued that they permit a strategy which reduces excessive overseas commitments and yet is not a retreat into a Fortress America. In their efforts to maintain manned aircraft, Air Force planners resisted accepting the role of personnel carrier for the ground forces. Instead, they emphasized the need for overseas bombers. For the Army, airborne units were emerging as the prestige units but were very expensive. As in the case of the Air Force, top planners pressed for the overseas bases which would in effect make possible the maximum number of traditional infantry commands.

Forward planning means that each unit must submit a rationale for its continued existence even if men cannot clearly foresee the future. The search for a mission is not a secret act but one which involves public relations, since Congressional support will have to be mobilized. In the fall of 1970, the Department of Defense announced that the nine-thousand-man Special Forces (Green Berets) would be reduced in time to six thousand. In the 1950's, under the Eisenhower–Dulles–Radford military strategy of rollback and massive retaliation, the Special Forces were organized as a small elite group designed to operate guerrilla movements behind the enemy's lines in time of war. Under the Kennedy–Rostow administration, the Green Berets assumed a dual role: on the one hand, they were to organize and lead indigenous forces in military operations against Communist guerrillas and even main force elements; on the other hand, they were to be an instrument of community development and nation-building. For the post-Vietnam period, the force has offered itself as an instrument of "stability operations," military aid, and training, including fighting bandits. Since open acknowledgment of training for work behind the enemy lines, in a period of strategic nuclear deterrence, sounds implausible, the second mission projected for the Green Berets is that of training teams to engage in armed reconnaissance in "disputed areas."

But the military establishment must respond to the political imperatives of civilian control and Presidential leadership. President Nixon's political appeal for a great power détente and the appointment of Henry Kissinger as Secretary of State have produced a new focal point in the formulation of strategy by military professionals. The impact of Vietnam started to recede in the light of the realities of a manpower shortage of an all-volunteer force. The military planner after 1972 developed a stronger interest in the problems of the NATO force.

The outline of U.S. foreign policy meant that only in Western

Europe would significant numbers of U.S. ground forces be stationed overseas. The mechanism and negotiation of the Strategic Arms Limitation Talks (SALT) and the resulting treaties, as well as the exploration of the Mutual Balanced Force Reduction scheme, have presented challenges which have consumed the energies of professional officers who aspire to higher command. The fact that détente would have to be explored while the Soviet Union pressed to the "limit" in the Middle East served to strengthen to some extent the pragmatic outlook.

Civilian Control

THE MILITARY pattern of strategic planning is conditioned by the imagery and the realities of civilian control. The term "military–industrial complex" has activated the professional officer's defensiveness. It reminds him of the important percentage of national resources which has been placed at the disposal of the military. And it implies that military weaponry has not been procured as a result of careful calculation in the public interest but involves fierce political struggles of which profits are an essential component. For the military man, the term is replete with ambiguities, since he is prone to believe that basic decisions are made by civilians for civilian "political considerations."

The professional officer does not realize that the term military–industrial complex, as employed in the work of C. Wright Mills, the independent "radical" sociologist, and of Malcolm Moss, liberal political scientist and Presidential speech writer, has become dated. In academic circles, it is generally recognized that the original decisions to intervene in Vietnam and to deescalate and to start negotiations rested in civilian hands and were under Presidential initiative. The military remained prepared to accept a firm decision to terminate hostilities by political arrangements, regardless of any officer's personal views. At most, the military were junior partners in formulating United States foreign policy. Such an orientation could be found in the writings of radical critics of American foreign policy, for example, Gabriel Kolko.[32]

In the 1960's, the formulations of the military as a pressure group, depicted in *The Professional Soldier,* came into sharper focus. The military is a unique pressure group because of the immense resources under its control and the gravity of its functions. In particular, research highlighted the well-known imbalance in the resources and effectiveness of the Department of Defense in contrast to the Department of State in managing both the day-to-day operations and the longer-term patterns of United States foreign policy.[33] The impact of the military as a pressure group is enhanced by its unified training and educational system, especially its higher schools, which develop a strong sense of corporate identity among its members.

Relations between the armed forces and the Central Intelligence Agency, on the other hand, are vague and under a screen of secrecy. It seems probable, however, that the Central Intelligence Agency often exercises the important initiative and influence in covert operations. Its realistic and pessimistic intelligence estimates in Vietnam were neglected both by the military and political leadership.[34] Paul Blackstock's comprehensive historical study of covert foreign relations in a variety of nations underlies the inherent three-way struggle among the officials responsible for foreign affairs (the Department of State), the professional intelligence services (Central Intelligence Agency)[35] and the covert operational personnel of the armed forces. The United States has not been immune to these most-difficult-to-control struggles and there is no reason to believe that an all-volunteer force will escape them.

The position and political power of the U.S. military in American society is directly linked to the exercise of the war-making powers of the President. U.S. involvement, first in Korea and progressively in Vietnam, resulted essentially from Presidential initiative rather than a conventional Declaration of War ratified by Congress. Opposition to the expansion of the President's war-making powers has "spilled over" in political criticism of the armed forces. The issue of the war-making powers of the President came sharply into focus in connection with the incursion into Cambodia and again with the resumption of the bombing of North Vietnam in 1972. In both cases, the U.S. military not only energetically responded to Presidential orders—as would be expected—but also gave indications that they welcomed the opportunity to make use of their military power.

Economic pressures have undermined any oversimplified notions of the military–industrial complex. In a period of continuous inflation, the business community has produced powerful sources of opposition to existing United States military policy, although it may be difficult to translate business opposition into political policy. Reduction in defense spending, a wide range of economists believed, would not reduce overall levels of economic activity in the United States. However, a small number of industrial concentrations with substantial vested interests in military spending would suffer more than other industries would gain. Stanley Lieberson's analysis has identified the states that would suffer from cuts in defense spending.[36] Senators from those states dominate the Senate Armed Services Committee, a base from which they are able to act as powerful agents on behalf of defense and defense-related industries. This coalition must compete with the other major "interests," and they have been able to do this with considerable success, since outside the Soviet bloc the United States spends a larger share of its gross national product and government budget on its military than any other nation except Israel.

In evaluating past and future trends, however, it needs to be noted that the proportion of the federal budget spent on military affairs was higher for long periods in the nineteenth century, that a large fraction of the expenditures in the second half of 1960–1970 were used to support the war in Vietnam, that conventional forces consume a larger share of the budget than do nuclear forces (to the extent to which the distinction can be made), and that even with the expansion of the military budget for the fiscal years 1968 and 1969, the military expenditures as a proportion of the gross national product declined up to 1973. The strain on U.S.–Soviet Union relations and the inability to implement SALT-II negotiations result in an increase in military budgets.

The military establishment was given vast resources to impose on Southeast Asia, by force, a logic of containment first applied to Western Europe. This military effort during a period of domestic social and political tension produced the most violent antimilitarism in modern United States history and exacerbated the cleavages in the American political system. The military, in turn, developed a defensiveness and a deep sense of strain. However, the impact of Vietnam on the military profession must be seen in the context of the military's gradual transformation since the end of World War II. After a half-century of increased interpenetration and convergence of the military and the civilian sectors, the trend toward "civilianization" has been slowed and may even have reached its limits in many aspects. As noted, each of the hypotheses about "civilianization" of the military with respect to authority and skill structure or with respect to social representation has reached a point of limitation. Technology and the changed role of the military in international relations, either actual or desired, mean the decline of mass armed forces.

The outcome is not predetermined. An all-volunteer system will result in a reduction in the size of the military force, and this in turn, will have a profound impact on international relations. In the first instance, the issue is conceptual; that is, a clearer understanding is re quired, by both the military profession and political leadership, of the potentials and limits within which force, especially United States force, has come to operate, and of the political consequences of every military act or intent.[87] In the first edition of *The Professional Soldier*, the concept of the constabulary force was offered to clarify what would be required by such a transformation of the military: "The military establishment becomes a constabulary force when it is continuously prepared to act, committed to the minimum use of force, and seeking viable international relations rather than victory because it has incorporated a protective military posture."

During the decade from 1960 to 1970, analyses of the constabulary concept and alternative formulations were diverted by the impact of Vietnam. However, it is striking to note the growth of a body of writing which postulates the potential involvement of the military in the pursuit of peace-keeping, arms control, and the long-range goal of a world without war. Many analyses have converged on the format of the constabulary force, or at least on the notion that the military function—the willingness to face danger, risk, and casualties—is an inherent aspect of the peace-keeping function.[88]

Military planners recognize that the pressure to plan for specific military purposes leaves little room for a pool of resources and men to be used in unexpected contingencies. In addition, military planners have resisted the notion that future military forces could be effective and their morale maintained if they had secondary functions. One such secondary, stand-by function is as an emergency force for natural and man-made disasters, including power failures, pollution emergencies, and the like. By 1970, the nation could not engage in emergency overseas relief programs (as in Jordan and Pakistan), clean beaches after oil mishaps, search continuously for lost survivors at sea, handle the aftermath of floods, or engage in a great variety of related tasks without the support of the armed services. However, military leaders preferred not to make these activities explicit in planning for the future.

Similarly, the military has effectively resisted efforts to use its facilities for educational and remedial programs. It felt that such efforts would divert it from its basic task, lower the quality of its manpower, and reduce its prestige. In a democratic society, funds cannot be allocated to the military which legitimately belong to civilian educational institutions. However, the military has traditionally served as a second-chance institution in its routine training functions. The military has failed to understand that, in this role, it is not expected to solve the unsolved problems of civilian society but rather to operate a small-scale demonstration effort—a by-product of its ongoing activities. The armed forces have been able to function as a remedial educational institution because they de-emphasize the social background and the prior failures of their recruits, make use of labor-intensive techniques, avoid excessive professionalization, and build on the social cohesion and self-esteem that military life affords their lower-status recruits.

An all-volunteer force will be smaller and more self-contained, and there will be a new pattern of civil-military relations. Although some dimensions of military life, such as its internal authority, will continue to converge with civilian society, its skill structure, its patterns of recruitment, its style of garrison life, and its search to maintain its heroic image will continue to differentiate it in important ways from civilian society.

Domestically, the all-volunteer armed force entails potentials of greater social separation and new political imbalances and tensions. The danger rests in highly selective linkages with civilian society—including a possible officer and enlisted body markedly unrepresentative of civilian society, excessive emphasis on in-service education, and narrow and uniform career experiences for top leaders. It rests in the possibility of an inbred force which would hold deep resentments toward the civilian society and accordingly develop a strongly conservative, "extremist" political ideology, which in turn would influence professional judgments.

There are many mechanisms by which the undesirable features of an all-volunteer armed force can be reduced. These include approaches such as one year in a civilian university for all academy cadets, a stronger emphasis on officer candidate schools, the development of five- and ten-year career officers, lateral entry into the military profession at middle-level ranks, an improved system of military justice, and more effective grievance procedures. The personnel problems of the military profession in the 1970's will be complex because of the declining career prospects and the problems of transition to a second civilian career. In particular, intellectual isolation from the main current of American university life may be one of the main trends that needs to be avoided. Much of the initiative to offset such isolation will have to be taken by civilian universities, if they are to remain centers of vigorous intellectual investigation and discourse.

There are civilian scholars who believe that the mechanics of the marketplace will correct the problems and difficulties of the military profession. They underestimate self-esteem and self-conceptions. The military think of themselves as civil servants in national service, and that is an essential ingredient of civil control. To be paid ade-

quately is essential for one's prestige; but the military resist the
idea that civilian society should assume that they are in the military
merely or primarily because of considerations of the marketplace.
Such a definition leads them to feel that they are mercenaries and
not professionals subject to internal and external control. A volunteer armed force will be much less likely to think of itself as
mercenary if military service is seen as part of a broader system of
community and national service based on voluntary participation.

MORRIS JANOWITZ

University of Chicago
Near South Side
Chicago, Illinois
September, 1974

Notes

1. Speier, Hans, *Social Order: The Risks of War*. New York: George W.
Stewart, 1952; Lowry, Ritchie P., "To Arms: Changing Military Roles and the
Military–Industrial Complex," *Social Problems*, Summer, 1970, pp. 3–16.

2. For a detailed analysis of these trends see Janowitz, Morris, "The Emer-
gent Military," in Sam Sarkesian (ed.), *Industrial Military Complex: A Re-
assessment*. Beverly Hills: Sage Publications, Inc., 1972; see also Janowitz,
Morris (ed.), *The New Military*. New York: John Wiley, 1967; Moskos, Charles,
The Enlisted Man. New York: Russell Sage Foundation, 1970, chapter 8;
Yarmolinsky, Adam, *The Military Establishment: Its Impact on American Society*.
New York: Harper and Row, 1971.

3. Resistance to redefinition of boundaries and functions is as much civilian-
generated as it is the result of self-interest of the military. The report of the
Fitzhugh Committee on the reorganization of the Department of Defense is a
case in point. This committee was charged with making recommendations to
Secretary of Defense Laird and President Nixon on simplifying and improving
the management of the military establishment. In the report, issued on July 1,
1970, there were no recommendations which might have removed any technical
and logistical functions from the jurisdiction of the military establishment. *Report
to the President and the Secretary of Defense by the Blue Ribbon Defense Panel*,
July, 1970. Washington, D.C.: Government Printing Office.

4. *The President's Commission on an All-Volunteer Armed Force*. Washington,
D.C.: Government Printing Office, 1970, p. 15.

5. Janowitz, Morris, "The U.S. Forces and Zero Draft." Adelphi Paper No
94 (London: The International Institute for Strategic Studies, 1973).

6. Beebe, Gilbert W., and DeBakey, Michael, *Battle Casualties*. Springfield,
Illinois: Charles C Thomas, 1952, p. 21.

7. According to Albert Biderman in an extreme formulation, "Being a soldier
as such is not a particularly hazardous occupation. Life insurance companies
do not charge special premiums for military personnel, with the exception of
those on flying or special hazardous duty." Biderman, Albert, "What Is Military?"
in Sol Tax (ed.), *The Draft: A Handbook of Facts and Alternatives*. Chicago:
University of Chicago Press, 1967, pp. 122–137.

8. Smith, Robert, "Disaffection, Delegitimation and Consequences: Aggregate Trends for World War II, Korea and Vietnam," Working Paper No. 166, Center for Social Organization Studies, October, 1970, pp. 3–4.

9. Moskos, Charles, *op. cit.*, pp. 134–156.

10. In a survey of 2,372 army enlisted personnel at the 22nd Replacement Battalion in Cam Rahn Bay in November 1969, one-half reported that they had used marijuana at least once and 17.7 per cent were regular users (that is, smoked the drug 200 times or more a year). The findings were reported by Captain Morris D. Stanton, psychologist, Fort Meade, to the U.S. Senate Subcommittee on Alcoholism and Narcotics, on December 2, 1970. This source indicated an extensive rise in marijuana use as a result of service in Vietnam. Major Kenneth E. Nelson, Letterman General Hospital, San Francisco, on the basis of his study of 1,064 combat soldiers, 173rd Airborne Brigade in Vietnam, described the average marijuana user in Vietnam as "age 21, rank E-4 (corporal), a draftee or non-career oriented enlisted man, of slightly less than high school education and a field soldier." See also Fisher, Allan H., Jr., "Preliminary Findings from the 1971 DOD Survey of Drug Use." Washington, D.C.: Human Resource Research Organization, 1972.

11. Zald, Mayer and Simon, William, "Career Opportunities and Commitments Among Army Officers," in Morris Janowitz (ed.), *The New Military*, pp. 257–288.

12. Wool, Harold, *The Military Specialist: Skilled Manpower for the Armed Forces.* Baltimore: The Johns Hopkins Press, 1968.

13. *Ibid.,* p. 43.

14. Sharp, Laure M., and Biderman, Albert D., *The Employment of Retired Military Personnel.* Bureau of Social Science Research, Inc., Washington, D.C.: 1966.

15. Lebby, David Edwin, "Professional Socialization of the Naval Officer: The Effect of Plebe Year at the U.S. Naval Academy." Unpublished Ph.D. dissertation, University of Pennsylvania, 1970.

16. "A Comparison of New Cadets at U.S. Military Academy with Entering Freshmen at Other Colleges," Office of Research, U.S. Military Academy, March, 1969, p. 1.

17. Lebby, David Edwin, *op. cit.*, p. 159.

18. Radway, Laurence I., "The Future of ROTC," Center for Social Organization Studies, University of Chicago, Paper No. 17, January, 1970, 23 pp.

19. Radway, Laurence I., "Recent Trends at American Service Academies." Unpublished paper, 1970, pp. 3–8.

20. Hecox, Captain Walter E., "A Comparison of New Cadets at U.S. Military Academy with Entering Freshmen at Other Colleges, Class of 1973." Office of Research, U.S. Military Academy, February, 1970, p. 24.

21. Janowitz, Morris, p. 24 of this edition.

22. Lovell, John, "The Professional Socialization of the West Point Cadet," in Morris Janowitz (ed.), *The New Military*, pp. 128–130.

23. Lucas, William A., "Anticipatory Socialization and the ROTC," in Moskos, Chas. (ed.), *Public Opinion and the Military Establishment.* Beverly Hills, Calif.: Sage Publications, Inc. (1971).

24. Radway, Laurence I., "Recent Trends in American War Colleges," Paper presented at Research Committee on Armed Forces and Society, Seventh World Congress of Sociology, Varna, Bulgaria, September, 1970, p. 18.

25. Grusky, Oscar, "The Effects of Succession: A Comparative Study of Military and Business Organization," in Morris Janowitz (ed.), *The New Military*, pp. 83–108.

26. Moskos, Charles, *op. cit.*, pp. 108–133.

27. Hodge, Robert W.; Siegel, Paul M.; and Rossi, Peter H., "Occupational Prestige in the United States, 1925–63." *American Journal of Sociology*, November, 1964, p. 291.

28. Taylor, Telford, *Nuremberg and Vietnam: An American Tragedy.* Chicago: Quadrangle Books, 1970.

29. Taylor, Maxwell D., *The Uncertain Trumpet.* New York: Harper and Brothers, 1959.

30. Furguson, Ernest B., *Westmoreland: The Inevitable General.* Boston: Little, Brown, 1968, p. 286.

31. Riva, D. R., "The Attitudes of Professional Military Officers Towards Arms Control and Disarmament." Unpublished Ph.D. dissertation, University of Missouri, 1967, pp. 61–62.

32. Kolko, Gabriel, *The Roots of American Foreign Policy.* Boston: Beacon Press, 1969.

33. For example, see Adam Yarmolinsky, "Bureaucratic Structure and Political Outcomes," *Journal of International Affairs*, No. 2, 1969, pp. 225–235.

34. Ransom, Harry Howe, *The Intelligence Establishment.* Cambridge: Harvard University Press, 1970.

35. Blackstock, Paul, *The Strategy of Subversion: Manipulating the Politics of Other Nations.* Chicago: Quadrangle Books, 1964.

36. Lieberson, Stanley, "An Empirical Study of Military–Industrial Linkages." *American Journal of Sociology*, January, 1970, pp. 562–584.

37. Janowitz, Morris, "Toward a Redefinition of Military Strategy in International Relations," *World Politics* (forthcoming).

38. The boundaries of the military need are not necessarily defined by pre-existing conceptions of the professional soldier or by current military strategy. It is worthwhile to speculate on the character of military organization under hypothetical conditions, as, for example, a world without war, or a world in which the military serve as effective inhibitors of war and collective violence by means of viable peace-keeping arrangements.

For example, in an extreme formulation, Walter Millis and James Real in *The Abolition of War* are concerned with eliminating war as an instrument of national policy. Yet they conclude with an organizational concept which they label a national police force. National police forces and not world police were offered as instruments for the abolition of war by these policy analysts, who believe themselves to be both realistic and radical innovators. Although there are substantial differences between the theoretical concept of the constabulary force and Walter Millis' notion of a national police force, there is also a wide fundamental area of convergence. These new utopians, the realistic utopians, not only acknowledge the permanent existence of the specialists in violence but (under whatever name) see him as having a role in arms control and disarmament. Under the hypothetical conditions of a more peaceful world, military institutions are seen as transformed in their duties and roles and, of course, reduced in scope but not as withering away. Millis, Walter, and Real, James, *The Abolition of War.* New York: Macmillan, 1963.

Preface

TO BELIEVE that the military profession in the United States anticipates no future alternative but an inevitable major atomic war is to commit a crude error. To believe that the military have become integrated with other leadership groups into a monolithic national political establishment is to commit a sophisticated error. But to believe that the military are not an effective pressure group on the organs of government is to commit a political error.

This study is an attempt to describe the professional life, organizational setting, and leadership of the American military as they have evolved during the first half of this century. Treating the military profession as an object of social inquiry enables a fuller and more accurate assessment of its power position in American society and of its behavior in international relations.

The military face a crisis as a profession: How can it organize itself to meet its multiple functions of strategic deterrence, limited warfare, and enlarged politico-military responsibility? First, there is the complex task of adapting the military establishment to continuous technological change. Second, there is the necessity of redefining strategy, doctrine, and professional self-conceptions. Maintaining an effective organization while participating in emerging schemes, such as nuclear test controls or regional security arrangements, will require new conceptions and produce new tasks for the military profession.

Education, career lines, and the realities of military authority all influence the logic and decision-making processes of military leaders. Despite its concern with managerial issues, the profession has been able to maintain its heroic posture, in varying degree, and

[lvi]

its public service tradition. Above all, it must operate in response to political controls which are so distinctively American.

The military profession is not a monolithic power group. A deep split pervades its ranks in respect to its doctrine and viewpoints on foreign affairs, a split which mirrors civilian disagreements. Instead, the military profession and the military establishment conform more to the pattern of an administrative pressure group, but one with a strong internal conflict of interest. It is a very special pressure group because of its immense resources, and because of its grave problems of national security. The military have accumulated considerable power, and that power protrudes into the political fabric of contemporary society. It could not be otherwise. However, while they have no reluctance to press for larger budgets, they exercise their influence on political matters with considerable restraint and unease. Civilian control of military affairs remains intact and fundamentally acceptable to the military; any imbalance in military contributions to politico-military affairs—domestic or international— is therefore often the result of default by civilian political leadership.

Recent striking technological developments in the military overshadow the important growth of a new intellectualism among military professionals: The military profession has become more and more dedicated to the development of a critical capacity and a critical outlook toward its tasks. The officer is taught that he must be realistic, that he must review the shortcomings of the past and the contemporary records of military affairs. Will this emphasis on critical capacities produce negativism, or will it lead to a concern with new solutions? The military profession, like any profession, runs the risks of confusing its technical and intellectual background with political expertness. One response already discernible is the search for a comprehensive ideology, at the expense of creative problem-solving. Another outcome would be an increased sense of frustration, which could become politically disruptive.

It adds very little to assert that few nations have succeeded in both adequately solving the political problems of civil-military relations and maintaining their political freedom. Great Britain is cited all too often as the special case; in that country political forms of civilian democratic control have remained intact over a long historical period which included extensive military operations. But since old-fashioned military dictatorships are unfeasible in modern industrialized societies, it is equally outmoded to think in terms of maintaining traditional forms of political control. The modernization of the agencies of civilian government is a continuous task, but it is not the direct subject of this study. Rather, the focus is on the military profession and its potentiality for development into a constabulary force which would enable it to perform its national security duties, and provide it with a new rationale for civilian political control. In the United States the task of civilian leadership includes not only the political direction of the military, but the prevention of the growth of frustration in the profession, of felt injustice, and inflexibility under the weight of its responsibilities.

I

AN ELITE IN TRANSITION

CHAPTER *1*

Professionals in Violence

THE CIVILIAN IMAGE of the professional soldier remains firmly rooted in the past. His style of life, his day-to-day tasks, and his aspirations change as the technology of war is transformed. Yet, outdated and obscure conceptions of the military establishment persist because civilian society, including the alert political public, prefer to remain uninformed. Military officers, especially those who occupy posts at the highest echelons, are only dimly perceived as persons, decision-makers, and political creatures.

In the United States the military profession does not carry great prestige. However, civilian political leaders are prepared to defer to the technical judgments of the military specialist, and the public at large is uninhibited in acclaiming a few conspicuous and dramatic military leaders as popular heroes. Despite a tradition of hostility against the military establishment, the electorate has demonstrated its willingness to make individual exceptions by repeatedly selecting generals as civilian presidents. Historians have suggested that compared to his fellow officers, the soldier turned president is often the least professional in manner and the most civilian in outlook.[1]

Significantly, civilian perceptions of the professional officer are not the same as perceptions of the military hero. In contrast to the public acclaim accorded individual military heroes, officership remains a relatively low-status profession. The results of a national

[3]

sampling of opinion in 1955 place the prestige of the officer in the
armed services not only below that of physician, scientist, college
professor, and minister, but also below that of the public school
teacher.[2] Yet one of every two adult civilians said that he would
be pleased if his son pursued a career in the military services.
Generally, the public prestige of the military is similar to that accorded government employees; the less educated and the younger
among the public hold the military, along with government employees, in higher esteem. Thus, whatever else the public may think
of the military profession, it sees it as another career opportunity,
and as one which offers an opportunity for social mobility for the
socially underprivileged.

Moreover, instead of political realism, a set of stereotyped assumptions has pervaded domestic politics with respect to the professional military. For example, it is typical to assert that the military establishment is the major source of thought or policy which
overemphasizes the use of force in the resolution of conflict,
whether domestic or international. Such an assumption overlooks
the extent to which the armed forces are a creation of the larger
social structure, and the extent to which they serve the economic
and political needs of the civilian population. It is a concept which
sees the military establishment as a sort of self-contained organ, as a
vestigial appendage, rather than a creation of contemporary society.
It is a view which is oblivious of the deep factional divisions in
strategic orientations within the military profession itself.

It is also typical to assert that the military professional is disci-
plined, inflexible, and, in a sense, unequipped for political compromise. In this view, since the perspectives of men are fashioned
by their daily tasks, the life of the military professional produces a
pattern of mental traits which are blunt, direct, and uncompromis-
ing. The military establishment is seen as an institution in which
"debate is no more at a premium than persuasion: one obeys and
one commands."[3] This may have been the environment of the military establishment of the past, but it hardly describes contemporary
military organization, where sheer size and technical complexity
require elaborate procedures to insure coordination.

Paradoxically, this obsolescent image is maintained despite the
vast flow of communication about military affairs. Congressional
scrutiny of the military establishment has become extensive and

continuous, although most often concerned with minutiae. The modern military establishment itself is thoroughly conscious of the importance of its public relations. Its press officers supply a vast flow of human interest material. Its ranking officers often engage in fierce inter-service rivalries, which produce an unending series of conflicting policy statements.

War and war-making have supplied major themes for serious modern novelists. However, as Malcolm Cowley points out in his analysis of post-World War II novelists, their efforts have been more an expression of personal frustration than an exploration of military life in depth.[4] An outstanding exception is James Gould Couzzens' *Guard of Honor*, which depicts intimate interpersonal relations at a rear-echelon Air Force training and experimental base, rather than the organizational dilemmas of war-making. Perhaps the most revealing sources of the logic of the military are the more thoughtful and reflective autobiographies of retired generals and admirals, which are to be read as indicators of professional beliefs rather than as historical records.

The university community has not been particularly concerned with the basic transformation of the military establishment, although it has produced a steady stream of historical writings about military operations and polemics about current policy. Pioneer research was conducted by Pendleton Herring in *The Impact of War* and by Louis Smith in *American Democracy and Military Power*.[5] With the publication of *The Soldier and the State*, by Samuel Huntington, in 1957, and *Arms and Men*, by Walter Millis, in 1956, a new focus in American scholarship became evident.[6] Strange as it may seem, it was the first time since Alexis de Tocqueville that American military institutions were being analyzed as an aspect of the American political process.[7]

Skill and Performance

THE OFFICER CORPS can also be analyzed as a professional group by means of sociological concepts. Law and medicine have been identified as the most ancient professions. The professional, as a result of prolonged training, acquires a skill which enables him to render specialized service. In this sense, the emergence of a pro-

[6]

fessional army—specifically, a professional officer corps—has been a slow and gradual process with many interruptions and reversals. Mercenary officers existed in the sixteenth century and the outline forms of professionalism were clearly discernible by the beginning of the eighteenth century; however, one cannot speak of the emergence of an integrated military profession until after 1800.

But a profession is more than a group with special skill, acquired through intensive training.[8] A professional group develops a sense of group identity and a system of internal administration. Self-administration—often supported by state intervention—implies the growth of a body of ethics and standards of performance. Samuel Huntington speaks of three essential elements in military professionalism: expertise, responsibility, and corporateness. "Professionalization" is a concept which implies an element of desirable behavior. As it applies to the military, it presents an ambiguous topic, for what is the import of ethics and responsibility for the professional combatant?

Clearly, the professional officer believes that responsibility operates during the conduct of war, including the taking of prisoners, and the concentration of force on military objectives. But the mass destructiveness of modern warfare often makes these professional reservations seem trivial. And what are the criteria of professional responsibility? Was the German general staff "professional" when it blindly followed orders which had little or no military purpose? Yet, to speak of professionalism clearly means that the conduct of warfare is given over to men who have committed themselves to a career of service, men who are recognized for their "expertise" in the means of warfare. It implies the decline of the gentleman amateur.

A small proportion of men within the military profession, as in any profession, can be thought of as constituting an "elite." The term elite refers to those who have the greatest amount of actual and potential power, if power is defined as control over the behavior of others. One must use the term with the greatest caution. Nevertheless, it is perfectly reasonable to examine the military in order to determine who are the elite in the profession.

Because of the formal structure of the military establishment, the military elite comprises the highest ranking officers. This is not to overlook the fact that some lower-ranking officers wield considerable power, or that most top officers rely on lower-ranking advisors and specialists who influence the outcome of military decisions. Nevertheless, the elite concept makes it possible to distinguish those members who use their skills to achieve social and political ends from those who are content to practice their profession for personal and immediate rewards.

De Tocqueville's analysis of the military profession in the United States during the nineteenth century proceeds almost exclusively in terms of social stratification. From what social strata do the officer and the enlisted man come? With what social strata do they develop an affiliation and common interest? Can the behavior of the military establishment be understood in terms of the needs and interests of dominant commercial and industrial strata? How can an upper-class military officer with aristocratic self-conceptions be reconciled with a middle-class political democracy?

But the social and political behavior of the military in the middle of the twentieth century cannot be understood as deriving only from the stratification of American society. Modern technology has produced such a high level of specialization that men are likely to think of themselves as members of a specific skill group, rather than as members of a social class. The growth of skill specialization produces professionalization, which, in turn, influences social and political perspectives.[9] This granted, the professional officer requires analysis in terms of variables which would be applicable to any professional or elite group: social origins, career lines, social status and prestige, career motivations, self-conceptions, and ideology. At the risk of oversimplification, one might assert that the sociological analysis of a profession is the systematic analysis of a biography—not simply the biography of a great leader, but group biography in an organizational setting.

Five Basic Hypotheses

FIVE WORKING HYPOTHESES supply the point of departure for an analysis of the military profession over the last fifty years, for to speak of the modern military in the United States is to speak of the last half century.[10] These working hypotheses were designed, in particular, for an understanding of the changes that have occurred in the political behavior of the American military. But the American military profession can be adequately understood only by comparison with the military profession of other nation states. The working hypotheses must be applied to the military establishments of other major Western industrialized nations as well. Comparisons between American military establishments and those in Great Britain and Germany, where the military has displayed notable differences in political behavior, are particularly appropriate.

To investigate these hypotheses, direct empirical research was required. Beyond reliance on historical and documentary sources, the social backgrounds and life careers of more than 760 generals and admirals appointed since 1910 were studied; opinion data were collected by means of a questionnaire administered to approximately 550 staff officers on duty in the Pentagon; and 113 officers were intensively interviewed as to their career and ideology.

1. *Changing Organizational Authority.* There has been a change in the basis of authority and discipline in the military establishment, a shift from authoritarian domination to greater reliance on manipulation, persuasion, and group consensus. The organizational revolution which pervades contemporary society, and which implies management by means of persuasion, explanation and expertise, is also to be found in the military.

It is common to point out that military organization is rigidly stratified and authoritarian because of the necessities of command and the possibilities of war. The management of war is a serious and deadly business. It is therefore asserted that effective military command permits little tolerance for informal administration. Moreover, because military routines tend to become highly standardized, it is assumed that promotion is in good measure linked to compliance with existing procedures. These characteristics are found in civilian bureaucracies, but supposedly not to the same extent and rigidity. Once an individual has entered the military establishment, he has embarked on a career within a single comprehensive institution. Short of withdrawal, he thereby loses the "freedom of action" that is associated with occupational change in civilian life.

The hypothesis concerning the shift in organizational authority, however, is designed to elucidate the realities of military command, since these realities condition the political behavior of the military elite. It is true that a large segment of the military establishment resembles a civilian bureaucracy insofar as it deals with the problems of research, development, and logistics. Yet, this hypothesis should apply even in areas of the military establishment which are primarily concerned with combat or the maintenance of combat readiness. In fact, the central concern of commanders is no longer the enforcement of rigid discipline, but rather the maintenance of high levels of initiative and morale.

It is in this crucial respect that the military establishment has undergone a slow and continuing change. The technical character of modern warfare requires highly skilled and highly motivated soldiers. In any complex military team an important element of power resides in each member who must make a technical contribution to the success of the undertaking. Therefore, the more mechanized the military formation, the greater the reliance on the team concept of organization.

What dilemmas does this shift in authority pose for an organization with traditions of authoritarian discipline and conservative outlook? If the organizing principle of authority is domination—the issuing of direct commands without giving tne reason why—the image of the professional officer is that of the disciplinarian. What are the consequences for the political perspectives of traditional military leaders, if they must operate under this new type of organizational authority?

2. *Narrowing Skill Differential Between Military and Civilian Elites.* The new tasks of the military require that the professional officer develop more and more of the skills and orientations common to civilian administrators and civilian leaders. The narrowing difference in skill between military and civilian society is an outgrowth of the increasing concentration of technical specialists in the military. The men who perform such technical tasks have direct civilian equivalents: engineers, machine maintenance specialists, health service experts, logistic and personnel technicians. In fact, the concentration of personnel with "purely" military occupational specialties has fallen from 93.2 per cent in the Civil War to 28.8 per cent in the post-Korean Army, and to even lower percentages in the Navy and Air Force.

More relevant to the social and political behavior of the military elite is the required transformation in the skills of the military commander. This hypothesis implies that in order to accomplish his duties, the military commander must become more interested and more skilled in techniques of organization, in the management of morale and negotiation. This is forced on him by the requirements of maintaining initiative in combat units, as well as the necessity of coordinating the ever-increasing number of technical specialists.

Furthermore, the military commander must develop more political orientation, in order to explain the goals of military activities to his staff and subordinates. He must develop a capacity for public relations, in order to explain and relate his organization to other military organizations, to civilian leadership, and to the public. This is not to imply that such skills are found among all top military professionals. Specific types of career lines seem to condition these broad managerial orientations, but the concentration of such skills at the top echelon of the military hierarchy is great, and seems to be growing. As a result, along with a narrowing skill differential between military and civilian elites, transferability of skills from the military establishment to civilian organization has increased.

3. *Shift in Officer Recruitment.* The military elite has been undergoing a basic social transformation since the turn of the century. These elites have been shifting their recruitment from a narrow, relatively high, social status base to a broader base, more representative of the population as a whole.

This broadening of the base of recruitment reflects the growth of the military establishment and the demand for larger numbers of trained specialists. In Western Europe, as skill became the basis of recruitment and advancement, the aristocratic monopoly over the officer corps was diminished. In the United States an equivalent process can be demonstrated, although historically, social lines have been more fluid. The air force, with its increased demand for technical skill and great expansion over a very short period of time, has offered the greatest opportunity for rapid advancement.

The question can be raised as to whether the broadening social base of recruitment of military leaders is necessarily accompanied by "democratization" of outlook and behavior. One aspect of "democratization" of outlook and behavior implies an increased willingness to be accountable to civilian authority. On the basis of European experiences, particularly in pre-Nazi Germany, there is reason to believe that "democratization" of entrance into the military profession can carry with it potential tendencies to weaken the "democratization" of outlook and behavior.

Are the newer strata in the American military establishment less influenced by the traditions of democratic political control? As the officer corps becomes more socially representative and more heterogeneous, has it become more difficult to maintain organizational effectiveness, and at the same time enforce civilian political control? And, finally, what does representative social recruitment imply for the prestige of the military? Historically, the officer's social prestige was regulated by his family origin and by an ethos which prized heroism and service to the state. What society at large thought of him was of little importance, as long as his immediate circle recognized his calling. This was particularly true of the British officer corps with its aristocratic and landed-gentry background and its respectable middle-class service families.

But, as the military profession grows larger and socially more heterogeneous, as it becomes more of a career, does not pressure develop for prestige recognition by the public at large? Every professional soldier, like every businessman or government official, represents his establishment and must work to enhance the prestige of his profession. In turn, a miiltary figure can become a device for enhancing a civilian enterprise. Do not such trends force the military to become more obtrusive and place a strain on traditional patterns of civilian-military relations?

4. *Significance of Career Patterns.* Prescribed careers performed with high competence lead to entrance into the professional elite, the highest point in the military hierarchy at which technical and routinized functions are performed. By contrast, entrance into the smaller group—the elite nucleus—where innovating perspectives, discretionary responsibility, and political skills are required, is assigned to persons with unconventional and adaptive careers.

This hypothesis is probably applicable to all organizations, for top leadership, especially in a crisis, is seldom reserved for those who take no risks. But among the military the belief in a prescribed career is particularly strong. An unconventional career, within limits, can imply a predisposition toward innovation, or, at least, criticism of the operation of the military establishment at any given moment. It implies that the officer has undergone experiences which have enabled him to acquire new perspectives, new skills, and a broader outlook than is afforded by a routine career. Unconventional or unusual careers, however, must be developed within the framework of existing institutions, since officers who express too openly their desire to innovate or to criticize are not likely to survive.

All types of elites must be skilled in managing interpersonal relations, in making strategic decisions, and in political negotiations, rather than in the performance of technical tasks. Yet, they enter these leadership roles through prescribed careers which emphasize technical tasks. If this is a correct hypothesis, then the study of career development in the armed forces should throw some light on the process by which a minority of military leaders departed from their prescribed careers to become concerned with broader military issues, and with the social and political consequences of violence in international relations.

5. *Trends in Political Indoctrination.* The growth of the military establishment into a vast managerial enterprise with increased political responsibilities has produced a strain on traditional military self-images and concepts of honor. The officer is less and less prepared to think of himself as merely a military technician. As a result, the profession, especially within its strategic leadership, has developed a more explicit political ethos. Politics, in this sense, has two meanings; one internal, the other external. On the internal level politics involves the activities of the military establishment in influencing legislative and administrative decisions regarding national security policies and affairs. On the external level politics encompasses the consequences of military actions on the international balance of power and the behavior of foreign states. The two aspects of military "politics" are, of course, intertwined.

Since the outbreak of World War II, career experiences and military indoctrination at all levels have resulted in much broader perspectives—social and political—than had been the tradition. Yet, what the consequences are likely to be for civil-military relations in a democratic society is very much an open question. It may well be that these experiences have had the effect of making the military profession more critical of, and more negative toward, civilian political leadership.

In particular, prevailing patterns of belief in the armed forces require careful examination. It is clear that in the United States current indoctrination in the armed forces is designed to eliminate the civilian contempt for the "military mind." The "military mind" has been charged with traditionalism and with a lack of inventiveness. The new doctrine stresses initiative and continuous innovation. The "military mind" has been charged with an inclination toward ultra-nationalism and ethnocentrism. Military professionals are being taught to de-emphasize ethnocentric thinking, since ethnocentrism is counter to national and military policy. The "military mind" has been charged with being disciplinarian. The new doctrine seeks to deal with human factors in combat and large-scale organization in a manner conforming to contemporary thought on human relations. In short, the new indoctrination seems to be designed to supply the military professional with opinions on many political, social, and economic subjects, opinions which he feels obliged to form as a result of his new role, and to which he was expected to be indifferent in the past.

Much of this indoctrination is designed to develop a critical capacity and a critical orientation. Will the growth of critical capacities be destructive of professional loyalties, or will it be productive of new solutions? Will the present increased effort to politicize the military profession produce negative attitudes? In the United States any such hostility is hardly likely to lead to open disaffection; it is more apt to cause quiet resentment and bitterness.

These hypotheses are designed to contribute answers to questions which focus primarily on politics and policy: How can the past political behavior of the military in the conduct of war and in domestic politics be explained? How adequate and well prepared are top military leaders for the continuing political tasks which must of necessity be performed by the military establishment?

Three issues are central in evaluating the political behavior of the military profession. First, in the past the military profession has been considered deficient in its ability to judge the political consequences of its conduct. The American military have been criticized for their lack of political sensitivity in directing and executing military tasks. Some of the sharpest criticism has come from military statesmen themselves. General Omar Bradley, in his memoirs, stated with considerable detachment, "At times, during the war, we forgot that wars are fought for the resolution of political conflicts, and in the ground campaign for Europe, we sometimes overlooked political considerations of vast importance."[11] In a deeper sense, the behavior of the American military was not so much unpolitical, as inappropriate and inadequate for the requirements of a world-wide system of security. The growth of the destructive power of warfare increases, rather than decreases, the political involvements and responsibilities of the military. The solution to international relations becomes less and less attainable by use of force, and each strategic and tactical decision is not merely a matter of military administration, but an index of political intentions and goals.

Second, somewhat paradoxically, the military have been charged with exceeding their proper role in a political democracy. The military profession is criticized as carrying too much weight and influence in the formulation of foreign policy, especially by over-emphasizing the function of violence. As compared with that of Great Britain, our military force seems much too active and out-spoken as a legislative pressure group and as a "public relations" force. Even a sympathetic military commentator, Hanson W. Baldwin, has asserted: "The influence of the military on public opinion —a necessary influence in the atomic age—has reached the point today where it is time to call a halt."[12]

The greater economic and human resources of the military establishment and its increased responsibility result in greater domestic political involvement. But to what extent does this expansion represent a response to a vacuum created by the ineffectiveness of civilian institutions and leaders? It cannot be assumed that such expansion represents "designed militarism." Designed militarism—the type identified with Prussian militarism—involves domination and penetration of civilian institutions by military leaders, acting directly and with premeditation through government auspices and other institutions. "Unanticipated militarism" develops from lack of effective traditions for controlling the military establishment, as well as from a failure of civilian leaders to act relevantly and consistently. Under such circumstances, a vacuum is created which not only encourages an extension of the power of military leadership, but actually compels such trends. Unanticipated militarism seems more likely to account for crucial aspects of contemporary problems in the United States.

Third, in the past the military profession has been judged deficient because of its social and intellectual isolation from civilian society. While the extent of this segregation is probably exaggerated, it is clear that before World War II this exclusiveness helped the profession to maintain its *esprit de corps,* and to retain its officer personnel during a period of civilian indifference. Contrary to popular belief, the resignation rate for academy graduates from the armed forces during the inter-war years was very low.[13] However, if since World War II the military profession has abandoned its social isolation, it has also experienced an increased exodus of younger officers, including academy graduates. By military standards, the rate is considered high.[14]

In 1957 official studies reported a shortage of 28 per cent of younger officers in the 4–14 year service group.[15] A study of Army lieutenants concluded that officers with higher potentiality for advancement tended to resign after completing their obligatory service, while those who were less qualified remained. To date, the lack of sufficiently qualified new junior officers has been compensated by substantial resources of trained and experienced officers carried over from World War II. By 1963, however, many of these officers, having completed twenty years of service, will end their active duty. In the meantime this trend in resignations of academy graduates has increased since 1951 to the level where one out of every four or five academy graduates leaves the service within five years after being commissioned.[16] Any evaluation of the military profession involves its ability to attract and retain superior personnel, a baffling problem in a political democracy, where the professional soldier holds an ambiguous position.

As a result of the complex machinery of warfare, which has weakened the line between military and non-military organization, the military establishment has come more and more to display the characteristics typical of any large-scale organization.[17] Nevertheless, the military professional is unique because he is an expert in war-making and in the organized use of violence. This primary goal of the military establishment creates its special environment and influences its decision-making process. Social background, military authority, and career experiences condition the perspectives of its leaders. The style of life of the military community and a sense of military honor serve to perpetuate professional distinctiveness. Recognition of the specialized attributes of the military profession will provide a realistic basis for maintaining civilian political supremacy without destroying required professional autonomy.

But the military have not emerged as a leadership group with a unified theory of war and a consistent set of tactics for influencing executive and legislative decisions. On the contrary, military leaders are sharply divided on issues of military strategy and the necessities of national security. The analysis of the military as a professional group should throw light on the career experiences and personal alliances which are at the root of these differing concepts of military doctrine.

Notes

1. Goebel, Dorothy and Julius, *Generals in the White House*. Garden City: Doubleday, 1945.

2. Public Opinion Surveys, Inc., *Attitudes of Adult Civilians Toward the Military Services as a Career*. Prepared for the Office of Armed Forces Information and Education, Department of Defense. Washington: 1955.

3. Mills, C. Wright, *The Power Elite*. New York: Oxford University Press, 1958, p. 196.

4. Cowley, Malcolm, "War Novels: After Two Wars," in *The Literary Situation*. New York: Viking Press, 1954, pp. 23–42. For similar conclusions, reached in a study of twenty-nine war novels published in the decade 1943–53, see Harry Postman, "The Perspective of American War Novelists." Unpublished paper.

5. Herring, Pendleton, *The Impact of War: Our American Democracy under Arms*. New York: Farrar & Rinehart, 1941. Smith, Louis, *American Democracy and Military Power*. Chicago: Univesity of Chicago Press, 1951.

6. Huntington, Samuel P., *The Soldier and the State*. Cambridge: Harvard University Press, 1957. Millis, Walter, *Arms and Men: A Study in American Military History*. New York: G. P. Putnam's Sons, 1956.

7. Under the direction of Professor T. R. Fox of Columbia University, a committee of the Social Science Research Council has pioneered in stimulating research in civil-military relations and in the politics of national security.

8. Carr-Saunders, A. M., & Wilson, P. A., *The Professions*. Oxford: Clarendon Press, 1933; Henderson, L. J., "Physician and Patient as a Social System." *New England Journal of Medicine*, 1935, 212, 816–23; Parsons, Talcott, "The Professions and Social Structure," in *Essays in Sociological Theory, Pure and Applied*. Glencoe: The Free Press, 1949, Chap. 8.

9. Lasswell, Harold, *Politics, Who Gets What, When, How*. Glencoe: The Free Press, 1951, especially Chap. VI, "Skill."

10. At the end of the nineteenth century, the American military establishment, like that of other industrialized states, became an integrated organization with an elaborate hierarchical structure, as the organizational concept of the general staff became an administrative necessity.

11. Bradley, Omar, *A Soldier's Story*. New York: Henry Holt, 1951, p. xi.
12. Baldwin, Hanson W., "When the Big Guns Speak," in *Public Opinion and Foreign Policy*, edited by Lester Markel. New York: Harper & Bros., 1949, p. 119.
13. On the basis of a questionnaire study of West Point graduates during the period from 1923 to 1933, the rate was not more than 5 per cent; details are presented in Chapter 7, Career Development.
14. Davidson, General Garrison H., *Report on Graduate Questionnaire*. U.S. Military Academy, July 1, 1958, p. 4.
15. Defense Advisory Committee on Professional and Technical Compensation, *Highlights of a Modern Concept of Compensation for Personnel of the Uniformed Services*. Washington: G.P.O., March, 1957, p. 4.
16. The West Point class of 1950 had only an 11.5 per cent resignation after five years, while the 1951 class had 20.9 per cent. It was estimated that about one-fourth of the 1953 and 1954 classes would resign within five years after graduation. Both the Annapolis class of 1952 and Air Force appointees from the West Point class of 1952 had resignation rates of 20 per cent after five years. *The Army Times*, July 27, 1957, 17, 188. Undoubtedly, these fluctuations, which go back to the first wave of resignations after the Mexican War, are closely tied to the state of the nation's economy: prosperity increases the rate; depression reverses the trend.
17. On the one hand, sociologists have insisted that all social organizations display fundamental uniformities as they strive to achieve their goals. This is particularly true of large-scale bureaucratic organizations such as the military establishment. No other theorist contributed as much as did Max Weber to stimulating social research into the processes of bureaucratic organization. For him, the essence of large-scale organization and bureaucracy rests with its hierarchical organization, rational legal authority, and impersonal procedures. Current sociological thinking has sought to emphasize the informal contacts and personal communications which soften official rules and sanctions.

On the other hand, sociologists have been concerned with an almost diametrically opposed approach to organizational behavior. They have sought to understand the variations in organizational forms which result from the pursuit of different goals: How does the decision-making process of a military unit differ from that of a business organization? Here the intellectual task is to discover the uniformities among classes of organizations grouped by their overt goals. This approach to the analysis of social organization has such diverse intellectual origins as economic determinism, cultural anthropology, and political science.

II

ORGANIZATIONAL REALITIES:
HEROIC AND MANAGERIAL

CHAPTER 2

Technology and Decision-Making

THE HISTORY of the modern military establishment can be described as a struggle between heroic leaders, who embody traditionalism and glory, and military "managers," who are concerned with the scientific and rational conduct of war.[1] This distinction is fundamental. The military manager reflects the scientific and pragmatic dimensions of war-making; he is the professional with effective links to civilian society. The heroic leader is a perpetuation of the warrior type, the mounted officer who embodies the martial spirit and the theme of personal valor.

Neither heroic leaders nor military managers perform as military engineers or technologists. As early as the nineteenth century technologists had important functions in the American military establishment. Since the turn of the century technological military developments have become so comprehensive that one can speak of an organizational revolution in the military, just as there has been an organizational revolution in industrial production. With the introduction of nuclear weapons and missiles, the military seem to have been almost converted into a giant engineering establishment. But, in actuality, the military establishment requires a balance between the three roles of heroic leader, military manager, and military technologist, a balance which varies at each level in the hierarchy of authority. Technical specialists can develop into men

who hold crucial leadership roles, but this requires modification of
their skills and outlook. As the military establishment becomes
progressively dependent on more complex technology, the importance of the military manager increases. He does not displace the
heroic leader, but he undermines the long-standing traditionalism
of the military establishment, and weakens its opposition to technological innovation. With the growth of the military manager, technological innovation becomes routinized.

Technological Innovation

IN EVERY PROFESSION there is a strain between traditional thinking and technical proficiency; but in the military profession conservative influences in the past have been particularly pervasive,
if only because the consequences of resistance to change appear
so obvious in retrospect and at times so disastrous. From their
earliest historical origins professional officers in Western Europe
and in the United States, except for outstanding unconventional
leaders, have tended to be conservative about both the means and
the ends of the military establishment. In regards to means, military professionals have a long record of resistance to technological
change, and have maintained outmoded organizational forms.[2] In
regards to ends, military traditionalism implies a rigid commitment
to the political status quo, a belief in the inevitability of violence
in the relations between states, and a lack of concern with the social
and political consequences of warfare.

The sources of traditional thinking in the military profession
and among its elite are varied and deep.[3] In the narrowest terms,
the military establishment is dependent on other dominant elites
for its very existence, for its economic resources, and for its privileges and emoluments. At least this has been the case in Western
Europe and in the United States since the breakdown of the feudal
unity of the military and the political. The dependence of the military on the status quo—whether that status quo is industrial
capitalism or communism—reinforces traditionalism. Traditional
attitudes are institutionalized by the requirements of military
organization and planning. When war-making becomes more technical, the military establishment requires years of preparation and

advance thinking. Sudden developments are resisted as disruptive, for it takes years to translate ideas into weapons systems.

Most fundamentally, the professional soldier is conservative, since his social origin is grounded in the history of the post-feudal nobility in Europe and its social equivalents in the United States. His prototype is the Prussian officer corps, so carefully documented by the German historian, Karl Demeter.[4] In the United States before the Civil War the southern "plantocracy" gave strong aristocratic overtones to the military profession. Interestingly, in the origins of the naval profession, as represented by the British Navy, there was greater reliance on middle- and even lower-class personnel in the officer corps, because men were needed to perform the arduous and skilled tasks of managing a vessel and its crew.[5]

It was hardly accidental that feudal aristocratic elements supplied the cadres of the military profession as it evolved in the nineteenth century. Although an aristocratic outlook slowed the introduction of modern technology, the nobility were available, equipped, and prepared to serve. Perhaps it would be more accurate to conclude that European military professionals fought to maintain their social position by monopolizing officership until their numbers ran out, and until they were displaced by the ever-increasing need for technical experts. Alfred Vagts, the social historian of militarism, is explicit as to the function the peacetime military establishment rendered for the landed interests:

To a very large extent the history of this post war militarism [Napoleonic] is again identical with the history of post-feudal nobility everywhere, even in America. . . The armies were the mainstay of large scale agriculture which, without the chance to provide grain and mounts to them and to place the younger sons in army and other governmental employs, would in many places have crumbled under the impact of industrialism. These classes, from which officers sprang, were favored by Corn Laws and other measures showing that the agrarian still exacted a price from society for his martial aid.[6]

The only appropriate ideology was a conservative one, whether in England, Prussia, or the United States.

In the nineteenth century the organizational behavior of the American military profession showed important differences from its European counterparts because of differences in the structure of civil society and national values. Historians have carefully docu-

mented the difference between the American military system and
the European continental system in the nineteenth century. The
American standing Army was kept small, almost minute, so that the
principal source of manpower was the state militia. The organization of land forces was directed toward employment in civil
disorder, pacification of Indian tribes, and useful engineering activities. Commercial interests and ambitions supported a Navy sufficient to fight pirates and protect commerce, but not to enforce
imperial aspirations. Facilities for the training of officers was eventually provided by the establishment of West Point and Annapolis,
but reliance on volunteers in peacetime meant that the lower strata
of society supplied the essential manpower. This military system
collapsed with the outbreak of serious warfare, and had almost to be
built anew. By contrast, the European system placed much greater
emphasis on standing armies, trained reserves, the professionalization of the officer corps, and preparation for intensive warfare between nations. Nevertheless, these differences between the United
States and Western Europe did not mean that the traditional orientation in the American military profession was weaker than in
Europe.

These sources of organizational conservatism among military
leaders are obvious. But there is a subtle and pervasive aspect of
military behavior which has continued to reinforce traditionalism,
even as the military professional developed and became more managerial after the termination of the Spanish-American War. To
prepare for war and to make war is to face continuous uncertainty,
fraught with grave consequences. The uncertainties of warfare are
so great that the most elaborate peacetime planning and the most
realistic exercises are at best weak indicators of emerging imponderables. Dogmatic doctrine is a typical organizational reflex reaction
to future uncertainties. What has happened in the past becomes a
powerful precedent for future engagements. Military leaders who
have successfully experienced combat develop prestige and reputations which can checkmate the advice of the scientist and the
technologist.[7]

Even after World War I, military history is replete with examples of opposition to military managers and their recommendations for organizational and technological improvement. The most
tragic example was probably the French Army, which entered

World War II with outdated armaments and inadequate military and organizational doctrines. There is no need to elaborate on the details of military directives in the United States which limited the airplane to a radius of a one-day march by the ground forces, or which blocked the development of the landing craft on which the entire strategy in the Pacific was based. The historic symbol of resistance to technology is the horse, the badge of the aristocratic and rural background of the military profession. Though the United States was able to assemble a modern military establishment of fifteen million men to defeat the Axis in 1945, Colonel George S. Patton, as late as 1938, was experiencing the "saddest day" of his life while he stood at attention with tears rolling down his cheeks as his old cavalry regiment marched by and stacked their sabers.[8]

When military leaders are not defending traditions, they are often seeking to establish traditions. During the opening phases of the Normandy campaign, when General Montgomery's armies were bogged down at Caen, together with the civilian, Professor Zuckerman, he prepared a plan for the use of heavy bombers to assist the ground troops. This plan had been envisaged in the early stages of planning the invasion, but when it was presented to the air marshals the response was negative.[9] Air Chief Tedder would not look at the plan. He was supported by Air Chief Marshal Harris in the contention that, if he helped Montgomery at Caen, Montgomery would be asking for help all the way to Berlin. General Spaatz, the responsible American air general, was even more hostile to the suggestion. He argued that "it was all very well for Bomber Command, which was part of a separate service, but if he helped the Army, the U.S. Air Force would never become independent of them." The plan was temporarily shelved, although ultimately bombers were used for this purpose.

However, for the most part, military technology follows closely the course of industrial technology.[10] The military establishment is marked by the same cultural lag and the same reluctance to adopt new technological innovations as is industrial enterprise. But the cultural lag of the military has had more dramatically disastrous effects, since the consequences of warfare are quick and deadly. Both institutions depend primarily on "outside" contributors, the military establishment depends on civilians, for revolutionary techniques. Even within the military establishment it has historically been the "outsiders," the marginal social groups and the unconvential persons, who have carried the innovating seeds. No case is more dramatic than that of the Prussian military system, where two of the innovating leaders, Scharnhorst and Gneisenau, were not of Prussian origin. In the period between 1820 and 1920 the leading personalities in the Prussian Army and general staff— Moltke, Waldersee, Hindenburg, Goltz, and Seeckt—came from impoverished, uprooted, landless families of the nobility, rather than the solid, successful, and traditional families from whom the image of the Prussian Junker is derived.[11] In the United States no example is more obvious or more controversial than that of Admiral Hyman Rickover, born of East European Jewish parentage—a member of the military who has persistently labored outside the conventional patterns of naval life.[12]

It must not be overlooked that most important developments have been the result of sheer improvisation during actual hostilities. More often than not the outbreak of war finds the available technology inadequate, and improvisation becomes the order of the day. The military staffs of Western Europe planned World War I with the utmost detail and care, particularly the Germans with their Schlieffen plan. But the great armies bogged down in 1914–15, and both sides set to work to develop new tactics to breach the system of trench defenses. The British developed tanks, but failed to exploit their invention.[13] The Germans modified their infantry tactics, emphasizing infiltration and machine gun fire, and as a result they almost succeeded in winning the war. The increased mechanization of warfare often calls for more, rather than less, on-the-spot improvisation. After the Allies failed to break out of Normandy, infantry divisions were retrained in the narrow bridgehead literally for hours before they were committed to battle, while ordnance teams redesigned new tanks to dig through the bocage.

Because from earliest times war has involved large-scale organization, military leaders have been concerned not only with technology, but also with organizational innovation. Since the early nineteenth century in Europe, and since the fiasco of the Spanish-American War in the United States, military managers have tried to develop organizational forms appropriate to the expanding boundaries of military enterprise. The basic element of large-scale organization, the distinction between staff and line, originated in the military and has been copied by economic and governmental enterprise. Managerial techniques based on statistics, mathematics, and the electronic processing of data, such as quality control and, more recently, operations research, flourished first in the military.

Although planning new forms of military organization is a major preoccupation of military staff, their efforts often have failed to anticipate important possible consequences. Elihu Root, a civilian, evolved a radical transformation of the Army high command, but World War I produced a complete collapse in strategic adminis-tration. The lessons of World War I were studied ceaselessly in staff courses. Yet, in 1942 the War Department required a complete reorganization, since the single-theater concept of war failed to hold up under the pressures of global war. Since the Navy exists as a fleet "in being," its organizational transition to hostilities has been less stressful.

However, by 1945 the classical view of the military professional standing in opposition to technological innovation was no longer applicable. And the present cycle of the arms race in nuclear and guided weapons has converted the armed forces into centers of continuous support and concern for innovation. It is true, of course, that the military establishment hardly presents ideal working con-ditions for the professional scientist or research engineer. The Springfield Arsenal and the New London Navy Yard have been re-placed by Atomic Energy Commission installations and the uni-versity-affiliated laboratory. Yet, the important point is that decision-making in the military establishment is no longer characterized by traditional thinking about technological requirements, The realistic assessment of needs and prospects has become as widely routinized and automatic as it is in civilian industry. The procedure of innova-tion in industry and in the military converge. Increasing specializa-tion and complexity make necessary the replacement of individual decisions by staff work and group research, with the result that extensive organizations are created whose vested interests press for continuous innovation.

However, routine, step-by-step innovation is not necessarily ra-tional and effective. The breakdown of traditional thinking has more often than not led to trend thinking, to a concern with gradually perfecting technical instruments, rather than the strategic re-evalu-ation of weapons systems. This orientation in itself is a form, though a modified one, of technological conservatism. Revolutionary developments are still likely to come from "outsiders." The development of air power conforms to this pattern, even though the Air Force thinks of itself as the most innovation-minded sector of the military services. To illustrate, an early revolutionary development in air power was that of the jet engine, yet neither the British nor the American Air Force grasped the importance of jet propulsion. Designed in 1929 by British specialists, and flight-tested in the United States by 1942, jets were not standard weapons until the Korean conflict. Although the first contract for the development of an intercontinental ballistic missile (Atlas) was given to Consolidated Vultee Aircraft Corporation (reorganized into Convair) in 1947, it was not until the formation of the "outside" von Neumann Committee in 1954 that the necessary reallocation of resources was effected to bring this new weapon into being. It took the impact of Project Lincoln, the work of a group of civilian scientists assembled by the Massachusetts Institute of Technology, to redirect Air Force thinking about air raid warnings and anti-aircraft defense systems.[14]

Whether the problem is missiles or manpower, planning toward the future tends to be a projection of existing trends, rather than an imaginative emphasis on revolutionary developments. Instead of exerting a direct effort to develop the intercontinental ballistic missile, military-stimulated technology has methodically sought to develop short-range and medium-range missiles and then to move to the perfection of the "ultimate" weapon. In the process trend thinking has led to the proliferation of a wide variety of prototypes and sub-prototypes, for each potential line of development must be perfected at the expense of the rapid development of a standardized system. Despite the mass production character of American society, standardization of technical equipment has not had priority in the United States military. Elaborate product differentiation and enforced technological obsolescence based on minor modifications are essential aspects of private enterprise in the United States. This orientation seems to have influenced decision-making in military technology.

There are, of course, interesting differences in the perspectives of military managers of the three services. In the past, when technology was simpler, both the Army and Navy placed great emphasis on their own development of weapon prototypes. Once weapons were developed and tested, they were subcontracted to private manufacturers. This philosophy was still operative in the concept of the Army's Huntsville Ballistic Arsenal. In 1958 efforts to remove the Arsenal from the jurisdiction of the Army were as much an expression of the opposition of private enterprise to the concept of a government arsenal as they were an attempt to achieve coordination in the missile program. The Air Force, on the other hand, is more closely tied to the aircraft industry for its research and development. The expansion of the Air Force has been more rapid, and its problems of technological development more complex, forcing it to turn to civilian enterprise. Under the terms of the unification of the armed services, certain technical functions, such as ordnance, chemical and biological warfare, and medicine were concentrated in the Army and Navy. However, the Air Force has preferred not to rely on the other services, and has turned to civilian contractors instead. Despite these differences, the common issue facing the three services is that the decision-making problem has shifted from resisting technological innovation to determining priorities among different lines of development and allocating resources for different requirements.

Under democratic political control, such decisions about priorities involve civilian authority. But since they are technical decisions, civilian political authorities are dependent on the staff work and expert opinion of specialists. One of the outstanding characteristics of the United States military establishment prior to the outbreak of World War II was that, except at the very top echelons, personified by the Secretary of War, the Secretary of the Navy, and their assistant secretaries, the hierarchy was essentially military. There was no equivalent of the civilian civil servant, working at a high level in the British War Office or Admiralty. In addition, many logistical and technical functions in Great Britain are under the jurisdiction of the civilian Ministry of Supply, whereas in the United States they reside in the military services.

When Franklin D. Roosevelt was Assistant Secretary of the Navy under President Woodrow Wilson, he advocated, without success, the creation of civilian jobs in the War and Navy Departments which would attract and retain able men. As President, he made no effort to carry out such a policy. World War II brought an influx of civilians to key jobs in these departments, and since then efforts to develop unification in the Department of Defense has served to make this staff a more permanent feature. Similarly, the creation of the Joint Chiefs of Staff was designed to overcome the limitations of thinking in terms of individual services. But the development of the autonomy of such a staff is a gradual process. In particular, the ability of civilians in the Department of Defense to assemble necessary data on which to base future policy for weapon development has seemed to lag.

The problems involved in the need to amass and analyze scientific data are at or beyond the frontiers of technology and basic science. One striking development of the military establishment after the end of World War II was the provision for the separate services to maintain semi-autonomous research centers committed to long-term operations research analysis. The Air Force organized the Rand Corporation, first as an adjunct to the Douglas Aircraft Corporation and subsequently as an independent unit; the Army established the Operations Research Office. The Navy, following its government arsenal tradition, continued its war-time operations research team within its organizational structure. At the level of the Department of Defense, a Weapons System Evaluation Group was established, along with an independent counterpart, the Institute for Defense Analysis, described as a "non-profit organization set up under private sponsorship." One strong pressure for such arrangements arises from the need to circumvent civil service salary levels and selection procedures. Although these agencies are dependent on the military service for funds, they have developed some measure of autonomy and enjoy high prestige in the military establishment.

Moreover, routine planning is not necessarily appropriate for handling the new missions of the military establishment—namely, deterring war, waging limited war, and defense against unconventional war. Mutual warning systems, inspection and disarmament procedures are not only crucial technical matters, but political issues as well. As in the past, much of the basic responsibility for innovation in these areas rests in the hands of outsiders. The formulation of proposals for an atomic test inspection system was first to be found in the pages of the *Bulletin of the Atomic Scientists*, a private publication. Considerable analysis of the problems of atomic armaments control has been stimulated and executed by civilian and university groups. One of the most comprehensive of such studies, *Inspection for Disarmament*, edited by Seymour Melman, was the outgrowth of research conducted by the Institute of International Order and the Institute of War and Peace Studies of Columbia University.[15]

Since each of the services is faced with the constant threat of danger, there are powerful pressures to continue routines, even if these routines now include innovation. In the Air Force, particularly, the technological routines involved in developing and manning the intercontinental ballistic missile system came to consume the attention of most of the key leaders. Apart from the problem of how to employ officers whose skills are no longer required, they recognized no organizational crisis. Thus, it is understandable that the Air Force is the most rigid in approaching the nuclear arms race, and the least concerned with exploring the social and political consequences of its military posture.* By contrast, the ground forces have been confronted with an organizational crisis, and have become outsiders, in a sense, in the military establishment. Again, it is understandable that they have been the most flexible, the most concerned with new approaches to the nuclear arms race and national security. The weakening of their traditional function has forced a widening of horizons and a greater concern with the consequences of warfare. In the Navy both the Air Force and the Army patterns of decision-making have operated simultaneously. A major concern has been with the technological routines of developing missile-carrying submarines and atomic-powered aircraft carriers. However, naval leaders recognize an organizational crisis, as do ground force generals, and for the same reasons.

The Persistence of the "Fighter Spirit"

IT MIGHT BE THOUGHT that continuous technological innovation would ultimately transform the military establishment into an engineering enterprise. Indeed, the impact of technological developments during the last half-century has had the consequence of "civilianizing" the military profession and of blurring the distinc-

* See Chapter 13, The Logic of War.

tion between the civilian and the military. Yet, are there no limits to this trend; is decision-making on technological matters likely to extinguish the "fighter spirit" which has characterized traditional military leadership, especially at the lower levels? The fighter spirit is not easily defined; it is based on a psychological motive, which drives a man to seek success in combat, regardless of his personal safety.

It is a commonplace that increased destructiveness of military technology tends to weaken the distinction between military and civilian roles. Weapons of mass destruction socialize danger to the point of equalizing the risks of warfare between soldier and civilian.[16] The complexity of the machinery of modern warfare and the requirement for their technical maintenance in the combat zone also tend to weaken the organizational line between the military and the non-military. The maintenance and manning of new weapon systems requires greater and greater reliance on civilian technicians. One striking example of the reversal of civilian and military roles is the personnel of the Distant Early Warning Line (DEW), the Arctic radar net for air defense. Ninety-eight per cent of this six hundred-man force are civilians, despite the assumption that such a crucial mission, under such extreme conditions, would be assigned to the military. However, the need for skilled personnel was so great and so immediate that the Air Force could not supply them for years to come, except by direct recruitment of civilians. By doubling civilian salaries, and offering a $1,000 bonus for eighteen months of duty, personnel needs were rapidly filled. But money was not the only attraction, for many civilians apparently saw this assignment of service on the DEW line as an adventure associated with military life.

The civilian character of the military establishment increases as larger numbers of its personnel are devoted to logistical tasks, which have their parallels in civilian enterprise. As long as the armed forces must rely largely on drafted personnel, or short-term reservists who have volunteered because of the pressures of the selective service system, the military establishment must accommodate itself to personnel who are essentially civilians. This constant flow of civilians into and out of the ranks of the military is a powerful influence against military traditionalism and authoritarian forms.

As the organizational revolution in technology increases the importance of the deterrence of violence, the military must concern itself with broad ranges of political, social, and economic policies. The stationing of troops in Allied countries, the conduct of international military alliances, and the development of military assistance programs, all have the consequence of modifying the purely military character of the profession.

Despite these developments, the military establishment has not lost its distinctive characteristics. The narrowing distinction between military and non-military bureaucracies has not resulted in an elimination of fundamental differences, and there is no reason to assume that these differences will be eliminated in the future. Despite the rational and technological aspects of the military establishment, the need for heroic fighters persists. The pervasive requirements of combat set the limits to civilianizing tendencies.

The distinction between the requirements of military roles and civilian roles remains intact, despite the "equalization of risks." Conventional combat-ready formations need to be maintained for limited warfare. These units may be surrounded by a military establishment which is built mainly on automatic weapons, and which is concerned with a complex of problems of logistical support. Yet, these units must have an organizational format and a fighter spirit which will enable them to operate effectively. Segregation from the main technological stream of military life contributes to the persistence of this "fighter spirit." Thus, the Marine Corps, which at the close of World War II seemed an organizational anomaly, has, by its very isolation, maintained its combat effectiveness for limited assault missions.

Moreover, naval and air units are required to carry on the tasks of continuous and long-range reconnaissance in order to detect enemy movements. While life on the round-the-clock air-borne radar picket mission, or the month-long submarine cruise, may appear to be more boring than hazardous, they require conventional military formations. Even with fully automated missile systems, it is still necessary to maintain conventional air crews, submarine teams, and air-borne assault units as auxiliary methods of delivering new types of nuclear weapons.

More important, no military system can base its expectation of victory on the initial exchange of fire power—whatever form that initial exchange may take. Military planners must assume that there will be subsequent exchanges which will involve military personnel—again, regardless of their armaments—who must be prepared to carry on the struggle as soldiers. That is, they must be prepared to subject themselves to military authority and to continue to fight, regardless of their own preferences. The automation of war civilizes wide sectors of the military establishment, yet the need to maintain combat readiness, and to develop centers of resistance after the initial outbreak of hostilities, insures the continued importance of military organization and authority.

What about the consequences of the increased importance of deterrence of warfare as a military task? Can the martial spirit be maintained if the military establishment is preparing to avoid hostilities? If the military is forced to think about avoiding wars, rather than fighting wars, the traditions of the "military mind," based on the inevitability of hostilities, must change, and military decision-making must undergo transformation as well.

Again, there are limits to the consequences of this trend. The role of deterrence is not a uniquely new mission for the military establishment. The balance of power formula operates, when it does, because the military establishment is prepared to fight effectively and immediately. With the increase in the importance of deterrence of hostilities, the military elite become more and more involved in diplomatic and political warfare, regardless of their preparation for such tasks. Yet, the specific and unique contribution of the military to deterrence is the plausible threat of violence, a threat which can be taken seriously because of the real possibilities of violence. Old or new types of weapons do not alter this basic formula. Effective deterrence is, in part, a political strategy. It is also a question of military decision-making—namely, the maintenance of an establishment prepared for combat.

Thus, as long as imponderables weigh heavily in estimating military outcomes, and as long as military operations involve a variety of tactics, short of nuclear warfare, the military reject the civilian engineer as their professional model. Of course, both the engineer and the technologist are held in high esteem. But the ideal image of the military profession continues to be the strategic commander, not the military technician. It is the image of a leader, motivated by national patriotism, rather than personal monetary

gain, a leader who is capable of organizing the talents of specialists for every type of contingency.

No bureaucracy ever conforms to the ideal model of rational
organization. And in the operational logic of the military establishment, as long as there are dangerous and irksome tasks to be done,
an engineering philosophy cannot suffice as the organizational basis
of the armed forces. Particularly in a free-enterprise, profit-moti-
vated society, the military establishment requires a sense of duty
and honor to accomplish its objectives. Heroism is an essential part
of the calculations of even the most rational and self-critical military thinkers:

A note of smugness was not missing from the remark all too frequently
heard during World War II: "We go at this thing just like it was a great
engineering job." What was usually overlooked was that to the men who
were present at the pay off, it wasn't an engineering job, and had they
gone about their duty in that spirit, there would have been no victory
for our side.[17]

Certainly, traditional loyalties are essential for all organizations,
but in the military establishment they are peculiarly powerful. The
development of a rational approach to innovation cannot supplant
an uncritical willingness to face danger—the essence of the martial
spirit. In a sense, the distinction between the military manager and
the heroic leader can easily be misunderstood. Military managers—
in the ground, air, and naval forces—are aware that they direct
combat organizations. They consider themselves to be brave men,
prepared to face danger. But they are mainly concerned with the
most rational and economic ways of winning wars or avoiding them.
They are less concerned with war as a way of life. Heroic leaders,
in turn, claim that they have the proper formula for the conduct of
war. They would deny that they are anti-technological. But for them
the heroic traditions of fighting men, which can only be preserved
by military honor, military tradition, and the military way of life,
are crucial.

As a result, the military profession is confronted with a persistent
dilemma, and this dilemma is deepened by the growth of automated
warfare. The profession must recruit and retain officers who are
skilled in military management for its elite, but, at the same time,
many of its officers, including the most conspicuous ones, must
be able to perpetuate the traditions of the heroic leader. It is,

of course, possible for one man to embody both roles, and World
War II did produce a number of officers of this variety who have
risen to key leadership positions. However, in tracing the impact
of military organization on the political perspectives of its leading
professionals, it is insufficient to point out that military managers
have grown in number and influence. The martial spirit continues
to give the military profession its distinctive outlook, and to mold
even its military managers. Modern trends make it difficult to imbue
the fighter spirit in the next generation of officers, and the civilian
population is often ambivalent about its implications. While civilian
leaders may be able to control the strategic policies of the military
establishment, they cannot dispense with heroic leadership.

Notes

1. Alfred Vagts makes the distinction in the alternative formulation of the
"military way" and the "militaristic way": "The military way is marked by a
primary concentration of men and materials on winning specific objectives of
power with the utmost efficiency, that is, with the least expenditure of blood
and treasure. It is limited in scope, confined to one function, and scientific in
its essential qualities. Militarism, on the other hand, presents a vast array of
customs, interests, prestige, actions and thought associated with armies and wars
and yet transcending true military purposes. Indeed, militarism is so constituted
that it may hamper and defeat the purposes of the military way." *The History
of Militarism*. New York: Norton, 1937, p. 11.
2. This is not to deny specific pioneering contributions of the military
profession, especially in managerial forms, or to overlook those historical
periods in which the profession was characterized by considerable ferment.
See Roberts, Michael R., *The Military Revolution, 1560–1660*. Belfast: Marjory
Boyd, 1956.
3. See, especially, Speier, Hans, *Social Order and the Risks of War*. New
York: George W. Stewart, 1952; Andrzejewski, Stanislaw, *Military Organization and Society*. London: Routledge & Kegan Paul, 1954; Williams, Richard
Hays, "Human Factors in Military Operations: Some Applications of the
Social Sciences to Operations Research," Technical Memorandum ORO-T-259.
Chevy Chase: Operations Research Office, 1954; *Report of the Working Group
on Human Behavior under Conditions of Military Service*, A Joint Project of
the Research and Development Board and the Personnel Policy Board in the
Office of the Secretary of Defense, June 1951. See, also, Van Doorn, J.A.A.,
Een Sociologische Banadering van het Organisatieverschijnsel. Leiden: H. E.
Stenfert Kroese N.V., 1956.
4. Demeter, Karl, *Das Deutsche Heer und Seine Offiziere*. Berlin: Verlag
von Reimar Hobbing, 1935; *Das Deutsche Offizierskorps in Seinen Historisch-
Sociologischen Grundlagen*. Berlin: 1930.

5. Elias, Norbert, "Studies in the Genesis of the Naval Profession." *British Journal of Sociology*, 1950, *1*, 291–309.

6. Vagts, Alfred, *op. cit.*, p. 164.

7. ¬here are exceptions, of course. In Sweden, where prolonged peace has eliminated veteran generals who can interpose their outdated personal experiences as a basis for planning for the future, technological innovation does not have to face this barrier.

8. See, particularly, Katzenbach, Edward L., "The Horse Cavalry in the Twentieth Century; A Study on Policy Response," in *Public Policy; A Yearbook of the Graduate School of Public Administration*. Cambridge: Harvard University Press, 1958, pp. 120–50.

9. McCloughry, Air Vice-Marshal E. J. Kingston, *The Direction of War*. London: Jonathan Cape, 1955, p. 144.

10. For an over-all summary of this concept, see Kaempffert, Waldemar, "War and Technology." *American Journal of Sociology*, 1941, *46*, 431–44.

11. Goerlitz, Walter, *History of the German General Staff, 1657–1945*. New York: Praeger, 1954, p. 56.

12. However, it is not by reference to individual case histories, but by a systematic review of career patterns that the importance of the unconventional career emerges. See Chapter 8, The Elite Nucleus.

13. Liddell Hart, Basil Henry, *The Tanks; The History of the Royal Tank Regiment and its Predecessors, Heavy Branch, Machine-Gun Corps, Tank Corps, and Royal Tank Corps, 1914–15*. New York. Praeger, 1959.

14. See Millis, Walter, *Arms and Men: A Study in American Military History*. New York· G. P. Putnam's Sons, 1956, p. 350.

15. Melman, Seymour, ed., *Inspection for Disarmament*. New York: Columbia University Press, 1958.

16. As the size of the United States armed forces has increased, the mortality rate in war has decreased, despite the greater destructiveness of modern warfare. Thus, the incidence of death from battle and disease has dropped from 104.4 per 1,000 man years in the Civil War to 5.5 in the Korean conflict. See *Veteran's Benefits in the United States, President's Commission on Veteran's Pensions, April 1956*, p. 82.

In limited warfare there is still a sharp mortality rate in one specialized military group and in one social grouping: The Korean conflict brought heavy and continuous casualties in the infantry, and, given the selection system into the infantry, this meant disproportionate risks to the lowest social strata. See Mayer, Albert J., & Hoult, Thomas Ford, "Social Stratification and Combat Survival." *Social Forces*, 1955, *34*, 155–59.

17. Marshall, S. L. A., *Men Against Fire*. New York: William Morrow & Co., 1947, p. 210.

CHAPTER *3*

Discipline and Combat Goals

IN THE *Journal of Military Service Institution,* for March 1895, there appeared a prize-winning essay by Captain Eugene A. Ellis, 8th U.S. Cavalry, entitled "Discipline: Its Importance to an Armed Force and the Best Means of Promoting or Maintaining It in the United States Army."[1] The essential component of discipline for Captain Ellis, appropriately, an officer in the tradition-bound cavalry, was rigid adherence to rules, regularity, subordination, and devotion to established government. In expounding a military discipline based on authoritarian domination, he held that it "may be necessary for a company commander to proceed to extreme measures to enforce his discipline." He objected to coddling and tinkering, and to the "unsettling results from concern with the privileges of enlisted men."

Only a decade later, in 1905, the *Journal of Military Service Institution* published a very different type of essay on discipline by Captain M. B. Stewart.[2] This article helps us to locate the time at which the proposition became relevant that military discipline and authority would shift from authoritarian domination toward a greater reliance on manipulation, persuasion, and group consensus. It represents the beginning of a more rational and more managerial approach to the problems of organizing men for combat. As of 1905, the Army was in the process of reorganization into a large-scale

modern institution. Captain Stewart, an infantry officer, was aware
that the social composition of the enlisted personnel would have to
change; modern armies could no longer be manned by the outcasts
of civil society. While he sought to undo the negative public image
of the military establishment and to make acceptable the notion of
citizen peacetime service, he was, at the same time, redefining for
his officer colleagues the essentials of military discipline. His formulations were prophetic of the "team concept" of morale: "Succinctly, the atmosphere of the army today is one of clean lives,
honorable dealing, an enthusiastic devotion to country, an atmosphere enforced by a system of rigid discipline whose object is the
correction and encouragement, rather than the punishment, of the
individual." He emphasized the positive techniques which he believed best insured military discipline: interest in the material
well-being of the soldier, the competence of leadership, and the
inculcation of "confidence and self-reliance."

By 1914, the doctrine of "positive" discipline was fully formulated by military spokesmen. In a sense, the military establishment had to confront its managerial dilemma even before industrial
organization developed a concern with rationalizing its "human relations." Indeed, the prize-winning essay of the year on "The
Attainment of Military Discipline" reads like a contemporary management manual based on applied psychology.[8] The basic concepts
are now perseverance, initiative, psychology, and morale. The
writer is forthright in facing the tensions between military discipline and democratic political processes. Military discipline is
justified only because of its importance during hostilities. "Nevertheless, military power is not absolute and military law protects
personal rights and liberties by limiting the powers of the commander." Whatever depresses morale weakens discipline. Training is
the central issue, since discipline rests on organizational efficiency
and technical competence. Traditional "spit and polish" is de-
emphasized. Precision in the execution of movement both in the
field and in combat exercises must be relaxed. Military authority
should be exercised to achieve fundamentals, and the commander
must not interfere with his subordinates in nonessential matters. In
the end, psychological effects are crucial, and every military commander "might study psychology with profit."

Since the military establishment is a reflection of civilian social structure, this transformation in military authority, which started before World War I, but which only came about, painfully, during World War II and the Korean conflict, reflects changes in the larger society. Popular demand for equality of treatment grows with industrialization. As the standard of living rises, tolerance for the discomforts of military life decreases. The skepticism of urban life carries over into the military to a greater degree than in previous generations, so that men will no longer act blindly, but will demand some sort of explanation from their commanders. Social relations, personal leadership, material benefits, ideological indoctrination, and the justice and meaningfulness of war aims are now all component parts of military morale.

From Domination to Initiative

MOST MILITARY PERSONNEL, especially those at the middle and higher levels, are engaged in administrative and logistical operations; yet, the organizational behavior of the military is not fixed by these operations. Military leadership, if it is to be effective, must strive to imprint the organizational format of combat units on the entire military organization. To understand the logic of military authority is to understand the practices of combat commanders, even though they constitute a minority. In theory, military operations are best served by a hierarchical organization which can enforce coordination of its complex units. In practice, the maintenance of initiative in combat has become a requirement of more crucial importance than is the rigid enforcement of discipline. In the formulation of S. L. A. Marshall, "The philosophy of discipline has adjusted to changing conditions. As more and more impact has gone into the hitting power of weapons, necessitating ever widening deployments in the forces of battle, the quality of the initiative in the individual has become the most praised of the military virtues."[4]

A military establishment which made use of close order formations, based on relatively low fire power, could be dominated and controlled by direct and rigid discipline. But since the development of the rifle bullet more than a century ago, the organization of combat units has been changing continuously, so as to throw the solitary fighter upon his own resources and those of his immediate comrades. Despite the proliferation of military technology, all three services are dependent on the achievement and initiative of a very small percentage of their fighting personnel, a percentage who are willing to press the attack under all circumstances. The Air Force discovered that less than 1 per cent of its military pilots became "aces"—five victories in battle—yet this 1 per cent accounted for roughly 30 to 40 per cent of the destruction of enemy aircraft in the air.[5] In World War II, and again in the Korean conflict, the command problem centered on developing the ability of the infantry soldier to make fullest use of his weapons. Group interviews with soldiers immediately after combat revealed, on the whole, a low expenditure of fire power by units in combat; less than one-quarter of the troops fired their weapons in battle, and victory depended on a handful of dedicated personnel. The infantry squad, the aircrew, or the submarine complement, all have wide latitude in making decisions requiring energy and initiative. The increased fire power of modern weapons causes the increased dispersion of military forces—land, sea, and air—in order to reduce exposure to danger. Thereby, once the battle has started, each unit becomes more and more dependent on its own organizational impetus.

The technology of warfare is so complex that the coordination of a complex group of specialists cannot be guaranteed simply by authoritarian discipline. Members of a military group recognize their greater mutual dependence on the technical proficiency of their team members, rather than on the formal authority structure. A dramatic and perhaps extreme demonstration of this process emerged from a psychological study of air cadet training by Donald T. Campbell and Thelma H. McCormack, two professional psychologists.[6] Assuming the authoritarian and traditional dimensions of the military establishment, Campbell and McCormack set out to inquire whether air cadet training would increase authoritarian predispositions among officer candidates. Since they assumed that the dominant characteristic of the Air Force was its authoritarian orientation, the consequences of participation in its training program must of necessity heighten authoritarian personality tendencies among those who successfully complete such training. Authoritarian personality tendencies imply both the predisposition to arbitrarily dominate others of lower status, and simultaneously to submit to arbitrary higher authority.

The results of the research, as measured by the well-known authoritarian "F" scale, showed, on the contrary, a decrease in authoritarian traits among cadets after one year of training.[7] Combat flight training requires an emphasis on group interdependence and on the team concept of coordination to insure survival and success.[8] Even in the infantry, these considerations apply.

Another study shows that the Marine Corps still attracts recruits who want tougher training, and who apparently prefer to submit to harsher discipline. Yet, after the death of six recruits in 1956 during basic training, the Marine Corps took steps to eliminate extreme forms of control, such as physical and mass punishment. For these reasons, the military establishment, despite its hierarchical structure, its exacting requirements for coordination, and high centralization of organizational directives, must strive, contrariwise, to develop the broadest decentralization of initiative at the lowest echelons. In the 1958 police action in Lebanon a non-regular lieutenant of Arabic parentage, in charge of a forward tank platoon, had the authority to judge whether rebel sniping was endangering his men. The authority to enlarge military operations, with all its political implications, rested in his hands, although after the fact higher officers could reverse his decision.[9]

The shift from domination to manipulation and persuasion involves the relative balance of negative sanctions versus positive incentives. Domination is defined as issuing orders without explaining the goals sought or the purposes involved. This was the spirit of the charge of the British Light Brigade. It came to an end only after the battles of the Somme and Paaschendale, when Allied civilian leadership began to see the pyrrhic victory such actions would bring. Manipulation implies ordering and influencing human behavior by emphasizing group goals and by using indirect techniques of control. While the terms manipulation and persuasion have come to be thought of as morally reprehensible, they describe the efforts of organizational management when orders and commands are issued and the reasons for them are given. It is impossible to analyze modern bureaucratic institutions without reference to a concept such as manipulation or persuasion, or some more socially acceptable equivalent. The objective of the effective military manager is not to eliminate differences in rank and authority. Instead, he seeks to maximize participation in implementing decisions at all levels by taking into consideration the technical skills and interpersonal needs of all concerned.

Military organizations, because their actions center on violence in situations of extreme crisis, reserve the right to exercise drastic sanctions against their personnel. But extreme and drastic sanctions are compatible with leadership which makes use of techniques of group consensus. The Nazi army was an effective armed force, not because of ideological indoctrination, but because its noncommissioned and commissioned officers were competent leaders who were able, due to their technical ability and demonstrated concern for their men, to develop cohesive social relations.[10]

The sheer weight of military organization insures that most soldiers and officers will not resist minimum compliance; indeed, they have no alternative. But whether they will demonstrate initiative and determination depends upon the managerial and organizational skill of the military profession. "Command" gives way to "leadership" in the language of the military. In fact, Army regulations speak of a "gradual shifting of emphasis from command to leadership, so that while the commander of a battalion or company is referred to as 'commander,' the commander of a platoon section or a squad is referred to as a 'leader.' "[11] An Air Force manual on discipline, prepared with the assistance of an academic expert on human relations in industry, Professor William F. Whyte, supplies the formulation, "We are on the discipline target when an airman feels he is living under rules which protect and support him."[12] The factors of discipline are enumerated as "self-respect, leadership, efficiency, motivation, productivity, loyalty, morale, esprit de corps and conceptions of mission."

The *Naval Officer's Guide*, unofficial manual for the service with the strongest traditions, presents advice to the new officer on how to give commands with a strong "group dynamic" and personnel psychology orientation:

In wartime and in many situations in peacetime, you cannot take the time to explain your decisions. You must say, briefly and even abruptly, "Go there. Do that. Now carry out my orders." Any reasonable man in a subordinate position will recognize the pressure of events and unhesitatingly do as he is told.

When there is more leisure, it is part of wisdom to temper your "No" with an explanation. With experience, an officer learns how to do this, without opening the way to fruitless discussion and argument. He states his reasons briefly and then gives his decision. Some officers become so adept at presenting unpleasant decisions that hardly ever does a person leave their presence unhappy or resentful.[13]

The transformation of military authority can be seen in every phase of organizational life; both heroic leaders and military managers must adjust to the requirements of group consensus. The so-called Doolittle Committee, convened to review and correct the abuses of military authority during World War II, codified this trend toward discipline based on manipulation and group consensus. Since, in some respects, the Air Force had made the most progress along these lines, it was fitting that the committee should be directed by an Air Force officer—General James Doolittle. The Committee sought to narrow the differences in privileges, status, and even the uniforms of enlisted men and officers, and to rewrite military law to build in greater protection against arbitrary action.

The tactical officer no longer corresponds to the image of the rasping-voiced cavalry officer, shouting orders to men whom he assumed to be ignorant. Rather, in all three services, he is a junior executive, confronted with the task of coordinating specialists and demonstrating by example that he is competent to lead in battle. When military discipline was based on domination, officers had to demonstrate that they were different from the men they commanded. Today, leaders must continuously demonstrate their competence and technical ability, in order that they may command without resort to arbitrary and ultimate sanctions. The slogan in the old armed forces was "Salute the bars, not the man," since authority was formal. But contemporary military roles depend on the qualities of the men who occupy professional positions.

The exercise of military authority varies from service to service, depending on technical problems and the type of recruits. In the American civilian image, the Air Force has the most "enlightened" policies of discipline and organization, the Navy the most traditional, and Army policies are in the middle. In actuality, there are important similarities between the Air Force and the Navy with regard to the basis of their military morale, despite the difference in their traditions. For one, in both services enlisted personnel are volunteers, although many have been influenced to volunteer as an alternative to induction under selective service. Secondly, internal social solidarity is enhanced by the intimacy of life aboard ship and airplane. The ground force has the most difficult task in adjusting to the new discipline, since it must rely most heavily on draftees. Its routine existence places it in closest contact with the civilian population, and its physical organization tends to disperse its personnel and weaken social cohesion. But these differences should not obscure the common trends present in all three services.

Consistent with managerial outlook, it is not strange that applied personnel psychology has been stimulated by the military services. The military sought to apply a "scientific" approach to human relations, even before a scientific base for management had been created. Frederick Taylor found avid exponents of his theories of scientific management in a circle of Army and Navy authorities. As early as 1909, long before the scientific management approach reached industry, General William Crozier introduced some features of the Taylor system into a government arsenal at Watertown, Massachusetts. At that time Crozier was Chief of Ordnance, having been graduated from West Point, and having served there as an instructor. The objections by trade unions, plus congressional action in 1915, put an end to this experiment. During World War I psychologists were given a chance to demonstrate their skills for the first time. In 1917–18 personnel specialists devised mass systems to ascertain intelligence, skill, and aptitudes as a basis for assigning men to military occupations. The experience of military psychologists of this period provided a foundation for the subsequent rapid development of personnel selection in civilian industry and business.

During World War II, in addition to erecting an elaborate machinery for matching men's skills to military jobs, the ground and air forces encouraged social scientists to broaden their interest beyond personnel selection and investigate motivational aspects of military life. Research on "morale" was by no means a new approach to the management of large-scale organization. But the armed forces undertook morale studies on a most extensive scale, and industry and business continued these studies as a tool of administrative management. In 1948 a presidential address at the American Psychological Association included the statement: "My first general observation is that during World War II, the profession of psychology came of age. . . ."[14]

Of greater consequence was the adaptation of psychiatric practice to the needs of military life. Initially, psychiatric practices in the military setting were ineffective and disruptive, since they only eliminated unsuitable personnel from service and from combat. But psychiatric theory is eminently suited to the needs of discipline based on manipulation. It assumes the group character of human motivation, claims that each person has a breaking point, and maintains that mental health is a responsibility of the military profession.[15] Once the psychiatrist was made part of the military establishment, he developed a broader view of the environment in which he was operating, and, by effective rehabilitation, contributed to the new forms of discipline. Psychiatrists have come to share fundamental authority with military commanders in defining standards of military behavior.

The Dilemmas of Command

ALL ORGANIZATIONS have inherent pressures toward human inertia. In the military establishment, in particular, technological innovation proceeds faster and more efficiently than does organizational change. It was inevitable that the rise of the military manager would generate new tensions and unresolved conflicts. As long as the professional soldier cannot accept the self-image of an engineer, there are powerful limits to a purely managerial philosophy. And, in fact, there is no reason to believe that the military establishment, with its combat goals, could be effective without a sense of social solidarity, grounded in tradition and sentiment.

Perhaps the greatest strain facing the military "manager" is the episodic character of combat. The sense of urgency, the reality of immediate combat, is a stimulus that makes military authority effective. In the cold war, once the immediate pressure of combat is removed, there is a tendency to slip back into older patterns of authoritarian discipline which are no longer effective. Only in those units which are constantly on the alert can the sense of urgency counteract organizational inertia, and in such units military managers must face the alternative disruption of hyperactivity and prolonged organizational tension. Size and complexity militate against organizational effectiveness and initiative. Because the military establishment—like other complex large-scale organizations—is so difficult to manage, and requires so many competent leaders, there is reason to believe that the introduction of enlightened policies may not necessarily produce commensurate positive results. On the contrary, the new managerial techniques require long periods of training and very high levels of organizational loyalty. Much confusion and tension exists in the military; officers with older traditions must adjust and readjust to the requirements of an increasingly technological organization.

To the foreign observer, the American military establishment—and this includes all services—appears to be a "mass produced" institution, in which little effort is made to build on previous loyalties and maintain organizational continuity. The replacement system handles men as individuals, rather than as members of teams, although in recent years there has been a conscious effort to deal with the problems of organizational stability. The turnover of personnel, as a result of the selective service system and the use of reserve officers, is probably no higher than it is in civilian establishments in a mobile society. However, personnel turnover in the armed forces is more disruptive, because of the requirements of greater social cohesion.

To infuse a sense of urgency and solidarity, military managers seek to invoke a combat philosophy and to strike an aggressive posture. At one time combat ribbons and insignia were designed for this purpose, but they have had a tendency to depreciate in value. Lieutenant General Truscott spoke of his deliberate selection of a bright leather jacket to dramatize his presence to his men.[16] General George Patton followed a practice of visiting the front in a jeep and returning home to his headquarters by plane, so that his troops would always see him advancing. Whatever deeper psychological meaning his pistols may have had for him, Patton was well aware of their symbolic value. He recommended to his more sober colleague and commanding officer, General Omar Bradley, that he give up his commonplace regulation Colt .45 pistol for a more "social gun."[17] As the Air Force became the dominant arm, it was necessary for commanders to continue to fly. They felt that they needed to demonstrate their combat potency, if they were to perform their administrative duties effectively. Thus, outside the office door of General Thomas White, commanding officer of the Strategic Air Command, was a chinning bar, as a symbol of his own physical fitness and that of his staff.

The persistence of outmoded forms of discipline is sometimes an expression of ideological beliefs among segments of the military elite. In the United States, and elsewhere, the military elite hold a conservative political orientation; as a result, they are often alarmed at and misinterpret the new requirements of military authority.[18] Some see these requirements as potentially undermining the entire basis of authority and coordination, and as potential barriers to decisions on the strategic level. They fail to see how manipulative techniques can supply the basis for developing the necessary strong sub-leadership required to operate effectively within a well-managed and closely supervised larger military formation. In fact, they fail to see that control of rank and file leadership, based on positive group cohesion, is essential to maintain both decentralized initiative and operational control over widely dispersed military formations.

It is not necessary to assume that indirect social control implies an inability to arrive at strategic or tactical decisions. On the contrary, staff work in support of the strategic commander has traditionally assumed a range of interplay before the responsible authority arrives at a decision. The contemporary requirements of command have pushed this form of decision-making down to the lowest operational units, and it is understandable that such a trend is resisted.

By the same token, professional soldiers resist a completely scientific management orientation on realistic grounds. The success of group discipline in the United States has—for better or worse—been linked to the development of applied personnel psychology. Unfortunately, scientific management has not been able to live up to its claims or the demands placed on it. The widespread reaction found in civilian society to the "organization man" has its counterpart in the reaction of the military establishment to the claims of psychology. Just as the military pioneered in applied psychology, they have also been early to recognize its limitations. After forty years of research and development of military personnel selection practices, it is now abundantly clear that there is no satisfactory and reliable technique for locating personnel with leadership potentials. Only the selection of specialists for particuar technical jobs, and the selection of combat aviators as aviators, not leaders, seems feasible. Efforts at scientific selection for military purposes were summarized by the psychologist Fillmore H. Sanford, with the distinctlv negative conclusion:

Much effort, both scientific and otherwise, has been invested in the attempt to select young men who will turn out to be good military leaders. It is fair to say that, in contrast to the obvious success scored in recent years in the selection of people for various kinds of specific jobs, no one has yet devised a method of proven validity for selecting either military or non-military leaders.[19]

Thus scientific management is reduced in the end to another aspect of organizational life which the successful professional soldier must master and incorporate into his administrative routines.

Because of the powerful pressures toward organizational tradition, there have been persistent attempts to resist change. Some quarters in the United States military establishment have pointed to the events in Korea as justification for traditional military authority and discipline. Most competent observers have agreed that troop behavior in Korea reflected the difficulties of a political democracy fighting a limited war. During the first phase of the conflict ground troops lacked sufficient exposure to realistic training more than they lacked ideological indoctrination.* The bulk of the prisoners of war who fared badly after capture came from these infantry units which were overrun during the first weeks of conflict. Moreover, the Air Force discovered that if combat flying remained a completely volunteer assignment, a prohibitive percentage of reservists sought exemption.

Eventually the ground forces retrained their troops into one of the most effective military forces in recent American history, but the adaptation had little to do with formal discipline in the traditional sense. Nor did the Air Force rely on authoritarian discipline to solve its organizational problems. The subsequent performance of military units in Korea is a striking example of how a professional officer corps, especially its junior elements, was able to prevent civilian apathy from influencing battle behavior.

* See Chapter 19, The New Public Relations, for an analysis of trends in ideological indoctrination in the military establishment

Ultimately, the reforms of the Doolittle Committee became the target of military criticism. Some of the objections were based on reasoned considerations, for example, that new procedures had unduly weakened the military command structure by limiting decentralization of authority, especially in restricting tactical commanders in their administering of "company" or "mast" punishment. But much of the reaction was merely an expression of persistent or renewed traditionalism.

The traditionalist point of view found its fullest expression in the Womble Committee of the Department of Defense, which sought to investigate the professional status of officers as an aftermath of the Korean conflict. Its report, issued in 1953, dealt with basic matters of pay and promotion, which had not kept pace with changes in civilian society.[20] But more than that, the report was written as a reaction to the Doolittle Committee, and, significantly, was headed by a naval officer. It contained strong overtones of concern with reviving traditional forms of discipline and officer prerogatives, and expressed an emphasis on formalism which seemed to be oriented toward past ideology, rather than the realities of military life.

A return to an organizational form based on domination is impossible. Given the cultural traits of American society, any massive reintroduction of old-fashioned repressive military discipline would mean that the officer corps would run the risk of losing its most creative intellects, while the non-commissioned ranks would attract mainly those who are unsuccessful in civilian life. Any widespread and conscious effort to reimpose authoritarian discipline is tempered by the political pressures available to draftees and reservists. Yet, in 1958, when a sample of potential members of the military elite (113 from the three services) were questioned as to whether they thought "that the authority of the company grade military officer has been weakened too much," the majority answered in the affirmative. These officers showed a greater willingness to attribute this decline in authority to changes in formal regulations than to acknowledge that the task of the tactical commander had changed and required more complex administrative skills.

The strains of military life do not lead to the perpetuation of the old order as such, but to the perpetuation of extensive ritualism, and to outbursts of organizational rigidity which remain baffling to the civilian outsider. Anachronistic survivals are practiced alongside highly effective procedures of military management. Much of the ritualism of the military profession—the constant, minute, and repeated inspection of person and property—are devices which are to be found in any occupation where the risks of personal danger are great. Ritualism is in part a defense against anxiety, but it is also a device for wedding tradition to innovation.

Civilian society learned of the impact of ritualism, for example, when the Air Force, despite its managerial emphasis, announced that Specialist Third Class Donald Wheeler, a member of the honor guard platoon in Tokyo, refused to get a "white sidewall" haircut and would therefore be court-martialed.[21] A white sidewall haircut leaves the head shaved bare from ears to crown, and is required to insure the uniformity of appearance of the honor guard platoon. Wheeler insisted on keeping his regulation length sideburns. The Air Force spokesman who claimed that "members of the honor guard should look alike" was contradicting the prize-winning essay on discipline of half a century ago, which laid down the doctrine that military authority should interfere in personal matters only when essentials were involved.

Nostalgia for the past also expresses itself in ceremonialism. The evidence and opportunities for increased ceremonialism are ample—ranging from the reintroduction of the dress sword for naval officers to more close-order military parades. Ceremonialism serves a purpose when it contributes to a sense of self-esteem and organizational solidarity. But at some point it becomes a substitute for problem-solving.

Many civilians still see the military profession as it existed in an earlier phase, when authoritarian domination was the typical mode of behavior. Despite the residues of ritual and ceremony, by 1945, members of the military profession who reached the top had demonstrated an ability to operate within the transformed system of military authority, even though they had to go through a painful re-education. Especially in such units as the Strategic Air Command, the paratroops, or in the submarine service, where realistic training is both strenuous and involves an element of danger, military leadership has had to adjust to these new professional requirements.

Notes

1. Ellis, Captain Eugene A., "Discipline: Its Importance to an Armed Force and the Best Means of Promoting or Maintaining It in the United States Army." *Journal of Military Service Institution*, 1895, *16*, 211–50.

2. Stewart, Captain M. B., "The Army as a Factor in the Upbuilding of Society." *Journal of the Military Service Institute*, 1905, *36*, 391–404.

3. Lane, Lieutenant Arthur W., "The Attainment of Military Discipline." *Journal of Military Service Institution*, 1944, *55*, 1–19.

4. Marshall, S. L. A., *Men Against Fire*. New York: William Morrow & Co., 1947, p. 22.

5. Gurney, G., *Five Down and Glory*. New York: G. P. Putnam's Sons, 1958.

6. Campbell, Donald T., & McCormack, Thelma H., "Military Experience and Attitudes toward Authority." *American Journal of Sociology*, 1957, *62*, 482–90. The data for this study were collected during the period from January 1953 to March 1954. Other efforts to describe the social relations in U.S. armed forces include: Stouffer, Samuel A., *et al.*, *The American Soldier*. Princeton: Princeton University Press, 1949, Vol. I, p. 55; Davis, Arthur K., "Bureaucratic Patterns in the Navy Officer Corps." *Social Forces*, 1948, *27*, 143–53; Rose, Arnold M., "The Social Structure of the Army." *American Journal of Sociology*, 1946, *51*, 361–64; Freeman, Felton D., "The Army as a Social Structure." *Social Forces*, 1948, *27*, 78–83; Brotz, Harold, & Wilson, Everett K., "Characteristics of Military Society." *American Journal of Sociology*, 1946, *51*, 371–75; Spindler, C. D., "The Military—A Systematic Analysis." *Social Forces*, 1948, *21*, 83–88; Page, Charles H., "Bureaucracy's Other Face." *Social Forces*, 1949, *25*, 88–94.

7. Adorno, T. W., *et al.*, *The Authoritarian Personality*. New York: Harper & Bros., 1950, pp. 222–80.

8. In fact, there is some empirical evidence, and there are ample observations, that selection boards in the Air Force tend to select for promotion the less authoritarian officers, presumably, in part, through selecting well-liked men. See Hollander, E. P., "Authoritarianism and Leadership Choice in a Military Setting." *Journal of Abnormal and Social Psychology*, 1954, *49*, 365–70. Richard Christie found only a slight and statistically insignificant increase in authoritarianism (California "F" scale) among a group of Army inductees after six weeks of infantry basic training. Christie, Richard, *American Psychologist*, 1952, *7*, 307–308.

9. Lieutenant John Eyd, Brooklyn, New York, in command of the 2nd Platoon, 3rd Battalion, of the 25th Armored Regiment was given the assignment of commanding a group of tanks located nearest the Beirut rebel forces. A non-regular officer, he was given the assignment because of his linguistic ability, having had a Syrian father and a Lebanese mother. He told newspaper reporters that "there was a time when a flip of a coin could have decided whether I gave an order [to fire] or not." Although he was fired on, he refrained from taking action. Some indication of Lt. Eyd's state of mind could be inferred from the following statement: "If I'd been an Irishman instead of an Arab, I would be in Mannheim, Germany, getting married to my German girl friend and fixing papers to get her into the States. As it is, I'm due out of the service in a couple of months and probably will go straight home and have to try to get her over from there." *New York Times*, August 28, 1958.

10. Shils, Edward A., Janowitz, Morris, "Cohesion and Disintegration in the Wehrmacht in World War II." *Public Opinion Quarterly*, 1948, *12*, 280–315.

11. War Department, *Leadership, Courtesy and Drill*, Field Manual 22–5. Washington: February, 1946, p. 4.

12. Office of the Air Provost Marshal, The Inspector General, Headquarters, U.S. Air Force, "Discipline in the U.S. Air Force." June 1955, p. 6.

13. Ageton, Rear Admiral, Arthur A., *The Naval Officer's Guide*. New York: McGraw-Hill, 1951, p. 293. See, also, *Naval Leadership*, prepared at the U.S. Naval Academy, under the direction of the superintendent. Annapolis: U.S. Naval Institute, 1949.

14. Guilford, J. P., "Some lessons from Aviation Psychology." *The American Psychologist*, 1948, *3*, 3–11.

15. Mandelbaum, David G., "Psychiatry in Military Society." *Human Organization*, 1954, *13*, No. 3, 5–15; No. 4, 19–25.

16. Truscott, Lieutenant General L. K., Jr., *Command Missions: A Personal Story*. New York: E. P. Dutton, 1954.

17. Bradley, Omar, *A Soldier's Story*. New York: Henry Holt, 1951, p. 5.

18. Brown, C. S., "The Social Attitudes of American Generals 1898–1940." Unpublished doctoral dissertation, University of Wisconsin, 1951.

19. Sanford, Fillmore H., "Research on Military Leadership," in *Current Trends; Psychology in the World Emergency*, Stephen Collins Foster Memorial Lectures. Pittsburgh: University of Pittsburgh Press, 1952, pp. 20–21.

20. Department of Defense, *Final Report—Ad Hoc Committee on the Future of Military Service as a Career that will Attract and Retain Capable Career Personnel*. Washington, Press Release, December 3, 1953.

21. Phillips, Wayne, *New York Times*, July 29, 1956

CHAPTER 4

The Military Hierarchy

IN BROADEST TERMS, the professional soldier can be defined as a person who has made the military establishment the locus of his career.[1] Since 1900, the United States officer corps—both regular and active reservist—has grown at a faster rate than has the population at large, and faster than most professions. The pattern of growth for the officer corps as a whole, as measured by its average size between hostilities, has been:

7,000	1900 to 1910
25,000	1920 to 1940
188,000	1948 to 1950[2]

As nuclear weapons and guided missiles become part of the technology of warfare, any flattening of the rate of growth of the officer corps is in part due to the transfer of activities to civilian personnel.

Since military forces must expand rapidly in time of war, the military professional is trained to assume command over vast numbers of reservist officers and citizen soldiers. The extent and speed of expansion of the United States military establishment in time of war, from its peacetime base, has been so immense and so rapid as to challenge most theories of organizational behavior. In September 1939, the Army, that is, the ground and air forces combined, had some fifteen thousand officers, and by July 1945, officer strength had reached almost nine hundred thousand. No more than 2 per cent of the officers were regular officers, and, of these, about half were graduates of West Point. Approximately 3 per cent came from the National Guard, and 15 per cent from the officer reserve. Another 13 per cent were commissioned from civilian life, as doctors, dentists, and other specialists, while the remainder—67 per cent— were recruited from the body of the Army, via officer candidate schools, cadet training, and direct commissions. For the Navy, the expansion of the officer corps during World War II was not of the same proportions, but the career professional still constituted a small fraction.

The American military establishment was able to operate during World War II because professional officers were selected for assignment to key command posts. The logic of the military establishment assumed that while many staff posts—including high ones —could be filled by citizen soldiers, the top command structure required career professionals. Beyond the training that regulars acquire in decision-making, professionalization means incorporation into an "iron frame" and indoctrination in a sense of assuredness and fraternity with other commanders, which can only be acquired over many years. The requirements of a permanent military establishment, capable of multiple functions—from strategic atomic retaliation to deployment for limited warfare—mean that the profession is permanently expanded, and that shifts in size are gradual and long term. Yet, in such a hierarchy officers are still not predominantly professional soldiers, if professionalization means lifetime career service. In 1950, before the outbreak in Korea, there were approximately 163,000 officers in command of a military force which numbered over 1,400,000. To man this establishment, the military profession consisted of approximately one-third regular professionals, in the sense that the government had accepted the responsibility of seeking to provide, although it did not necessarily guarantee, 20 years of service and an opportunity for continuous promotion only for this group. The other two-thirds consisted of a wide stratum of voluntary and involuntary reserve officers with varying obligations for service, who were concentrated at the lower ranks and in more specialized assignments.

Since 1950, the ratio of regulars to non-regulars has risen to the point where, in 1959, 42 per cent were regulars. The variations between the services has tended to decline. The Air Force, because of its rapid expansion, had the lowest concentration; yet, by 1959, it had reached the level of the Army with one-third of its officers being regulars. The Navy, being the most stable in size and in personnel practices, had over 65 per cent regulars.

Thus, during the decade from 1950 to 1960 the officer corps was able to meet its personnel requirements because it had two major sources of non-regulars. One stable group was the reservists, who had accumulated an investment in a military career as a result of their service in World War II and Korea, and subsequently elected to serve for twenty years. The other group of non-regulars were the short-term officers, who selected ROTC service and other forms of commissioning as an alternative to selective service in the enlisted ranks of the ground forces. These officers serve from two to four years and then return to civilian life.

While both of these sources of personnel will undergo radical changes in the future, the military hierarchy will continue to be based on a balance between regulars and non-regulars. The long-term goal of the military profession is to achieve a 50 per cent balance between regulars and non-regulars. Non-regulars who were incorporated into the military as a result of their World War II service will depart in large numbers in 1963 after twenty years of service. The adequacy of the short-term reservists has been declining rapidly, as junior officers must be trained for longer and longer periods before they can be effective. Therefore, the ROTC programs will be required to change their function from training reservists to producing regular and non-regular career officers.[3] To meet the requirements of technical personnel for the lower ranks of their hierarchy, the Navy and the Air Force have developed extensive cadet programs which enable high school graduates to become officers. Perhaps one of the most striking responses to the pressures of procuring officer personnel is the extent to which the services have opened entrance into the officer ranks to those enlisted personnel who specialize in technical occupations. In the Navy, for example, in 1957, of the approximately 13,000 officers commissioned, 2,698 or 20.9 per cent were enlisted men integrated in the officer corps.

Professionalization of the officer corps means more than a lifetime career commitment. The history of professionalization of military leadership has established the principle that top posts should be assigned to graduates of the service academies—West Point and

Annapolis, and, in the future, the Air Force Academy. Graduation from a service academy is assumed to insure that the officer will understand and appreciate the importance of command and military "generalship."

The Mexican War first saw the emergence of the professional soldier into the higher ranks of the Army. Nevertheless, when the Civil War started not a single graduate of West Point held a general officer's commission in the regular Army. The Confederacy, by contrast, made greater use of West Point graduates in top posts. When the conflict had ended, sixteen of the seventeen regular generals in the Union Army were academy graduates.[4] While the Civil War established the dominance of West Point professionals in the ground forces, the politics of the National Guard perpetuated the semi-professional general until World War II. The control of senior officer appointments was a form of honest patronage of which Congress and state politicians were reluctant to deprive state governments. The inherent consequences of rapid expansion and contraction of the ground forces meant that entrance into the top military cadre would be open to persons who did not attend a service academy, but who were incorporated as a result of wartime experience. A tabulation of ground force commanders in World War II highlights the fact that West Point graduates managed field operations as a result of their assignment to the highest posts, but their numbers were too few to establish an exclusive monopoly.[5]

	No.	West Point Graduates	Percentage
Supreme commanders	3	3	100
Army group commanders	9	7	77.8
Army commanders	20	11	55.0
Corps commanders	31	20	64.5
Division commanders	92	48	52.2
Total	155	89	57.4

By contrast, the naval academy was able to establish and maintain its complete dominance of the elite cadre at a relatively earlier period. The Navy did not have to cope with the equivalent of the National Guard. More important, the relatively larger and more stable size of the fleet "in being" supplied a more extensive basis from which to draw academy graduates for the highest positions in time of war.

These basic features of a professional officer corps stand out in sharp relief in periods between armed conflicts. For purposes of empirical investigation, the years 1910, 1920, 1935, and 1950 present appropriate sample points for identifying the size, skill, and composition of the top military cadre, which constitutes the central focus of this study. Table 1 lists the number of general officers in this sample and the lowest ranks.*

Table 1

Sample of U.S. Military Leaders, 1910–50

	1910	1920	1935	1950	Total
Army	14 (Brig. Gen.)	51 (Brig. Gen.)	64 (Brig. Gen.)†	166 (Maj. Gen.)†	295
Navy	29 (Rear Adm.)	67 (Rear Adm.)	61 (Rear Adm.)	204 (Rear Adm.)†	361
Air Force				105 (Maj. Gen.)†	105
Total	43	118	125	475	761

† Includes temporary rank.

This group of top military leaders can be thought of as the "elite cadre." They are a professional elite, in that they are responsible for the management of the armed forces, yet, they are a cadre, in that from within their ranks are recruited the strategic leaders— the elite nucleus—who give the military establishment its direction.

As of 1950, the military establishment was on the eve of an atomic reorganization. The temporary ranks of major general in the Army and Air Force, and of rear admiral in the Navy, could be taken as a cutting point for identifying the top military cadre, although any formal definition is only a starting point. In 1950 this group comprised a total of four hundred seventy-five men. All were regulars, in the sense that the military was their major career and that they had spent the bulk of their lives in military service. Only a scattered few (2.7 per cent) had interrupted their military career with civilian employment. Moreover, these top military leaders had entered the military profession during World War I, or soon thereafter, and had experienced the severe retrenchment of the 1920's. Of the Army generals, only 11.4 per cent were too young to have participated in World War I; the corresponding percentages for the Navy and the Air Force were 36.0 and 48.1 per cent respectively.

The Navy stands in contrast to the Army and the Air Force in terms of reliance on academy training for its key leaders. As of 1950,

* See Methodological Appendix for details.

the Navy was, in effect, completely inbred at the top level, (Table 2). In the elite cadre the posts of fleet admiral, admiral, and vice admiral were reserved for graduates of Annapolis. Among the one hundred fifty-five rear admirals of the line, 95.5 per cent were graduates of Annapolis. Thirty-seven rear admirals with technical specialization were listed in the annual register after the ensigns of the line, as a dual-status hierarchy. Only four of this group were academy graduates, since they were composed mainly of doctors, dentists, chaplains, and supply specialists. If these specialist rear admirals are included, the percentage of academy graduates in the top naval leadership would still total 82.2 per cent. Only approximately half of both the Army and the Air Force groups were West Point graduates. The 58.4 per cent for the Army generals included about 10 per cent who graduated from military colleges favored by the War Department, and which have served as equivalents for West Point.[6]

A subtle, but important, difference existed between the leaders

Table 2

Military Leadership, 1950: Education in Service Academies[7]

Rank	Total	West Point	Special Military Schools	Annapolis	Per cent Academy-Grauated
Army					
General of the Army (5 stars)	3	2	1		100.0
General (4 stars)	4	3	1		100.0
Lieutenant general	35	19	5		68.6
Major general	124	56	10		53.2
Total	166	80	17		58.4
Navy*					
Admiral	11			11	100.0
Vice admiral	39			39	100.0
Rear admiral	154			147	95.5
Total	204			197	96.6
Air Force					
General	4	2			50.0
Lieutenant general	13	5			38.5
Major general	88	44	3		53.4
Total	105	51	3		51.4

* Excludes thirty-seven rear admirals who were in the specialists corps, only four of whom were academy graduates.

of the Army and the Air Force, in that the very top grades of full
general and lieutenant general in the Air Force were more available to outsiders. But, in general, the higher the rank, the greater
was the concentration of academy graduates.

Thus, the expansion of the military establishment has prevented
both the Army and the Air Force from relying exclusively on
academy-educated officers for top leadership. In this respect the
United States military establishment differs from both the British
and the German professional officer corps. While this means greater
heterogeneity in top leadership, non-West Point graduates nevertheless entered the military profession early in their career, many
of them during World War I, and participated in most of the other
phases of career training. The trend of the future indicates that the
Army and the Air Force will more and more parallel the practices
of the Navy. In 1957 the armed forces commissioned some 46,000
officers, and the sources for these commissions were typical of the
post-Korean conflict period. Some 22,000, or 48.6 per cent, came
from the various ROTC programs, while 1,319 were trained by the
academies. Future military leadership will be predominately
recruited from this annual segment of less than 3 per cent.

Ascription versus Achievement

UNDER FEUDALISM, because of a primitive skill structure and a
relatively static organization, military leadership and authority
could be based on tradition, custom, and, most important of all, on
social position. The feudal military establishment had a strongly
ascriptive hierarchy. Ascription meant that an individual's position
in the military depended on his social characteristics, and not on
his personal achievements. Men were born into the officer class, or
they were excluded. Seldom could they earn such a position through
performance. The transformation of the feudal military establishment into a professional armed force meant that the traditional
ascriptive basis of military position and leadership had to become
modified toward an increasing reliance on the criteria of individual
achievement.

By the turn of the twentieth century, the skill structure of the
military profession had undermined the effectiveness of ascribed

authority. Yet, in the United States armed forces promotion by strict seniority, on the basis of age and service, was a keystone in the persistence of an ascriptive hierarchy. As the profession became more achievement-oriented, personnel records began to supplant social pedigree. In the contemporary armed forces belief in merit criteria is as strong as it is in most civilian enterprise, and no less difficult to achieve.

The decline of the seniority system has been a long, gradual, and tortured process. The system of blanket promotion of junior grades, especially as developed by the Navy, had an apparent logic, since it gave young officers an opportunity to adapt to military life and to develop and demonstrate their capacities. Blanket promotion by seniority, especially at the lower grades, was an expression of the concept of an officer as a "gentleman." If a person had the proper background to be selected as an officer, and if he behaved appropriately, it could be assumed that he would have the proper abilities as a naval officer.

The persistence of promotion by seniority in the face of the growth of professionalization served to separate military self-images from civilian ones. In a private enterprise society, which placed such emphasis on personal achievement, a rigid system of promotion by seniority seemed particularly stupid and unjust. In the Army seniority promotion up to the grade of colonel persisted long after World War I; in the Navy seniority was a guiding principle for the whole hierarchy.

If the theory of seniority promotion was considered unjust, its actual practice often horrified the civilian outsider. In peacetime seniority was the key to a higher standard of living and the emoluments of military life. The professional officer corps was not merely segregated as to rank. Within each rank, date of appointment, down to the specific day of the month, was a matter of crucial concern. From the allocation of housing to the assignment of seating arrangements, captains and majors had to be sorted in terms of their date of rank. Frequently, a family would be settled on a post in housing appropriate to their rank, only to learn that they were being displaced by another officer of higher rank, or of the same rank but of greater seniority.

Decisions as to who would be assigned a command were also crucially influenced by date of rank. The manipulation of promotion dates became a device for protecting favorites, and maintaining the hold of service academy graduates on key assignments. General Claire Chennault recorded with undisguised bitterness his recall orders in the China-Burma Theater, when his Flying Tigers were incorporated into the regular armed forces:

My own orders to active duty arrived on April 9, promoting me from captain to temporary colonel. Nine days later I was promoted to temporary brigadier general. Although I had been senior to Bissell in the Regular Army, his promotion to brigadier general was dated one day earlier than mine so that he then became senior to me. It was an old and effective Army routine.[8]

Even under the principles of seniority, some measure of flexibility was possible, however. Seniority was compatible with selection out, and the Navy has always answered its critics by pointing to the elaborate system of examination and review it had built into its seniority system. In the Army the President has, for a long time, been free to choose any officer of the rank of colonel or above for promotion to any position. Before World War I, by the manipulation of temporary ranks, isolated examples of rapid promotion, such as that of John J. Pershing, were accomplished.

Retirement of older officer personnel at the very top is always possible, but it takes the stress of a great crisis to accomplish such a drastic step. The events of Pearl Harbor and its aftermath resulted in the rapid retirement of elderly military commanders. Of the thirty-one top-ranking naval commanders during the year 1941, 94 per cent were of age sixty or over. On July 1, 1944 the corresponding percentage was only 39 per cent. Similar retirement of top-ranking Army and Marine officers occurred after Pearl Harbor.[9]

Selection out and forced retirement would not have been adequate to meet the necessities of World War II. Any complex bureaucracy, if it is to be effective, must make use of achievement criteria, so that those with outstanding managerial skills and technical expertise can be promoted rapidly. In the early days of rebuilding the United States armed forces for World War II, General George Marshall was able to get Congress to amend basic legislation, so that selected rapid promotion became possible. During subsequent years of combat the careful and traditional balance of age and rank was all but destroyed for the Army and Air Force, under the pressure to promote "up and coming" officers.[10] In the

Air Force the average age of general officers, as of July 1, 1945, dropped to 46.9, with Brigadier General Clinton D. Vincent being the youngest at the age of 28.[11] In the Army the average age was somewhat higher—51.4 years—with the youngest, Brigadier General Frank S. Besson, Jr., of the Army Service Forces, being 34. In the Navy, with its greater organizational rigidity, the average age for flag officers of the line, as of May 1945, was the highest—56.4 years—while the youngest admiral was 42 years of age.

These data reflect the expansion and rapid promotion of wartime, but these experiences formed the basis for the Officer Personnel Act of 1947, in which the modification of the seniority system was, in effect, formally accepted.[12] While standards for the appropriate age of each rank, up to lieutenant colonel were maintained, the emphasis was shifted to promotion by merit. By placing the retirement age at 62, over-aging of the military leadership cadre was prevented. As a result, in 1950, the average age of general officers in the top three ranks on active duty was: Army, 56.3 years; Navy, 54.8 years; and Air Force, 51.2 years (Table 3).

Table 3

Military Leadership, 1910–50: Age Distribution

	Average Age	Range	Number
Army			
1910	57.8	50–64	(14)
1920	56.7	50–64	(51)
1935	61.1	55–64	(64)
1950	56.3	43–62	(166)
Navy			
1910	61.2	59–62	(29)
1920	59.3	51–64	(67)
1935	59.9	55–65	(61)
1950	54.5	49–62	(204)
Air Force			
1950	51.2	41–62	(105)

With the decline in promotion by strict seniority, narrowly age-graded leadership at the top has been replaced by a much more heterogeneous group. In the Navy, as of 1910, the age of the elite was limited to the narrow range of 59 to 62, and it has been broadened drastically to 49 to 62. Similarly, in the Army the minimum effective age of becoming a general in 1950 was in the early 40's, a marked reduction from 1910 when 50 years of age was the bottom. The weakening of the seniority system reflected that pressure for performance which has become an over-riding consideration, at the expense of military honor and tradition. Members of the top military cadre are successful men by the standards of their organization, and organizational realities force them to be continuously concerned with managerial skill and achievement.

Skill and Rank

MILITARY COMMANDERS at all levels, but especially at the top, are now charged with directing and administering an organization whose personnel have specialized skills which are more and more transferable to civilian structure. When, in the nineteenth century, the military profession began to introduce more complex instruments of destruction, the required skills were not only relatively simple, but had little relevance to civilian life. With the exception of a few military engineers, the accomplished soldier—both officer and enlisted man—had an enforced career commitment to the military. It would be fair to say that, as long as technology was relatively simple, the officer's position in society was ascribed because he was a soldier, rather than because of any specific skills he had achieved.

Occupational specialization since the Civil War demonstrates that the skill structure of the military has become not only more complicated, but also more transferable to civilian society (Table 4). Military type occupations for enlisted men accounted for 93.2 per cent of the personnel in the Civil War, but after the Spanish-American War civilian type occupations began to predominate. By 1954, only 28.8 per cent of the Army enlisted personnel were engaged in purely military occupations. This same pattern holds for the officer group, and to an even greater extent for both the Navy and Air Force. Indeed, this trend is present in all the armed forces, and reflects the expansion of logistical and maintenance functions. However, the trend is more marked in the United States military establishment because of the higher standard of living of the armed forces and the greater emphasis on specialized mechanical instruments and devices.

Table 4

Occupational Specialization in Army Enlisted Personnel, Civil War to 1954[13]

Occupational Group	Civil War %	Span.-Amer. War %	WW I %	WW II %	Korean War %	1954 %
Civilian-type occupations						
Technical, scientific	0.2	0.5	3.7	10.1	10.7	14.5
Administrative, clerical	0.7	3.1	8.0	14.6	19.2	17.5
Skilled mechanics, maintenance, etc.	0.6	1.1	21.5	15.8	16.9	20.3
Service workers	2.4	6.5	12.5	9.7	11.5	10.4
Operative, laborers	2.9	2.2	20.2	13.6	8.6	8.4
Military-type occupations	93.2	86.6	34.1	36.2	33.1	28.8

This proliferation of skill—which continues at a rapid rate, with the introduction of guided missiles—has changed the hierarchical organization of the profession. In theory, and in image, the military rank system is a continuous and sharp pyramid with direct and clear-cut lines of authority from top to bottom. In actuality, because of the need to find places for greater numbers of specialized personnel, the military hierarchy is no longer a pyramid. In the days when technology was simpler, the most numerous rank was the private and the able-bodied seaman, both of whom performed relatively standardized tasks. The number of enlisted men dropped off progressively and sharply with each higher level of rank to a very small apex. Only the handful of top noncommissioned officers "outranked" the junior officers in administrative and technical skill. In such a hierarchy the number of ranks could be few, the lines of authority could extend directly from the apex to the very bottom, and managerial skills were not at a premium.

As late as June 30, 1935, the rank of enlisted personnel of the Army conformed to this idealized pyramid.[14]

	Number	Percentage
Master sergeant	1041	.8
First sergeant	1143	.9
Technical sergeant	1676	1.3
Staff sergeant	4493	3.6
Sergeant	11673	9.4
Corporal	11266	9.0
Private first class	31831	25.5
Private	61612	49.5
Total	124735	100.0

By contrast, the distribution of enlisted grades in a typical highly technical bomb squadron was reported at the end of the Korean hostilities as follows:[15]

	Percentage
Master sergeant	7.0
Technical sergeant	10.3
Staff sergeant	15.2
Airman first class	24.4
Airman second class	28.1
Airman third class	13.5
Basic airman	1.5
	100.0

This diamond-shaped pattern of rank distribution now obtains, to varying degrees, in all combat and technical units of the armed forces.

By 1920, for the officer corps as a whole, lieutenant and captain, and their naval equivalents, had become the most numerous ranks, and this diamond-shaped structure has persisted (Table 5). The changed pattern of rank gives the impression of an inflation in rank, and a corresponding diminution of authority. A comparison of the actual rank distribution in the Army and the Navy in 1920 and in 1950 shows that the "upper middle ranks" of colonel and lieutenant colonel (of captain and commander in the Navy) have increased proportionately, while the lowest officer ranks have correspondingly declined (Table 5). This parallels the changing pattern of civilian social structure, where the upper middle class proliferates because of the expansion of new professional and skill groups.[16] In part, this represents an effort to raise the status and income of the soldier. In part, it represents a tendency of organizations to grow internally. Basically, this expansion of the middle strata of ranks—officers and enlisted men—is a typical manifestation of organizations which have grown more complex.

The new skill structure does not permit such a simple hierarchical command structure, although the military commander both issues and obeys direct orders and regulations. Clearly, as the destructive power of the armed forces increases, channels for issuing orders to make use of weapons become more and more centralized. But, simultaneously, the task of military authority more and more often involves the coordination of diversified units, rather

Table 5

Officer Corps, 1920–50:
Hierarchy of Ranks

	Army		Air Force			Navy	
	1920	1950	1950			1920	1950
	%	%	%			%	%
General	.4	.8	.5	Admiral		1.3	.8
Colonel	4.1	9.4	4.3	Captain		4.4	6.8
Lt. Col.	4.7	11.5	10.0	Commander		7.6	10.9
Major	14.9	20.7	17.8	Lt. Cdr.		14.4	18.3
Captain	35.9	34.9	34.6	Lieutenant		32.8	28.8
First Lt.	32.6	13.9	26.4	Lt. (J. G.)		16.6	24.0
Second Lt.	7.4	8.8	6.5	Ensign		22.9	10.4
	100.0	100.0	100.0			100.0	100.0

than the exercise of direct control of the highest echelons over the lowest ones. Thus, the military establishment, like most other large-scale organizations, displays a centralization in basic decision-making, but at the same time a decentralization in implementing operations.

To illustrate, if we consider a typical operation in the Korean conflict, where an infantry combat team required air support from naval carrier-based planes, it is clear that direct orders of a hierarchical authority are being augmented by complex lateral coordination. In the range of tasks from strategic deterrence to preparation for limited warfare, from military assistance programs to international planning, much military leadership consists of planning and coordination, rather than issuing orders. The academic directors of the new Air Force Academy are dedicated to the assumption that they are training "future commanders of missile squadrons and not space cadets."[17] The command task of such officers will consist almost exclusively of the coordination of technical specialists.

The size and complexity of the hierarchy is so extensive that the traditional distinction of staff-command no longer fits the realities of military administration. Organizations in which the role of staff officer is limited to that of adviser may have been effective as long as the technology of warfare developed slowly. But the commander has greater and greater difficulty in assessing the performance of his technical subordinates, and, consequently, is forced more and more to use his staff officer in supervisory as well as advisory roles.

In a highly suggestive study of organizational strains, Samuel A. Stouffer, Andrew F. Henry, and Edgar F. Borgatta investigated the attitudes toward staff-command relations in the Air Force.[18] The authors charted the opinions of twenty-five hundred Air Force officers as to the conditions under which they believed a higher-echelon staff officer should handle a problem in a lower-echelon staff section through the staff channel. The alternatives were dealing directly with the lower staff officer, as contrasted with the approved approach of handling the problem through command channels. The conclusions reveal that, in the normal course of events, informal and unofficial staff intervention would be used and the classic distinction between staff and line overlooked.

As might be expected, regular officers were most prone to report that they would use command channels, the volunteer reserve officer less prone, and the involuntary reserve officer the least prone. However, the magnitude of these differences was not striking, indicating that the weakening of staff-command relations operates for all types of officer personnel. The managerial skill of the officer in the immediate situation is as important as his formal authority. The higher the level in the military establishment, the more likely are the lines of staff and command to become mixed and confused.

Division of Labor

THE HYPOTHESIS that the top military elite are increasingly apt to develop skills common to civilian administrators and civilian leaders does not mean that all general officers are primarily concerned with techniques of organization, negotiation, and maintenance of organizational effectiveness. The four hundred seventy-five members of the 1950 sample of top military leaders can be classified into three skill groups on the basis of career lines and major assignments: technical support, staff officer, and command. Among these three groups, the type and degree of emphasis on managerial skill varies. The technical support officer is the most specialist-oriented, although the engineering officer who rose to the head of a bureau must have acquired some managerial skill. The staff officer is essentially a specialist in coordination, while the commander at this level is the "generalist" in decision-making.

The distribution of officers in each of these categories was roughly equal for the Army and the Air Force; about 20 per cent fell into the technical support category, while the remainder were divided between staff officers and commanders—operational and strategic (Table 6). While the Navy had the same proportion of officers in charge of technical support, commanders greatly outnumbered staff officers.

Table 6
Military Leadership, 1950:
Division of Labor

	Army %	Navy %	Air Force %
Technical support	18.7	17.1	19.0
Staff	30.7	21.9	35.8
Command	45.2	60.2	37.7
Not classifiable	5.4	.8	7.5
Number	(166)	(204)	(105)

At any given time, however, only a minority of generals and admirals in the expanded peacetime military establishment are in command positions, that is, in charge of military fighting units. In 1953 the Army had five hundred general officers. Roughly one-third of these were assigned to command positions with strategic or tactical units in the United States and overseas, while the remainder held administrative posts.[19] A similar pattern operated in the Navy, where three out of four admirals were assigned to administrative work, and in the Air Force where the ratio was three out of five. Aside from the complex administrative tasks of the military establishment, the armed forces in peacetime do not have enough combat units to accommodate all the senior officers.

A functional breakdown of the administrative and planning tasks performed by the military elite reveals strategic planning, military assistance, logistics, manpower, research and development, legislative liaison, and public relations, aside from the vast array of technical military assignments in research and development, engineering, ordnance, logistics, personnel management, and education. Alternatively, the division of labor can be seen in roles developed mainly since World War II, which primarily involve responsibility for dealing with international security and international politico-military affairs. While every military task ultimately impinges on international politics, some officers have tasks which involve direct political planning and political negotiation.

Every ranking field commander stationed abroad is, by virtue of his very position, a political agent. At the Department of Defense the international security affairs unit includes generals and admirals drawn from a variety of staff and command background, who are concerned with strategic political-military matters affecting the United Nations, the North Atlantic Treaty Organization, etc. The Joint Chiefs of Staff, as principal military advisers, are thoroughly enmeshed in political estimates as they prepare their strategic plans. The same pattern repeats itself in strategic planning units of the three services and in the overseas commands, but at these levels, in addition, the administration of military alliances and military assistance programs increases the number of general officers involved in political affairs.

It is difficult to report precisely how many general officers have such politico-military assignments at any given time, since job titles are sometimes misleading. Yet, the pattern can be inferred from assignments, as, for example, among the Army general officers in 1953.[20] One out of four officers, at a particular time, had assignments which extended well beyond the hardware aspects of warfare into matters of international politics. As warfare becomes more technological, the number of military command assignments decreases while "military" management and politico-military assignments increase.

Interpersonal skill is of the essence for those who must operate in the ever-changing environment of the higher levels of military administration. In fact, at each higher level of military administration, as the lines of authority become more complex, assignments more diffuse, and contacts with other agencies more elaborate, the relative importance of interpersonal skill comes to be valued more highly than substantive knowledge. In 1954 a sample of approximately 576 Army, Navy, and Air Force officers on staff duty in the Pentagon were asked the question, "Generally speaking, do you feel that substantive knowledge or interpersonal skill is more im-

portant in your type of work?"* The results reveal that, for officers
from all three services, the higher the administrative level, the
greater the emphasis on interpersonal skills.[21] At the Office of the
Secretary of Defense a greater premium was placed on skills in
negotiation; by contrast, officers assigned to service headquarters
valued substantive knowledge more and tended to be "task oriented." Officers serving on committees with civilians, or with officers
from other services, placed relatively greater emphasis on interpersonal skill than did officers without such assignments. Hard-
bitten commanders such as General Mark Clark decry the recent
introduction into the American scene of "British conference method
of threshing out problems in round table talkfests, a custom
which . . . has become popular since the war in our own military
establishment, at the sacrifice of speed and efficiency."[22] The conference technique is not a foreign importation, but an inevitable
aspect of modern managerial techniques.

The development of "oral briefing" as a part of the decision-
making process is military in origin. Despite the military profession's
concern with authoritative communications, it has gone far in
institutionalizing informal oral briefings. At these informal meetings
decisions are arrived at by elaborate compromise, and, therefore,
the skill of oral presentation is crucial. The oral briefing is a response to the speed with which events transpire. It is also a reflection of the fact that the official flow of upward communication is
less adequate in the military than in other bureaucracies. The oral
briefing is a rapid and flexible device for upward communication,
which permits a more or less informal exchange of information.
Since briefings are attended by many officials, they serve to bypass
any single person who might block the upward flow of information.
The presence of younger staff officers at the important briefings
guarantees that coordination between staff officers can take place on
an informal level, regardless of the official position of the nominally
responsible officer.

Communication skills are required not only for the mechanics
of internal decision-making, but also because the contemporary
military commander must have representational ability. Early in
his career General Douglas MacArthur was, in effect, the first War

* See Methodological Appendix for details regarding this sample.

Department press officer. General Mark Clark personally shook the hand of each prisoner of war who was returned from Chinese camps during Operation Little Switch. Commanding officers of basic training centers in the United States hold open house, just as business corporation executives do, but the mothers and fathers of selectees are invited to attend, rather than stockholders.

To identify the managerial aspects of top military command does not deny the important element of tension which exists between the emotional, physical, and technical requirements of many initial assignments of a combat officer—such as the fighter pilot or the paratrooper—and the requirements of higher command. Most members of the contemporary military elite have had to display the ability to shift from the skill requirements of lower echelons to the requirements of higher rank. The breakdown of discipline based on domination, the weakening of the strict seniority system, and the shift away from a pyramidal hierarchy leave no alternative. For future generals and admirals, the gaps between heroic leadership and military management becomes smaller as administrative pressures increase at the lower levels. Ultimately, under the new skill structure, the struggle between the combat type officer and the military manager gives way to a fusion of roles. The crucial difference becomes that between those officers whose capacities and experiences limit them to management of small tactical units, and those who are able to manage large and complex organizations. When asked the question, "Do you think it more important for a military officer to be a good leader of men or a good administrator?," the majority of the sample of 113 officers—the sample of the future elite—felt that both "skills" were essential, or that a good leader was, in effect, a good administrator.

This process of transition of roles from tactical to large-scale operations is perhaps most difficult in the Air Force. A study by Raymond Mack, a research sociologist, underlines the observation, well known to every alert military commander, that in the Air Force flying has more prestige than decision-making at the lower echelon.[23] But this system of prestige does not extend throughout the entire hierarchy. Although a combat ideology pervades the highest echelons, the prestige of decision-making and planning increases as the individual advances in position. Thus, an air officer must readjust his values, often with great difficulty, as his career unfolds. One of the main functions of higher education in staff and command school and war college is to assist the officer to adjust to the prestige patterns and values of higher echelons.

The more rapid the advancement into the highest echelons, the less time is available to retrain officers for their new duties. The air officer is certainly likely to reach the rank of general much more quickly than officers in the other two services, and he is therefore much more likely to carry with him the attitudes and responses of the tactical combat officer. In the 1950 sample of military leaders, 49 per cent of the Air Force officers reached the rank of general officer with twenty-one years or less of military service. In the Army the percentage was 6.6, and in the Navy 1.5.

Emerging tensions within the military profession may well divide those leaders with broad managerial orientation from the new military scientists who are concerned with the technical development of weapons systems. Many competent officers in the military establishment are now following scientific careers. Their number is growing, their prestige is rising, and their position in the hierarchy is assured. These officers have a narrower definition of their task and role than do the military managers.

To speak of the new skill structure is not to imply that efficiency is or can be the guiding criterion. As described earlier, combat goals are still the ultimate consideration of the military establishment.* Given the ends of war, and the imponderables of war-making, managerial skills must operate without day-to-day criteria of success or failure. In the business corporation profits are reputed to be a specifically calculable criterion for evaluating the utility of a manager. Everywhere in the military cost accounting and operational analysis are used as stimuli for increasing the efficiency of military operations. But the profit criterion is missing in the military profession.

C. W. Mills suggests that contemporary military leaders are like corporation managers, and are even, in a sense, managers who are interchangeable among various types of organization, thus creating a power elite. There is little to be learned from a theory which can be reduced to the simple formula that a manager is a manager, regardless of his organizational environment. The organizational revolution in warfare means that the process of advancement and

* See Chapter 2, Technology and Decision-Making.

promotion is not merely the result of technical and combat skill, but also the result of communication, persuasion, and negotiation—and these are, to be sure, the practices of all types of organizational leaders. The professional soldier, like the corporation manager, must learn that interpersonal issues are crucial in the internal effectiveness of his organization. He must learn that the success or failure of his particular organization depends in part on representational skills in dealing with other military organizations and with civilian groups.

Yet, the purposes of military organization are profoundly different from those of business organization, and the loyalties and logic of the professional soldier in his managerial capacities are also different. Merely to state that the military elite are managers throws no light on who is recruited into the military, on how military education and a military career fashion the outlook of the professional soldier.

Notes

1. See Lewis, Michael, *England's Sea Officers: The Story of the Naval Profession*. London: Allen & Unwin, 1939. Lewis traces the historical development of the British naval officer. The author defines professionalism in the military exclusively in terms of career considerations: Provisions for the continuous entry of young officers, a system of training the young officer, regular employment of the trained officer, reasonable chances of the officer's gradual rise in professional, financial, and social status, steady exodus at the upper end of the service, retirement.

2. Thus, in a 50-year period the size of the officer corps expanded approximately 27 times. By contrast, the personnel of the Department of State, including the foreign service, expanded from 1,836 in 1913 to 16,443 in 1949, or an increase of 9 times.

3. For an analysis of officer education and procurement, see Lyons, Gene M., Masland, John W., *Education and Military Leadership: A Study of the ROTC*. Princeton: Princeton University Press, 1959.

4. Dupuy, R. E., *Men of West Point*. New York: William Sloane Associates, Inc., 1956, p. 120. Four of the first major generals of the volunteers commissioned by September 1861 were civilians; twenty-four of the seventy-one brigadier generals had had no previous military experience; while perhaps one colonel out of each twenty appointed had significant military credentials.

5. Compiled from the records of the West Point Alumni Foundation and published in the *Register of Graduates and Former Cadets of the United States Military Academy*, 1947–51. (Dupuy, R. E. *op. cit.*)

6. These schools include Norwich University, Pennsylvania Military College, Virginia Polytechnic Institute, Virginia Military Institute, North Georgia

College, Clemson Agricultural College, The Citadel, and the Agricultural and Mechanical College of Texas.

7. Official Army Register, Adjutant General's Office, 1950; Register of Commissioned Officers, Naval Personnel Bureau, 1950; and Air Force Register Office of the Air Adjutant, 1950.

8. Chennault, Claire Lee, *Way of a Fighter: The Memoirs of Claire Lee Chennault.* New York: G. P. Putnam's Sons, 1949, p. 177.

9. Lehman, H. C., "The Age of Eminent Leaders: Then and Now." *American Journal of Sociology,* 1947, 52, 342–56.

10. For a general discussion of age in the military profession, see Vagts, Alfred, "Generals: Old and Young." *Journal of Politics,* 1942, 4, 396–406.

11. Metropolitan Life Insurance Company, "Age of Military Leaders: The Army." Statistical Bulletin, August 1945, pp. 2–4; "Age of American Military Leaders: The Navy." June 1945, pp. 1–3.

12. Grant, Myles S., "Promotional Policy in the U.S. Army: A Case Study." Defense Policy Seminar, Harvard University, May 28, 1957.

13. Report on Conditions of Military Service for the President's Commission on Veteran's Pensions, Question IV (Nature of Military Duties). Washington, December 28, 1955.

14. Annual Report of the Secretary of War, Washington, 1935.

15. Mack, Raymond, *Social Stratification on U.S. Air Force Bases,* Technical Report 4, Air Force Base Project, Institute for Research in Social Science. Chapel Hill: University of North Carolina Press, undated, p. 10.

16. The same pattern holds true at the enlisted level. For example, an infantry regiment in 1939 had three master sergeants, while in 1955 a single infantry company had five. In 1939 the infantry squad leader was a corporal; in 1956 he was a sergeant first class.

17. Blasingame, Colonel Benjamin Paul, Head, Department of Astronautics, Air Force Academy, *New York Times,* September 21, 1958, p. 79.

18. For this study, the Air Force created the conditions for a social scientific investigation of a basic aspect of its organizational behavior. The findings are available in the Final Report of Contract AF33 (038)–12782: Staff Command Conflicts and Other Sources of Tension in Relation to Officer Leadership and Organizational Effectiveness.

19. House of Representatives, 83rd Congress, 1st Session, Committee on Armed Services, Hearings, March 5–August 3, 1953.

20. Adapted, in part, from Masland, John W., & Radway, Laurence I., *Soldiers and Scholars.* Princeton: Princeton University Press, 1957, pp. 515–16.

21. The percentages choosing interpersonal skill were as follows:

	Army %	Army N	Navy %	Navy N	Air Force %	Air Force N
OSD	51	(53)	55	(33)	50	(30)
Joint Staff	34	(38)	24	(33)	39	(36)
Service Headquarters	34	(106)	18	(123)	33	(94)

22. Clark, Mark, *Calculated Risk.* New York: Harper & Bros., 1950, p. 133.

23. Mack, Raymond, "The Prestige System of an Air Base: Squadron Rankings and Morale." *American Sociological Review,* 1954, 19, 281–87.

III

CAREER PATTERNS:

AVENUES OF ASCENT

CHAPTER *5*

Social Origins

THE OFFICER CORPS has comprised a cross section of American society. Selection was on a geographic basis, and competitive examination came to play an important role in recruitment. Thereby, the danger of military officers becoming a self-perpetuating clique, or representing a privileged group, has been avoided. Such is the self-image of the professional soldier. To some extent this self-image is grounded in reality, since American social structure never had the opportunity to produce an extensive aristocratic stratum with a special stake in the military, such as was the case in Western Europe, even after the development of capitalism.[1]

In the pre-Civil War period, southern military influence, grounded in an American equivalent of European aristocracy, weighed heavily in the military establishment. James Franklin Hope, in *The Militant South*, marshals historical evidence to demonstrate that the plantation system, with its internal security problem over its slave population, produced a cadre of men who displayed aristocratic-like manners.[2] If one relies on the more profound analysis of James Cash in *The Mind of the South*, the concern with violence and with the military profession was an expression of agricultural and rural traditions which pervaded the entire social structure, and which were destined to persist until the South became industrialized.[3] In any case, did not the defeat of the South and the congressional system of appointment destroy this influence and create a representative officer corps? Samuel Huntington asserts: "Both those entering the officer corps and those reaching its highest ranks in the years after the Civil War were a cross section of middle class America."[4]

Such a credo is most appropriate for democratic political control of the military establishment. It implies that there is nothing in the professional soldier's social background which would endanger internal democracy. If the officer corps were a representative cross section, they would hardly harbor intentions to upset the political balance. They could not be accused of imperial ambitions, beyond those sanctioned by the popularly elected legislators. The idea of the representative origins of military leaders is a part of the general belief in the humble origins of American leadership.

The belief that the officer corps, including its top stratum, mirrors the nation's credo has served the needs of the internal administration of the military establishment. In times of conflict this means that draftees and volunteers are led by their own kind, and not by any special social strata, whose traditions or aspirations might be suspect. Yet, the military has never been fully at ease with this self-image of its representativeness. And their more alert members recognize its variance with social reality. They have also come to believe that, in some respects, they are superior to the bulk of the population. More secretly than publicly, they hold the self-conception of standard bearers and conservators of great traditions in a changing social environment. One cannot be average and still fill such a role. Somehow, social heritage must have been at work.

No profession resists inquiry into its social origins as stubbornly as does the military. To inquire directly about social background, especially about religion, is resented as impolite. With the exception of some data about West Point students, published sources, including individual biographies, seldom contain the needed information. Only by extensive correspondence and inquiries, plus an elaborate search of documentary sources, was it possible to collect data on the social origins and changing composition of the military elite.*

* See Methodological Appendix.

Can it be argued that this topic might better remain undisturbed? If only to ascertain the consequence of congressional action to recruit on a geographical basis, such an inquiry would be justified. But the analysis of the social origins of the military is a powerful key to the understanding of its political logic, although no elite behaves simply on the basis of its social origin. In the end, since the military really has very little to hide, these data contribute to a new and perhaps more relevant credo. If the military elite have not been a cross section of society in the past, in the contemporary scene the military offers opportunities for social mobility to the dedicated and to the proficient, even if they are of lowly origin.

It was assumed that, instead of a representative social background, the American military would have many of the characteristics of the business and political elite. They would be heavily recruited from native-born, Anglo-Saxon, and upper social stratum parentage. Upper social stratum would not mean the most elite business families, but rather the prosperous, the professional, and the upper middle class. It was expected that the Navy would be the ranking service in terms of the social background of its officers, the Air Force the lowest, while the Army would be somewhere in the middle.

The empirical data collected on the 1910–50 sample of 761 Army, Navy, and Air Force general officers confirm these assumptions, and, in the case of the Army, amplify similar conclusions of C. S. Brown, the historian, who studied the social background of 465 generals from 1898 to 1940.[5] However, important differences between the military leaders and other leaders emerge, which help to explain the position of officers in American social structure. In addition, the hypothesis required systematic investigation into whether, since the turn of the century, the military elite has been shifting their recruitment from a narrow, relatively high-status social base to a broader, more representative, and lower status base. This would be a consequence of the mere growth in the size of the military establishment, and the need to recruit increasing numbers of technical specialists. It is generally the case that submerged social groups select technical training as an avenue of social mobility. Therefore, it seemed reasonable to assume that the Air Force would have gone the furthest in broadening its recruitment base.

Nativity

THE MILITARY PROFESSION and its elite members, with rare exceptions, are native-born. The fact that entrance into the military takes place at an early age tends to exclude those born abroad. Since the military profession is an expression of national identity, only those with strong feelings of nationalism tend to enter. By the same token, only the native-born can be entrusted with such service. As can be seen from Table 7, less than 2 per cent of the historical sample of military elite members were born abroad, excluding the few who were born as sons of Americans on duty overseas. There is no difference between the three services in this respect, nor is there any sharp historical trend from 1910 to 1950.

Table 7

Military Leaders, 1910–50:
Native-Born versus Foreign-Born

	Army	Navy	Air Force	Total
	%	%	%	%
Native-born	99	97	97	98
Foreign-born	1	3	3	2
Total	(100)	(100)	(100)	(100)
Number	295	361	105	761

Armed forces in the throes of national revolution have traditionally opened their ranks, including the very top, to sympathetic foreigners. This has been the case from the American Revolution to the most recent Spanish Civil War. But the native-born character of military elites is a universal characteristic of the modern nation state. Italy is a relative newcomer to modern nationalism, yet, among a sample of 138 army generals drawn from the period 1910 to 1939, not a single officer was born abroad, even of Italian parentage.[6] Germany presents the same picture, except that persons of German parentage who lived in areas under disputed rule were drawn into its military elite. Nevertheless, the number of persons from these peripheral areas is indeed small. Of the top two hundred fifty generals on active duty in 1941, they did not total more than 6 per cent, including Austrians incorporated after the annexation.[7] In the more revolutionary para-military and military formations of the Nazi party, the concentration of foreign-born Germans (*Volkdeutsche*) was considerably higher.

Within the geographical definition of the empire, the British military elite could incorporate Britons from the dominions and the colonies with considerable ease. In fact, as of 1950, of the twenty-eight leading generals, the inner nucleus of the British ground establishment, less than half were born in England, Scotland, or Ireland, while the majority had been born and spent their formative years in the colonies.

The native-born character of military leadership has special meaning in a new nation as Israel, whose whole existence—illegal and legal—is less than a generation, and whose population is overwhelmingly composed of new immigrants. Nevertheless, to be a real Israeli means to have been born in Israel and to have attended Israeli primary and secondary schools. While most of Israel's top political and economic leaders were born abroad, mainly in Eastern Europe, the military generals are overwhelmingly native-born or at least have had their main education in Palestine.[8]

But the real measure of the depth of nativity is not merely being native-born, but having many generations of native-born parents. All available biographical and autobiographical data underline the overwhelming preponderance of old settler stock—especially British and German—to the exclusion of newer post-1880 waves of immigration. The three services have been almost devoid of generals and admirals with names from southern and eastern European culture areas; they were heavily recruited from the descendants of early migrations from England, Ireland, Germany, and northwest Europe. Examination of numerous military biographies and autobiographies reveals a wealth of additional detail. Frequently, genealogical links to the Civil War period are reported, and reference to the Revolutionary war period is not an isolated occurrence.[9]

In the introduction to the Stilwell papers, Mrs. Winifred A. Stilwell wrote, "General Stilwell was descended from Nicholas Stilwell who came to New Amsterdam in 1638. Records and family documents carry the name back to 1456. Among those Stilwells who followed Nicholas, there were many who served this country as soldiers, so it was perhaps natural that my husband chose a military career."[10] General George Marshall's biographer described his ancestors as follows: "With John Marshall of the Forest, the family emerges from obscurity. Born in 1700, he became a large planter, married the daughter of the sheriff of Westmoreland County, and sired nine children."[11] Although the Marshall ancestry is long and distinguished, the author points out that "they belonged to the class known in Virgina as 'good people,' a label which distinguished them from the aristocratic estate of 'good families.'" Exemplifying another tradition, General Claire Lee Chennault recorded in his memoirs, "My ancestors were Huguenots who left Alsace-Lorraine in 1778 to fight with Lafayette in the Revolutionary War."[12]

Representative of German stock was General Robert L. Eichelberger, whose forefathers "emigrated to the American colonies in 1728. The Eichelbergers had lived for several generations near Heidelberg, but they were originally German Swiss from Basle. They were honest and good people who fought in the American Revolution and lived in Pennsylvania and Maryland before moving to Ohio."[13]

As the military establishment grows in size, the number of persons ~vailable from the oldest American stock becomes much too limited to fill all the posts, yet the emphasis on nativity can still persist. Many more sons of Eastern European families have entered the profession, particularly the Air Force. But the percentage of the 1959 and 1960 cadet classes at West Point shows the stamp of native American traditions. More than 65 per cent are third generation or more—that is, at least their grandparents were born in the United States. In Table 8 a comparison of these cadets with the

Table 8

West Point Cadets, 1959 and 1960: Generation of Nativity[14]

	West Point Classes 1959–1960 %	Total White Population %
Foreign-born	1	6.7
First-generation (one or both parents foreign-born)	8	26.2
Second-generation (parents or grandparents native-born	91	67.1
Total	100 (1448)	100

equivalent age grouping in the population shows the more extensive native tradition.

By contrast, American business and political leadership is more accessible to the foreign-born. In Lloyd Warner's study of a 1952 sample of top business leadership, he found that 5 per cent were foreign-born. Another 20 per cent were first generation, having had fathers who were born abroad.[15] There can be no doubt that a long native-born background of many generations has been a distinguishing characteristic of the professional soldier. These traditional family attachments are one important reason why men have chosen a military career.

Rural Background

FROM A HISTORICAL and theoretical point of view, there was every reason to believe that the military would be heavily recruited from nonindustrialized areas—from agricultural communities and small towns. First, the experience of the United States should not be very different from that of the nations of Western Europe. Second, the emphasis on native-born personnel would, in itself, imply an over-representation of officers from rural and small town backgrounds, since the foreign-born and second generation concentrate in the metropolitan areas. Third, and most fundamental, there has been an integral association between military institutions and rural society. The out-of-doors existence, the concern with nature, sport, and weapons which is part of rural culture, have a direct carry-over to the requirements of the pre-technological military establishment. But in the final analysis the link between rural social structure and military organization is based on the more central issue of career opportunities.

The military profession was an alternate channel of mobility for the ambitious, wherever there was a relative absence of economic opportunities. In rural areas traditions and requirements for a military sense of honor could be expected to flourish, in opposition to the ethic of private profit of urban commercialism. At the same time, a simpler kind of patriotism prevails in rural areas. While it was expected that, in general, the military elite would be recruited disproportionately from nonindustrialized communities, it seemed reasonable that this would be less the case for the Navy. The Navy has had the longest technical tradition, and maritime activities must of necessity take place on the sea coast, close to urban centers.

The data on the place of birth of military leaders indicates that they are overwhelmingly of rural and small town origin (Table 9). High-ranking officers, especially in the Army, tend to come from small towns located in agricultural communities, removed from major industrialized metropolitan areas. Military officers who did come from urban sectors tended to come from smaller cities, rather than larger urban centers. As the nation became urbanized, military leadership shifted its pattern of recruitment. Nevertheless, in 1950 almost 70 per cent of the Army leaders came from rural backgrounds, while, as we expected, the naval percentage had declined to approximately 56 per cent. The Air Force leadership followed the same pattern as the Army, in part, because in 1950 most of the Air Force generals were recruited from the Army.

Table 9
Military Leaders, 1910–50:
Rural versus Urban Background—
Size of Place of Birth*

	Army 1910	Army 1920	Army 1935	Army 1950	Navy 1920	Navy 1935	Navy 1950	Air Force 1950
	%	%	%	%	%	%	%	%
Farm	22	22	16	4	9	7	2	2
Small town (under 2500)	64	51	49	57	45	52	53	65
Military site	—	4	9	5	3	8	1	3
Total rural	86	77	74	66	57	67	56	70
Total urban	14	16	25	33	40	25	44	30
Not ascertained	—	7	1	1	3	8	—	0
Total %	100	100	100	100	100	100	100	100
Number	(14)	(51)	(64)	(166)	(67)	(61)	(204)	(105)

* As of time of birth.

It can be argued that this concentration of rural background merely represents the national population at the time of birth of these officers. As can be seen in Table 10, at the approximate time of birth of the 1950 sample, 60 per cent of the total population was living in rural areas (communities under 2,500).

However, the essential conclusion is that military leadership is of a rural background, when contrasted with other elite groups.

Table 10
Military and Civilian Leadership, 1950: Rural versus Urban Background— Size of Place of Birth

	Army 1950	Navy 1950	Air Force 1950	Business 1952	U.S. Population 1900
	%	%	%	%	%
Farm and rural	66	56	70	26	60
Urban	34	44	30	74	40
Total	100	100	100	100	100
Number	(166)	(204)	(105)	(8,300)	

Comparison with Lloyd Warner's 1952 business leadership group highlights the marked difference. In contrast to the almost 70 per cent of contemporary military leaders with social backgrounds from rural settings, only 26 per cent of the business leaders have rural backgrounds. In addition, more recent recruitment of younger leadership is still heavily from rural and less industrialized communities. Thus, nearly two-thirds of the officers in the Air Command and Staff School in 1949 either were born, or spent the ten years prior to their military service, in communities of less than 50,000 population.[16]

Since the rate of economic and industrial growth in the United States has been unequal, is there any evidence of a regional concentration in the backgrounds of the military elite? To what extent is the South over-represented, not only because of the persistence of a military tradition, but as a consequence of slower industrialization? A regional bias in the background of military leaders should be strongly mitigated by the congressional apportionment system.

Nevertheless, using the formal definition of the United States Census, there was still, in 1950, an over-representation of southern-born officers in the Army, and, to a lesser extent, in the Navy leadership. In calculating regional representation, the Negro population was excluded, since, in effect, they were not candidates for admission into the military profession at the time of the birth of the 1950 sample. From Table 11 it can be seen that the South had at least one-third more representation in the Army than would have been expected on a purely white population basis. In addition to the South, the West was also somewhat over-represented in the Navy. But, again, a fuller measure of the southern component of the military elite can be seen by a comparison with business leaders who came from the South. In Warner's 1952 business leadership sample, only 16 per cent came from the South; in other words, the South was sharply underrepresented in business leadership, as contrasted with its position in the military.[17]

Table 11

Military and Civilian Leadership, 1950:
Regional Background at Time of Birth*

	Army 1950 %	Navy 1950 %	Air Force 1950 %	Business 1952 %	Percentage White Population 1900
North east	23	27	25	38	31
South	34	31	25	16	24
North central	37	30	43	40	39
West	6	12	7	6	6
Total	100	100	100	100	100

* Of those born in the U.S.

Since the turn of the century, official state boundaries have proven to be a poor index to southern regionalism. If, instead of state borders, a social-cultural definition is used, which includes the borderlands of southern Illinois, Ohio, and parts of Indiana and Pennsylvania, the concentration of southern over-representation in the military elite is more pronounced. In order to arrive at a valid indication of geographical affiliation, officers were classified, not only on the basis of birthplace, but also as to where they received their formal education, exclusive of academy attendance.† This produces a fuller picture of the southern affiliation of both the Army and the Navy (Table 12). For the Army southern affiliation declined from 90 per cent of the elite sample in 1910, to 46 per cent in 1950. Even though this represents a marked shift, generals with southern affiliation were roughly twice over-represented. This measure of affiliation does not include location of relatives or marriage into southern families which, on the basis of incomplete data, would further raise the figure. The southern connections of the 1950 naval sample are almost equally as strong: About 44 per cent could be classified as affiliated with the South. By contrast, these definitions do not reveal an over-representation of southern affilia-

† The few southerners who received a northern education were classified as "non-southern."

tion in the new elite of the Air Force. Thus, the Air Force, as a new career opportunity, despite its heavy recruitment from rural areas, is most representative in terms of region.

Table 12

Military Leadership, 1910–50: Southern Affiliation*

	Army 1910 %	Army 1920 %	Army 1935 %	Army 1950 %	Navy 1910 %	Navy 1920 %	Navy 1935 %	Navy 1950 %	Air Force 1950 %
Southern affiliation	93	42	56	46	38	45	38	44	28
Non-southern	7	58	44	54	62	55	62	56	72
Total	100	100	100	100	100	100	100	100	100
Number	(14)	(51)	(64)	(166)	(29)	(67)	(61)	(205)	(106)

* Based on area of birth and place of pre-military education.

Social Strata

RECRUITMENT from rural communities does not necessarily imply humble social origin. On the contrary, American military leaders traditionally have come from the more privileged strata. However, recent trends in their social background supply striking confirmation of the decline in the relatively high social origins of the military, and of its transformation into a more socially heterogeneous group.

That the military profession at the turn of the century was recruited from the privileged strata, despite the introduction of the congressional appointment system in the 1830's, presents no mystery. Congressmen could only appoint those men who sought admission. Progressively, since 1900, wider and wider interest has developed in a military education, but it took the great depression to transform the system. It is understandable that congressmen, because of personal contacts, associations, and interests, tended to select from among the more privileged strata. Some, particularly in the South, made it their responsibility to recruit those they thought were the "proper type." In his memoirs Colonel T. Bentley Mott recounts a letter his family received from their Virginia congressman:

"If you can suggest the name of a gentleman's son whose antecedents
indicate him to be the material out of which good officers are made,
send him to Alexandria. I am holding a competitive examination there
for West Point, and I want a boy selected who has the right qualifications
and who can graduate."[18]

Father's occupation, plus income and status, were used as the
measures of social origin, and provided the basis for locating each
officer's parent somewhere in the social pyramid, from the upper
stratum to the lowest.[19] Of the three services, the Navy has the
highest social base of recruitment, the Army the next, while the Air
Force is decidedly lower (Table 13). The Navy, like the Army, has
a small group—very small indeed, in that it comprises less than 5
per cent of its membership—drawn from the upper class, while the
Air Force has no such group. In the Navy these upper-class officers
come from older eastern families, with socialite connections and
wealth derived from long-established business enterprises. In the
Army the upper-class background is derived more from southern
family tradition, and is based on regional social position and political service.

Table 13
Military Leadership, 1910–50:
Trends in Social Origin

	Army 1910–20 %	Army 1935 %	Army 1950 %	Navy 1950 %	Air Force 1950 %
Upper	26	8	3	4	—
Upper middle	66	68	47	57	30
Lower middle	8	23	45	34	62
Upper lower	0	1	4	5	8
Lower lower	0	0	1	0	0
Total	100	100	100	100	100
Number	(38)	(49)	(140)	(162)	(60)

In the United States the line between upper middle class and
"upper class" is indeed a thin one, and often based on self-des-
ignation. According to one account, written in 1880, under the title,
"Ladies and Officers of the U.S. Army," the Army was a "domain of
its own, independent and isolated by its peculiar customs and discipline; an aristocracy by selection and the halo of traditions."[20]
In fact, as of 1910, Army and Navy elite were strongly upper middle class (Table 13). Although adequate quantitative documenta-

tion could be collected only for the Army, the pattern of infusion of persons from lower middle-class backgrounds has been gradual, but steady, in both the Army and the Navy. By 1950, lower middle-class Army generals had risen to 45 per cent, from less than 10 per cent in 1910. The rate of influx of the lower middle-class into the ranks of the admirals was almost as great. Air Force leadership has been most heavily recruited from the lower middle class (62 per cent) and it has the largest percentage of working class sons (8 per cent). While these data deal only with military personnel who have risen to the high ranks, they reflect the different social stratification of the officer corps of the three services.

With regard to specific middle-class occupations, it has been the professional and managerial groups, rather than the business groups, which have contributed to the military, reflecting the clash between business and military values (Table 14). Sons of military officers,

Table 14

Military Leadership, 1910–50: Father's Occupation

	Army 1910–20 %	Army 1935 %	Army 1950 %	Navy 1950 %	Air Force 1950 %	West Point Class, 1960 %
Business	24	16	29	32	26	15
Professional and managerial	46	60	45	38	38	50
Farmer	30	16	10	7	15	—
White collar	—	6	11	8	16	13
Worker	—	2	5	5	5	19
Other						3
Total	100	100	100	100	100	100
Number	(37)	(49)	(140)	(162)	(60)	(765)

awyers, doctors, public officials, and, of particular interest, teachers and ministers, were most prominently represented. Before World War I in the United States, as in Europe, the military profession, by offering a good education and a suitable career, offered a solution to many a well-bred farm and plantation family facing economic decline. In the 1910–20 army sample the sons of farmers came predominately from better suited middle-class families, at least socially, and those out of the South came from the very "best" families. With urbanization, the percentage of farmers' sons declined, and they tended to come from more modest, but essentially middle-class backgrounds. The broadening of the social base has brought in the lower middle-class, white-collar families—sons of salesmen and clerical workers—plus a smattering from the working class. Whereas in the Army elite of 1910–20, these occupations were completely absent, by 1950 they constituted 16 per cent, and in the Air Force they were even more numerous (21 per cent).

The occupational background of the cadets at the United States Military Academy of the class of 1960 indicates that these trends toward greater social representativeness will continue.[21] Contemporary recruitment determines the social composition of future leadership. Among the cadets—the generals of the future—the number of sons of businessmen continues to decline. Lower-status occupational backgrounds, namely the white-collar and the working class, continue to grow. Of those with working-class backgrounds, the majority come from skilled trades, such as the sons of machinists and printers, but some are from the very bottom of the social pyramid. In other words, offspring from the lower social strata constitute more than 30 per cent of the new personnel entering the military academy, and there is no reason to assume that this is at marked variance with the other services. Thus, there is considerable justification for the belief that the military establishment is becoming an avenue of social mobility for those of lower social origin and from newer immigrant families.

Despite this trend toward a broader base of social recruitment, however, the military elite is still not as open an elite as is the business elite. Lloyd Warner's sample of top 1952 business leaders included 15 per cent whose fathers were from the working class, as opposed to 5 per cent for the military (Table 15). Likewise, the other low-status group, comprising the sons of white-collar families, was larger among the business elite than among the generals and admirals (19 as compared with 11 per cent).

Data on trends in the social origins of political leadership are not very complete. One study of the 1949 United States Senate indicates that this group has the same predominately upper middle-class social background as the military. Members of the House of Representatives, as well as state and municipal political leaders, represent somewhat lower social origins and greater ethnic heterogeneity.[22] The main feature of the background of congressmen, as

Table 15

Military and Civilian Leadership:
Father's Occupation

	Military 1950 %	Business 1952 %
Small business		18
Large business		8
Total business	30	26
Professional and managerial	44	29
Farmer	10	8
White collar	11	19
Worker	5	15
Other		2
Total	100	100
Number	(362)	(8,300)

well as that of other political leadership groups, is that an overwhelming majority are trained as lawyers.

The major European military elites have been subject to the same broadening of their social base of recruitment. At the end of the Napoleonic wars, aristocratic elements still supplied the bulk of the military elite, although even then the influx of middle-class elements into the officer corps was well developed. Quantitative data on the social transformation of the officer corps in the nineteenth century is available for Germany and Sweden.[23] In the Prussian military establishment of 1824 the military elite consisted almost exclusively of nobility, while the corps as a whole was more than 40 per cent middle class (Table 16). A very similar pattern can be seen in Sweden. The broadening of the social base of recruitment took place in all the European countries, although the rate varied to some extent from nation to nation. In each country, efforts were made to preserve and enlarge the cadres of inherited nobility by ennobling outstanding heroes in battle, but the trend could hardly be resisted. By the outbreak of World War II, the nobility had become a minority of the military elite in all major Western European nation states. Both in Germany and in England, the percentage had declined to about one-third, and of these, about one-half were from the newer lesser nobility and landed gentry. In Sweden and Italy the number had fallen to an even lower percentage of around 20 per cent.

Table 16

Western European Military Leaders, 1824–1950:
Aristocratic versus Middle-Class Origins*

| | Germany | | Sweden | | Gt. Britain | Italy |
	Elite Officer %	Total Corps %	Elite Officer %	Total Corps %	Elite %	Elite %
1824			**1823**			
Nobility	97	58	70	54		
Middle class	3	42	30	46		
Number	(111)	(5,230)				
1872			**1865**			
Nobility	94	49	62	46		
Middle class	6	51	38	54		
Number	(178)	(11,034)				
1898			**1890**			
Nobility	81	40		40		
Middle class	19	60		60		
Number	(254)	(14,778)				
1911			**1913**		**1914**	**1914**
Nobility	67	33	35	30	40	50
Middle class	33	67	65	70	60	50
Number	(263)	(16,979)			(40)	(32)
1925			**1923**		**1920**	**1919**
Nobility	38	20	33	24	25	20
Middle class	62	80	67	76	75	80
Number	(149)	(3,606)			(60)	(25)
1932					**1935**	**1930**
Nobility	33	20			37	13
Middle class	67	80			63	87
Number	(149)	(3,766)			(35)	(47)
1939						
Nobility	34					
Middle class	66					
Number	(177)					
1944			**1943**			
Nobility	18		25	13		
Middle class	82		75	87		
Number	(230)					
					1950	
Nobility					7	
Middle class					93	
Number					(26)	

* Scattered cases of working-class origins are included for this table in the middle-class group.

The aristocracy first gave way to the middle class in the artillery and the technical services, where specialized technical training was required. In the more honorific cavalry, with its natural link to

feudal life, the upper social stratum concentrated its numbers in
the face of military expansion. As in the United States, the new
recruitment came heavily from rural areas, and often with a strong
regional overtone, namely, from that part of the nation which had
experienced the least industrialization. In Germany, from 1911
through 1944, never more than 15 per cent of the military elite came
from urban communities, despite continuous industrialization of
the country. The regional concentration was traditional because of
Prussian dominance. At the outbreak of World War II, 40 per cent
of the *Wehrmacht* generals were still Prussian in origin. In England
the professional military and its elite members were mainly recruited from the southern rural counties. Of the top thirty generals
in Great Britain as late as 1950, every one who had been born in
England was from the southern counties and only eight had urban
backgrounds. In Italy the rural and regional background meant
either southern Italy, or the northwestern provinces of Piedmont
and Lombardy. Southern Italy and the mountainous northwestern
region accounted for 80 per cent of a sample of fifty Italian World
War II generals.

Another aspect of social origin is the proportion of military
leaders who have entered the profession through self-recruitment—
namely, the sons of professional soldiers. The percentage of self-
recruitment rose in the Army from 7 per cent in 1910 to 23 per cent
in 1935 (Table 17). As a consequence of rapid growth and the war-
time recruitment of officer personnel from civilian society, the percentage dropped to 11 in 1950. For the Navy, the extent of
self-recruitment in 1950 was somewhat lower—7 per cent; for the
Air Force, as might be expected, it was the lowest—5 per cent.

Comparison with self-recruitment in the German military elite,
the epitome of the professional military, demonstrates that in the
past the American system has not produced a self-perpetuating
elite. Self-recruitment from among the sons of professional officers
was extremely widespread among the top-ranking German generals
from 1911 until the collapse of the *Wehrmacht* in 1945. While the
long-term trend moved away from self-recruitment (more than
50 per cent in 1925), at the close of World War II about 30 per cent
of the *Wehrmacht* general officers were recruited from the sons of
professional officers. Not only was self-recruitment extensive, but
throughout this period almost half the German military elite who

Table 17

American and German Military Leadership, 1910–50:
Percentage with Fathers Who Were Officers

	U.S. Army %	German Army	%
Period 1910	7	1911—General officers	17
		Officers	27
		Total per cent	44
Number (14)		Number (136)	
Period 1920	10	1925—General officers	27
		Officers	29
		Total per cent	52
Number (51)		Number (42)	
Period 1935	23	1933—General officers	22
		Officers	29
		Total per cent	51
Number (64)		Number (94)	
		1939—General officers	15
		Officers	15
		Total per cent	30
		Number (177)	
		1941—General officers	14
		Officers	16
		Total per cent	30
		Number (250)	
Period 1950	11	1944—General officers	15
		Officers	14
		Total per cent	29
Number (166)		Number (230)	
West Point, class of 1960	25		
Number (565)			

came from military families were sons of generals, implying an even tighter circle of internal recruitment.

Indicative of the future, as shown in Table 17, 25 per cent of the cadet class of 1960 at West Point are sons of Army officers—either academy graduates or non-academy regular Army officers. (Including sons of reserve officers of the National Guard would raise the figure another 10 per cent.) Sons of military officers can enter the service by the normal channels, but they are assisted by the system of presidential appointments, since the percentage appointed by Congress has gradually declined. For the Navy, it has dropped from 96 per cent to 67 per cent in 1957, while for the Army it has declined to 82 per cent. The result has been to increase the opportunity for sons of military officers to enter the profession via the military academies; and, therefore, in future years the military profession may be more self-recruited than it was in the past.[24] Thus, these findings refine the conclusion on increased social representativeness in the recruitment of the military elite: Along with a broadening of the base, there has been at least a temporary increased reliance on self-recruitment.

Religion

RELIGIOUS AFFILIATION and belief is an index which gives deeper meaning to social background. The data on religion are not as full as they are on other measures of social background, since there is a tendency among leaders in a political democracy, and especially among the military, to resent being questioned about their religious background. Yet, the essential conclusions are well documented.

First, the American military elite has been overwhelmingly a Protestant group. Recruitment from rural communities and from older families directly implies such religious affiliation. Second, as the social composition of the military has begun to draw more heavily on lower-status groups, the concentration of Catholics has begun to increase, but the lag has been considerable.

Thus, the ratio of Protestants to Catholics among those for whom data are available in the 1935 Army sample is 88 to 12 per cent (Table 18). C. S. Brown's data on his sample of Army generals from 1898 to 1940 disclosed a ratio of Protestants to Catholics of 91 to 9 per cent. The persistence of Protestant dominance can be seen by the fact that, in the 1950 Army sample, the ratio remained unchanged and was exceeded by the 20 to 22 percentage in the population at large. The same pattern holds true for the admirals in 1950. The transformation in social composition becomes apparent in the Air Force, where, for those on whom data could be collected, the percentage of Catholics has risen to 16 per cent. Future trends are indicated from data on the West Point cadet classes of 1959, 1960, and 1961, where the percentage of Catholics has risen to 29. These figures reflect the influx of those from white-collar and working-class background, and may signify an over-representation.[25] With this broadening of the base, a Jewish segment of approximately 2 per cent becomes part of the new cadet corps.

Table 18
Military Leaders, 1935–60:
Religious Denomination

	Army 1935	Army 1950	Navy 1950	Air Force 1950	1959	West Point Classes of 1960	1961
	%	%	%	%	%	%	%
Protestant	88	89	90	84	67	63	64
Catholic	12	11	10	16	27	33	29
Jewish	—	—	—	—	3	1	2
Other	—	—	—	—	1	2	3
None	—	—	—	—	2	1	2
Total	100	100	100	100	100	100	100
Number	40	138	163	49	667	755	731
No data	24	28	42	57	14	10	
Total number	(64)	(166)	(205)	(106)	(681)	(765)	(731)

When Julius P. Garesche entered West Point in 1837, he was the only Catholic in the cadet class, although not the first Catholic at the academy. As might be expected, he was from an old upper-class and honorable French family which had transplanted itself to Wilmington. His father had a record of government service. Thus, except for his religion, he conformed to the pattern of recruitment. Yet his behavior was deviant enough by Catholic standards to induce his son to write his biography, giving the grounds on which a Catholic of that period chose a military career.[26] The theme of incorporation of the Catholic into the American military in the nineteenth century is one of deep complexity, and Julius Garesche's full incorporation through the ordeal of the Civil War reflects the gradual social transformation of the military establishment. The Protestant chapel at West Point is called the Chapel. It was not until 1900 that a Catholic chapel was built.

This analysis of religious background requires one more step, since the Protestantism of the military reflects the social structure of the rural South, from which the military elite has been so heavily recruited. In 1950, 40 per cent of the Army group and 42 per cent of the Navy group reported that they were Episcopalian (Table 19). In the group of Army generals from a somewhat earlier historical period, studied by C. S. Brown, almost half were Episcopalian. There is good evidence that a substantial minority adopted the Episcopalian faith, rather than having been born into it. This affirms the importance of this denomination in both the Army and the Navy. Interestingly enough, the concentration and importance of Episcopalians (22 per cent) in the Air Force is much less, again reflecting the greater heterogeneity of the newer establishment. The conservative, traditional orientation of the religious background

Table 19

Military Leaders, 1950:
Religious Denomination

	Army %	Navy %	Air Force %
Traditionalist	63	56	43
Episcopalian	40	42	22
Other*	23	14	21
Pietistic**	18	13	23
Revivalist†	—‡	—	—‡
No denomination	8	21	18
Catholic	11	10	16
Total per cent	100	100	100
Number	(138)	(163)	(49)

* Other Traditionalist includes Presbyterian, Congregationalist, Lutheran, Evangelical.
** Pietistic includes Baptist, Methodist, Disciples of Christ.
† Revivalist includes the various fundamentalist denominations.
‡ Less than one per cent.

of the military is further underlined when the denominations are classified into traditional, pietistic, and revivalist, with revivalist including the more modern fundamentalist groups. Fundamentalist sects are wholly unrepresented among the military elite.

Is there any special significance in the concentration of Episcopalians among the military elite, a concentration which, until recently, dominated organized military religion? Is Episcopalianism merely the religion of a special social stratum which produced men who sought professional careers in the military establishment? Religious symbolism is found in many aspects of military life, in part because of the danger of death. But the Episcopalian doctrine, with its strong emphasis on authority, ceremony, and mission, supplies a positive religion for the military profession. Thus, in the catechism of the Episcopalian Church it is written:

To submit myself to all my governors, teachers, spiritual pastors and masters . . . to order myself lowly and reverently to all my betters and to do my duty in that state of life into which it shall please God to call me.

In summary, these data, and their comparison with European military elites, describe a growing social representativeness and make it clear that, on the basis of social origins alone, the military elite has had a distinctive character beyond the impact of professional training. The military elite has been drawn from an old-family, Anglo-Saxon, Protestant, rural, upper middle-class professional background. This social setting has operated as the equivalent of the European aristocracy in supplying the cadre of military leaders. Until the outbreak of World War II, these social factors lay at the root of the conservative political beliefs held by the American military. They helped to maintain the heroic fighter tradition in the face of growing technological and managerial pressures. But analysis of the ideology of the military elite will demonstrate that, in the absence of an effective feudal tradition, there were fewer barriers to the development of a flexible attitude toward social and political change, as compared with European counterparts. However, these social origins clearly imply that the development of a cosmopolitan outlook would be slow and would require considerable effort.

As in the case of Europe, because of the increase in the size of the military establishment and the need for trained specialists, social patterns of recruitment have been transformed. The trend has been in the direction of greater and greater representativeness, but a strong emphasis on second- and third-generation, native-born, nonindustrial background still persists. There has been very little self-perpetuating of professional military elite in the United States, because alternate avenues of social advancement have been so great that the sons of the military have sought a wider range of occupations than have their German counterparts, for example. The recruitment into the officer corps since the end of World War II seems, on the one hand, to involve a much greater reliance on the sons of professional soldiers, and, on the other hand, the opening of greater opportunity for the sons of the lower middle and working classes.

Some increase in self-recruitment is inevitable in a society where commercial, rather than public-service, values predominate. Only by reaching further down in the social pyramid to search for talent will the military establishment find new sources of officers interested in the advantages of a military career and attracted by public service. Yet, more so in the past than in the present, those who have been recruited into the elite have been strikingly homogeneous as compared with other elite groups.

In Europe, when aristocratic elements predominated, the political behavior of the military had a clear-cut group basis. As the social basis of the military became transformed, its political behavior was less and less conditioned by social background and more by professional considerations. Similarly, in the United States the social origins of the professional military set limits on their links with other elite groups, and on their potentialities for political behavior. The professional military has not operated on the basis of any narrow social class alignment, since it could never speak for any special social strata, as it could in Europe. However, as long as the military profession had a narrow social base of recruitment, it had a relatively uniform social and political outlook. Not only has the growth in social representativeness of the military profession assisted in the development of the military manager, it has also contributed to the growth of a diversified social and political outlook within the military profession.* The politics of the professional soldier has become the politics of an organization—of a pressure group—rather than the mere expression of the interest of a social stratum. But social backgrounds still condition and fashion conservative political perspectives in the profession, and set limits on the links with other elite groups.

Notes

1. Demeter, Karl, *Das Deutsche Heer und Seine Offiziere*. Berlin: Verlag von Reimar Hobbing, 1935.

2. Hope, James Franklin, *The Militant South*. Cambridge: Belknap Press of Harvard University, 1956.

3. Cash, James, *The Mind of the South*. New York: Albert A. Knopf, 1950.

4. Huntington, Samuel, P., *The Soldier and The State*. Cambridge: Harvard University Press, 1957, p. 227.

5. Brown, C. S., "The Social Attitudes of American Generals, 1898–1940." Unpublished doctoral dissertation, University of Wisconsin, 1951.

6. Data collected by Richard Le Blond, Jr., Department of Sociology, Temple University.

7. Data on the social background of the *Wehrmacht* were collected by the author from published sources and from personnel records assembled for the Nuremburg War Crimes Trials.

* See Chapter 12, Political Beliefs.

8. Based on data supplied by Professors S. N. Eisenstadt and Joseph Ben-David, Hebrew University, Jerusalem.

9. Documentation of this point is also supplied independently by C. S. Brown's analysis of the social background of American Army generals. *Op. cit.*

10. White, Theodore H., *The Stilwell Papers.* New York: William Sloane Associates, Inc., 1948, p. ix.

11. Payne, Robert, *General Marshall: A Study in Loyalties.* London: William Heinemann, 1952, p. 2.

12. Chennault, Claire Lee, *Way of a Fighter: The Memoirs of Claire Lee Chennault.* New York: G. P. Putnam's Sons, 1949, p. 2.

13. Eichelberger, Robert L., *Our Jungle Road to Tokyo.* New York: Viking Press, 1949, ix.

14. Data collected by Medical Research Project, United States Military Academy. This comparison underemphasizes the importance of nativity in the military profession, since the census data only permit tracing to the second generation. Similarly, only 2 per cent of the members of the 1949 staff and command school class of the Air Force were born abroad, excluding the territories of the United States. The number of first generation personnel was 7.5 per cent, which is roughly comparable to the West Point class of 1959 and 1960. Source: Van Holmgren, Major Tanner, "Background Study of Some of The Available Data Concerning The Student Officers of The Air Command and Staff School," Class 1949-B, Air University, Maxwell AFB, Alabama. Unpublished.

15. Warner, W. Lloyd & Abegglen, James, *Occupational Mobility in American Business and Industry.* Minneapolis: University of Minnesota Press, 1955, p. 87. Similarly, the percentage of first-generation members of the Senate and House of Representatives in recent years has been around 18 per cent. See Matthews, Donald R., *The Social Background of Political Decision-Makers.* Garden City: Doubleday, 1954, p. 26.

16. Van Holmgren, Major Tanner, *op. cit.*

17. Warner, W. Lloyd, & Abegglen, James, *op. cit.,* p. 70.

18. Mott, Colonel T. Bentley, *Twenty Years as a Military Attache.* New York: Oxford University Press, 1937, p. 24.

19. The distinction between blue collar and white collar supplied the basis for classifying occupations as either lower or middle class. In the lower stratum the distinction between lower lower and upper lower was made on the basis of skill, and thereby of income. In the middle class income and prestige divided the lower middle from the upper middle. To be placed in the upper stratum required some explicit evidence of considerable wealth, or high social status, or both. By this approach, it was possible to classify the sons of businessmen and farmers in their appropriate social stratum, ranging from upper class to lower middle.

20. Greene, Duane M., *Ladies and Officers of the U.S. Army; American Aristocracy. A Sketch of the Social Life and Character of the Army.* New York: Central Publishing Co., 1880.

21. The distribution of father's occupation for the class of 1961 is, in effect, the same.

22. Matthews, Donald R., *op. cit.,* p. 23.

23. Carlsson, Sten, *Ståndssamhälle och ståndspersoner, 1700–1865.* Lund: 1949.

24. Occupational inheritance at the military academies is somewhat higher

than it is in the medical profession, where less than 20 per cent of medical students are sons of doctors. Source: Rogoff, Natalie, "The Decision to Study Medicine," in *The Student Physician*. Cambridge: Harvard University Press, 1957, p. 112

25. Data collected by Medical Research Project, United States Military Academy.

26. *Biography of Lt. Col. Julius P. Garesche*, by his son. Philadelphia: J. P. Lippincott Company, 1887.

CHAPTER *6*

Career Motivations

GIVEN the prevailing emphasis on commercial values and business success in the United States, selection of a military career is often believed to be a weak career choice. Among segments of the civilian public, entry into the military is often thought of as an effort to avoid the competitive realities of civil society. In the extreme view, the military profession is thought to be a berth for mediocrity. Pendleton Herring, writing on the eve of the attack on Pearl Harbor, stated the issue with the complete tact of a Harvard professor of political science:

. . . The place of secondary importance to which we relegate military affairs meant inevitably that the best talent and the most enterprising and ambitious young men would not seek to make the profession of arms their life career. They went into business and the well-rewarded professions. A few military families quietly carried on a tradition of service in the Army or Navy, but this made little imprint on the broad picture. Thus, when we have resorted to war in the past we have not only been unprepared in the obvious ways of lacking arms and equipment, but in the more fundamental ways of trained talent and appropriate institutions. This is no reflection on our Regular Army.[1]

Contrariwise, many a military officer sees his career as filling some special mission, rather than as just a job. Since civilian society and its political leaders must rely so heavily on the advice and com-

petence of professional soldiers, these conflicting images are a source
of extensive tension.

The selection of a military career, like the selection of any
career, represents the interplay of opportunity plus a complex of
social and personality factors. In one sense, to say that the military
is a mediocre career choice is an expression of a liberal ideology
which holds that, since war is essentially destructive, the best minds
are attracted to more positive endeavors. Even the more judicious
statement that the military has not been able to attract its share
of alert minds, is almost a truism. All elite groups could make use of
more effective personnel. The military profession has produced
individual leaders of great stature, and after twenty years of public
neglect—between World War I and World War II—the number of
outstanding officers who were available was quite remarkable.

In assessing the selection of a military career, two rather specific
empirical questions could be investigated. First, is it true that during the period in which the 1910–50 leaders were recruited, the
military profession attracted persons whose basic intelligence was
not equal to the intelligence of those in other professions? Second,
is the issue perhaps not mainly one of sheer intelligence, but of
motivation? Could it be that the underlying motivation for a military career is an expression of "careerism," whereby a person seeks
what he believes to be a noncompetitive and protected route to the
achievement of limited ambitions?*

Only a partial answer can be given to our first question as to
the intellectual level of officer candidates. For the Army, recruitment into the top military leadership until World War II was overwhelmingly through entrance into West Point (Table 20). By 1950,
however, the concentration of West Point graduates in the Army
leadership group had decreased to about one-half, plus another 10
per cent from those selected military schools whose graduates were
eligible for direct commission. In 1950 the concentration of West
Pointers in the Air Force leadership group was roughly the same
as in the Army. By contrast, recruitment into the Navy via Annapolis has been, and remains, almost exclusively the general rule.

Thus, in the past, the examination system of the service acad-

* In Chapter 7, Career Development, the subsequent question is raised:
Even if the military profession gets its fair share of talent, does it succeed in
holding the most intelligent, and does it continue to develop their capacities?

emies has created a set of minimum standards which, although specialized in emphasis, were clearly equal to, and probably superior to college entrance requirements in many civilian institutions of higher learning in the United States. These standards, of course, were not necessarily met by those who entered the military group via other routes. The academies can point to the intellectual prowess of their cadets by tabulating the number of Rhodes scholars. However, this is hardly convincing evidence of the overall intellectual level of military cadets or midshipmen. Instead, the impression exists among educators that the intellectual level of those entering the military profession via the service academies reflected the effective and adequate minimum standards, rather than any extensive concentration of students at the upper end of the intelligence continuum. In recent years the average intelligence

Table 20

Military Leadership, 1910–50:
Educational Background

	Army				Navy				Air Force
	1910 %	1920 %	1935 %	1950 %	1910 %	1920 %	1935 %	1950 %	1950 %
West Point or Annapolis	79	86	81	48	90	96	98	97	48
Military school	—	—	5	10	3	1	—	—	3
College and university	7	4	8	27	—	—	—	1	22
Non-college graduate	14	10	6	15	7	3	2	2	27
Total per cent	100	100	100	100	100	100	100	100	100
Number	(14)	(51)	(64)	(166)	(29)	(67)	(61)	(205)	(106)

quotient of midshipmen and cadets has been significantly better than that of average college freshmen on the graduate record examination administered by the Educational Testing Service.[2] Still, average performance is not an adequate index to the concentration in service academies of superior students.

It is insufficient to focus merely on intellectual skills and academic performance. Success in middle- and top-level assignments in the military, or for that matter in any bureaucratic organization, requires intellectual skills and training different from those which the colleges afford. The fact that follow-up studies in the military demonstrate a low correlation between academic performance and career advancement is inconclusive, since this would be typical of many other professions, and certainly of the development of elite leadership.*

With regard to our second question, the evidence contradicts civilian assumptions concerning career motives of the professional soldier, especially for the first quarter of the century. Up to the period of 1950, the meaning of career choice for the military elite suggests the following hypothesis: While for many persons, and perhaps even for a majority, the military career represented the pursuit of a relatively secure, safe, and promising prospect, more or less similar to other professions, for a substantial minority, at least, the choice of a military career was a strong decision. To speak of a strong career choice means that a person feels that a particular occupation is singularly important to him, since he believes that it will give him the rewards and gratifications he wants.

For such persons, the military career had overtones of a "calling," with a sense of mission. It represented a deliberate rejection of what was believed to be the prosaic and limited horizons of the business world. In the urban commercial centers the selection of a military career was frowned upon. Yet, through their families many urban candidates were exposed to an atmosphere in which being a soldier was thought to be honorable. But it was the rural background that gave special meaning to, and legitimized the military career. In the hinterlands the notion still persisted that there was glory other than that to be gained from profits in the market place. The virtues of physical prowess, social protocol, and a general ideal of service to the community were still valued. The military career offered the strong-willed an opportunity to achieve these values; and, in turn, such career motivation made it possible for the armed services to perpetuate the martial spirit.

Direct empirical investigation of career motives was undertaken by intensive interviews conducted in 1958 on the sample of 113

* When these data are examined in detail, in Chapter 7, Career Development, they reflect the fact that military education at the academies has been technical, and oriented to the immediate, initial assignments that the officer must perform.

colonels and brigadier generals (and their naval equivalents) whose service records indicated they would be prospects for continued ascent.* These men were officers who had been recruited during the 1930's or integrated after World War II, and for this reason would reflect the increased social heterogeneity of the officer corps. Even after long deliberation, an individual is often unaware of the real motives which have guided his decision. Yet, to the degree to which the officer was aware, or could be made aware, of some of the personal and social pressures that were operating within him, he revealed them. Of course, the psychological analyst would hold that these responses are still suggestive of hidden motives. The rapport that was established in these interviews is reflected in the typical candor, albeit singular content, of one high-ranking officer's response:

I went to a [service academy] and I often wonder about my motivation. I did have the opportunity to graduate from a great prep school. I was undecided as to what college to go to. I was very impressed by the men that I knew who went to [service academy] but I was appointed to [service academy] by a clerical error. I asked a senator for some information on [service academy] and instead he sent me an appointment. I probably would not have gone to the academy otherwise.

Published memoirs of older leaders supplied an additional important source. Numerous personal interviews by the author over a decade and a half provided further essential background on the complexities of career motivation.

The Expression of Missionary Zeal

FOUR MOTIVE PATTERNS, singly and in combination, were of consequence for those who rose to the level of general or admiral by 1950: tradition, or more precisely family and social inheritance; sheer desire for education and social advancement, with or without a career commitment to the military; experience in a military setting; and "boyhood" ambition. The potential officer's career choice was further influenced not only by his feeling that the armed forces had a vital function, but by the fact that the military had offered

* See Methodological Appendix for details.

an adequate and respectable level of personal security in peacetime. Nor should one overlook the intermingling of these motives with a diffuse desire for an active, athletic-type career.

While the relative importance of different motives is difficult, if not impossible, to reconstruct, one can infer that the effects of tradition and social inheritance were very widespread among those who entered the military profession before 1920. An official questionnaire study of 7,800 graduates of West Point, conducted by the superintendent of the academy, concluded that "relative to compelling factors for entering West Point, almost half indicated that prestige and traditions of West Point or the Service was the most important reason."[3]

Social inheritance meant, first of all, having a father who was a professional soldier:

It was in my blood. I was an army brat. I even oriented my high school curriculum to that. So probably from age of 13. At 15 I took a preliminary physical exam to go to West Point. . . . I didn't decide myself but I'm not sure youngsters choose their careers at this age on a sound basis. I was a pre-World War I brat and as a Lt. in the army he [father] was sought after by the local "400" in San Francisco.[4]

Social inheritance also meant having relatives who were military officers, and family tradition. Often, family traditions were transmitted via uncle, cousins, or other relatives. In each case a personal relation between an officer and the youngster had been at work. One is struck by the number of officers who report that stories by and about their grandfathers helped influence them decisively:

Oh, as a school boy determination. . . . Oh, I think the fact of a grandfather who fought in the Civil War and read me stories about military had a lot to do with it. Most of my family, however, were civilian soldiers.[5]

In the broadest sense, social inheritance could be based on regional factors alone.

I'm afraid I'd say a mixture of reasons. I grew up in a small southern town and living next to me were a couple of old confederate soldiers. Across the street was a marine hospital. These two things impressed me. Also I knew two men from West Point who told me it was a fine place. Also my parents didn't have the money to send me to college. Also the war between the states was completely over in the minds of the people and I was excited by the monuments and historical sights. And in addition, Robert E. Lee went to West Point.[6]

Such a response demonstrates a typical mixture of motives, and especially the difficulty of separating out the educational attraction of the service academies. The questionnaire study of West Point graduates reported "educational opportunities" as the second or third reason listed most frequently for attendance at West Point. Clearly, these opportunities were factors in attracting young men in the past. Until the growth of the outstanding civilian technical institutes, the military academies offered as good an education in engineering as was available anywhere. But there were relatively few among those who entered the academies before 1920 and attained high rank who in retrospect claimed that they "went for a good education," with little or no interest in a military career. This theme became frequent among those who entered after 1930—in the period of the depression. Instance upon instance, these older generals and admirals, who came from upper middle-class families, elected deliberately to attend a service academy, rather than to study medicine or law or enter the clergy. Often, this required that they have sufficient funds to enroll in one of the preparatory schools with a reputation for preparing a boy to pass the specialized entrance examinations which the academies administered. The conspicuous minority from the lower middle and even the working classes, for whom an appointment was the only possibility for higher education, had to prepare by their own efforts, or with the assistance of local public school teachers.

For a number of Army and Air Force leaders, military experience during World War I, rather than attendance at West Point, supplied an entrance to a military career. For them, it was the experience of military life that generated the desire to make it a career. Among these, for example, are officers such as General Bedell Smith, for whom military service was the first occupational experience. Others, such as General L. K. Truscott, Jr., had already started on a civilian career as a country school teacher in Oklahoma.

Finally, a small minority revealed that the decision stemmed from a boyhood dream or ambition, a pre-adolescent fantasy, which in some cases could even be established as having formed by the age of ten. Such boyhood dreams can be generated without direct family contact with military tradition:

Basically, it stems from my reading interest as a small child in history and biography. As a youngster I went to a camp and liked it and thought I would try the Army as a career.[7]

But any of these responses—social inheritance, educational opportunity, military experience, boyhood ambition—can have an ambiguous meaning. Each response could have meant either that the person had followed through on a career which he had felt he strongly wanted and would pursue with zeal, or that he had embarked on a career which was one among many he could choose from, and had selected it without a consciously purposive decision. These intensive interviews produced data which indicated the relative power of career choices.

To follow in the tradition of one's father could very well mean no more than a passive, conforming response to pressure. For example, one officer of military parentage reported:

I was born in the army. My father graduated in 19—. I suspect I always thought in that direction. I made my decision actually when I graduated from high school. He pointed out the disadvantages as well as the advantages. . . . But my father was an army officer—this had its effect. However, I didn't live any differently than civilians even though my father was in the army. I frankly have only real memories of living on an army post while we were in Hawaii but from what I knew then I didn't like it.[8]

Such a response is not the product of strong motivation, or the reflection of a sense of mission. To follow a tradition, if one has been coerced, often leaves a residue of dissatisfaction, a feeling that no choice was ever really made. Acting on tradition and social inheritance can mean mere compliance without personal convictions:

Let's go back. My grandfather was in the army. He had two sons. My father was in the army and my father's brother was in the marines. With this kind of a background I thought I would like the navy. I graduated from Annapolis in 19—. Also I was in the Boy Scouts and there I learned to dislike hikes and that's the reason for the navy because it's a clean life. Later I was in the Sea Scouts and this also interested me. My dad was not a West Pointer but the midshipman's crew was in San Francisco in 19— and my mother liked the uniform and she convinced dad I should go to the academy [Annapolis].[9]

In contrast, the memoirs of General Matthew Ridgway indicate how tradition based on positive parental identification can operate to produce a sense of dedication appropriate for a strong leader. He writes:

Though my father did shape and guide my interest in many ways, he never by word or overt act sought to persuade me that I should follow in his footsteps as a career soldier. This, I think, in no way reflected his own attitude toward the Army, for he was a soldier to the core, for all his kindliness and gentleness. It did reflect his belief that a boy was an individual, a new being on the earth, with his own traits of character and personality, and he should be allowed to choose his life work without interference—a procedure I hope Penny, my wife, and I will be able to follow in the rearing of our small son. Nor do I recall feeling any strong inner compulsion to take up the trade of arms as a career. I do think I sensed, deep down, that my father would be happy if I should choose to go to West Point, where he had graduated in 1883, and it was, I think as much an effort to please him as it was any burning desire on my part to become a soldier that led me to make application for an appointment in the class of 1912.[10]

To have been attracted to the service academies because of the superior education they offered could also involve a variety of psychological motives. For the son of a prosperous professional, who had the continuous benefit of family support and an adequate secondary school preparation, especially in mathematics, the selection of West Point or Annapolis was hardly an index of a strong personality. It was merely a sound step in his struggle to advance himself in the professional world. But for the son of a less privileged family, coming from a background which was socially atypical, preparation for West Point or Annapolis could be the expression of great personal drive. This might be the kind of strong career choice which foreshadows determination to perform some sort of mission rather than to merely serve in a post.

Rear Admiral Hyman Rickover was born of a Polish Jewish family, which had migrated to the United States in 1906 and settled in Chicago. Although his father was an expert tailor, because of the system of sweatshops then in existence the family had a most frugal existence. By the time Hyman Rickover reached high school he had worked at a variety of jobs. He was able to attend high school only because he held down an eight-hour-a-day job; from three in the afternoon until eleven at night he worked as a Western Union messenger. According to Clay Blair, Jr., who wrote a biography of Rickover, his life consisted of a grinding work schedule, and, though he studied diligently, he was not an outstanding student. In fact, one year he failed two subjects because "he had been too sleepy to absorb the material."[11] He made up the lost credits by attending summer school.

When, in 1918, Congressman Adolph Sabath, through the intercession of a family friend, offered Rickover an appointment to the Naval Academy, young Hyman had the opportunity for a college education, which for financial reasons would not otherwise have been available. But his high school preparation was inadequate for the entrance examinations. Using $300, which represented his boyhood savings, Rickover enrolled in a prep school near Annapolis in order to cram for the entrance examinations. After two weeks' study at the school, he quit, having decided that the course was inadequate and would never enable him to pass. Instead, he closeted himself in his boarding-house room and studied intensively for two months. He took the examination at the appointed time with other students from preparatory schools and passed. During his first year at Annapolis he continued to cram, since soon after entering the Academy he fell ill with diphtheria. When he was able to join his classmates several weeks later he discovered that they were far advanced and that he could catch up only by studying late at night, which was strictly against the rules and irritating to the other midshipmen as well.

Case history evidence abounds to identify those officers who entered the military with a powerful sense of zeal and mission. For some, even boyhood ambition, which psychologists might argue is merely fantasy, proved to be an index to the strength of their decision. George C. Marshall was scarcely in his teens when he decided to become a soldier. Because of his family and social environment, as well as the letters he received from his older brother already enrolled at the Virginia Military Institute, the imaginary battles with his boyhood friends had a strong element of reality.

Claire Lee Chennault, in his memoirs, did not hide his desire to excel:

Although born in Commerce, Texas, in 1890, my earliest recollections are of roaming the oak woods and moss draped cypress swamps of the Mississippi flood plains in Northeast Louisiana. . . . My mother died when I was five and my father, John Stonewall Chennault, who lived to be eighty, had a fine understanding of the love of a boy for the woods. . . . Without conscious impulse, I constantly strove to be the first in anything I undertook. I simply had to run faster, jump farther, swim faster, dive deeper, catch the longest string of fish, shoot better, make the best grades in all my classes, do the most work on the farm, and read more books than any of my contemporaries. . . . I had an insatiable urge to win, to lead in any activity in which I engaged, to instruct others who were less proficient, but I never felt elated when I won. . . . While still in grade school I pored over history books in my grandfather Lee's library, reading about the Peloponesian and Punic wars. Although I had no idea where Greece, Carthage, and Rome were, I was enthralled by the charging elephants, armored warriors, and burning ships in the colored engravings of the battle of Thermopylae, Zama, Cannae and Salamis. . . .

My first taste of military life came while a freshman cadet at Louisiana State University, where I enrolled in the agricultural course. I had no desire to be a farmer, but all the grade school at Gilbert could offer, plus a year of extra study, left me with insufficient credit for any other college course.[12]

Chennault, fearful of the confinement of academy life, withdrew in the middle of his examinations for Annapolis, and ultimately entered the military profession through the "back door" as an aviator during World War I.

William "Billy" Mitchell was the son of Senator John Lendrum Mitchell, who declared at the official launching of the battleship Wisconsin, "I have had a horror of guns since the Civil War." Yet, for his son, who enlisted as a private in the First Wisconsin Regiment at the declaration of war against Spain, "nothing could just then be more glorious than the adventure of war."[13]

General H. H. Arnold's father was a successful doctor, "who in 1898 laid aside his practice temporarily in order to serve as Lieutenant and Surgeon of the Pennsylvania Cavalry in Puerto Rico." He decided thereafter that one of his sons should go to West Point, and "he was able to bring a bit of influence to bear toward procuring an appointment." However, the father's decision was for the older brother to enter West Point, while H. H., after attendance at Bucknell College, was slated to become a minister. In the end, Arnold took the examination in his brother's place, and entered West Point. Of this change in career he wrote:

I have never understood why my friends laugh when I tell them this. As my career did work out, it came to require as much sheer faith as any preacher's. Or perhaps I should say, as any other preacher's, since it actually took as much evangelism, and maybe more years, to sell the idea of Air Power as it would ever have taken me to sell the Wages of Sin.[14]

Military officers frequently made reference to linkage between their profession and the ministry. One Army colonel, when asked about the gratifications of military life, said: "It is not too different from priesthood or ministry in serving a cause." In a letter a retired naval captain wrote to his son, which was widely distributed, the analogy is spelled out in detail:

The naval profession is much like the ministry. You dedicate your life to a purpose. You wear the garb of an organized profession. Your life is governed by rules laid down by the organization. You renounce your pursuit of wealth. In a large measure you surrender your citizenship; renounce politics; and work for the highest good of the organization. In the final analysis your aims and objects are quite as moral as any minister's because you are not seeking your own good, but the ultimate good of your country. You train the men under you to be good and useful citizens, and, like the minister, what you say must conform to the rules of the organization.[15]

It has not been unusual for a young man to have to make a decision as to whether he would enter the ministry or the military. In the United States, and more often in Europe, sons of clergy have frequently taken up a military career.[16] Conversely, officers who resigned from the military have found in the clergy an expression of their desire to "do service and to perform in the name of a great cause."[17]

Finally, the desire to excel usually expresses itself in high school. The appointment system to the academies tended to recruit students who had attracted some recognition in high school because of scholarship, athletic success, or because of their personal qualities. The questionnaire study of West Point graduates disclosed that about one-fourth had been elected to either of two elective offices (president, vice-president, or equivalent) in their last two years in high school. In addition, about one-fifth had been either valedictorian or salutatorian of their high school graduating class. On the basis of self-selection, appointments went to the energetic and ambitious students, and not to those who were indifferent to their status in society.

For many of those in the military profession who had entered the elite by 1950, available data clearly establish that the military was more than an occupation. It was, in fact, an opportunity to satisfy strong motivations. These observations are more often than not based on those who have been successful. But this is precisely the issue. Not only is the choice of a military career a strong choice for an important minority, but, as in any social institution, the stronger the motivation, the more likely is the possibility that the person will rise to the top. The sense of mission has been strongest among the elite nucleus—the minority of prime movers on whom the success or the failure of the military establishment has depended. But when, as in the case of General "Billy" Mitchell, missionary zeal oversteps ultimate organization forms, the individual runs the risk of expulsion or internal exile. Has this sense of mission been diluted as a career motive among those who are in the potential military elite, and among the contemporary cadets?

The Growth of "Careerism"

THE EVENTS of the depression of the 1930's marked a transformation of American social structure, and among these changes was the recruitment pattern of the military. The immediate effect was an increased interest in the free education available at the service academies. Applicants and aspirants were no longer limited to members of service families and to those social circles which carried military traditions. Many who won entrance had little or no interest in the military, although the impact of military indoctrination and the outbreak of World War II subsequently influenced a number of them to make the profession a career goal:

I decided to go to West Point in high school but not to become a professional officer. This was in 1932–1933 and I didn't have enough money to go to college. I did the necessary studying and took the examination to go to West Point with no intention of staying in the Army. I felt I would be happy to stay in the three years but then get out and teach. . . . After two years I had decided not to stay in. I found the common run of officers was not too impressive and decided to get out in three years. But I graduated in 1938 and would have gotten out in 1941 but the war started and I had to stay. Now during the war I had opportunities which I wouldn't have elsewhere. Also during the war I had a good group of commanders and also I had the rank and career ahead of me when it would have been silly to get out.[18]

The phrase "silly to get out" betrays a careerist orientation based on the evaluation of the conditions of employment, rather than any sense of calling or missionary zeal.

Economic pressures were but one dimension in the larger organizational revolution that was going on in American society with particular consequences for the military profession and its system of recruitment. The older patterns of informal and interpersonal connections guiding the selection system could no longer operate. For example, when, in 1904, Lieutenant General Holland Smith sought entrance to an officer appointment, he was able to speak directly with the Secretary of the Navy, who could personally interview him and take notice of his qualifications and his "suitable" family background.

The prospect of the Secretary of the Navy being personally engaged in recruiting and counseling officer candidates for the Marine Corps in the 1950's seems not only remote, but would be thought to be a demonstration of personal favoritism. The expansion in the size of the military, as well as the large and heterogeneous base from which recruits must be drawn, requires formal and bureaucratic techniques of selection. The organizational revolution thus weakened the older system, based on tradition, interpersonal connections, and private cram schools.

Some effects of the transformed selection system can be seen in the career motives of potential members of the military elite. Those who see the military profession as a calling or a unique profession are outnumbered by a greater concentration of individuals for whom the military is just another job. The interview responses in the group of 113 potential members of the military leadership are at variance with the views of older members of the profession.

The important minority who selected their careers for traditional reasons, or because of social inheritance, is still clearly present. While the number interviewed and the basis of selection limits generalizations, it can be noted that about one-quarter of the Army and Navy officers fell into this category (Table 21). However, among the Air Force, the influence of tradition was not very widespread. Again and again, Air Force officers indicated that the educational opportunities of the service academies, or the support for education from college reserve programs, had attracted them to Air Force careers. This motive pattern was prominent for about one-half of the Air Force officers.

So pronounced were careerist aspirations, and so legitimate is the expression of such aspirations, that for a sizable minority—

about 20 per cent, or one out of every five—no motive could be discerned, except that the military was a job (Table 21). For these persons, the choice of a military profession constituted weighing the advantages and disadvantages of such a career against what they could, or thought they could, attain in other jobs. Many of them continued their military career simply because they had accumulated so much seniority that they felt they could not cut their investment. Undoubtedly, this type has always been found in the

Table 21

Potential Military Leaders, 1958:
Basic Career Motivation

	Army %	Navy %	Air Force %
Tradition	26	22	3
Educational opportunity	22	18	51
Careerist	22	22	15
Military experience*	17	22	31
"Boyhood" ambition	12	16	0
Other	1	–	–
Total per cent	100	100	100
Number	(54)	(32)	(27)

* Includes those who sought adventure.

military, as in all bureaucracies. Such officers make little pretense or effort to hide their motives. For example, an energetic Air Force officer, with a law background, commented:

After I had completed five years of service in World War II, I came back to my law practice and then two years later I went back into service as a regular officer. . . . I'm from somewhat a military background, as my father was a military academy graduate and he was a general officer. However, this is not material in my case. When I returned to my civilian work, I found I was a little spoiled for civilian work and preferred the work in the Air Force without the pressure of civilian life.[19]

The reserve system, with its unpredictable career consequences, fosters a careerist orientation. Although it is difficult to separate reality from rationalization, the remarks of one naval officer are revealing:

I didn't decide. I was called up in April, 1941 and served five years, and had no idea of coming back. But then I was called back in 1948 and I felt I might as well get my 20 years in. I had two cracks at lucrative jobs and was stopped, so I think I may as well stay in.[20]

Among careerists, the importance of public service is reduced from an end-in-itself to one factor to be weighed with other factors in judging the worth of the military profession:

In 1945, I made up my mind to stay in because I would have had to start all over again in civilian life. The salary in the service might not be the best, but you do get security. Also, there is the public service aspect. You are volunteering to defend your country, which makes it honorable. So measuring this public service against the civilian life, I thought I would be honorable.[21]

Apart from the careerists, there is a minority who seemed never to have made any decision, but who just drifted into the military. Having had some previous military experience, such as college reserve training or membership in National Guard Units, they felt little concern with the career aspects of their work, but had found life in the military satisfactory:

I never really made up my mind. When I got out of high school in 1939, I went into active duty and stayed on until 1945. In 1947, I received a regular commission. When I first went into service, I had no intention of staying in.[22]

That's hard to answer. I enlisted in the service in 1937, shortly after leaving high school. I decided to spend a year in the Army and get out. However, I was quite impressed and decided to stay on. I was made a First Sergeant in 1942 and was made a Warrant Officer and later commissioned a Second Lt. After the war, I was given a regular commission in 1947. I liked the discipline, the degree of integrity of the military, and the future.[23]

The questionnaire study of West Point graduates indicates that in recent years there has been an increase in the percentage of military cadets who have had previous military experience and college education. Such trends do not necessarily imply greater career commitment or stronger career motives. On the contrary, many of these men have drifted into the military as a result of immediate experience and available opportunity. For example:

I decided to go to West Point in 19—. I refused to go to college after high school and worked. I belonged to the Connecticut National Guard

—a cavalry outfit. After about three years of working, then I realized that there were things I didn't know. So examinations for West Point came out and I was eligible. So I tried. A couple of non-coms taught me math to get by the exam. Apparently, everyone was illiterate and perhaps also my family influence helped and I passed. So then I had to pass West Point's entrance exams against smarter guys. The Borden's School—a prep school for West Point—a cram school I attended then. Having no math in high school I needed this. I was convinced I failed but I didn't. I got into West Point in 19—... After one year at West Point, I decided I didn't like it but my father made me promise to sit for two years. He felt I had an obligation to stay and I said I would. So it was an accidental choice.[24]

The organizational revolution has not, however, eliminated the presence of those who attest that boyhood "ambition," based on pre-adolescent fantasy, conditioned their choice. The desire to be a great general or a famous admiral still persisted in the post-World War I period. Perhaps it was the absence of great flying generals in the story books of that time that accounts for the absence of any Air Force officer who would admit motivation from such boyhood images.

There is always the danger of imputing more complex motives to our subjects than were actually at work. In the vast military establishment, membership in the potential military elite is open even to those who were motivated by sheer adventure. This is especially the case for Navy and Air Force personnel, although Army officers spoke of the opportunities for outdoor life and for hunting. An Air Force colonel in an important staff post gave such a reason for deciding on a military career:

Nothing except a "young buck" reason that it looked like a lot of fun.[25]

A naval officer commented:

I was always interested in boats and the water, like participating in Gold Cup Regattas.[26]

One Army general felt:

Even after I left West Point, I wasn't sure I would stay in. I have often said I joined the Army to get outside.[27]

Original career motives aside, what commitments has professional experience created among the members of the potential elite? Although all 113 members of the sample have some potential for promotion, obviously, those most likely to rise are the men with the strongest commitment to the military profession. The mechanisms of promotion, whatever their defects, operate in this direction.

When confronted with the question, "If you had an opportunity to do it over again, would you choose another profession?," more than 80 per cent were unequivocal in their positive response. Only an isolated case expressed fundamental antagonism; the remaining minority revealed realistic indecision. But this is a defensive question, which would tend to minimize expression of career dissatisfaction. Perhaps a more meaningful response was that given to the question, "If you had a son, would you like him to have a career as a military officer?"[28] Positive commitment to the military profession declined in all three services, but the drop was hardly marked (Table 22). Those who said "yes" ranged from 76 per cent, among naval officers, to 68 per cent among Army officers. It would be highly revealing if comparable data existed for other professions. Yet, these percentages are striking, in the light of the specific sources of dissatisfaction with conditions of service, such as salary and frequent changes of station. Nor can these responses be dismissed as "public relations," for the same interviews produced revealing candor as to underlying career motives. Instead, there is initial evidence for an ever-recurring theme—the effectiveness of the military indoctrination system.

The officer indoctrination system involves more than service academies and schools of higher military education, although they

Table 22

Potential Military Leaders, 1958:
"If you had a son, would you like him to have a career as a military officer?"

	Army %	Navy %	Air Force %
Yes	59	54	46
Yes, but let him decide	9	22	25
Total yes	68	76	71
Uncertain	2	6	7
No	24	12	15
No answer	6	6	7
Total per cent	100	100	100
Number	(54)	(32)	(27)

are central. The daily routine of military existence is part of the indoctrination system. Whether one enters the military because of a sense of mission or for careerist reasons, constant preoccupation with combat engenders a distinctive self-conception. The fact that the professional soldier considers himself distinctive explains why, in a society in which the military is held in doubtful esteem, social inheritance of the profession—whether coerced or voluntary—takes place at all.

All professions are faced with competition in the recruitment of personnel, and seek to attract those who are dedicated, or who can be indoctrinated with zeal. Similarly, all professional leaders decry the diminishing of career commitments among their new recruits. The development of strong career commitments is a real problem for any profession, and especially for the military. The staffs of the military academies admit privately that, although the intelligence level of new recruits rises year by year, there is no concurrent increase in the sense of career commitment. To judge from the number of junior officers who resign after completing their required services, the contrary is clearly the case. British sources, which are more candid, report that 60 per cent of all entrants to the Royal Military Academy who "successfully pass the necessary examinations and the Regular Commissions Board are graded before arrival as 'likely to make a below average officer,'" mainly because they lack motivation and leadership potential.[29]

The service academies no longer provide the best available technical education; those who select them are not following strong desires for technical and scientific education. Except in special cases, congressmen no longer take a personal interest in their academy appointments, or in using them as political patronage. Instead, it is easier, and politically more useful, to announce a public examination and choose successful candidates on the basis of academic achievement, thereby avoiding the charge of favoritism. The new system may be fair, and may even produce more intelligent cadets, but it hardly guarantees the selection of those who are strongly motivated toward a military career. The older informal system was undoubtedly more effective in this respect. An occasional congressman has gone so far as to use personnel selection tests, but there is no valid scientific procedure for selecting heroic leaders or for screening military strategists.[30]

Thus, it is understandable that the academies seek to reserve openings for those who have demonstrated "leadership" ability in high school athletics and student life, and to de-emphasize academic achievement. It is also understandable that the academies seek to draw on the sons of military officers. Private cram schools have declined, and the services now operate their own preparatory schools where those with appropriate background are specially prepared. Increased selection from the enlisted ranks also represents a search for persons with strong career commitments and a heroic outlook. Yet, even those who come from military families seem to be acting less in terms of tradition and more in terms of the rational calculation that an education at military academies and at government expense is the "smart" gambit. Like medical school deans, academy commandants have become deeply concerned about the number, quality, and the commitment of applicants.

In 1955 the United States Naval Academy launched an "Operation Information" to recruit more acceptable candidates. The ratio of applications to vacancies had dropped to about two to one, and two years later, as a result of this effort, applications had increased to about five to one. The recruitment procedures follow the techniques of civilian universities. Each Christmas, one hundred first-class (senior) midshipmen get a few days extra leave, in order to talk to civic groups and organizations in their communities. The information program includes various types of public relations paraphernalia: pamphlets; a television program, entitled "Men of Annapolis"; and an improved intercollegiate football team.[31] The United States Military Academy has fashioned a similar recruitment and public information program. Recruits who have been attracted to the military profession by "public relations" require the most intensive indoctrination, and the service academies deem themselves well equipped for this task.

Notes

1. Herring, Pendleton, *The Impact of War*. New York: Farrar & Rinehart, 1941, p. 12.
2. Masland, John W., & Radway, Laurence I. *Soldiers and Scholars*. Princeton: Princeton University Press, 1957, p. 233.
3. *Report on Graduate Questionnaire*, July 1, 1958, p. 6.

4. Interview No. 38.
5. Interview No. 20.
6. Interview No. 36.
7. Interview No. 28.
8. Interview No. 31.
9. Interview No. 98.
10. Ridgway, Matthew, *Soldier: The Memoirs of Matthew B. Ridgway*. New York: Harper & Bros., 1956, p. 22.
11. Blair, Clay, Jr., *The Atomic Submarine and Admiral Rickover*. New York: Henry Holt, 1954, p. 35.
12. Chennault, Claire Lee, *Way of a Fighter: The Memoirs of Claire Lee Chennault*. New York: G. P. Putnam's Sons, 1949, p. 7.
13. Levine, Isaac Don, *Mitchell: Pioneer of Air Power*. New York: Duell, Sloan & Pearce, 1943, p. 3.
14. Arnold, H. H., *Global Mission*. New York: Harper & Bros., 1949, p. 6.
15. Niblack, Captain A. P., "The Letters of a Retired Rear Admiral to His Son in The Navy, 'Does It Pay to Be A Naval Officer?' " May 30, 1913.
16. More than one hundred twenty-five of those who applied for admission to West Point from 1842 to 1891, and of the cadets admitted to the academy from 1892 to 1899, were the sons of clergymen. Larned, Charles W., "The Military Genius of West Point," in *The Centennial of the United States Military Academy at West Point*. New York: 1802–1902; Washington: 1904.
17. One of the most famous soldier-ministers was Leonidas Polk, who resigned from the Army to become a Protestant bishop. In 1841 he wrote that in the past few years, "as many as twelve or fifteen officers of the Army, and it is believed some from the Navy, have laid aside the military profession for the more peaceful, but not less arduous, vocation of the Christian ministry." Polk, Leonidas, *Army and Navy Chronicle*, November 4, 1841, 11.
18. Interview No. 50.
19. Interview No. 62.
20. Interview No. 113.
21. Interview No. 34.
22. Interview No. 75.
23. Interview No. 74.
24. Interview No. 56.
25. Interview No. 75.
26. Interview No. 84.
27. Interview No. 2.
28. Alternative version, as required: "If your son is already in the military, are you pleased that your son has chosen a military career?"
29. "Sandhurst and the Schools," *London Times*, February 4, 1953, p. 7.
30. Sanford, Fillmore H., "Research on Military Leadership," in *Current Trends; Psychology in the World Emergency*, Stephen Collins Foster Memorial Lectures. Pittsburgh: University of Pittsburgh Press, 1952, pp. 20–21.
31. Baldwin, Hanson, "Annapolis Aweigh," *New York Times*, April 8, 1957, p. 2.

CHAPTER 7

Career Development

ENTRANCE into the military elite comes only after many years of professional education, training, and experience. Military career lines are highly standardized, as compared with other professions. By examining the crucial switch points in an officer's life history, it is possible to understand the experiences which molded his life chances and regulated his opportunities for ascent. The successful officer feels that the civilian population cannot possibly understand the intricate mechanisms of education, selection, and promotion But the career experiences of generals and admirals are matters of public record, and this information is an essential part of the civilian control of the military profession. On the basis of published memoirs, and through interviews, it was possible to reconstruct the main outlines of the informal standards which operate behind the official procedures of selection and promotion.

In tracing career lines and the mechanics of advancement into the military elite, the importance of organizational accident can easily be understated. In retrospect, it makes a great deal of difference to a graduating cadet when war breaks out, for a difference of one or two years can be crucial in determining his chances for promotion. Thus, to have graduated from West Point or Annapolis in the years before the United States entered World War I meant that a young officer's chances were greatly enhanced; his availability was then timed to mesh with the expanded need for more generals and admirals during World War II. A tabulation of the chances of becoming a permanent major general, for example, rose and fell with statistical precision between the classes of 1905 to 1917.[1] Up to, and including the class of 1907, the chances of a cadet's becoming a major general were approximately five to seven out of one hundred. For the class of 1908, the chances began to rise sharply through the 1940's, and continued to rise until the "magical" years of the class of 1912, which had three times the chances of the class of 1907—eighteen out of one hundred. For the class of 1916, the chances reverted to the normal pattern (5.6 per cent) when World War II came to a close.

In addition to one's being in the appropriate academy class, one's career depends on being available at the right spot when new opportunities suddenly develop. For example, at the time he commanded the 25th Division at Guadalcanal, General J. Lawton Collins was a major general at the age of forty-eight. Collins discovered he was far too young for the Pacific, since General MacArthur, aged sixty-four, preferred contemporaries in his command. Since there was little likelihood, therefore, of Collins' commanding a corps in the Pacific because of his age, General Marshall recommended his transfer to Europe, where there were sufficient posts for permanent lieutenant colonels to continue their career advancement.

Organizational and personal accident aside, in each service the military career is grounded in an idealized notion of the appropriate sequence of assignment. In theory, the steps in a military career consist of rotation from command to staff assignments, with the prize staff assignment being service in the operations and planning sections of the Washington command post. In actuality, the military career could better be described as a progression of educational experiences, as student and teacher, interspersed with operational military assignments. In contrast to the concentrated single dosage of professional education in medical or law school, an officer, as he moves up the hierarchy, is sent to various schools, at prescribed intervals, to acquire new skills and new perspectives. Before World War II, aside from attendance at a service academy, the typical professional spent as much as one-quarter of his career in school or in training situations. The amount of educational training continues to increase in the post-World War II period. A survey of graduates from the Fort Leavenworth staff and command school who averaged thirteen years of service revealed that, on the average, these officers had spent one-third of their careers in command positions, one-third in staff positions, and one-third in schools and training experiences.

The Meaning of an Academy Education

EDUCATION at a service academy is the first and most crucial experience of a professional soldier. The educational experiences of the cadet cannot obliterate his social background, but they leave deep and lasting impressions. Although attendance at a service academy is not universal for generals and admirals, the academies set the standards of behavior for the whole military profession. They are the source of the pervasive "like-mindedness" about military honor and for the sense of fraternity which prevails among military men. The professional military perspective until 1950 must be understood as an amalgam of the conservative background of its cadets and the technical and engineering curriculum of West Point and Annapolis.

The professional officer enters a career in which a single authority regulates all of his life opportunities. Indeed, the officer candidate finds that the full cycle of his daily existence comes under the control of this single authority, for military life is institutional life. Beyond the technical skills that he acquires, the academies must prepare him for the particular style of life of military existence and indoctrinate him in the importance of heroic leadership. They must seek to weaken regional ties and develop a sense of broader national identity. Once the potential officer gains admittance and survives the ordeals of initiation, the purpose of an academy education is to transform him into a member of a professional "fraternity." West Point, Annapolis, and, more recently, Colorado Springs must implant in the officer recruit a concept of professional honor. Since graduation from an academy means entrance into a group which disperses very gradually—the officer is always associated with a particular graduating class—academy education means acquiring lifetime colleagues and the necessity of accommodating to them. The graduates of Harvard, Princeton, and Yale become scattered, but the lives of academy graduates continuously cross and recross.

If the goal of academy education is initiation of the officer recruit, the task has become more and more complex. When the military profession and its elite members were recruited from the narrow base of an upper-status social background, with traditional family connections, the service academies encountered little resistance to their definitions of military honor. As the recruits have become more and more representative, however, the effectiveness of indoctrination cannot be taken for granted. The aspiring officer, from more humble social origins and with more of a careerist orientation, must be instructed in a great deal more than the meaning of professional honor. He must also be convinced that a military career is materially worthwhile, personally rewarding, and socially useful. The military profession, like other professions, is composed predominantly of officers who are, essentially, experts and specialists, absorbed in their specific tasks.[2] Thus, it is an unspoken assumption that the military academy must instill in the officer recruit the importance of career success through continuous hard work, self-education, and a concern with the "big picture."

In order to ascertain whether cadets have those military traits presumed necessary for officers, most armed forces have developed elaborate systems of inducting new members. In the past, at both West Point and Annapolis, the techniques of initiation have been of the same variety: strict discipline, detailed regulation of the recruit's daily routines, a fanatical concern with athletics, and indoctrination in military traditions and professional etiquette. Colonel Sylvanus Thayer, a founder of West Point, initiated such rigid discipline that he was reported to have been denounced by President Andrew Jackson: "Sylvanus Thayer is a tyrant. The autocrat of all the Russias couldn't exercise more power!"[3] The traditions of Colonel Thayer persisted until after 1920, when military leaders of World War II were in attendance. It is appropriate to quote one general's recollections, since he was able to articulate what many others endured in silence:

I entered West Point on the 14th of June 1913, and was immediately plunged into the ordeal which faces every plebe—the six weeks of rigorous mental, physical and spiritual testing known as "beast barracks." The first class men and the yearlings drive you pretty hard during that period, and there is many a night when a man, sore and bruised both physically and emotionally, doubts the wisdom of ever having entered West Point at all. I know I did. But I managed to get through by giving myself little pep talks as I lay there in my bunk after lights out.[4]

From the memoirs of retired military leaders and numerous sentimental histories of the service academies, it is not difficult to read between the lines for an understanding of the sense of accomplishment that mere survival for four years brought the newly commissioned ensign or second lieutenant. Transition to academy routine is sharp and sudden, and therefore often seems repulsive to the outsider. Gradually, physical force has been eliminated, but strict discipline persists. One cadet can still order another cadet to exercise until he is physically exhausted. The system of hazing continues to operate, so as to effect a quick transition from civilian life to the military profession. The new recruit is given a number of weeks of intensive exposure to the rigors of military life, and is a candidate for hazing during his first years. The academy authorities vested with the responsibility for maintaining traditions see these survivals as trial demonstrations which permit the recruit to determine the depth of his commitment to the military profession.[5]

The endless routines and the "plebe" system of hazing is justified as a device for teaching self-control, as well as resistance to panic. One participant, whose relative detachment is attested to by the fact that he resigned from a promising military career, assessed the system:

One of the principle methods of hazing used at West Point is the so-called clothing formation. The way this works is this. There are no elevators in West Point barracks and the plebes tend to live in the 4th floor. In the basement of most of the barracks, except the very new ones, the showers are, the washbasins and so on. On a Sunday afternoon plebes who have done something wrong or made some mistake are turned out for clothing formation. They go down in the basement and a bunch of upper classmen brace them, that is, make them stand in an exaggerated posture of attention. Then one of these upper classmen will say you have 2½ minutes to go to your room, change into full dress uniform and be back down here. Now this is a perfectly preposterous demand. It takes much longer than that to get up to your room, change into full dress and come down, but if you show an indifference or any unwillingness to try to reach this impossible goal they will jump all over you and make you go to clothing formations for the rest of the year. Indifference is another thing they are trying to eradicate. There is no worse crime than indifference. Well, the cadet dashes upstairs, changes into his full dress uniform, dashes down again. He must do this under a terrible pressure of time and when he comes down and the upper classman finds that he has forgotten something or that his belt isn't tied right, then he catches unmitigated hell. This accustoms a man to panic, to having to do things that require a lot of coordination, to remember a great many details and to do it under great time pressure. Cadets learn by this to be familiar with the feeling of panic, to control it. They learn to do things at a very fast pace, but calmly so as not to forget any details. It doesn't take much imagination to see the utility of this for a war situation. I never once saw the significance and purpose of the clothing formation when I was a cadet, but I had occasion to remember it in the war and my understanding of the significance of it came after I was actually in combat.[6]

Undoubtedly, realistic military training, whether it be paratroop training, fleet exercises, or aerial gunnery demonstrations supply the same type of experience. These initiation exercises at the academies —including the new Air Force Academy—serve also as an entrance requirement to a select fraternal group.

As excessively harsh discipline has declined, athletics has taken over, since sports involve a team spirit and are appropriate preparation for military life. Mass athletics is supposed to prepare the officer for the task of handling civilians as citizen soldiers. Athletics is the symbolic analogy of personal involvement in combat. Therefore, it is not accidental that both service academies began to emphasize athletics around the turn of the century, when both the Army and the Navy were beginning to organize themselves into large-scale institutions. Emphasis on athletics gradually spread throughout the services, and soon penetrated into the enlisted ranks. Following the pattern of civilian colleges and universities, a strong overtone of semi-professionalism developed in the search for successful performers.

In fact, a military career requires considerable physical vigor. An educational institution built around the theme of vigorous athletic activity serves to attract the physically fit and the athletically inclined. The letters of a retired naval officer to his son indicate the extent to which physical development became part of the curriculum at Annapolis at one time:

As soon as you enter the academy, the testing dynamometer at the gymnasium, in about half an hour, shows you how you stand as to every group of muscles. Ten groups are tested in each arm, eight in each leg, eight in the trunk, and three in the chest. Of course your height and weight are taken, because your total strength varies as the square of your height in inches, and if you are deficient in any group beyond a certain limit, you automatically pass into the "weak squad." Your card will also show what machine, by number, you should use in the gymnasium to make good your deficiencies so that you can pass the required test on the dynamometer. Meanwhile it is your fate to spend, in the gymnasium, the time that otherwise would be spent in watching, or playing football or baseball, or outdoor athletics. . . . I am glad to see at Annapolis that the actual gymnasium apparatus, under this Americanized Swedish system is utilized for the good of and the actual physical development of each midshipman exactly as he needs it. . . . Whatever interest the government takes in this physical development, it gets back in future service from each officer. . . .[7]

The mechanics of professional indoctrination are equally comprehensive. Special courses in military history are taught, and exposure to the appropriate behavior of the military professional is an essential part of academic and tactical training. However, it is the very physical and historical surroundings that produce the most lasting impressions on undergraduates. Cadets and midshipmen use the rooms once occupied by great generals and admirals. At West Point there is the old chapel with the British colors seized in the Revolution; historical monuments also abound at Annapolis. As at Harvard or Princeton, the campus gives the image of unending stability. American undergraduate education, especially in the eastern private schools, seeks to produce loyal alumni. Not only do the service academies at West Point and Annapolis have the same features of sentimentality, they also have the assistance of powerful historical traditions.

In the absence of such assets, the Air Force Academy at Colorado Springs presents a picture of "gracious living and a picture window view of the Rocky Mountains." The theme is the modern age. Indirect lighting has been installed in the classrooms, with the corridors acting as a buffer, graduating the light "from the mountain brilliance to the proper indoor reading levels." As one enthusiast reported, "the two-man cadet rooms rival the finest modern hotel accommodations, with eye-level bookcases and vinyl plastic floors." The absence of an historical tradition does not mean the absence of ceremonialism, however. The Air Force Academy compensates for such deficiencies with an emphasis on "spit and polish," protocol, and military etiquette.

It was in this context of discipline, athletics, and professional traditionalism that West Point and Annapolis developed their academic curriculum. As mentioned previously, early in the nineteenth century it could be claimed that West Point was ahead of its time in offering first-rate engineering and mathematical education. Enthusiasts have even recorded that the early forms of instruction, which made use of small classes and daily recitation, were marked advances in pedagogy. Until the outbreak of World War II, both of the service academies still offered the bright student an effective education in engineering. The implicit assumption has been that "the real professional education" of an officer begins after graduation, in his practical experience and in the specialized schools of the armed forces. Those of the faculty who argued the importance of a general education were in the minority. As long as the instructional staff was limited to professional soldiers with no advanced academic training in the humanities and the social sciences, general education was limited, if not impossible. At West Point Colonel Herman Beukema chaired a department of economics, government, and history after 1926, and served as a pioneer in the effort to reorient the curriculum toward more general education.

Because the military academies are highly autonomous and governed, to a considerable extent, by self-perpetuating academic boards, the efforts by academy educators to update the curriculum have been gradual. Yet the long-term trend has been toward a greater and greater emphasis on general education and on the inculcation of those interpersonal skills which a military manager requires. Today, professional requirements are such that an old fashioned trade school education is no longer sufficient. Moreover, the cadets insist that, in addition to their technical training, they get some exposure to the content of civilian collegiate courses, for they are no longer prepared to see themselves as entering a profession which is apart from the rest of society. The search for a balance between general education and professional preparation is reflected at West Point by the faculty's reference to the "whole man" conception—based on the assumption that a synthesis of educational objectives is possible. Annapolis has remained more traditional and technical, while West Point has sought to press in the direction of a more balanced curriculum. The Air Force Academy, with the fewest traditions to overcome, has developed the curriculum which, with the exception of military subjects, is closest to that of the average civilian university.

Therefore, the education which officers who rose to be generals and admirals in the decade from 1950 to 1960 received, was basically a technical and engineering education. Paralleling civilian education, its intellectual assumptions were optimistic, since students were drilled in the belief that the fact that the United States had never lost a war was due to the determination of its professional soldiers and their ability to work out scientific and technical solutions to military problems. Furthermore, personal and controlled self-assuredness was implanted in the academies.

Despite contemporary trends in the curriculum, the academies, especially West Point and Annapolis, still emphasize an engineering content. As of 1958, one West Point academic administrator felt obliged to acknowledge in public print that the 425 hours devoted to mathematics were not essential for educational aims.[8] The academies realize that even engineering has become too complicated for them to compete with specialized civilian institutes, so they make it possible for their graduates to go on to civilian schools for postgraduate study. The study of languages has increased, but with probably no more startling success than in civilian universities. Since the end of World War II, social science has found its way into the curriculum, mainly in the form of military economics and the analysis of the current balance of power in international relations. Perhaps the most important development is the increase in the number of civilian instructors, and the increased opportunity for officers to study at civilian universities before becoming instructors at military academies.

Both the military academy and the civilian university have had to assume greater responsibility for training in interpersonal and social skills, which once were thought to be the responsibility of the family. In 1922 General Douglas MacArthur, superintendent of West Point, announced that the cadets had been granted the privilege of an occasional six-hour pass and $5.00 per month for spending money. In his annual report for that year he wrote:

They [the cadets] are no longer walled up within the academy for two years at a time. They acquire by their small business transactions and by their contact with the outside world the beginnings of an experience which would be of value to them when they graduate. Without such opportunities of business and social activity, the cadet is graduated and thrust out into the world, a man in age but a high school boy so far as his experience goes. . . . These few privileges extended to the cadet in recent years will go far to break down the walls of isolation and broaden their experience.[9]

Since 1955, applied courses in human relations and group psychology have been offered at all three of the academies, and stand as a testament to the fact that the requirements of the organizational revolution have penetrated the military profession. Training in public speaking, through classroom instruction or extracurricular activities, is essential for the military manager of the future. An elaborate pattern of social life, extracurricular activities, and a broadening concern with "current events" are part of the pattern.

With the exception of a few individual cases, there is little evidence to link intellectual superiority at the academies with subsequent performance in a career. In fact, it has been repeatedly found that academic and scholastic achievement are unrelated to military leadership at the tactical and intermediate levels. These characteristics are neither a basis for selection nor rejection of a tactical officer. This observation was first documented by research carried out during World War I, and has been reaffirmed in numerous studies.[10] One study on recent West Point graduates is reported to have shown little or no correlation between academic records and later efficiency reports.[11] But do these observations relate to performance at the higher levels of administration and command?

Again, it was anticipated that, with the exception of a few individual cases, the association between academic performance and entrance into the nucleus of the military elite in the past would not be pronounced. (General Douglas MacArthur's outstanding academic record is repeatedly cited as the special example.) The data contained in Table 23 on the academic standing of generals

Table 23

Military Leadership, 1950: Class Standing in Military Academy

	Army	Navy	Air Force
	%	%	%
Upper quarter	36.4	50.8	21.3
Middle range	46.7	38.7	59.5
Lower quarter	16.9	10.5	19.2
Number	(77)	(191)	(47)

and admirals in the 1950 sample do reveal that those graduates who were in the lowest quartile of their class are under-represented. Higher class standing somewhat assists promotion to the top, more so in the Navy than in the Army, but not for this sample from the Air Force. These results are confirmed by a more detailed study by James L. Howerton of one hundred seventy major generals who graduated from the military academy during the period 1904–17:

"A cadet's chance to become a future general is slightly greater if he stands above the 50th percentile in general merit, but where above that point does not seem to make an appreciable difference. On the other hand, his chances are slightly less if he stands below the 50th percentile but they are by no means ruled out."[12] General merit included performance in both military and academic subjects, yet, more detailed analysis revealed no difference in chances for promotion as between the two subject matter areas. Moreover, those in the very highest levels—lieutenant general and general— had no record of particularly outstanding academic performance. Instead, a larger percentage of generals participated in extramural athletics than did their classmates, indicating that to have been outstanding in athletics at West Point was the best indicator that a cadet would become a general.

To some degree these data underline that the military profession in the past has placed higher emphasis on "doing" than on "intellectual" accomplishment. Roger Hilsman, a West Point graduate whose career included combat leadership in Burma, and a professional academic career as a political scientist at Princeton and Johns Hopkins University and as head of foreign affairs research for the Legislative Reference Service, Library of Congress, formulated his experience as follows: "There are, of course, intelligent generals, highly intelligent ones; but intelligence is not the same as intellectuality. . . . Military men are not thinkers."[13] Intellectuality is not a highly prized trait because, in training a modern armed force, and in battle, decisiveness and interpersonal and executive skill are more essential. Yet, the military has respect for the educated man, especially for his expertise.

These data merely confirm that the military academy is no different from other professional schools, in that there is a tremendous gap between its curriculum and the realities of professional life. The content of professional education in law and medicine has been a continual source of controversy, as to what best prepares a graduate for his responsibilities in a changing society. In the case of the service academies, the low correlation between intellectual performance and subsequent careers in the past may, in effect, be the result of what has been described as a low conceptual level in academic instruction and an emphasis on rote learning, rather than an emphasis on analysis and creative problem-solving. Furthermore, in the process of indoctrination, and in the effort to create a sense of professional loyalty, the cadet must learn to conform. According to one academy psychiatrist, the cadet is a more dependent personality than is the average college man.[14]

This does not imply that the academies have not provided training in ambition. On the contrary, the elaborate system of grading and ranking, of heavy academic assignments and elaborate reference to the cadet's class position, have supplied plenty of opportunity for those who wished to demonstrate their energies and drive. But initiative must be expressed within the confines of a detailed and elaborate daily schedule which leaves the officer recruit only seconds for reflection and privacy. Given the system of rigid "lights out," and the absence of adequate library facilities, cadets and midshipmen have often been driven to do their burning of the midnight oil in the basement latrines.

By its own standards, military education has been effective in forming a base for solidarity in the military profession. There was much less exodus from the military profession by academy graduates up to 1939 than might have been anticipated. Given the values of American society, with its emphasis on success in business, this is indeed an accomplishment. More adequate data are available on West Point than on Annapolis in this connection. At the outbreak of World War I, after a period of 115 years of operation, West Point had produced 5,601 cadets. From this group, 2,895 were still alive and if one subtracts 414, who were retired, the exodus by resignation was no more than 12.5 per cent. At the outbreak of World War II the number of graduates had increased to 12,663, of whom 8,446 were alive. After subtracting the 898 who had retired, the percentage who had resigned from active duty had increased to 14.9.[15]

In recent years the exodus of academy graduates from the profession has increased to a point where, five years after graduation, between 20 and 25 per cent have resigned. Moreover, there is every reason to believe that the graduates of the Air Force Academy with its more civilianized forms will demonstrate an equal propensity to change professions, especially as the skills between the Air Force and civilian society become more transferable.

The common identifications forged in four years produce strong like-mindedness and a network of close personal contacts. All large-scale organizations develop factions, but the military profession is unique in that only academy education generates this basic divide—between graduates and non-graduates. To reserve officers, who have not attended the academies, academy graduates are thought to be members of a "mutual protective society." To academy graduates, the system is not thought to manifest undue favoritism, and is believed essential for the effectiveness of the profession. The skill structure of the military has made it possible for considerable numbers of non-academy graduates to penetrate into the highest ranks in the Army and the Air Force. The outstanding person is recognized with only limited regard to academy attendance. But when all other factors are in balance, the service academy graduate has the advantage. The same mechanism operates in university life, since there are a selected number of graduate schools which dominate the appointment system.[16]

Thus, a report by the Human Resources Research Institute demonstrated that approximately equal percentages of West Point graduates and non-West Point graduates who stood at the top third of their class at the Air Corps Tactical School became generals. However, among those officers who stood in the middle and lower third of their classes, the academy graduate, rather than the non-academy graduate, was more likely to become a general.[17]

The system of academy education to which the military elite of the mid-twentieth century was exposed was decidedly traditional in its definition of soldierly honor. In its essentials, this boiled down to "never refuse a combat assignment." This sense of honor kept many in the military, even though there were lucrative opportunities for economic advancement available outside. Again and again, when probed in informal interviews as to why they had stayed in the service during the stagnation years of the 1920's, military leaders replied that they wanted to repay the government for their free education. Such a response appears naive, but in reality it is an expression of a sense of honor and satisfaction with public service. These men were not thinking of repayment in financial terms, but rather that their free education had given them a sense of group solidarity and a way of life, in return for which military service seemed a reasonable price to pay.

Military honor is inevitably rooted in a sense of nationalism and in national traditions, and the service academies have contributed to the professional definition of nationalism. In the nineteenth century nationalism was not primarily a political concept for the military profession. On the contrary, it has a social and ethnic definition which emphasized appropriate ancestry—namely, native-born, older "Anglo-Saxon" stock. By the turn of the century, the newer Catholic groups were no longer outsiders, although the data on social origins indicate that it was not until World War II that they began to enter the military profession extensively. Negroes have always been excluded, but the national society expected this. Despite the elimination of segregation in the armed forces, the increase of Negroes at the service academies has been slow, but not because of discrimination. Negroes are under-represented in all professional schools because of a lack of adequate prior preparation. Moreover, as Professor E. Franklin Frazier, the sociologist, has argued, Negroes in the United States overidentify with white values and accept business success, rather than professional success, as the most desirable route for social ascent.[18]

Since the turn of the century, the crisis in national identity at the academies has centered around exclusion versus inclusion of Jews. Aside from the conventional sources of hostility toward the Jew, at the service academy he was likely to be stereotyped as over-intellectual, and therefore unsuitable for an active profession. Not having had any previous nationality, he could hardly become a true American in the minds of those who saw nationality in terms of geo-political definitions. In turn, Jews displayed little interest in a military career. Up through the events of the 1930's, when the academies were extending the base of their social recruitment, anti-Semitism persisted on an informal basis. This was especially the case at Annapolis.[19] Today, anti-Semitism is no longer an issue at the academies, no more than at Princeton or any civilian university with upper-class traditions. The military institutions reflect changes in the larger society, and in turn help speed up social change by seeking to de-emphasize the importance of the social backgrounds of those who have been admitted into the profession.

It is striking that the most powerful consequence of academy military education in the past has been the inculcation of a mechanical acceptance of civilian supremacy. If the cadets themselves were not taught to think about the political dimensions of warfare, this was thought to be appropriate for a society in which the military was a profession under democratically elected civilian leaders. The concept of submission to civilian authorities centered about the understanding that political authorities decided who was the enemy, when war was to start, and the terms of peace. But, until 1939, the selection system, the narrow emphasis on military history, and the social isolation of the academies produced a breed of political conservatism or political indifference among cadets.* Those officers who developed broader interests were influenced by higher military education or by their own inclinations.

The academies have never concerned themselves with the broader task of inculcating a belief in the importance of accepting on-going civilian administrative supervision of the military establishment. They have never sought to establish principles for limiting the political activities of the military profession as a pressure group on its own behalf for more appropriations. Cadets and midshipmen are implicitly taught not to have open party preferences. But, more explicitly, they have been taught that Congress traditionally starved the military establishment, and that, therefore, it was the duty of the profession to press continually for maximum allocations in the name of military preparedness. Since the academies have necessarily emphasized service loyalty, rather than identification with the national military establishment, the fierce inter-service rivalries of the American military profession have been fostered by academy education.

Higher Military Schools

Since the military hierarchy is divisible into three levels—tactical officers, middle-level commanders, and senior-level generals and admirals—the sequence of professional education fits this division. First, a college education, military or civilian, plus training in the specialized service schools within a period of five to ten years after commissioning, is designed to equip the professional for the initial tasks of tactical officership. Second, at command and general staff school (post-graduate school in the Navy), ten to fifteen years after commissioning, he is retrained for the duties of middle- and high-level commander. Finally, in order to train a general or flag officer, the curriculum of the war college of each service is oriented to strategic matters.[20] These schools operate to identify and train those officers who have the capacity to become military managers, rather than just "military mechanics." In addition to a host of specialized schools, on a service-wide basis the armed forces op-

* See Chapter 12, Political Beliefs.

erate the Industrial College of the Armed Forces, with an economic mobilization curriculum, and the National War College, which is concerned with the integration of national security strategy. The need for higher and higher levels of skill specialization is so great that a central element in the professional education of the officer is the rapid post-war development of the practice of sending officers to civilian schools for their master's and doctoral degrees. More than 40 per cent of the recent West Point graduates have, within ten to twelve years after graduation, attended a civilian graduate school for one or more years, and the percentage is as high, if not higher, in the Air Force and the Navy.

The link between academic performance at the service academies and subsequent career success is difficult to discern; however, performance at the higher military schools plays a greater role in elite selection. The skills that are required for success at these higher military schools bear more directly on the real task of the military administrator. Students are encouraged to produce new solutions to old problems; the level of analysis is much higher than at the military academies. Concern with military tradition is tempered with an emphasis on a critical approach, and this seems to have been present even in the 1930's. The educational procedures of contemporary higher schools in the military, as well as the observations of many civilians who have served as instructors, attest to the particular form of academic debate and inquiry that is present.[21]

It is precisely because these higher institutions supply an opportunity to build a reputation that they operate so effectively in the career management of the professional soldier. Attendance at a higher military school brings together officers who have been scattered throughout various military installations. Superiors and peers have an opportunity for mutual judgment, and these judgments form part of the formal and informal record on which promotions are based. The classroom atmosphere of a war college is a close equivalent to that of the staff conference and the oral briefing. The skills on which a reputation at the war college is built are highly applicable to the real life of a military manager. At these schools new alliances and personal friendships develop which are important for career advancement. When the group of 576 officers on staff duty at the Pentagon in 1954 were asked, "Have the friendships you made at school (war colleges and National War College) been of specific and concrete value to you in your present job?," they answered overwhelmingly in the affirmative.

The Army has emphasized a formalized system of higher professional education to a much greater degree than has the Navy. The Air Force has modeled itself after the Army only in terms of aspirations. From Table 24, it can be seen that, of the military leadership

Table 24

Military Leadership, 1950:
Higher Professional Education

		Command & General Staff School %	War College*' %
Army	Attended	92.4	70.1
	Did not attend	7.6	29.9
		(157)	(157)
Navy	Attended	**	33.0
	Did not attend		67.0
		(203)	(203)
Air Force	Attended	57.5	22.5
	Did not attend	42.5	77.5
		(98)	(98)

		Technical Support %	War College Staff %	Commander %
Army	Attended	61.3	74.5	70.7
	Did not attend	38.7	25.5	29.3
		(31)	(51)	(75)
Navy	Attended	8.5	46.7	33.3
	Did not attend	91.5	53.3	66.7
		(35)	(45)	(123)
Air Force	Attended	25.0	21.0	22.5
	Did not attend	75.0	79.0	77.5
		(20)	(38)	(40)

* Includes officers who attended a war college of a different service.
** Many admirals of this period had some post-graduate training, but because of the variety of forms this training took, no single percentage would be meaningful.

cadre in 1950, almost all had attended middle-level management schools, the command, and general staff school, while in the Air Force the percentage who have been exposed to this educational experience was much lower and amounted to little more than half. Comparable figures for the Navy are not feasible, since before

World War II there was a wide variety of post-graduate schools and courses, many of which represented training in technical and engineering subjects.

The service difference persists at the war college level. While 70 per cent of the Army leadership in 1950 had attended the Army War College, only a third of the naval leaders had had an equivalent opportunity. Because of the rapid expansion in the Air Force, and the emphasis on combat at the highest echelons, it is understandable that less than a quarter of the Air Force leadership in this period had attended a War College. In Table 24, War College attendance is also classified by type of military function. As might be expected, officers charged with technical support missions are somewhat less likely to have participated in the higher military educational system. They were more likely, instead, to have received advanced education in civilian universities.

The greater exposure of ground force officers to higher education, especially at the war college level, is but one of the many indices to the increased orientation of Army commanders to the political aspects of warfare, as compared to the two other services. These data help to explain the greater flexibility of Army thinking, and the greater degree of criticism of official national security doctrine from Army spokesmen during the post-World War II period. An outstanding feature of the war college system is the increased use of civilian experts from universities and government agencies as instructors.

The hierarchy of military schools has been subjected to repeated self-criticism and outside evaluation. The two most important efforts have been the comprehensive study, *Soldiers and Scholars,* by the political scientists John Masland and Laurence Radway, who sought to describe the entire system as it related to politico-military tasks, and the report of a curriculum study group of the Air University, organized by the educator Ralph W. Tyler.[22] First, a persistent difficulty is that the system of higher education reflects, rather than modifies, the fierce inter-service rivalries of the military establishment. The war colleges tend to implement and develop a service point of view. In 1947 the National War College was established as an institution committed to a "broad military establishment" point of view. A decade after its establishment, the National War College stands officially, but not in fact, at the apex of military education. While it has the highest prestige in civilian circles, in the career development of an officer it merely serves as an alternative for attendance at the war college of his own service. Nevertheless, examination of the curriculum and intellectual content of the three service war colleges indicates that the broadest approach to national policy issues obtains at the Army War College, with the narrowest at the Air War College.[23]

Second, contemporary military education—from the academy to the war college—especially in the Army and the Air Force, seeks a sophisticated approach to the international political scene. The political aspects of the curriculum focus on a current-events analysis of diplomacy and international relations.* However, in assessing the role of higher military schools in fashioning the political behavior of the military profession, one is struck by the fact that the curriculum does not focus on specific political consequences—past, present, or future—of military action. There is little or no attention given the problem of the immediate political impact of the United States world-wide military system. Topics such as the consequence of stationing troops in allied countries, the political and economic effects of military assistance programs, political problems of managing military alliances, the propaganda consequences of the actual deployment of United States armed forces and of public statements about these deployments are not seen as political behavior. In fact, none of the war college focuses on the management of political warfare—that is, the practices involved in the coordination of military action with political persuasion.

Third, there is no evidence that military educators are concerned with civilian criticism that the military exceeds its role in fashioning public opinion and as an administrative pressure group before Congress. Little attention is given to the complex problems of civilian supremacy and to the political basis of United States governmental forms. In other words, there is no concern that the new type of education might contribute to fashioning a generation of highly political colonels who will be ill at ease with the traditions of civilian political control. On the contrary, the informal curriculum of the three service war colleges is geared to the notion that the professional soldier must be fully equipped to present vigorously to the public and to opinion leaders—in and out of

---

* Political and social assumptions which the three services have evolved regarding the role of violence in international relations are analyzed in Chapter 13, The Logic of War.

government—his service's point of view on budget matters and on military policy.

Finally, outside evaluations of the higher military schools as they deal with politico-military matters point out that these institutions, reflecting the procedures of civilian education and the technical outlook of the profession, place great emphasis on the mechanics of instruction. Teaching methods, semantics, concern with communication skills divert attention from subject matter and analytical skills.

In addition to attendance at professional schools, higher military education includes experience as instructors at these institutions and at the military academies. On the negative side, this often has the consequence of decreasing the level and adequacy of instruction; self-instruction tends often to become inbred. On the other hand, for those who are instructors, it constitutes an additional experience, and a further opportunity for mastering multiple roles. In the prescribed career, instructorship at West Point or Annapolis precedes attendance at command and staff school, and selection is based heavily upon the officer's performance while a student at the service academy. Of the 1950 leadership sample, 26 per cent of the Army generals had instructed at West Point, 32 per cent of the admirals had instructed at Annapolis, and only 8 per cent of Air Force generals had instructed at the military academy. Instruction at specialized service schools, at ROTC and naval reserve units, at command and general staff school, and at war college, supply numerous additional teaching experiences. In all, it is a rare Army general (less than 5 per cent) who has not been a teacher at some time in his career. In the Air Force more than 80 per cent of the leadership sample have had some teaching experience; in the Navy almost half have had such assignments.

If training military managers implies mastering multiple roles and adapting to new situations, the switch from soldier to student, and from student to teacher, is a realistic educational experience. J. W. Getzels, a research psychologist, studied the instructional staff at the Air University and found that the more authoritarian officer was under greater role conflict in his capacity as teacher, and performed less well as a result. Contrary to expectation, regular officers of the Air Force, as compared with reserve officers, were less troubled by the role conflicts in shifting from operational tasks to a teaching assignment.[24] When considered together with the research of E. P. Hollander, which concluded that selection boards of the Air Force tend to select and promote less authoritarian officers, presumably in part through selecting men who are well liked, one gets additional information on the necessary interpersonal skills in the prescribed career line.[25]

The Tactics of Promotion

EVEN when the military profession was small, homogeneous, and governed by seniority rules, informal lines of communication and personal reputation were important in molding an officer's career. As the military profession became more and more managerial, those who wanted to rise had to establish a reputation based on their skill or on their heroic qualities. In building a reputation, each younger officer has the task of coming to the attention of important superiors. Similarly, superior officers were continuously concerned with discovering those officers whom they wished to have serve as their sub-commanders and their staff officers. Before 1941, senior officers, including General George Marshall, kept such lists of men who they had personally observed, or who were reputed to have the qualities for important commands. The process could best be described as a system of "tapping," by which men were recognized as potential members of the elite.

As a result, the military profession is today engaged in a continuous process of informally rating their superiors, peers, and subordinates. The system of peer rating, which the psychologists thought they were introducing in Officer Candidate School has been a long-standing informal selection procedure. Before World War II, mutual contact among officers was widespread since the profession was small, and therefore the informal system was completely pervasive. The officer had to establish his individuality, but within the confines of narrow and acceptable limits. The result was to reinforce conformity in social behavior, for excessive individuality would injure one's reputation. Because of its growth alone, the military establishment has been forced to erect an elaborate and formal personnel system to control promotions and career development. But for a realistic understanding of career development, it is impossible to separate the formal procedures from the elaborate informal screening that goes on simultaneously. As the size of the professional officers' corps has grown, and as the system of promotion by seniority has weakened, there has been a corresponding growth in the complexity of official record-keeping. When official personnel records were first collected, before the War of 1812, commanding officers were brief and perhaps overly forthright. It sufficed to record in a man's dossier, "A good man, but no officer," or, "A knave, despised by all."

Army regulation number 600–185, issued on June 16, 1948, which governs the filing of officer efficiency reports, is a formidable document. In addition to describing the officer's last job in detail, supervising officers are obliged to estimate the officer's capacity along nine dimensions using a five-point scale. His job efficiency is recorded according to nineteen factors; twelve of these are on the basis of "forced comparisons" with all officers in his unit, and seven are determined by means of a ten-point scale. Furthermore, his job evaluation requires the judgment of eighteen personal qualities; twelve of them are made on the basis of "forced comparisons" with all other officers in the unit, and six are on a ten-point scale. This makes possible, presumably on the basis of machine tabulation, a three-digit over-all score. It has been unofficially reported that under such a system justification of promotions can involve differences of one point in the third digit. When, at the close of World War II, the Air Force was faced with the task of selecting fourteen thousand officers, it signed a contract with the American Institute of Research, under the direction of Dr. John Flanagan, and produced an elaborate technique based on the so-called "critical incident" device.

Most responsible social scientists would claim that there is no theoretical or empirical justification for such elaborate personnel testing devices, and that they have come into being only because of the organizational necessity for some manageable criterion. It is understandable that there is widespread unfavorable criticism of the efficiency report system.[26] In reality, the efficiency report and a suitable dossier are merely additional barriers or handicaps that must be surmounted in the race for career promotion. By the same token, it is understandable that elaborate informal devices persist to make such cumbersome systems workable.

The informal "tapping" system continues to operate in the contemporary military establishment, even at the lower levels. At the bottom, where the processing of service records proceeds on a mass basis, the young officer hopes that some higher officer will take a special interest in him and will make an entry on his record, or informally report some meaningful comments beyond the formal ratings. By the time a young officer is a captain in the Army or Air Force, or a lieutenant in the Navy, he may have already established a reputation as an "up and coming" officer, and this reputation is communicated both to him and to his superiors. The search for talent is as intense in the military as it is in any other profession, and to be a sponsor for an outstanding young officer is to the advantage of the more established professional.

At the middle levels, where careers are made or broken, informal networks of communications operate in the context of the activities of official promotion committees and personnel officers. The aspiring officer retains considerable initiative in directing his career, and he seeks out those assignments which are reputed to be part of the successful career. Early in his career he learns that the road to the top, at least to the level of one or possibly two stars, is not through assignment to the specialized technical services, but by being an unrestricted line officer. In the Army the Corps of Engineers occupies a special position. It has high prestige, offers interesting work in peacetime, selects the top graduate from West Point, and enables an officer to find increased employment opportunities after retirement. While the Corps of Engineers has supplied generals who served as administrators and military technologists, it is not a major route to military leadership. Instead, the aspiring officer believes that the prescribed career is in the combat arms, although the fortunes of particular weapons systems change with technological progress. He believes it is important to have command duty, and to be involved in operations when assigned to staff duty. Informal communications play an important role in the allocation of these desired assignments, especially for the middle-level officer who has built a reputation for his skill and potentiality for promotion. At the highest levels, of course, colleague reputation and informal contacts outweigh personnel records as the basis of making assignments.

Practices vary among the services, but it is in the Air Force, strangely enough, that informal contacts are the most crucial in counterbalancing personnel record-keeping. This is due, in part, to the greater mobility of the Air Force officer who has an opportunity to maintain wide contacts, and to literally shop around for his next assignment. In general, until recently, the expanding horizons of the Air Force gave each officer greater latitude and greater power over the management of his career.

In each service, personnel officers and selection boards have more or less clear-cut images of what constitutes the ideal career for the aspiring professional officer. More often than not, these images are firmly rooted in past experiences. The events of each war have weakened them, but they continue to operate with powerful effect in peacetime. What evidence exists to indicate that in the past selection boards and personnel officers have had special talents in estimating the future needs of the military profession? To describe the prescribed military career does not fully encompass the life history of that smaller segment within the military elite who in effect transformed the profession during the last half century.

Notes

1. Howerton, James L., "West Point Generals of the Wartime Army: Their Performance While Cadets at the U.S. Military Academy." Unpublished master's thesis, department of education, George Washington University, 1945.

2. Vagts, Alfred, The History of Militarism. New York: Norton, 1937, p. 319.

3. Dupuy, R. Ernest, Where They Have Trod: The West Point Tradition in American Life. New York: Frederick A. Stokes Company, 1940, p. 205.

4. Ridgway, Matthew, Soldier: The Memoirs of Matthew B. Ridgway. New York: Harper & Bros., 1956, p. 206.

5. Research evidence was collected in 1952 by Richard Christie in a field experiment involving infantry troops at Fort Dix which indicates that, other things being equal, a sharp break with civilian ties assists, rather than retards, socialization into the military community. See Christie, Richard, "An Experimental Study of Modification in Factors Influencing Recruits' Adjustment to the Army." New York University, Research Center for Human Relations, 1953.

6. Personal communication.

7. Niblack, Captain A. P., "The Letters of a Retired Rear Admiral to His Son in the Navy." May 3, 1913.

8. Lincoln, Colonel G. A., & Jordan, Jr., Lt. Col. A. A., "Leadership to Provide for The Common Defense." Public Administration Review, 1957, 17, 258.

9. Report of the Superintendent of the United States Military Acaaemy, 1922, pp. 7–8.

10. Kohs, S. C., & Irle, K. W., "Prophesying Army Promotion." *Journal of Applied Psychology*, 1920, 4, 73–87.

11. Tayler, E. K., *Research on Military Leadership*. Department of the Army, unpublished and undated, p. 43.

12. Howerton, James L., *op. cit.*, p. 9.

13. Hilsman, Roger, "Research in Military Affairs." *World Politics*, 1954, 7, 502.

14. Masland, John W., & Radway, Laurence I., *Soldiers and Scholars*. Princeton: Princeton University Press, 1957, p. 243.

15. The official questionnaire study of West Point graduates presented a somewhat lower rate of resignation. It also concluded that officers who gained entrance through congressional nomination were slightly more likely to resign than those who entered from non-congressional sources, such as presidential nomination, honor military and naval schools, as sons of deceased veterans, etc. These latter appointees were more likely to have come from families with military background and experience. The rates of resignation reported for graduates from West Point between 1923 and 1933 included: congressional appointment, 6.2 per cent; non-congressional appointment, 3.2 per cent. The rates for graduates from West Point between 1945 and 1949 included: congressional appointment, 19.7 per cent; non-congressional appointment, 14.5 per cent.

16. Caplow, Theodore, *The Academic Marketplace*. New York: Basic Books, 1958.

17. Human Resources Research Institute, Report No. 15, p. 11.

18. Frazier, E. Franklin, *The Black Bourgeoisie*. Glencoe: The Free Press, 1957.

19. One story widely circulated and even reported by a highly reputable national journalist reflects the spirit of the social pressure at the naval academy. The man who stood second academically in the class of 1922 was a Jew. "His picture in the classbook was printed on a perforated page for easy removal." See Wallace, Robert, *Life*, September 8, 1958, p. 109.

20. See Masland, John W., & Radway, Laurence I., *op. cit.*, for a detailed factual description of the structure of military education in the United States.

21. *Ibid*.

22. Tyler, Ralph W., "Analysis of the Purpose, Pattern, Scope, and Structure of the Officer Education Program of Air University," Technical Memorandum, OERL-TM-55-6. Air Force Personnel and Training Research Center, Maxwell Air Force Base, Alabama, May 1955.

23. At the Army War College the final problem students are asked to solve is the development of a "national security strategy" which would involve not only the military potentials of the three services, but also the political and economic dimensions.

24. Getzels, J. W., & Guba, E. G., "Role Conflict and Personality," *Journal of Personality*, 1955, 24, 74–85.

25. Hollander, E. P., "Authoritarianism and Leadership Choice in a Military Setting." *Journal of Personality*, 1955, 24, 365–70.

26. For example, see Herron, C. D., "Measuring Men by Slide Rule." *Infantry Journal*, 1948, 63, 33–36.

CHAPTER *8*

The Elite Nucleus

IN AN ORGANIZATION as large and complex as the armed forces the prescribed career line gives the young officer a concrete image of the successful military professional. The prescribed career line further enables the establishment to develop a cadre of like-minded young men to perform essential functions. Although for each service the details of a prescribed career become fixed in the minds of the aspiring officer, the content of this prescribed career is inevitably based on past experiences. Yet, the military establishment adapts to change precisely because its most outstanding leaders anticipate future requirements, and expose themselves to experiences which are outside the prescribed career. Thus, one of the basic hypotheses for the period from 1910 to 1950 was that prescribed careers, performed with high competence, led to entrance into the professional elite, the highest point at which technical and routinized functions are performed. By contrast, entrance into the smaller group of prime movers—the nucleus of the elite—where innovating perspectives and skills are required, is open to persons with unconventional careers. Such a proposition seems to have special importance in accounting for those officers who became involved in politico-military affairs during a period when these matters were not defined as part of the role of the professional soldier.

The formulation of Arthur K. Davis in this connection is undoubtedly correct in principle, but far too extreme: "The effectiveness of military leaders tends to vary inversely with their exposure
to a conventional routinized military career."[1] Most officers who
have entered the top one-half of 1 per cent of the hierarchy have
complied with conventional career forms; but, in addition, they
have frequently had specialized and innovating experiences which
have increased their usefulness to the military profession. Among
these leaders, the men who have been most decisive are characterized by even more pronounced unconventionality in their career
lines.

Leadership Models

THE RULE-BREAKING MILITARY LEADER of unconventional background has a long history in American military affairs. In the
instance of George Washington it is impossible to unravel reality
from myth, yet, he has come to stand for a Cincinnatus—the civilian
surveyor and farmer who took up arms, and who in his very person
embodied the unconventional genius. During the Revolution "Mad"
Anthony Wayne and "Swamp Fox" Marion established the tradition
of the fighting hero, who had the ability to improvise on the spot.
Andrew Jackson personified the military leader who was more concerned with the superiority of native American "frontier" skills than
with the formalities of the military profession. He made his contribution to the tradition that the combat commander should be
"one of the boys."

While the Civil War was the first major armed conflict managed
by military professionals, the unconventional type was represented
at crucial times. Victory for the North hinged, in no small measure,
on the contribution of the untidy figure, U. S. Grant, who emerged
gradually from obscurity, and who succeeded where professional
soldiers of established reputation had failed. Grant was, of course,
a product of West Point, but his career was marginal at best, by
professional standards. He spent much of his time in low-prestige
quarter-master-type assignments, which were nevertheless appropriate in sensitizing him to the tasks of large-scale warfare. His
personal difficulties made him such a problem to the profession

that he resigned from military service, until the Civil War reopened his career. The Civil War also produced a plethora of men in the heroic model, with Stonewall Jackson and Jebb Stuart as the prototype of men who were truly maverick individualists and whose strength rested in their passionate dedication to the "cause."

The conspicuous military figure during the Spanish-American War was not even a professional soldier, but a civilian—Theodore Roosevelt. In the years before the outbreak of World War I, Leonard Wood emerged as a prime mover in his effort to convert the ground forces from a collection of Indian fighters into a modern army. Leonard Wood was, of all things, a doctor, and to have a doctor appointed to the post of Chief of Staff during a period of growing professionalization was deeply resented by the insiders. But it required an outsider who was uncommitted to the traditions of the past to serve as a catalyst. Leonard Wood, like John Pershing who was to follow him, maintained the outward facade of the heroic cavalry officer. He took the opportunity to become a real soldier by participating in a grueling—but essentially romantic—year-long chase of Geronimo, the last of the warring Indian chiefs. His career is worthy of the careful attention of aspiring young officers, because it is a study in decision-making and deliberate neglect of the rule book. In Cuba, and in the pacification of the Philippines, he combined repressive tactics with a benevolent administration to set an American pattern of military government. After serving as Chief of Staff, he stymied his career by taking the risk of breaking the professional rule of partisan neutrality; in seeking the presidency, he prematurely overcommitted himself to the Republican party.

John Pershing's career was closer to the professional military formula, but was much more than a prescribed career. While on duty as a junior officer in the Philippines during the period of the pacification, he was almost the only one of the officers of a considerable garrison who became very much interested in the rebellious Moros. While other officers were following the social protocol of an overseas garrison, he was associating with the natives, studying them, and learning their language. Pershing became well known and influential among the local native leaders, and attracted the attention of General George W. Davis, who was in charge of developing a form of civil-military government. Because of his knowledge and experience with the native population, Pershing was placed in an important staff post as the superior of many older officers.

His career, further developed through influential connections achieved by his marriage, demonstrated that he was a military organizer who recognized the administrative dimensions of warfare, although he displayed a warrior demeanor. His network of military associates included others with a managerial orientation: James G. Harbord, who rose from the enlisted ranks to serve as his Chief of Staff, and who left the Army to become president of The Radio Corporation of America, and General Frank Ross McCoy, a West Point graduate, who became central logistical manager and who later served in numerous politico-military posts.[2]

World War I offered Douglas MacArthur his first opportunity, as a brigade commander in the 42nd Rainbow Division, to establish his reputation as an individualist. Even then his costume was as notorious as his tactical skill: a floppy cap, a riding crop, and often a sweater with a huge wool muffler around his neck—all unorthodox, but attention-producing. Another outstanding rule-breaker of World War I was the exponent of air power—William "Billy" Mitchell.

Under democratic political control, as it has operated in the United States, the unconventional military leader represents selection by civilian authorities. Particularly in the Army, because of its greater potential for involvement in politics—both domestic politics and politico-military affairs in war-time—civilian authorities have had a tendency to select those who embody managerial perspectives for strategic positions, rather than those who glorify war-making. The profound popular suspiciousness, or at least ambivalence, toward the professional soldier has helped insure that such atypical soldiers would rise to the top. These innovators, whose perspectives are not captured and blocked by the traditions of the profession, bear the responsibility for adapting the military to new tasks.

In the military establishment the fighter spirit itself tends to become extinguished. Those who make a successful career of seeking to renew it are also innovators, in a sense, although they may draw their stimulus from the past rather than the future. As one advances in the military hierarchy, with its endless routine and prolonged periods of peace, it takes an act of strong assertiveness and individuality to maintain the fighter spirit. A successful military establishment must be run by military managers, but must include in its very elite a leaven of heroic leaders.[3]

In the absence of a crisis, and lacking civilian pressure, the management of the military profession between World War I and World War II reverted to narrow professionalism. Only one of the four chiefs of staff of the Army, Douglas MacArthur (1930–35), could be called a powerfully motivated person, but even his admirers admit that during this period he played a conventional role by his own standards.[4] The other chiefs of staff remain almost completely unknown organization men.[5] This observation could be stated in reverse. The type of leadership of the inter-war years was hardly predictive of what would emerge during war. With the advent of hostilities, dozens, if not hundreds, of ranking officers were pushed aside in the effort to advance younger and more creative officers whose thinking had not been confined by military routines.[6]

The conspicuous leaders in World War II and its immediate aftermath were not representative men, but rather exaggerations of the conflicting themes in the military profession. Regardless of the struggles for glory, the military managers maintained positions of effective authority. The dominant image of the military manager was embodied in such men as Dwight Eisenhower, Omar Bradley, H. H. Arnold, Walter Bedell Smith, William D. Leahy, and Ernest King. These were the men who reflected the technical and pragmatic dimensions of war-making. The heroic leaders who gave dramatic leadership to strategic and operational commands were represented by such men as "Bull" Halsey, George Patton, Jonathan Wainwright, James Doolittle, and Curtis LeMay.

Yet, in World War II contradictory images of the military elite were represented by the contrast between George Marshall, the prototype of the military manager, and Douglas MacArthur, who fused both roles, but who often performed as the heroic fighter.* The contrast is more than a contrast in leadership style, for, in the end, each man and his disciples developed a conflicting political outlook which deeply influenced the management of World War II. The reams that have been written about the differences of char-

* See Chapter 14, Coalition Warfare.

acter, skill and style of Marshall and MacArthur tend, however, to obscure certain crucial similarities. Both men were self-consciously prime movers who were concerned with mobilizing the military profession to achieve national objectives.

Douglas MacArthur was the son of a professional Army officer, who rose to be a general and communicated a sense of mission to his son. MacArthur's powerful ambition and his superior intellect set him apart from the typical professional, although throughout his career he displayed outward conformity to the standards and protocol of the old Army. No simple explanation suffices to account for the detachment that George Marshall was able to develop toward the military profession. Many point to the fact that he attended the Virginia Military Institute because he was refused an appointment to West Point, that his father was a Democrat in a Republican stronghold. But Virginia Military Institute graduates stood high in military circles. He was, furthermore, a tall gangling youth, awkward and uncoordinated physically—a great handicap in the military profession. At VMI he was subjected to the most fearsome hazing, and efforts to master his physical deficiencies required considerable self-denial. U. S. Grant once wrote, "I hear Army men say their happiest days were at West Point. I never had that experience. The most trying days of my life were those I spent there and I never recall them with pleasure." Marshall would undoubtedly have agreed that his military education was equally trying, although in the end he achieved recognition as a cadet at VMI.

Two incidents—real or mythical—highlight the different use to which these men put their strong personalities and their skepticism of formal authority. MacArthur was concerned with maintaining his heroic self-image; Marshall with developing the concept of the effective military professional. In the words of one of his most ardent admirers, General George C. Kenney, the reputation MacArthur had for "insisting on his rights and incidentally for winning most of the arguments, started almost at the beginning of his Army career."[7] Kenney recounts a characteristic episode at West Point which reveals not only a willingness to take risks, but also a personal definition of honor and obedience to military authority MacArthur objected violently to a professor because he believed that he had been erroneously put on a list of class "goats" for poor work in mathematics, and because he had been ordered to take additional make-up examinations. He felt that he had met his mathematics requirements, although he had not taken the requisite number of examinations. Challenging a direct order, he is reputed to have stated, "I have not failed my mathematics course and I will not have my name listed with those who failed. Orders can be rescinded and if my name is not removed from that list by nine o'clock tomorrow morning, I will resign." The next day his name was removed and, as the MacArthur story would have it, while his roommate was so worried that he could hardly close his eyes, MacArthur slept through the night soundly. In myth and reality, MacArthur's career was based on a flouting of authority, although he demanded strict obedience from his subordinates. MacArthur resisted military authority when it involved an affront to his honor and, by inference, to his fighting spirit.

The image of George Marshall is formed from episodes which reflect a different attitude toward challenging traditional authority. As an unknown lieutenant in the Philippines, he made a bet with a fellow lieutenant that he could name three trivial faults the inspecting officer would find when he inspected the men on parade.[8] Furthermore, Marshall stated that during field exercises he would commit three grave errors in tactics which would pass unobserved. The bet was accepted, and Marshall listed the three errors on an envelope. Having committed these errors, Marshall observed that no one saw anything amiss, and therefore collected his bet. Such behavior reflected his attitude toward his superiors and his willingness to challenge them for professional goals, rather than for personal honor.

Marshall's two chief subordinates—Dwight Eisenhower and H. H. Arnold—were also unusual officers who did not conform merely to the prescribed model. Contrary to the belief that he did not demonstrate his capacities before 1939, Eisenhower had clearly displayed his skill in representation and negotiation. In 1929 the 71st Congress passed the House Joint Resolution No. 251 to establish the War Policies Commission as a long-range planning group. The members of the committee included Secretary of War Patrick J. Hurley, as Chairman, and Secretary of the Navy Charles F. Adams, plus the Secretaries of Agriculture and Labor, the Attorney General, and selected senators and congressmen. Major Dwight D. Eisenhower was chosen as assistant executive secretary for this important committee because he could interpret the military to the political leaders and vice versa. When he went to the Philippines, General MacArthur appointed Eisenhower to his staff to help with legislative and public relations matters. Eisenhower had many specialized assignments and very few prescribed troop command posts. But he was more than an efficient staff officer who could be trusted with assignments with political overtones. In World War I he had shown great interest in tank warfare, and his executive talent began to emerge at command and general staff school.

Like Marshall, his sponsor, he had a sense of detachment about his profession, and Marquis Child, the biographer, has faithfully recorded his spirit, which was apparent even at West Point:

Eisenhower was a roughneck. He broke the rules just as often as he dared. Law abiding classmates were shocked at his daring. . . . His conduct was that of the tough boy from the wrong side of the tracks, defying the code and yet managing by his resourcefulness to live with it.[9]

Eisenhower did not come from a solid upper middle-class family, but truly from the other side of the tracks. His father was an unsuccessful merchant turned railroad worker. Even his religious background—he belonged to a fundamentalist sect—was out of place in a setting still dominated by Episcopalians. While he was gradually molded into the manners of the military profession, he never lost the detachment which made him a civilianized general.

H. H. Arnold met the social standards for recruitment into West Point: His father was a prosperous small town doctor from a family with a long social tradition in southern Pennsylvania.[10] His mother was a staunch member of the local county D.A.R. Arnold entered the military service with the attitude of a would-be cavalier; like Eisenhower, he early displayed his contempt for the rituals of military discipline. At West Point, instead of engaging in exemplary military behavior, he joined the Black Hand—a secret society which operated at night—in collegiate pranks which landed him in solitary confinement.

Arnold's career was launched in a dramatic effort at resistance to military regulation which made him famous even before he joined his first regiment. When he was assigned to the infantry instead of the cavalry, his senator and congressman called on the

Adjutant General to effect a change in his assignment to the cavalry. When the Adjutant General refused, reminding Arnold that as a second lieutenant he would do whatever anyone in the Army ordered, Arnold replied, "No, Sir, I am not a second lieutenant in the U.S. Army. I haven't accepted my commission." The senator ushered Arnold out of the room, and a compromise was arranged; Arnold remained in the infantry, but at least he was assigned to the Philippines where his youthful vigor might more easily find expression.

It was inevitable that Arnold would be attracted to the airplane, and he was among the first to receive flight training. His career development was not that of a pilot, however. From the outset, he found himself involved in administrative, staff, and intelligence duties connected with the development of air power. By 1911, Arnold was returning to his desk at Washington in the evening, after flying during the day, to collect and translate French and German reports of aerial development, including the first military use of air power in the Balkan Wars. During World War I he worked exclusively as a staff officer. He never took as extreme a position as did Billy Mitchell, but he was more effective because he knew the techniques for circumventing traditionalism. The crucial point in his career came in 1924, when he was offered the opportunity to become the president of a new air line—Pan American. But his zeal for military air power was too great.

As conspicuous heroes in American history, admirals have conformed more closely to the prescribed model. Of the four leading figures in the emergence of the naval establishment during the period of the Spanish-American War—George Dewey, Alfred T. Mahan, Winfield Scott Schley, and William T. Sampson—only Mahan was a true nonconformist. He falls into the category of the military intellectual, rather than the category of innovating military manager, whose reputation, at that time, resided more in civilian circles than in the naval establishment. The Navy's activities in World War I were routine and were dominated by traditionalists, with the notable exceptions of Admiral Bradley Fiske and Admiral William Sims, the iconoclastic advocate of air power.

When, in January 1941, much to the surprise of naval insiders, President Franklin D. Roosevelt directed that Ernest King be made an admiral and saved from retirement in preparation for his assignment as Chief of Naval Operations, the Navy came under the command of a nontraditionalist. King, because of the powerful pressures of naval traditions, could hardly be thought of as a maverick, yet, his career reflects extensive civilian contacts and a continuous concern for innovation. Born the son of a railroad repair shop foreman in a small southern Ohio community, the idea of joining the Navy was dramatized for him by reading *Youth's Companion*, a Boston publication which printed articles glorifying the naval profession. Thus, like Eisenhower, he came from more humble social origins than his typical classmate, and, like Eisenhower at West Point, he collected his full quota of infractions at Annapolis.

In the Navy, King was a deviant because of his conceptual, almost intellectual approach to naval problems. He had done well in his academic subjects at Annapolis, graduating fourth in his class. As a junior officer, while others were engaged in developing their skill in naval protocol, he studied books, such as Captaiin A. L. Wagner's textbook on organization and tactics, and had the opportunity to experiment with the administration of small ships since he had developed the reputation of being an expert. As a junior officer in 1908, King wrote an essay entitled "Some Ideas of Organization on Board Ship," which received a prize from the United States Naval Institute. These accomplishments led to an unusual situation: A junior officer in the Navy was able to establish a wide reputation on the basis of intellectual achievement.

Throughout his career in the Navy, King was concerned with academic matters; he edited the Naval Institute *Proceedings*, was deeply involved in reorganizing naval education, and pioneered in bringing outside civilian experts to lecture at the post-graduate school for officers of the line. His administrative skill and expertise provided him with extensive opportunities for experience as a staff aide and as a staff officer. But the remarkable aspect of King's career was that he served with all of the emerging weapons— destroyer, submarine, and airplane—and he rose to the top while the Navy was still dominated by battleship admirals.

The Marine Corps produced its maverick in the person of General Holland M. Smith. By Marine Corps standards, he was a managerial type. Smith prided himself for his hostility toward the Navy and his reckless dissent: "But I was a bad boy. I always have been a bad boy in inter-service arguments and I often am amazed that I lasted so long in the Marine Corps."[11] While H. Smith's career was of necessity filled with troop command assignments, he spent considerable time in planning and staff posts. He was a pioneer in the development of amphibious warfare and wrote the basic manuals for assault landing which later were taken over by the Navy and the Army. As he was prone to point out, these tactics were perfected on purely "theoretical" grounds, since there was no successful precedent in modern times. His career was in essence a fierce struggle to overcome the resistance of the Bureau of Ships in the naval establishment to larger and more efficient landing craft.

But the elite nucleus consists of more than a few conspicuous leaders. In 1943 Walter Millis, the military historian, wrote a perceptive introduction to a book, entitled *These Are the Generals*,[12] whose table of contents could be taken as one indicator of the elite nucleus at the midpoint of World War II. Of this group, the military managers—strategic, diplomatic, and logistical—were in the majority. Partly because the United States had engaged in little prior combat, most of them were without extensive field experience. But, of necessity, the highest posts were of the "staff" variety. Millis points out that only seven of the seventeen commanded troops in battle.

The course of the war revised and enlarged the list. Some men were killed in operational accidents; others had their careers wrecked by military and diplomatic reverses; new names were added as the result of personal achievement or organizational accident. In the end, the American military traditions repeated themselves. The members of the top elite, taken as a whole, do not present a picture of Prussian-type staff officers, but rather of civilianized military managers. The heroic leaders were conspicuous, since opportunities for combat command proliferated, but they were decidedly in the minority. While generalizations about such a relatively small group are hazardous, two observations seem possible. First, more often than not military managers were characterized by a social background at variance with the traditional pattern of recruitment from upper middle-class rural and old family stock. They tended to come from the families of lower social status or more marginal circumstances. Heroic leaders could often be identified with the survival of "aristocratic-like" traditions, if only as perpetuated by service-connected family backgrounds. Second, these men—whether military managers or heroic leaders—were characterized by powerful impulses to dissent and to challenge the structure of military authority as it had evolved during peacetime.

In the ground forces the men who developed reputations as primarily administrative and management experts included Brehon Somervell, Lesley McNair, Joseph McNarney, Lucius Clay, and Alfred Gruenther. Jacob Devers, too, belongs to this group, although he also served as a field commander. Of the field commanders, Omar Bradley, of modest social origins, represented the model of the civilianized general, while George Patton, appropriately of an aristocratic Virginia background, was the prototype of the heroic leader. Army commanders who conformed more to the military manager image included Alexander Patch, Robert L. Eichelberger, Walter Krueger, Courtney Hodges, William Simpson, and Leonard Gerow. By contrast, in the martial fighter category were Simon Buckner, Ben Lear, and Jonathan Wainwright. Such men as Mark Clark and L. K. Truscott, Jr., although they bore the imprint of the dashing soldier, accommodated themselves to managerial requirements. Conversely, although Joseph Stilwell thought of himself as an innovator, he probably fits best as a heroic fighter, if he fits at all.

The distinction becomes more elusive when applied to the Air Force generals, but it is still relevant because involvement in new technological weapons could still be compatible with persistence of a romantic self-image. Many Air Force generals rose rapidly in the profession on the basis of combat flying skills. As a result, in 1950 the concentration of heroic leaders among the top elite was greater in the Air Force than in the Army or Navy. Interestingly enough, the heroic spirit was most apparent among those associated with heavy bombers, the prestige weapon of the Air Force. Air Force officers who fitted the military manager model usually were associated with the tactical air force and with military air transportation, or had developed wider perspectives because of their participation in joint operations.

The events of World War II and its aftermath seem to have had the consequence of developing officers, especially in the ground forces, who fused the two styles. First, the opportunity for specialized and politico-military assignments greatly increased. Second, as the analysis of military discipline has sought to demonstrate, this merger was possible because the skills of air staff work and combat tend to overlap in important dimensions, and, as a result, authority comes to involve a decline in domination. A plethora of top leaders emerged whose actual experiences permitted them to present themselves as both military managers and successful combat commanders. General Ridgway's career typifies the pattern of the innovating officer who fused both images, but in which the military manager was ultimately dominant. His professional development was replete with experience which was unusual for an army officer.

Ridgway was born in 1895 at Fort Monroe, Virginia, where his father was a colonel in command of a battalion of field artillery. After graduation from West Point with the class of 1917, he felt that he was off to a good start when he was assigned to the Mexican border with the Third Infantry Regiment, and given command of a rifle company. As rumors were current that his regiment was to go to Europe, he believed that he would have an opportunity for the rapid advancement which combat brought to the professional soldier.[13]

However, instead, he received orders to report to West Point as an instructor and was assigned to teach Spanish, since apparently he had done well in that subject as a cadet. Instead of combat experience, he stayed at West Point for six years, first as a language instructor, then as a tactical officer, and finally as faculty director of athletics. While teaching Spanish at West Point, he was deeply concerned that he might lose contact with his specialty—the infantry. After some garrison service with the Fifteenth Regiment, then on duty at Tientsin, he sought to take up a traditional line of military duty and volunteered for the 1928 Olympic Army Squad. Instead, General Frank McCoy sent for him, and requested that Ridgway accompany him to Nicaragua where McCoy was going to supervise the elections. (In addition to the fact that by this time Ridgway spoke Spanish fluently, he had the personal qualities for such an assignment.) This was the second time he was diverted from traditional activities to opportunities which, in the long run, proved more useful to his career. After Nicaragua, he served once again with General McCoy on the Bolivian-Paraguayan Conciliation Commission.

His next assignment was to the advanced infantry course at Fort Benning, where he came under the influence of General

Marshall. By this time, he was clearly designated for a politico-
military career. On completion of the course he was sent to
Nicaragua again, and then assigned to the Philippines as technical
adviser on military matters to Governor General Theodore Roosevelt, Jr. The remainder of the 1930 period was spent at staff
assignments, including an assignment to the Army War College in
Washington. When war broke out at Pearl Harbor, Ridgway was
serving at the War Plans Division in Washington; he had recently
accompanied General Marshall to Brazil on a special mission designed to strengthen resistance to the Nazi penetration.

During this entire period Ridgway felt most uncertain about
his future career, since he had had no combat experience. "Here
at last was my chance to wipe out that blot on my record—or
rather fill in that blank on my record where it said 'combat service,
none'—a lack that had always made me vaguely uncomfortable in
the presence of officers who had seen action in World War I"[14] But
the administration of the War Department had already tabbed him
for higher command. In February of 1942 he was appointed Assistant Divisional Commander under General Bradley, who was
then organizing the 82nd Infantry Division. Thus, after having had
practically no prior troop experience, he was given a command
well above his expectations. The remainder of his career involved
rapid advancement, first, through strenuous divisional assignments
to higher corps responsibilities, and culminating in assignments as
the strategic commander of the 8th Army in Korea, Supreme Commander of SHAPE, and Army Chief of Staff.

The success of the professional officer is not achieved through
mechanical compliance with orders from higher headquarters. As
the Allied invasion of Italy was being prepared, the Italian government began negotiations for surrender. One aspect of the planning
for surrender procedures involved dropping Ridgway's 82nd Air-
Borne Division into the Rome area. Ridgway calculated that this
was an impossible mission. Yet, the opportunity and the hope for
dramatic success in the Italian campaign had led the entire Allied
High Command to underwrite this operation. When Ridgway
presented his reasons for the impossibility of the operation to General Harold Alexander, he was told, "Don't give this another
thought, Ridgway. Contact will be made with your division in
three days, five at the most."

Instead of accepting this reassurance from the High Command, Ridgway not only continued to resist his orders which, as it turned out, would have been disastrous, but also felt impelled to develop some workable plan for resolving the opposed pressures. He proposed to General Walter Bedell Smith, Chief of Staff, that an officer go on a secret mission to Rome to visit with Marshal Badoglio and learn whether the Italians were able to support the landing operation. Consequently, just a few hours before the air-borne operation was to take place, the Allied emissary in Rome, General Maxwell Taylor, was able to report, first-hand, that the mission was impossible. Ridgway's determined resistance to the orders only increased his stature and reputation as a field commander.

The pragmatic concern for innovation which Ridgway represented hardly implies a denial of the special characteristics of the military profession. Ridgway epitomized the fighter spirit and sought to keep it alive for organizational ends, rather than for personal honor. When his division was slated to become the first air-borne unit, he immediately had himself "checked out as a paratrooper." Attached to one side of his parachute harness were hand grenades, and, appropriately for the military manager, a first-aid kit was attached to the other side. Even in his heroic image, he was realistic and pragmatic.[15]

With the introduction of nuclear warfare and guided missiles, a new type of professional has entered the elite nucleus—the military technologist, a conspicuous example being Admiral Hyman Rickover. The military technologist is not a scientist, or for that matter an engineer; basically, he is a military manager, with a fund of technical knowledge and a quality for dramatizing the need for technological progress. As long as the concept of the military generalist predominated, the technologist was excluded from the highest ranks. The promotion of Rickover to a three-star admiral represents departure from this tradition, and is further evidence of the changing compostion of the military elite.

As described earlier, Rickover was an outsider in the naval profession, but his personal, social, and professional "marginality" did not bar his making a profound identification with the naval organization. His career was completely atypical, or at best no more than that of a "mere" technical specialist. He worked prodigiously, he commanded the fierce loyalty of his staff members, and he was civilianized to the point of disregarding naval protocol. His continued success was, to a considerable extent, based on outside support from congressional leaders, which support Rickover had the ability to mobilize: Rickover was able to maintain the confidence of congressional leaders when crucial decisions were at stake. When a congressman asked him, "Haven't you prepared for this hearing?," Rickover is reputed to have replied, "Certainly, I shaved and put on a clean shirt. . . . You can't fool a congressman for long. Sooner or later he will find out whether you're telling the truth. If you are, he'll help you. If not, you get the meat ax. . . ."

The three key officers in the military development of guided missiles—Bernard Schriever in the Air Force, John Medaris in the Army and William F. Raborn, Jr., in the Navy—all obviously conform to the managerial type. Schriever, a product of the ROTC and not West Point, received a few years of flight training and then was returned to civilian life. During the war he flew on bombing missions, and in his first post-war assignment he gained a reputation for his criticism of the B-52 program. (He advocated a lighter bomber which could shoot missiles.) By the time the von Neumann Committee in 1954 recommended highest priority for developing missiles, Schriever had identified himself as the Air Force expert and was given the key missile assignment. Medaris, too, had a deviant career by Army standards. He served as an enlisted man in the Marine Corps and became an officer without having attended West Point or any other higher military school. His career involved extensive service in the Ordnance Corps; he also served as Chief of the Military Mission to Argentina. Admiral Raborn followed the prescribed career of the naval generalist, and became involved in missile development late in his career.

Adaptive Career Experiences

THUS FAR, the analysis of the inner elite has been based on case studies—the most dramatic, if not necessarily the most representative. Could a systematic approach be used to test the extent to which unusual career experiences were found among the elite nucleus? The sociological perspective toward an elite group requires an analysis of biography in depth. Of course, the inner elite in an organization as large as the military profession would be composed extensively of officers who had followed the prescribed career pattern. But what were the relative proportions, and were there differences between the services?

In the ideal definition of the prescribed career line, constant rotation back to service with troops or aboard ship is assumed to be essential. In actuality, the ranking military leaders displayed an early and persistent propensity for staff work. While the typical young officer who was destined to rise to the rank of Army colonel or naval captain was serving in the field, future members of the military elite were more often military aides.*

Quantitative data on the time which members of the military elite spent at staff duties yield little insight into the processes of preparation for career advancement. The amount of staff duty is less important than the type and content of the duty, since a wide variety of staff assignments could hardly be called problem-solving assignments. For example, before 1941, operations and planning staff duty on the War Department general staff or with the Chief of Naval Operations had particular importance.

In addition, relevant assignments were those which required communications skills, trained the officer in negotiation, had strong political overtones, and involved relating the military to some outside organization. Before World War II, these specialized staff assignments were often looked upon by most officers as unusual, tedious, and even likely to interfere with career development. Many who were to rise to the very top took pains to avoid such posts as intelligence officer, military attache, language officer, posts involving congressional liaison and public relations, liaison with foreign armies, and military government. Actually, these preparatory assignments served as a general education in military management, and oriented the officer to the broader emerging political tasks of the armed forces. Officers who got these assignments were often recognized as men whose interests extended beyond those of the average narrowly oriented professional. To achieve specialization in such areas was, of course, detrimental to an officer's "career." Yet, these assignments, which required symbolic skills, and were so different from routine military tasks, assisted the officer to master

* Almost a third of a sample of the four-star generals of World War II and the subsequent period served as military aides.

multiple roles. In general, successful leadership requires the ability
to shift from one role to another with ease. In the current military
establishment such specialized assignments are more and more
common, but for the period when our sample of the 1950 military
leaders were developing their careers, to have sought, or even to
have accepted, such assignments revealed a strong propensity to
excel and to innovate.

Thus, it is understandable that among the 1950 leadership
sample there was an important minority of officers who had had
these assignments as part of their preparation for higher command.
The incidence varies by military service to the following extent:
in the Army, 39.3 per cent; in the Navy, 23.5 per cent; in the Air
Force, 19.6 per cent. These data reveal that much greater "on-the-
job training" for politico-military assignments was afforded ranking
officers in the Army, even though by this period the Air Force had
become the ascendant arm of the military establishment.

The concentration of these preparatory assignments varied
greatly, depending on the functional role of the officer. Generals
and admirals who specialized in technical support missions had
very few such assignments. While the number was somewhat higher
among operational commanders, it is in the careers of the higher
staff officers and strategic commanders that these symbolic skills
become more widespread. In turn, the concentration among strategic commanders was greatest in the Army—67.7 per cent as compared to 35.3 per cent for the Navy, and 38.1 per cent for the Air
Force. It is not argued that these assignments were the cause of
ascent into the elite nucleus. Most officers who had such assignments never rose to the highest echelon; no single type of career
experience is a powerful predictor of career success. The observations can be made, however, that officers with ambition and
innovating perspectives benefited by mastering such assignments,
and that the frequency of such assignments among the nucleus of
the elite is striking. The fundamental point is that the "myth" of the
prescribed career is not universal for the strategic personnel of the
military profession. No doubt, the same holds true for other professions.

But a still more systematic test of the impact and importance
of an innovating and unusual career experience is possible. It was
necessary, first, to identify the top 15 to 20 per cent who comprised

the elite nucleus from among the 475 officers who constituted the 1950 sample, by virtue of their rank as major general or rear admiral and above. Since this analysis rejects the conspiracy theory of the elite, 87 officers, or 18.3 per cent, were identified as prime movers by fellow professionals and informed observers. In no case were they selected simply because they held the highest rank. They were selected because of their contributions to the decision-making process. If there is any bias—and undoubtedly a different panel of experts would produce somewhat different results—it is in the direction of de-emphasizing the role of heroic leader types whose contributions were mainly in preserving the traditions of the warrior.

What were the relative proportions of this nuclear group whose careers were prescribed, routine, or what might be called adaptive? First, by prescribed career we mean a career in which the officer has followed the idealized pattern: more particularly, he has attended command and staff school and war college; he has had the proper command and staff assignments; and he has avoided low-prestige tasks. Second, short of the prescribed career, one might identify a routine career as follows: Such a career applies to officers who had followed the rules of the game, but who, at crucial points in their careers, were not given the opportunity to attend higher schools, or who refused to accept those staff posts which have come to be thought of as part of the prescribed career. Yet, these officers rose to be two-star generals and rear admirals, usually in command of technical services or specialized support formations. Finally, there were those careers which could best be described as adaptive. These officers had the essential elements, or most of the essential elements, of the prescribed career, but, for their time, they had additional and unusual experiences. They were officers who reached for the future by associating themselves with experimental weapons. (For example, in the Navy, they took courses in flight training during a period when the big battleship men dominated.) They were officers who, early in their careers, had unique educational experiences or politico-military assignments, which, though thought to be barriers to the successful career, in the end helped them to enter the military elite because they had been taught negotiative and innovative skills. If our hypothesis was correct, the elite nucleus would have a high concentration of men who had followed such adaptive or "individualist" careers.[16]

For the 1950 sample, the hypothesis holds true that the careers of the elite nucleus show a marked difference from the rest of the top professionals (Table 25). One-third of the top professionals

Table 25
Military Leadership, 1950:
Career Patterns

	Elite Nucleus %	Top Pro- fessionals %	Total Per Cent %	Total Number %
Total Sample				
Prescribed	32.0	32.1	32.2	147
Routine	10.2	66.0	55.6	254
Adaptive	57.8	1.9	12.2	56
Number	(87)	(370)	100.0	(457)
Unclassifiable				18
Total				(475)
Army				
Prescribed	20.0	33.0	29.9	47
Routine	7.5	64.5	49.7	78
Adaptive	72.5	2.5	20.4	32
Number	(40)	(117)	100.0	(157)
Unclassifiable				9
Total				(166)
Navy				
Prescribed	27.6	29.8	29.6	60
Routine	17.2	69.0	61.6	125
Adaptive	55.2	1.2	8.8	18
Number	(29)	(174)	100.0	(203)
Unclassifiable				1
Total				(204)
Air Force				
Prescribed	63.2	35.4	41.3	40
Routine	10.5	63.3	52.5	51
Adaptive	26.3	1.3	6.2	6
Number	(18)	(79)	100.0	(97)
Unclassifiable				8
Total				(105)

had followed prescribed careers. However, more than half of the elite nucleus had adaptive career experiences, thus demonstrating the extent to which entrance into the very top echelons of the military profession was not dependent on following the rules of the game.

Striking indeed was the different degree of opportunity available for such deviant careers in the three services While for the

1950 sample one-fifth of the Army top leadership can be classified as having had adaptive careers, in the Navy the percentage is 8.8 and in the Air Force 6.2 (Table 25). In part, this is due to the fact that for both the Navy and the Air Force, the command structure had produced a narrower definition of a professional career. Throughout the period of World War II, the Navy and the Air Force, to an even greater extent, were essentially technical services wedded directly to their major weapons systems; by contrast, the Army had collected a wide range of functions and politico-military commitments which gave expression to atypical careers.

In the Army, with its greater latitude for career diversification, and its wider range of functions, almost three out of every four members of the nuclear elite had atypical or adaptive careers; in the Navy the ratio was one out of every two. In the Air Force, however, where the top leaders were recruited because of tactical combat skill and combat performance, rather than politico-military assignments or a combination of combat and such assignments, the nucleus had more officers who followed prescribed career lines than those who deviated from them. Paradoxically, the Air Force, with its great technological base, lagged behind in the development of managerial generalists who had been exposed to multiple roles and skills. This over-riding combat-mindedness was crucial in setting the political perspective of Air Force leaders during the period 1950–60.

In the past, involvement in assignments which made for an unusual or adaptive career was often self-imposed and self-generated. Officers often accepted specialized assignments of a quasi-political nature, or those involving negotiation or communications skills, not because of narrow careerist opportunities, but because they were genuinely interested in such assignments. For example, in the old Army and Navy those who studied foreign languages often did so on their own initiative and were willing to incur short-term risks to their career development for long-term requirements.[17] Currently, language training is widespread in the military establishment, and is not so much an expression of a creative outlook. Similarly, the military establishment is currently seeking to make political education part of the prescribed career development.

Many of the contemporary tasks of politico-military administration require such technical expertise that the services have created specialized occupational categories to do essential staff work. In

1953 the Air Force created the occupational code category of international politico-military affairs officer.[18] The Navy, in turn, has created the title of international affairs officer.[19] The Army, due to its more extensive history of operational responsibility in political administration, has a variety of political occupation categories, such as civil affairs-military government officer and psychological warfare officer. All three services have intelligence officers and diplomatic attaches whose duties involve political intelligence. However, officers in these categories tend to become staff specialists, are cut off from the basic pattern of career development, and are not likely to be the military statesmen of the future. Nor is there reason to suppose that the military statesmen of the future are receiving their most decisive experiences at the higher military educational institutions which are teaching current doctrine. There is every reason to believe that training for the future will continue to involve a strong element of self-imposed initiative.

Notes

1. Davis, Arthur K., "Bureaucratic Patterns in the Navy Officer Corps." *Social Forces*, 1948, 27, 143–53.

2. Probably the most striking career of a non-traditional officer in World War I was that of Lord Trenchard. After an early life of sport and adventure, and after failing the entrance examination into the British Army several times, he entered the service by way of the militia. His advancement was most rapid, and by the end of 1915 he took over command of the Royal Flying Corps in France, without having had any of the essential career experiences.

3. Analysis of the core of decision-makers and innovators in the military profession must draw the line between innovation and amateurism. In academic life it is well recognized that those who engage in interdisciplinary research do so from two different sets of motives. Some have mastered their discipline and recognize its limitations; therefore, they seek to restructure knowledge by challenging old concepts and traditional divisions between the disciplines. Others are "second" raters who, failing to achieve recognition in their discipline, join in interdisciplinary efforts as a second chance at career success. In the military the very same pattern is present, so that the mere expression of individualism hardly indicates an innovating professional; it may in effect be no more than a pose.

4. Deweerd, Major H. A., *Great Soldiers of World War II.* New York: Norton, 1944.

5. John L. Hines, 1924 to 1926; Charles P. Summerall, 1926 to 1930; and Malin Craig, 1935 to 1939.

6. The experiences of Major General Sir Percy Hobart, although drawn from the British Army, are typical of those professionals whose thinking was too advanced. Hobart was a forceful advocate of armored divisions. As the commander of the original tank brigade, created in 1935, he had worked out

tactics and doctrine of tank warfare similar to those applied by the Germans. In Britain, however, the traditionalist generals were determined to curb, if they could not cripple, the growth of tank forces. Accordingly, when an armored division was formed, its command had to be given first to an artillery officer and then to a cavalryman. In 1938, when Hobart's claim to advancement could no longer be denied, he was shunted off to Egypt. There, he created the famous 7th Armored Division, but in the process he so outraged the orthodox that he was recalled before he could test his theories in action. Driven into premature retirement in 1940, he became a corporal in the Home Guard. He was rescued from oblivion by the personal intervention of Winston Churchill, but it was not until 1943 that he was given a meaningful opportunity to employ his exceptional talents.

7. Kenney, George, *The MacArthur I Knew*. New York: Duell, Sloan & Pearce, 1951, p. 228.

8. Payne, Robert, *General Marshall: A Study in Loyalties*. London: William Heinemann, pp. 32–33.

9. Child, Marquis, *Eisenhower: Captive Hero*. New York: Harcourt, Brace, 1959, p. 31.

10. Arnold, H. H., *Global Mission*. New York: Harper & Bros., 1949, p. 9.

11. Smith, Holland M., *Coral and Brass*. New York: Scribner's, 1949, p. 52.

12. *These Are the Generals*, foreword by Walter Millis. New York: Alfred A. Knopf, 1943.

13. Based on material presented in Ridgway, Matthew B., *Soldier: The Memoirs of Matthew B. Ridgway*. New York: Harper & Bros., 1956, pp. 18ff.

14. *Ibid.*, p. 49.

15. The creative military commander must always be prepared to challenge the fundamentals of military organization. If the personnel replacement system which is at the core of military organization is obviously inappropriate, then a commanding officer, such as Ridgway, seeks to find his way around it. Before his 82nd Air-Borne Division was dropped into Normandy, he had made arrangements, over strong protests, but with the support of General Bradley, to leave behind in England a small cadre who would take charge of the volunteers coming into his organization. He was anxious to establish continuity, and to overcome the inefficiency of the infantry replacement system. "My purpose was to indoctrinate each new man, not only with the proud spirit of the division as a whole, but with the spirit of each smaller unit which was then in combat" (Ridgway, *op. cit.*, p. 15). Such a move required extreme initiative and profound insight into the basis of military morale. It was an act which anticipated the findings of social scientists concerning the importance of primary group solidarity for military morale.

16. The classification of career lines into the categories of prescribed, routine, and adaptive, was based on a summary overall judgment by the author, with the assistance of informants from the three services.

17. Linguistic skill assisted entrance into the top elite among the top military commanders of World War II: for example, Mark Clark, French; George Patton, French; Stilwell, Mandarin; Ridgway, Spanish; Halsey, French; and Wedemeyer, German.

18. Department of the Air Force, *Officers' Classification Manual*, AFM 36–1. (as revised). January 1, 1952.

19. *Manual of Navy Officer Billet Classifications*, Navpers 15839. Revised June 7, 1954.

IV

THE MILITARY COMMUNITY:

THE PERSISTENCE OF MANNERS

CHAPTER *9*

Style of Life

THE MILITARY PROFESSION is more than an occupation; it is a complete style of life. The officer is a member of a community whose claims over his daily existence extend well beyond his official duties. In fact, any profession which performs a crucial "life and death" task, such as medicine, the ministry, or the police, develops such claims. The deadly mission of warfare has required that the officer be prepared at short notice to abandon his routine and personal commitments. This is obvious and commonplace. However, somewhat less explicit is the fact that any profession which is continually preoccupied with the threat of danger requires a strong sense of solidarity if it is to operate effectively. Detailed regulation of the military style of life is expected to enhance group cohesion, professional loyalty, and maintain the martial spirit. In good measure, military indoctrination has been effective because of the relatively closed community environment in which the military have lived. In turn, the style of life of the military community contributes to the self-consciousness and self-assurance of the military elite.

Traditionally, the military community has been more sharply segregated from civilian life in the United States than in the major nations of Western Europe. This social isolation has helped the military profession to maintain its distinctive characteristics and values. The influence of aristocratic traditions was weak; the commercial and capitalist ethic, which discounted the virtues of the professional soldier, was powerful. During much of its past history, the Army was located at remote frontier posts, fighting Indians. The minute size of the professional officer corps, as compared with the standing armies of Europe, helped to produce social isolation. The system of stationing the bulk of the ground forces in remote posts, partly because of tradition, partly because of economy, also reflected the civilian desire to remove the military, at least from visibility. The United States never had its counterpart of the continental garrison cities where federal troops were stationed for possible intervention in domestic politics.

But the social isolation of the Army and Navy officer can be overdrawn. During the inter-war years, officers were frequently assigned to civilian universities as military instructors, and some served at arsenals and depots where they developed civilian friends. Before World War II, the majority of the military posts were located in the South and in the West, where the civilian social elite developed extensive contacts with higher officers, or with those officers who came from the "better" families. Even in the larger metropolitan centers, "upper crust" social life often included judicious contact with the "right" Army families. The Navy, centered in the eastern seaboard and the two major western ports, had much greater contact with civilian society, and naval officers were an accepted part of the protocol of socialite circles. It would be accurate to describe these contacts with civilian society as ceremonial and social, rather than professional or political.

One is struck by the extent to which the military profession has been able to maintain many of its unique characteristics and heroic traditions in the face of technological and political changes. Old-timers are convinced that the "old Army" and the "old Navy" are gone. Yet, to the outside observer, it would appear that the military profession has been able to maintain much of the protocol and style of life of the old Army and Navy. In particular, it is striking to note the extent to which the Air Force has sought to impose the forms of the traditional military community on its members. This has been feasible only because the military establishment has wide powers of self-regulation, and is able to set standards of behavior for its members which go well beyond the conditions of work.

However, although traditional rules of social behavior persist in the military community to guide the style of life of the officer, they do not operate as effectively as they did in the past. Thus, it is necessary to investigate the consequences of the hypothesis that the officer corps has shifted its style of life from a relatively isolated group, residing mainly in its own community, to a profession with elaborate, though transitory, contacts with civilian society. Of course, new patterns of social integration are essential for the new roles that military managers are now called upon to perform. But the breakdown of the social isolation of the military community strains the effectiveness of traditional protocol in maintaining the military style of life. In an organization as complex and as large as the military establishment, elaborate military protocol contributes to reducing administrative frictions. How do protocol and gentlemanly manners operate in the face of broadening civilian contacts?

In a free enterprise society the military profession cannot compete with the private sector in monetary rewards for its elite members. Professional commitments therefore depend on the persistence of a style of life, and a belief in the superiority, or at least worth, of that style of life. To what extent has the breakdown of the exclusiveness of the military community been accompanied by increased dissatisfaction with the military style of life? The tensions and role conflicts in the military profession—in the cadre of future leaders—have come to involve the attitudes of the military wife, who now has a perceptible basis for comparing her lot with that of her civilian counterpart, and who has become disposed to conclude that she is disadvantaged.

Work and Residence

THE INTIMATE SOCIAL SOLIDARITY of the military profession, which civilians often both envy and resent, is grounded in a peculiar occupational fact. Separation between place of work and place of residence, characteristic of urban occupations, is absent. Instead, the military community is a relatively closed community where professional and residential life have been completely inter-

mingled.* The sharp segregation between work and private life has
been minimized in the military occupation.

Sociologists strongly believe that some of the basic tensions of
industrial society result from the absence of adequate mechanisms
for bridging the gap between the requirements of work and the
requirements of residence and family. In the "old Army," and in
the "old Navy," occupation and family life were closely linked. The
realities of the profession pervaded family and social life, and, in
turn, the military community was comprehensively organized to
assist family relations. The result was not only relative social
isolation, since military families tended to have more contact among
themselves than with outsiders, but also a powerful *esprit de corps*
among professional officers. The problem of choosing between work
and family life did not exist.

The organizational revolution in the military establishment has
gradually altered social relations within the military community. A
combination of developments has enlarged the military community
and weakened its social cohesion. First, there is an increasing trend
toward the civilian pattern of separation of work and residence,
because the military base is no longer able to accommodate all
personnel. Furthermore, military personnel are now more often
stationed at civilian institutions—government, research, industrial,
and educational—away from military communities. Second, the
sheer increase in numbers makes it more difficult to maintain professional solidarity. Each service has many more military installations, and the size of many installations has grown to the point
where they take on some of the impersonal characteristics of an
urban metropolis. At the same time, the more representative social
recruitment has meant a decline in the sense of social exclusiveness.
In the past, when the officer corps was dominated by a Protestant
Episcopalian upper middle-class background, the "outsiders" either
transformed themselves, or were few enough to be merely tolerated.
With a larger number of officers from more humble social backgrounds, plus a greater variety of religious, ethnic, and racial backgrounds, the military community has become more of a melting pot.

Third, the old military community was composed almost ex-

* This characteristic is also found among a few other highly specialized
professions, such as religious orders, and among some members of the artistic
and literary profession.

clusively of military personnel and their families. The contemporary military establishment has large numbers of civilians who occupy an ambiguous position in their desire to have the best of both worlds. Their presence enlarges and dilutes the military community. The same can be said for the limited presence of the women's auxiliary corps, for the traditional military profession was based on the solidarity of an all-male fraternity. Fourth, in the past the military community was based on sharp class consciousness, as between enlisted man and officer and within the hierarchy of ranks. Even an ardent spokesman, such as Colonel Richard E. Dupuy, describes the Army of 1904 as "Class conscious . . . from the Chief of Staff down to the most junior corporal who even impressed his fist upon a slothful recruit, and from 'Mrs. General' to the corporal's wife." The Navy was even more rigid in its distinctions. Such social relations could operate as long as military organization involved discipline based on domination. With the growth of managerial authority, the rank system remains intact, especially the line between officers and enlisted personnel, but efforts are now made to prevent status from being too obtrusive in the life of the military community. Enlisted personnel and their wives no longer can be taken for granted in an institution which operates on the basis of a "team concept"; they must be fitted into the social scheme and their presence acknowledged.

The handbooks, official and unofficial, on military custom and protocol are significant indices to the realities of the military community. A comparison of the content of the manuals issued at the turn of the century with contemporary editions reveals little change in the prescriptions of behavior for the officer and his wife. The one striking change lies in the fact that the audience has been enlarged, so that the manuals are now addressed to both commissioned and noncommissioned officers; nor do those manuals directed to officers' wives overlook the wives of noncommissioned officers. Nancy Shea, the unofficial Emily Post for the Army and Air Force is open and candid in her effort to minimize friction between the wives of commissioned and noncommissioned officers:

I feel it is important early in your married life, Connie, that you, as an enlisted man's wife, understand and accept the relationship too. Most Army men instinctively understand, so get Tony to present his side of the system to you first. There is nothing snobbish or antisocial about it; so from the beginning be careful not to be supersensitive or to carry the proverbial "chip on your shoulder." There will be times when you, as an NCO wife, will work with officers' wives on various post projects; simply be cooperative, polite and gracious.[1]

Since the Navy community is the most traditional, enlisted personnel are more taken for granted, and there is less concern with the status or attitudes of their wives.

With explicit effort, steps have been taken to weaken the impact of hierarchical distinctions on the next generation. In the old Army the rank system influenced the social relations of the children of service families; some outranked others on the basis of their father's status.[2] Enlisted men's children were strictly isolated. In the contemporary military establishment, children are of course fully aware of the status of their fathers. However, in both the Army and the Air Force, especially at overseas installations, the children of enlisted and officer personnel are not segregated in the schools managed by the services. The son of every military family is potentially an officer and the educational system serves to strengthen this potentiality. In part, this is a consequence of the open social class system of civilian society. In part, it is due to the fact that the new discipline of the profession has begun to seep through the military community.[3]

Changes in the mechanics of military life have also strained professional solidarity. At one time, the military style of life was leisurely; the typical officer's work day in the inter-war years ended by noon, although office routine developed after World War I. Freedom from an 8.00 A.M. to 4:00 P.M. routine, and opportunity for extensive leisure and sports, were compensations for the rigors of training exercises and frequent separations from one's family. If military honor required gentlemen as professionals, the military occupation made it possible for the officer to have a gentleman-like routine.

But the officer is being transformed into an officeholder. Those who occupy command and combat positions in military units which are on the alert are subject to continuous and extreme tension and live a highly intense life. Those in key positions are under all the pressures of "crash programs" and "administrative flaps." The system of rotation in assignment spreads these tasks, but the up-and-coming officer can no longer afford to behave like a "gentleman." Being an aspiring military manager means living like his civilian counterpart; it means taking work home at night (or rather going back to the office in the evening because classified documents must be left in the office), or working toward continuous self-improvement through reading and correspondence courses. Of course, many members of the officer corps are more or less detached about their careers, and continue to limit themselves to an 8:00 A.M. to 4:00 P.M. routine, but even they must now be careful not to give the impression of under-employment.

Since military commitments have become world wide, the frequency of changes and the distance between assignments have become extensive and disruptive. "Lack of stability for my family caused by frequent moves" was the second most frequent reason given by a sample of West Point graduates for their resignations from service.[4] The lack of sufficient housing also weakens the solidarity of the military community; many officers on duty in the United States live in civilian communities. Because of the greater transferability of skills to civilian employment, plus increased contacts with civilian agencies and private enterprise, the professional officer is more constantly challenged as to the validity of his career choice. He is more likely to judge himself, not only by the standards of the military community, but also by the standard of civilian society.

Standard of Living

THERE IS a widespread belief among military professionals that their standard of living has not been adequately maintained since the end of World War II. They are beset by a sense of "subjective deprivation," and feel that the material welfare of the rest of society is somehow advancing more rapidly than is their own.

Comparisons with the pre-1941 period and with civilian occupations are difficult to make, since so many different and incomparable elements are involved. In particular, it is difficult to evaluate the fringe benefits which accrue to the military profession. Two trends, however, which contribute to these feelings of discontent are clear. The income level of the military profession, like all professions except medicine, diminished somewhat, compared to the entire full-time labor force.[5] In 1929 Army officers' earnings were, on the average, 2.98 times that of all full-time civilian employees, and by 1949 the ratio had dropped to 2.53. The corresponding figures for lawyers were 3.89 in 1929 and 2.82 in 1949; and, for physicians, 3.68, rising to 4.10. Second, the depression and the post-war economic expansion had different consequences for the salaried and the independent professions. During the depression, the salaries of professionals, including teachers and military officers, fell hardly at all, while those of the independent professions dropped by as much as two-fifths. After 1942, the relationship was almost reversed: the salaries of teachers and officers increased by one-half and one-third respectively from 1940 to 1950, but the earning of physicians more than doubled, and those of lawyers almost doubled. Thus, in comparison to workers and self-employed professionals, the military have benefited less from economic growth.

Beyond these trends, the growth in discontent is linked to an increased tendency for military officers to compare their lot with that of industrial managers—in part, because the skills of the military manager are now more transferable to civilian industrial and commercial enterprise. In such comparison, military salaries are progressively disadvantaged. One management survey demonstrated that in the Air Force, from 1951 to 1955, brigadier generals' salaries increased 6 per cent, while "a comparable sample of industrial executives had increased their salaries by 26 per cent."[6]

In 1958 the pay scale of the military was revised and substantially improved in order to make the military more competitive with civilian employment and reduce turnover (Table 26). Actually, turnover in the military profession is not much higher than in civilian employment, except among very selected technical electronics specialists in the enlisted ranks; however, personnel turnover is much more disruptive to military organization than it is to civilian enterprise. For a long time, the military have received special incentive rewards for combat and hazardous duty. The revised pay schedule added a category of "responsibility pay" which ranges in amount from $50 to $150 per month, for officer specialists in the ranks of captain to colonel.

As a result, starting salaries for officer personnel became comparable to those offered college graduates in other fields. The effective range was increased so that senior colonels and naval

Table 26
Military Monthly Pay Scale, 1958

	Monthly Salary Under 2 yrs.	Monthly Salary Over 26 yrs.	Monthly Subsistence	Monthly Quarters †
General — Admiral	$1200	$1700	$47	$171
Lt. Gen. — Vice Adm.	1063	1500	47	171
Maj. Gen. — Rear Adm. *	963	1350	47	171
Brig. Gen. — Rear Adm. **	800	1175	47	171
Colonel — Captain	592	985	47	136
Lt. Col. — Commander	474	775	47	136
Major — Lt. Commander	400	630	47	119
Captain — Lieutenant	326	525	47	102
1st Lt. — Lt. (JG)	259	380	47	94
2nd Lt. — Ensign	222	314	47	85

† With dependents.
* Upper half.
** Lower half.

captains drew over $13,000 annually, including their allowances, aside from all the various fringe benefits such as medical services. The handful at the very top received over $20,000. Yet, the military —as a public-service profession—affords markedly curtailed opportunities for economic advancement, as compared with business and selected self-employed professions. It has lower ceilings, a longer time is required to reach these ceilings, and no opportunities exist to break through these ceilings. Moreover, the evidence points to a long-term trend in which there has been a greater increase in the lowest military salaries as compared with the highest salaries. The percentage increase in privates' salaries from 1908 to 1948 was 400 per cent; 57 per cent for second lieutenants; and 11 per cent for major generals.[7] Although the 1958 schedule decelerates this trend, it still remains an aspect in which the military community has marked equalitarian practices, as compared with civilian social structure.

Undoubtedly, the outstanding officer is deprived, as compared with his civilian counterpart in industry and business. For the whole profession, the feeling is ever present that they missed the chance of "good money," which is believed in civilian life to be a matter of chance and luck. In addition, increased responsibilities are believed to go unrewarded in the military. The claim is argued by the results of a survey prepared to justify higher military salaries. In the Air Force, in 1955, the brigadier general reported to have earned $12,230 on the average, had 2,400 employees under him, and was responsible for an inventory of 35 million dollars. By comparison, industrial executives earned an average of $59,300, managed 1,000 employees, and had an average inventory of 2.5 million dollars.

The fringe benefits of the military have suffered. In particular, as compared with the pre-World War II period, housing has deteriorated markedly. The rapid expansion of the military establishment has left a backlog of unfilled needs, and, as in civilian society, the standards of the new construction have been lowered. It is no exaggeration that first lieutenants in the inter-war years had housing comparable to that assigned to colonels in 1959. On the other hand, there has been an expansion of many auxiliary services, particularly medical assistance, but rising expectations mean that these increased benefits are taken for granted and thought to be minimum necessities.

Aside from the shrinkage in actual time available for leisure, recreational fringe benefits are no longer as attractive. Many of the features of a country club—swimming pools, officers' clubs, polo and horseback riding in the Army, and yachting and boating in the Navy—had been built into the military community. Some of these facilities have been curtailed, particularly horseback riding and polo playing, but others, such as private swimming pools and club house life, are now more widely available in upper middle-class suburban communities. Instead, travel abroad has become a reward of military life. Because of the cultural perspectives of the military, residence abroad is heavily preoccupied with tourism, sightseeing, and shopping. The military professional's view of foreign lands is epitomized in the report of an Army general's wife:

Tokyo usually is called a man's town, but there were some wonderful things for women there, too. The shopping, of course, was wonderful, with silver shops, pearl shops, silk shops, curio shops, and art shops among the finest in the world. Then the Army itself provided us with fine services. At the post exchange beauty shop, where I went, they had Japanese girls who were expert operators. And the price was astounding. It cost only sixty cents for a fine shampoo or a wonderful manicure or even a pedicure. One Japanese service that Americans learned to love was the massage at which the Japanese are expert. . . . They work on nerves and nerve ends, using some of the same principles that Japanese jujitsu wrestlers use in their matches. The study of the nerves of the body, applied with equal effectiveness to jujitsu and massage, is an ancient art in Japan, and surprisingly enough, an hour long massage in our own homes cost only a dollar.[8]

Residence abroad implies a higher standard of living and, because the military community is relatively detached from the immediate environment, a more gentlemanly status.[9]

The pension system, which once was thought to be so important for the military profession, has also lost much of its attraction. In the past, the military retirement system was special, since civilian occupations were without these benefits. In 1958 two-star generals and rear admirals with long service records were receiving annual retirement pay of approximately $7,000. While free medical care after retirement continues to be an important benefit, with the development of social security and elaborate civilian retirement plans, the military system is but one pension system among many, although in dollar value it is much superior to most. The threat and actuality of inflation, however, depreciates its value. The military have become particularly sensitive because rotation of job assignment makes it impossible for them, as compared with civilians, to acquire real estate, thereby depriving them of what they consider an important way of meeting the pressures of inflation. As a result, investment in the stock market is widespread in the military community, and *Wall Street Journal* is standard reading, not only for financial news, but for political guidance as well.

Consequently, the entire concept of retirement has undergone a change. No longer is retirement the final phase of a gentleman's career, a continuation of the military style of life. It is merely another step in career management. The Army no longer speaks of retirement, but of a "second" career. Traditionally, the bulk of military professionals, when they separated from military service, actually did retire; civilian employment was incompatible with their self-conception. These self-conceptions were important in view of the limitations in their actual skill. The social origins of the older generals and admirals also contributed to a desire to settle in a small agricultural town or resort environment. Since most officers had served for thirty years, such retirement was economically feasible. The pinnacle of a military career, particularly for the

Army officer, was to buy a farm in the Virginia area or a ranch in Texas, since Washington and Fort Sam Houston were the focal points of social life in the old Army.

The retirement age has now been lowered, so that many more officers, including those who entered into the leadership cadre, do not serve the full thirty-year term. These officers *must* take another job. Preoccupation with retirement pervades the military establishment, because of uncertainty about the future of particular weapons systems. The technical specialist is believed to have greater employment possibilities in civilian society than does the military generalist, and this reverses the traditional internal prestige system. Attendance at command and general staff school and the service colleges are thought of as more than career steps into the military elite. They are certificates of management training which are acceptable in civilian enterprise. Since much of officer life is spent in school or in teaching, many officers seek assignments which will permit them to take university instruction while in the service and certify themselves for future teaching jobs. Assignment to Washington and the urban centers is thought of as a possibility for part-time university study, particularly in law. Concern with a second career undermines the value of the original career choice and weakens professional commitments. Yet, the aspirations for a second career are still modest, and in fact limited, except for those Air Force officers who hope for "great things" in the aircraft and missile industry.*

None of these trends means that the military community has given up its aspirations for a gentlemanly style of life. Wherever possible, the old traditions are retained, but they may be reserved for the very top, and for the new formations that have risen to power and prominence. For example, Camp Crook, outside Omaha, was an elite Army cavalry station in the days before World War I. It has been renamed Offut Air Base, and the headquarters of the Strategic Air Command are located there. The massive, beautiful old homes of the cavalry colonels have been carefully preserved and renovated, with modern air-conditioning, and are occupied by flying generals. With the assistance of private servants—enlisted men from the commissary—an aristocratic style of life is possible

---

* See Chapter 18, Civilian Alliances, for details of civilian employment after retirement.

for the moment. Since SAC generals have been stationed all over the world, and since their wives usually have the professional assistance of interior decorators, the furnishings and decor have, in fact, been improved. The whole setting is an indication that the military establishment strives to preserve a standard of living for some of its elite that will maintain traditions for the next generation.

Family Relations

THE TRADITIONAL MILITARY COMMUNITY molded family life to the requirements of the profession. The fact that in recent years the military profession has produced men who hold public-service leadership positions outside of their military roles is due in some measure to the family patterns in the military community. In a society in which the tradition of public service is weak, the military community was organized so that family relations supported the officer in his conviction that he had—more than a job—some special mission or calling. Conflicts between family and career obligations were held to a minimum.

Army and Navy wives were precursors of the organization man's wife, in that they were consciously involved in the careers of their husbands. In her autobiography General Mark Clark's wife, Maurine Clark, writes with pride of this role:

Life on an Army post in peacetime gives the Army wife far more opportunity, and probably more obligation, to help her husband in his career than most wives find in civilian life. The reasons are fairly obvious. An Army post is something like a company town. Everybody is working for the same outfit. Everybody goes to the same post clubs and chapels and movies and buys their food at the same commissary and miscellaneous articles at the same post exchange. Living on the post, the husband is never far from either his home or work. The people the wife sees at night, at parties or in her home, are the people her husband works with or for. Army protocol requires that the wife get to know the commanding officer and his wife socially. And it is quite common in Army life for the wife to call the ranking officer by his first name while her husband must address him by rank, as "colonel or general."[10]

Army and Navy lore is full of stories of wives actively intervening in service affairs and in service politics. Among the more famous is that of George Patton's wife who, having a command of French, assisted him in translating textbooks used by the French cavalry schools, thereby enhancing his military reputation as an advanced thinker. Another well-known account deals with a colonel who had his wife memorize Army regulations, so that he would have a readily available reference source. Colonel T. Bentley Mott, who was involved in a variety of important political assignments as a military attache during World War I, relates an anecdote which is more typical of the role of the petticoats in the old Army. Mott had sought repeatedly, and without success, to get a transfer to the Army artillery school where he could advance his career and find relief from the intellectual boredom of his troop assignment:

I then bethought me of a promise Mrs. Wesley Merritt, the Superintendent's wife, had made me when I graduated [from West Point]. "If you ever want something that is proper for you to have and you need help, write to me," she had said. So I wrote. My colonel nearly fainted when a week later, he received a telegram ordering me to the Artillery School. Mrs. Merritt had written to her friend Mr. Endicott, the Secretary of War.[11]

Undoubtedly, the wives of officers contribute to professional solidarity by weakening the artificial barriers generated by the rank system. Occasionally, the wives have even influenced minor personnel decisions. A proper marriage by a young officer to the daughter of a high-ranking officer was a relevant step in building a career, and service wives worked hard to screen potential candidates. On the other hand, family and kinship ties have often encouraged generals to place sons and relatives on their personal staffs. Indeed, this practice was so extensive, and so disruptive, that early in World War II General George Marshall issued a specific order preventing such appointments. But a good deal of this lore about officers' wives and family connections must be recorded as legend rather than reality.

It is necessary to look elsewhere, and at more prosaic matters, to describe how pre-World War II military families served professional requirements. It is not possible to determine whether the military family was more stable than the civilian family, or whether military officers were less faithful to their wives than were civilian husbands; nor is there any reason to assume that this was the case. The important issue is that the military family was a mixture of traditional forms and many of the characteristics of the emerging "companionate" family, which Ernest Burgess, the sociologist, saw as a form more appropriate for the requirements of industrial and professional society. First, modern social structure stripped the family of traditional support from extended kin and from close community support. However, before World War II the military family, like the companionate family, was not dependent on its own social resources. The "companionate family" receives assistance from its neighbors, from voluntary associations, and from governmental agencies. The social and community services which are now gradually being made available to civilian families have long been provided to the military family.

Second, the military family, like the companionate family, had duties beyond child raising. Many of the welfare and recreational activities of the military community—to assist newcomers, to help sick wives and children, etc.—involved active participation of the military wife. She had a role outside of the household, short of employment in the labor market. The role may have been limited, formalized, and dull by standards of modern "gracious living," but it was a recognized and accepted part of the military style of life.

Third, the military family was deeply involved in the transmission of military tradition. Again and again, in data amassed from interviews and memoirs, one is struck by the extent to which women internalized the values of military honor and military ceremony. This remains true even in the post-war military community. The wife speaks with as much fervor as her husband when she says, "Fort Monroe was real Army, the honor guard marched frequently in the morning with the band. It was a grand sight to see the spick and span soldiers marching across the green of the parade grounds with the magnificent Chesapeake for a background."

Fourth, the curious mixture of traditionalism and modernity in military family life kept romantic love in bounds. Marriages were carried out with respect to protocol, and with an eye to perpetuating the traditional forms of social life. The service manuals specifically designated what could be said and done when young girls visited West Point and Annapolis, and elopements were incompatible with duty rosters and assignments in the field.[12] These dampers on romantic love were effective because officers married relatively late in life, due to financial considerations, and because a service wife had to fit in. Officers tended, after graduation from the service academies, to select their wives from among service families, or among those socially connected with service families. This system served to maintain the social and regional exclusiveness of the military profession. Since, for some, entrance into the academies was an effort at upward social mobility, or reflected a desire to maintain one's family status, marriage on the basis of academy ties was a validation of status aspirations. To be without a wife was a real career handicap, and a grave inconvenience in the circumscribed life of the military community where family and professional relations were intertwined. If a first marriage was terminated because of the death of a partner or due to personal discord, remarriage was essential and often arranged.

Family relations in contemporary military life do not adhere so closely to professional requirements. The greatest strain is to be found in the Air Force while the Navy seems least transformed. The percentage of graduates who marry immediately upon completion of their academy training has increased, with the consequence that many officers face the problems of starting a professional career and a family simultaneously. Earlier marriage often means that the officers select their wives from among their home-town girl friends, rather than from among service-connected families, thereby increasing problems of assimilation into the military community.

Indeed, the strains on family life are considered so important that ranking officers and special staff sections (Personnel Services Division) have been given the responsibility of developing programs to strengthen family relations, reversing the traditional assumption of the military community that the family will help to fill the needs of the profession. Tension between family and profession has become a real issue.

The subjective feeling that the military profession does not offer an adequate standard of living is a powerful source of tension, but the causes run deeper. For one, the military mechanics of the cold war constantly disrupt family routines. In the critical services, especially in the Strategic Air Command, where disruption of family life is greatest, the military establishment has responded by extending the greatest material benefits and the most extensive familial assistance. A commander of a strategic bomber squadron in the cold war leads a more disrupted family life than that of the commanding officer of a destroyer during the inter-war period. But from the testimony of operational officers, the disruption of family life, except in rare cases, does not interfere with operational efficiency, or with performance in staff assignments or military school.

Both officers and their wives complain of the irrationality and pressure of training schedules, but their criticism reflects a deeper concern with whether a military career is "worth while." Discontent is a reflection of a lack of self-esteem. It is a reflection of the ambiguity of the military career in a free enterprise society. In the past, the strains were less disruptive because the military family had a style of life which had its own internal consistency.

Very like the professional social worker, military authority has sought to "assist" the family to adjust to the military community. In the face of increased family disruption and discontent, the military community has been literally converted into an advanced form of the welfare and social service state. The actual extent of family disruption is not known. One study of a Strategic Air Command unit where career pressure and tension is most intense reported that in a sample of 52 families, 15 had one or both spouses who had been divorced.[13] In any event, in the military community it is assumed that the solution of family problems has become essential for professional solidarity. Since the military profession requires high levels of solidarity, this assumption is probably warranted.

The military community has become too large, too mobile, and too impersonal to rely on voluntary mutual self-help. Instead, elaborate arrangements and professional personnel have been introduced to handle family welfare. As in civilian society, the efforts of voluntary charity organizations, and even semi-voluntary groups such as the Red Cross, have been found to be too limited in scope. Thus the Air Force has organized its Dependent Assistance Program, with a paid staff of personnel affairs officers, whose job it is to move, receive, and resettle families while their husbands are involved in military duties. These officers, together with voluntary helpers (DA's), serve as specialists in referring families to the appropriate military agency for assistance, for the typical officer's wife could never master the mass of regulations governing their constantly changing rights and privileges. Within security limits, these specialists are informed in advance about military missions, so that they can act as informal grapevines to wives in regard to the arrivals and departures of their husbands. In addition to the long-standing services provided by the commissary and post exchange, the military community organizes infant nurseries, teen-age clubs, and a variety of recreational and educational activities. The chaplain has been augmented by the psychiatrist and the mental hygienist, and the military doctor seeks to substitute for the family doctor, despite the objections of the American Medical Association.[14]

Social services also include assistance in mate selection. At one time, the Air Force required men on duty in Great Britain to get their commanding officer's consent for marriage. With the marriage rate at three thousand per year in 1958, written consent was given only after a security investigation of the fiancee's moral and political background. In order to eliminate prostitutes, criminals, and subversives, a medical checkup and a confidential pre-marriage interview by a chaplain were required to select out incompatibles and to prevent marriages based on unreasonably coerced decisions.

The belief persists in the military, especially in the Air Force, that the wife has a role in assisting her husband's career and his military mission. However, there is a large gap between ideology and reality, for the wife sees few practical measures by which she can assist her husband. In an interview, one Air Force wife presented her perspective:

When they are in England, his letters—or the lack of them—tell me more than he realizes. But again, how am I to help? So many of the problems which the men face seem to be due to SAC policies and practices over which only the top command has control. We wives may be only women but we do see some of the outcome when competition is the keynote in all of the work relationships.[15]

Even the marginal role of the wives of top leaders as informal communication links has been reduced. The military establishment is too large and too fluid, and the principles of administration of efficient military management are too well developed for women to write effective letters to the Secretary of War about misplaced junior officers.

Instead, the main task of the service wife is to manage the details of family life, which, despite the facilities of the military community, can become a burdensome task. The logistics of family life in an operational command involve endless readjustments to new environments, and uncertainties which fall heavily on the wife. While her husband may find satisfaction, and even "adventure," in his official duties, her reaction may involve a mixture of resentment and boredom with the constant routine of family life. In fact, some military wives, especially those whose husbands entered with careerist motives, seem detached from the professional content of their husbands' lives. Instead of any real understanding, a "disaster" psychology often operates which leads them to feelings of apathy or hostility.

The breakdown of the isolation of the military community also means that the officer's wife has increased opportunity for comparing her lot with that of civilian professional families. Yet, the ability of the military family to transmit military tradition depends on a belief in the profession, rather than on a comparison with civilian standards of living. Informal interviews with wives of officers who were attending service war colleges, and who therefore had the greatest career potentials, produced highly uniform responses to the question of whether they wanted their sons to be officers. In contrast to their husbands,* the wives were vague and highly tentative. Most thought an academy education would be desirable only because it provides a superior education, and they left unstated that it was at government expense. Beyond that, few felt strongly positive about the prospect.

Strains within the military community are reflected in the extent to which deviant personal behavior comes to the attention of civilian society. Deviant behavior kept within the military community is more readily tolerable. War inevitably produces a lowering of standards of personal behavior among civilians and soldiers, which can be tolerated as a temporary relapse. However, in the cold war conspicuous and persistent deviant social behavior undermines the profession. One indication, although no doubt an extreme one, is the report by five social scientists on "Behavior Standards in the United States Air Force in Europe," completed in 1952.[16] Overseas assignments, especially where prolonged separation from family was involved, had produced such extensive deviant behavior in the Air Force that military authorities no longer hid the facts, but rather sought assistance from civilian "experts." These civilians were charged with examining the "nature, extent and cause of changes in behavior standards that take place in Air Force personnel assigned to overseas service."

* See Chapter 6, Career Motivation:

The social scientists found that certain varieties of black-market activities were widespread among Air Force personnel, but only black-marketing in currency was viewed as morally wrong. Drinking was reported to be extensive for all ranks in the officer corps, and was a standard way of spending one's free time, although alcoholism was infrequent. While the study group was unable to carry on any extensive sampling, their results showed extremely widespread extramarital sex relations among officers after they arrived overseas. At the root of these behavior patterns was the fact that, for the bulk of the officers, residence abroad meant no, or few, meaningful contacts outside the military community.

Black-marketing was eliminated by economic recovery in Europe and the imposition of tighter currency controls by military authorities. The end of separation from family ties, or the return of the officer to the United States, usually decreased deviant social behavior to more acceptable levels. Moreover, the greater his commitment to the profession—graduation from a service academy or permanent military status—the less likely was the officer to deviate from acceptable standards. By 1955, public concern with the standards of military personnel had diminished, and the issue remained one of professional self-regulation.

In fact, to some extent, standards of personal behavior in the military profession have tightened. When the military mission is to deter enemy aggression, and the officer is responsible for managing highly destructive weapons, the personal image of the professional soldier must be a responsible and socially proper one. The availability of the professional soldier for leadership both inside and outside the military establishment centers on the concept of the soldier as a dedicated public servant, free from personal corruption. Personal misconduct in allied nations becomes a political liability. Thus, the pressure for proper personal behavior has increased during a period in which the style of life of the military community is under increased stress.

There is every reason to believe that some of the strains in the military community are transitional. As the establishment becomes more and more automated, life will become more tolerable and regularized. As the military becomes more mobile, the air-borne officer will find his life more closely tied to home base, and, as in the Navy, his tours of duty more regularized. Moreover, the profession has its system of military protocol, etiquette, and honor, which are as essential for its stability and traditions as are its family relations and standard of living.

Notes

1. Shea, Nancy, *The Army Wife*. New York: Harper & Bros., 1954, xi.
2. H. H. Arnold reports that after World War I the rivalry between the Air Corps and the regular Army even extended to boyhood fights among the officers' children. But there were fights between the sons of the officers of Company A and Company B as well. (*Global Mission*. New York: Harper & Bros., 1949, p. 122.)
3. An interesting note on social stratification in the military community is the fact that, as in civilian society, a given family may find itself spread across class lines. For example, of his eight surviving children by his first wife, one of General Claire Chennault's sons became a colonel, another a major, and a third a master sergeant.
4. Davidson, General Garrison H., *Report on Graduate Questionnaire*. U.S. Military Academy, July 1, 1958, p. 26.
5. Department of Commerce, *Survey of Current Business*, National Income Supplement. Washington: 1951, Table 26, p. 184.
6. Report by McKinsey & Co., September 17, 1956.
7. Advisory Commission on Service Pay, *Career Compensation for the Uniformed Forces*. Washington: December 1948.
8. Clark, Maurine, *Captain's Bride, General's Lady*. New York: McGraw-Hill, 1956, p. 215.
9. The automobile becomes a particularly important symbol of status. Like members of a minority group who are deprived of a permanent residence as a sign of conspicuous consumption, the military family reaches for a more prestigeful car.
10. Clark, Maurine, *op. cit.*, p. 33.
11. Mott, Colonel T. Bentley, *Twenty Years as a Military Attache*. New York: Oxford University Press, 1937, p. 46.
12. See, for example, Banning, Kendall, *West Point Today*. New York: Funk and Wagnalls, 1937, Chap. X, "What Every Femme Should Know."
13. Lindquist, Ruth, "Marriage and Family Life of Officers and Air Men in a Strategic Air Command Wing," Technical Report Number 5, Air Force Base Project. University of North Carolina: Institute for Research in Social Science, October 1952.
14. Burchard, Waldo, "Role Conflicts of Military Chaplains." *American Sociological Review*, 1954, 19, 528–35.
15. Lindquist, Ruth, *op. cit.*, p. 19.
16. Maccoby, Nathan, *et. al.*, *Behavior Standards in USAFE Personnel*, Report No. Hr-18, Maxwell Air Force Base. Human Resources Research Institute, August 1952.

CHAPTER *10*

Etiquette and Ceremony

PARALLEL to the detailed operating procedures of the military establishment are the elaborate rules of etiquette and ceremony which govern personal relations. In both cases there is, of course, a gap between prescribed rules and actual practice, but in both cases the prescribed rules supply a frame for molding social behavior. The military are energetic socializers, and they work hard at their ceremonial obligations. No other occupation, with the exception of professional diplomacy, is so concerned with courtesy and protocol. "Old fashioned" politeness and formal manners survive, although they have been adapted to the realities of modern organizational life.

Men who must work and live in the closest physical proximity become concerned with their comrades' personal habits. The concepts of honor and of martial spirit are grounded in rituals of colleagueship. These rituals are but one of the devices of a profession which must control its anxiety due to its concern with death. The fact that these specialists in violence are so concerned with etiquette is a paradox, explainable only in that the elaborate forms of personal intercourse are designed to hide harsh realities, as well as boredom from endless routine. The stability of the military profession cannot be understood without reference to the importance of protocol. The self-conception that the military profession is "special," implanted in cadets by the service academies, is kept alive by these forms of etiquette and ceremony. If the military profession is unique because of its focus on violence, protocol must operate to reinforce professional self-concepts.

Since each officer is a member of a single organization, all contacts—official and social—are likely to repeat themselves. Without deliberate purpose, no officer can afford to offend, or even reject, contacts with other officers, especially those of equal or higher rank. Intimate contacts and wide friendships with one's colleagues are the building blocks of a successful career in any profession. But in the military the potential circle of contacts is immense, and the rules of social intercourse are well defined. The officer and his wife must have the ability to go far enough without going too far. One observer has commented, "A man should be able to tell a good story, but he should not be a notorious braggart; a man should be able to drink a lot, but he should not be an alcoholic; it is good to be well educated, but not to show off your education."

The civilian image of the military man as a loud mouth who uses foul language is outmoded, especially in regard to the potential member of the military elite. It may still be appropriate to swear— in fact, necessary—but the officer must know when it is not permissible. Most members of the military elite, including those with highly atypical careers, seem always to function within the framework of military protocol. In fact, many of them conform closely to the social code in order to achieve greater professional freedom.

In the past, sociability was facilitated by the small size of the military establishment and by the narrow base of officer recruitment. However, the organizational revolution has weakened the system of military courtesy. The old-timers and the dedicated decry the decline in etiquette and protocol, and readily express their annoyance with those who are more detached. In 1956 Major Mark M. Boatner, the son of a regular Army officer with an appropriate "landed" residency, "Penrith Plantation, Jackson, Louisiana," issued a volume, codifying military customs and ceremony. His introduction reflected a defensive posture:

You might expect a professional soldier to start a book like this with a long blast on the importance of military customs and traditions. I will refrain. Not because I don't feel strongly about it, but because the effort would probably be wasted.[1]

Yet, during the last half century the details of protocol have remained strikingly stable. A comparison of the contents of portions of the *Officers Manual* published in 1906 by Lieutenant Colonel James A. Moss with its contemporary counterparts reveals more persistence than modification.[2] In fact, the proportionate number of pages devoted to social customs, protocol, and ceremony has increased. On the basis of memoirs and expert opinion, the changes that have occurred have, for the most part, mainly reduced the number of formal occasions. Opportunity for the officer to evade and escape social obligations has increased, but the patterns of etiquette and ceremony remain relatively intact.

It is, of course, difficult to assess the cost in loss of creative personnel who dislike such etiquette, or to infer the impact of such practices on intellectual processes. For those who survive the acculturation of service academies, military protocol comes to be taken for granted. In the West Point investigation of officers who resigned, "dislike for military social structure and interpersonal relations," did not figure as a central reason. Only 2.0 per cent gave it as the most important reason; 11.5 per cent gave it as the second or third most important reason.[3] These data underline that other dissatisfactions with military life were of more consequence in motivating officers to resign.

The effectiveness of military etiquette and protocol is enhanced because the ceremonial functions of the military are valued by civilians, even in a democratic society. The professional soldier has a double public image. Despite the relatively low prestige that the military profession has for civilians, conspicuous display of the military uniform has its civilian audience. In a world in which rationality and efficiency seem to have triumphed, uniformed officers are important ceremonial appurtenances. Sociability and manners make them effective participants in the nation's diplomatic life and at overseas missions. The attendance of soldiers and officers are required more and more at public ceremonies and national displays. In recent years they have formed the largest element of the presidential inauguration parade, and are also present at the installation of state governors.[4] The military is aware of the importance of this role and is, in fact, prepared to enhance it. The return of the formal-dress uniform in all services, and the authorization of the dress sword for the naval officer, serve to increase the ceremonial usefulness of the profession.

Prescribed Sociability

TRADITIONS and ceremonials vary in form and detail among the services. Naval practices are the most formal, partly because life aboard ship is more compatible with such formality than is service in the field. The Navy has the highest concentration of officers who are academy graduates, and training in social behavior has been particularly strong at Annapolis. The importance of the ceremonial function of the military officer is well argued by Leland P. Lovette, a naval officer:

The matter of poise, bearing, address, dancing, formal ballroom etiquette, formal dinners, receptions and after-dinner speaking, all come within the scope of training the midshipman, because the professional life of the officer is occupied with considerable formality. It is well and good to speak of endeavoring to make most affairs informal, but presidents and sovereigns, ambassadors and high clerics, yes, generals and admirals do not prefer delicious informality. It is not a case in the Navy of what one wants to do; it is a case of conforming to good usage. The midshipman is taught early to learn the best usage, for aside from the diplomatic corps, he will meet in his career more foreign notables than any other class of government officials.[5]

Contrary to public image, the Air Force is highly sensitive about military customs and has fashioned its practices after Army traditions. As the newest service, and in its own image the most important one, it displays all of the concern and rigidity of the newly arrived. The personal code is less formal, but all the outer trappings of protocol operate.

In all three services etiquette and ceremony are organized around two basic themes. First, the code is designed to fuse the official and the private sphere, since such fusion is a basic feature of professional military life. In fusing the officer's official and private roles, obviously and explicitly, the military social code gives higher priority to the official role. Simultaneously, official contacts with fellow officers and with outsiders are not limited merely to the professional task at hand, but tend to be transformed into personal intercourse. It is as though all professional contacts in civilian life had to be enlarged into social contacts. When one is stationed aboard ship, or at an isolated military post, there is no alternative; but the code is applied throughout the military establishment. In specific detail, protocol covers the required courtesy to be extended between members of the military elite, as well as to outside political and foreign "dignitaries." The system extends all the way down the hierarchy.

Second, the code is designed to instruct the officer and his wife in the appropriate behavior for every phase of the life cycle, from engagement to burial. Custom guides the use of swords at a military marriage, the patterns of visiting, and the ceremonies of retirement, although in the expanded military establishment only the very top echelon receives the privileges of full protocol. Such rules make available arrangements for avoiding personal embarrassment. But the protocol of social behavior has a deeper significance, for it is designed to prevent the undue display of impulse or emotion.

In Army circles, when death occurs, there is no outward display of mourning except in the observance of the military customs of the service. There are no drawn shades, crepe-hung doors, muffled bells, or hushed voices, despite the deep sorrow of the family of the deceased.[6]

Some of the forms are carry-overs from old-fashioned "high society," after which the military sought to model itself. Other forms seem to be advance models of social life in the modern corporation concerned with the loyalty of its personnel; they are perpetuated, in part, to protect the military from the discomforts and frustrations ·of continuous residential mobility. To have lived in twenty different posts and stations in the course of a lifetime means to be apart from the rest of society. The web of social relations that military etiquette produces not only binds its members together, but acts as a filter through which the outer world is perceived.

Social relations within the military establishment operate on the assumption that once an officer is admitted into the system, he is assured of essential acceptance. The essence of the social code is not its exclusiveness, but rather its pervasiveness. At the highest levels, social exclusiveness begins to operate as much on the basis of personal characteristics as on social background. While excessive "shop talk" is considered to be in bad taste, the professional milieu dominates every form of social intercourse—formal entertainment, social calling, life in the officers' club, even friendship. The private life of an officer, including a member of the military elite, is no more or less hedonistic than that of his civilian counterpart. But the social code which regulates his private life is not based on the conspicuous display of "fun morality," which characterizes the "gracious living" of the upper and middle reaches in civilian society. It is rather an almost archaic concern with the persistence of manners; and the higher the station in the military hierarchy, the greater the importance of manners.

At the center of military protocol are such devices as the formal reception, designed to perpetuate the impression that all officers are in intimate contact and members of a fraternity. Katherine Tupper Marshall, the wife of General George Marshall, in her autobiographical sketch, presents a revealing portrait of these social arrangements.[7] When she married Colonel Marshall, a reception was given by General and Mrs. Campbell King on the lawn of the commanding general's quarters at Fort Benning. In preparation, she was thoroughly briefed by her husband as to his special friends, to whom he wished that she "show particular attention when they came down the receiving line." There were, first, the officers who had served with him in China and their wives; another group consisting of the Infantry School instructors and their wives; then, his daily riding companions; his older Army friends; and the like. When the list was expanded to include all those who had sent her flowers, the new bride was aghast, until Marshall informed her of the system:

"It will be quite easy," he assured me, "for I will be on your left and General King on your right. As they pass down the receiving line, he will give you their names and I will say 'China,' or 'flower' for example. All you will have to say is, 'You served with Colonel Marshall in China, didn't you?' or 'Thank you for your lovely flowers.' It will be most flattering to them."[8]

Mrs. Marshall recalls that she did very well for the first five hundred or so, but after that "the smile began to freeze on my face." General Marshall had a powerful memory, especially for names and faces; in many military families the roles were reversed, with the wife being responsible for the details of social protocol.

Another conspicuous pattern of social obligation in military life was the system of calling. In the old Army transfer to a new post required the new arrival, together with his wife, to call upon his commanding officer. In turn, members of the post called on the new officer and his family. During World War II calling was suspended, and subsequent Army regulations gave the local commander discretion in requiring these forms. But the trend in the Army is toward a revival of these practices, and the military manuals outline in detail the tactics of calling: the hours at which to make calls, the method for keeping a list of callers, the time limit for returning calls, and the firms that are best equipped to supply properly engraved cards—Tiffany in New York, and Bailey, Banks, and Biddle in Philadelphia. The transfers of Air Force personnel are so extensive that calling has never been effectively revived, but officers must still inquire as to the commanding officer's desires and practices.

The officers' club is the locus of a continuously organized social life. Protocol is oriented to the endless task of introducing new personnel, since the military establishment is now so large and so mobile that nothing can be left to chance. The instructions set forth in *The Army Wife* on how to introduce people at parties demonstrate some of the necessities, if the forms of social intimacy are to be kept alive in a vast bureaucracy:

Another snag in the introductions crops up when an Army man has taken a new wife. This can be particularly startling in a receiving line. Mentally, you wonder if Mary died, if they were divorced, or just what the score is. Socially, both men and women should take care to mention their current spouses early in the conversation, just to set the other fellow straight. This would avoid a lot of mental gymnastics.[9]

Nor is it absurd to include rules for handshaking, since it cannot be taken for granted that all men who are officers and who aspire to top commands, or their wives, have been adequately exposed to the proper forms:

When one shakes hands, it should be done with warmth and friendliness. A limp hand suggestive of a clammy fish is irritating. However, no one enjoys a bone-crusher. Shake hands as though it were a pleasure but not as though you were a drowning man going under for the third time.[10]

Life in a "company town" demands that all possible sources of dissensus be repressed. The conspicuous display of worldly goods,

beyond that suitable for one's status and rank, is particularly
frowned upon.

After gay talk at cocktails, we moved into the dining room and if the
roof had caved in I couldn't have felt worse. The voice of a colonel's
lady, speaking to another woman, floated through the room loud and
clear with the terrible words: "What a vulgar display of silver for a
junior officer."[11]

Religious practices are fashioned to serve the military community. Every person is assumed to have a religious affiliation. But
differences in denomination among Protestants, and between Protestants and Catholics, are de-emphasized, for the military community prefers a nondenominational military church. The mechanics
of the military establishment make it difficult for every Protestant
faction to be adequately supported at public expense. But more
important, religion, just as the social code, must serve professional
solidarity. The drift toward a unified Protestant military church has
produced outspoken opposition by fundamentalist and conservative
groups, some of whom are particularly antagonistic to the use of
the unified doctrinal and religious educational material which the
armed forces have produced.[12]

The increased presence of the Negro in the military community
puts the social code to its utmost test. Occasionally, a Negro enters
the military elite. As tactical officers in the ground forces and as
flying personnel in the Air Force, they rise regularly to the rank
of field grade officer, and military etiquette requires their acceptance into the social fabric. The military community is truly as un-
segregated a society as human beings have been able to create by
decree. The facilities of the military community, including all
social arrangements, are fully available to Negroes. In this respect,
the military is ahead of civilian society. However, the student of
race relations will observe that military etiquette makes it easier
to assimilate the Negro as an officer. Personal prejudice persists
under the rationalization that Negroes are not judged by the same
standards as whites: they get away with "murder." Yet, the system
works, because the Negro officer in turn has committed himself to
accept the system of protocol.[13]

Patterns of friendship are equally dominated by the military
style of life. Many contacts involve no more than surface intimacy,
since physical proximity and availability are determining factors in

the patterns of friendship. In the mobile military community, friendship cliques develop on the basis of prior civilian geographical ties. Even the distinction between rebels and Yankees (the rest of the nation) still operates as an informal basis for inclusion and exclusion.[14] At the same time, each officer has a small circle of acquaintances with whom he remains on intimate terms throughout his entire career. Such friendships result from having attended a particular school, or having participated in certain command or staff assignments together.

By the time the officer reaches the rank of general officer or admiral, he has made lasting friendships of deepest intimacy, for without them there is no real integration into the military profession. Upward social mobility into any elite position requires a careful shedding of older friends. However, in the military profession, as the officer moves up the hierarchy, personal friends continue as part of the informal selection system, as trusted advisors or as potential staff subordinates. As described later in this volume, friendships and personal alliances, born of organizational accident, develop into groups which express strategic and political points of view.*

Social Integration

IF THE MILITARY STYLE of life strives to produce an internally cohesive community, at the same time, it thwarts social integration with civilian society. Despite its increased size, and its elaborate organizational alliances with other civilian leadership groups, the military profession and its elite members are not effectively integrated, on a social basis, with other leadership groups.** There is little evidence to support the argument that the military forms an integral part of a compact social group which constitutes the power elite. Rather, in fact, the contrary seems to be the case: namely, the political behavior of the military in the United States is still deeply conditioned by its social isolation. Much of the "public relations" efforts of the military have been an effort to gain social access

* See Chapter 14, Coalition Warfare.
** See Chapter 18, Civilian Alliances, for an analysis of the political links of the military with other leadership groups.

to other, newer elites, particularly to scientific and academic circles.

The elite in the United States comprise highly diffuse social elements because of the sheer size of the nation, regional differences, ethnic and religious heterogeneity, and the rapidity of mobility into leadership positions. It is a much less integrated social grouping than, for example, "the establishment" in Great Britain, with its elaborate family ties, common education, and intimate patterns of social intercourse. There is no evidence that military leadership since 1900 has become more socially integrated with other elite groups. The broadening social composition of the officer corps, its separate educational system, the military style of life, and the growth in the size of the armed forces limit social integration of the military with older and even newer elite groups.

At the turn of the century, however, those social contacts that did operate seemed extensive enough to give the small military elite a sense of direct contact with the "upper strata." Even though such contacts were highly ritualistic and protocol-based, they helped to fix the position of top-ranking Army and Navy officers in the social structure, and even conditioned their self-conceptions. Thus, the aide-de-camp to General Wesley Merritt in the 1890's described the general's social contacts when his headquarters were in Chicago as follows:

We had rooms at the Auditorium Annex and we took our meals at the Chicago Club. The famous Round Table was then in full swing there and every day at luncheon one would see gathered about its ample bosom, Marshall Field, George Pullman, Peter Palmer, John Clark, Robert Lincoln, and all the rest. They were together for years, but nearly every one of them continued to address the other as "Mister"—Mr. Pullman, Mr. Palmer, Mr. Lincoln. Of course, Merritt was always "General."[15]

When General Merritt was transferred to Governors Island, his circle of contacts included "the Sloanes, the J. P. Morgans, and the Hamilton Fishes."

Since the Air Force has become the most representative of civilian social structure, Air Force commanders at their operational bases present prototypes of the social position of the new military manager. The military air base has its own form of social isolation, equivalent to the Army post and the naval station of inter-war years. Social isolation results from the constant turnover of personnel, from the limited range of contacts military leaders have with the surrounding communities, from the inbred patterns of leisure, and from the absence of suitable means for access to local and regional elite groups.

The constant turnover of personnel means that all levels of personnel, including those at the very top, have little opportunity to develop stable contacts off the base. Air installations are often remote from urban centers, and the trend is toward greater decentralization. Wherever the air base is located, military personnel are viewed by local business interests as "fair game." The time has long passed since Congress found it necessary to pass a law,* imposing a $500 fine on commercial establishments which posted notices stating, "No Soldiers Admitted," or which refused to cater to military personnel.[16] The purchasing power of the military community is too large and too important. Nevertheless, as one sociological investigation of relations between local communities and air bases reveals, the military community remains a kind of foreign settlement, and relations are uneasy and even exploitative in such matters as housing.[17]

The search for opportunities to educate their children provides military personnel with one of their major contacts with the life of the surrounding community, especially those personnel who live off the base. As with officials in large corporations who move into new communities, the needs and aspirations of the children draw the parents into community affairs. But even such contacts as these are limited, since military personnel move on. They seldom become officers in local Parent-Teacher Associations and they almost never run for positions on the local school board. Moreover, the top Air Force commanders in the field do not even have these contacts, since their children are likely to have graduated from public school and gone off to college. Air Force wives are denied, because of their "rootlessness," access to women's clubs of any social status. Instead, the Air Force relies on its own resources and has its officers' wives club. The general's wife is normally the honorary president, and the function of the club is to supply relaxation from the tedium and tension of military life.

Even leisure-time activities and sports fail to supply linkages between the air base and the local elite. In the old Army, polo and

*Act of March 1, 1911, chapter 187, 36 Stat. 963–964.

horseback riding were an important bridge; yachting and boating still play an important role in outside contacts in the Navy. General Curtis LeMay has a sports car, and auto racing carries some prestige in the Air Force. But sports car racing leads nowhere socially, except to the local automobile dealer, who, in fact, very often participates in the social life of the air base. Air Force social circles have spread out into the entertainment and mass communications industry, if only because the Air Force is public relations conscious. But, in the main, the Air Force must rely on its Army and Navy connections for access to upper socialite circles.

In the end, the social role of a commanding general in the surrounding community is even more detached than that of a branch manager of a national corporation, and no more prestigeful. Personal contacts with the local and regional elite are limited to speech-making before businessmen's lunch clubs and "public relations" participation in Armed Forces Day demonstrations. The bulk of day-to-day community contacts falls on staff officers, and is likely to be organized along managerial lines.

A case study of a typical Air Force base located in a southern state is presented by Floyd Hunter in an article which documents the lack of social integration of the military elite with the community and regional upper class, even in the South.[18] The military commander must be prepared to work out an accommodation with the adjoining community, as exemplified by his account:

When we first got to Plain City, all the local people were interested in was the money they'd get out of the Air Force. We put on a conscious campaign to get Plain City on the ball. We had several staff officers join each of the civic clubs. We used psychology on them, kept telling them what a wonderful reception they were giving the men—all the dances, parties, and so on, to keep the boys off the street—while actually they were doing nothing. This made them wonder who was doing all this and they got busy themselves. Now they have dances at the club for officers and a club for enlisted men in town. Police, instead of throwing men in the jug, now call up the base and say "come and get him." The police try to soft pedal the behavior of military personnel and say they "really aren't bad."[19]

But a persistent social barrier exists between the military and the prestige groups in the community. Occasionally, in Plain City, the wife of a high-ranking Air Force officer was asked to serve on the board of a social agency which had a military-oriented program.

The military command was sometimes used to "flavor" some of the social functions, but this does not necessarily mean they were fully accepted. On the contrary, there is a distinct tone of "good service" in these invitations:

Last year Mrs. Smith was entertaining some of the debutantes in her home. It was decided that it might be nice to have a few men in uniform attend the party. Mrs. Smith called Mrs. Green and told her that if she would have the General round up some of the lonesome and loose second lieutenants, they would be glad to have them at the party. General Green lined up six young officers and sent them to the party.[20]

None of the military professionals from the base belonged to the exclusive local clubs. Mrs. Jane J. Manly, a member of an old family in Plain City, described the situation as follows: "The military tend to remain pretty much to themselves and the townspeople do the same." In fact, in Plain City, despite its strong southern traditions, marriage to an officer in the Air Force is not considered as socially desirable an opportunity as marriage to an Army or Navy officer was considered to be in the past. The Air Force is large, and its officers come from all strata, so that it is not thought to be a "select organization."

If the Air Force general is assigned to a major technical installation in a large metropolitan center, however, he is likely to find that his job generates more civilian contacts, and that these afford a wider range of social contacts. But since his tenure is limited and his social position doubtful, he seldom develops any sense of real involvement, although he may in fact be expanding his roster of useful civilian contacts for obtaining a post-retirement position.

Army generals and admirals continue to have somewhat more extensive social roots in civilian society. Professional routines in the Army, and especially in the Navy, are more regularized than they are in the Air Force, although the differences can easily be overstated. The same broadening of the base of recruitment, the same pattern of constant job rotation, and the same emphasis on military community life operate to separate the Army and Navy elite from civilian leadership groups. The basic difference lies in the fact that residues of older traditions and patterns of family and personal connections continue to give members of the Army and Navy elite limited access to the socialite groups and to families of inherited wealth. The older aristocratic upper class, based on in-

herited wealth, has been noted to persist most extensively in economically declining cities, specifically Boston, Charleston, and to a
lesser extent, Philadelphia. These are the centers of those naval
installations where traditional patterns of social contact between the
Navy and the older upper-class families persist. The same is true
for a few of the older Army posts located in the South and in the
Washington area. These social contacts were once very important,
and they continue to operate with some consequence.

If the *Social Register* is taken as an indicator of integration with
aristocratic families, the military is at best peripheral. This index
demonstrates most sharply the different social position of the military in the United States, as compared with Germany, France, and
even Great Britain. For 1951, in New York, Boston, and Chicago,
the number of military officers listed in the *Social Register* is less
than 1 per cent. In Philadelphia and San Francisco the percentage
is between 1 and 2. Just as first-generation accumulation of wealth
is no basis for listing in the *Social Register*, professional military
achievement is insufficient by itself. This is demonstrated by the
fact that there is no emphasis on higher rank in the *Social Register*.
Instead, social pedigree—inheritance and social connections—is
essential. The link between the military and the socialite elite is
mainly centered in Washington, where 10 per cent of the names in
the *Social Register* have professional military affiliations.

As might be expected, Navy personnel outnumbered Army professionals in the *Social Register* of five of the six metropolitan
centers examined, including Washington, the exception being New
York. Moreover, the percentages for 1920 and for 1951 for all the
cities, except Washington, have been relatively stable. Thus, while
the size of the military establishment and its elite has grown many
fold, its involvement in the established socialite circles has not increased. Only in Washington has the percentage increased from 1.4
in 1920 to 9.9 per cent in 1951.

If the military leaders were an integral social part of a power
elite based on inherited wealth, the extensive intermarriage between their sons and daughters and the children of top businessmen and outstanding governmental and political leaders could be
expected. Such a web is rare indeed, and the pattern of social
recruitment makes a trend in this direction unlikely, or at least
very slow to develop. As an exception, one could point to Vice

Admiral William Glassford, 2d, who served as commander of the naval forces in the southwest Pacific in 1942. Glassford was a well-connected admiral who acted as President Franklin D. Roosevelt's personal representative at Dakar in 1943, when a "conservative" naval type was needed to contact the French. After his retirement, he became the European manager of the Radio Corporation of America, with headquarters in London. His daughter married Jacob Beam, the career ambassador to Poland, while his brother, Pelham D. Glassford, rose to be an Army officer of general rank. The more typical pattern is marriage into another service family or into another professional family, for the military are like "second cousins" to the established upper-class socialite families.

Service in Washington involves the military leader in the civilian social structure more conspicuously, mainly by means of formal protocol. The mechanisms of protocol do not insure social integration; in fact, they are designed to substitute for it. Yet, the Washington community does serve to bridge the social gap between various elite groups and the military. Many military officers retire in Washington or its suburbs, or have taken civilian assignments there, and they act as social expediters for officers who have more limited assignments in the area. Moreover, Washington socialite circles have a stronger interest in ranking governmental officials and assimilate military personnel more readily into their ranks.

Officers' manuals hold out the attraction of the Washington social "whirl," yet warn against its dangers:

Washington is an area of very considerable social activity. You can embroil yourself in social events to the point of exhaustion. Restrain the inclination to enjoy the multitude of entertainments available to you in the Washington area.[21]

At best, these arrangements can be said to maintain an elaborate pattern of entertainment, but they do not necessarily integrate the military into the "upper class." In the United States upper-class gentility is based on inherited wealth and not on public service alone, and the military profession is no road to wealth. Given the fact that the military are educated in service academies, their assimilation into the strata of inherited wealth is difficult. While the service academies do assist in upward social mobility, this mobility seldom extends to the top moneyed elite.

Nevertheless, the military profession, especially at the upper levels of its hierarchy, does perpetuate a leadership tradition. The source of this elite self-conception is grounded in military honor and re-enforced by military etiquette and the milieu of the military community. In particular, the distinctive quality of the military life makes it possible to perpetuate the martial spirit. To survive, the martial spirit must be taken for granted, and not constantly subjected to critical evaluation.

But the military establishment requires a balance between heroic leaders and military managers. Although both of these roles are performed in the same institution, or, for that matter, by a single person, there is an important element of antagonism between them. The military manager requires a sense of cosmopolitanism and detachment which is inhibited by the style of life in the military community. The forms of military social life, plus the social origins of the profession, make the development of a cosmopolitan outlook difficult. One who is well traveled is not necessarily cosmopolitan. Where cosmopolitanism does develop in the military, it results from educational experiences and conscious personal effort rather than from the social life or protocol of the military community.

Notes

1. Boatner, Mark M., *Military Customs and Traditions*. New York: David McKay, 1956.

2. Moss, James A., *Officers Manual*. Springfield: F. A. Bassette Co., 1906.

3. Davidson, General Garrison H., *Report on Graduate Questionnaire*. U.S. Military Academy, July 1, 1958, p. 26.

4. At the inauguration of Governor Nelson A. Rockefeller of New York on January 1, 1959, in addition to a professional military escort, "three ornate military units right out of a Viennese operetta—the Veterans Corps of Artillery and the Old Guard from New York and the Citizens Guard of Troy—made their entrance, complete with scarlet tunics and fur hat." *New York Times*, January 2, 1959.

5. Lovette, Leland P., *School of the Sea; The Annapolis Tradition in American Life*. New York: Frederick A. Stokes, 1941, p. 189.

6. Shea, Nancy, *The Army Wife*. New York: Harper & Bros., 1954, p. 319.

7. Marshall, Katherine Tupper, *Together, Annals of an Army Wife*. New York: Tupper & Love, 1946.

8. *Ibid.*, p. 6.

9. Shea, Nancy, *op. cit.*, p. 175.

10. *Ibid.*, p. 175.

11. Clark, Maurine, *Captain's Bride, General's Lady*. New York: McGraw-Hill, 1956, p. 35.

12. Reverend Engebret O. Midboe, a leading Lutheran authority on the military chaplaincy, has claimed the rise of a unique nondenominational "military church" in the United States armed forces. The "service church" reflects few of the doctrinal characteristics of those individual denominations which supply military chaplains. While he accused no one of fostering a break between the chaplains and their home churches, he pointed out that "it is rather a general drift away from the denominational mooring into a type of religious community which seems to operate with the least tensions in the military service." Until 1952, a military chaplain had to have a re-endorsement by his denomination each year in order to continue to serve in the armed forces. Under a revised system, once he is approved by his de-nomination as a chaplain, he may continue to serve until military retirement. Reverend Midboe has pointed out that the hymnal used in armed services is on a nondenominational basis, that the materials used in Sunday School, prepared under the Joint Chaplain Board, are almost required, and that chaplains who deviate from the "fairly well defined worship format" of a "general Protestant program risk administrative consequences and criticisms."

13. Given human nature, one would expect some subtle limitations on desegregation practices to persist. There is complete intermingling in the mess halls, in sports events, and in the social life of the officers' club. Etiquette requires that Negro officers do not dance with the wives of white officers, and vice versa. Personal rejection is thereby avoided, and the system acknowledges that professional solidarity does not eliminate all personal preferences.

14. Simpson, Richard F., *Friendship Cliques in the United States Air Force Wings*, Technical Report Number 3, Air Force Base Project. University of North Carolina: Institute for Research in Social Sciences, undated.

15. Mott, Colonel T. Bentley, *Twenty Years as a Military Attache*. New York: Oxford University Press, 1937, p. 50.

16. Ganoe, William, *The History of the United States Army*. New York: Appleton-Century, 1936, p. 438.

17. Barth, Ernest A. T., "A Typological Analysis of Ten Air Force Bases—Host Community Situations." Unpublished doctoral dissertation, University of North Carolina, 1955.

18. Hunter, Floyd, "Host Community and Air Force Base," Air Force Base Project. University of North Carolina: Institute for Research in Social Sciences, November 1952. While Hunter's generalizations about community power structure tend to be misleading, his observations about patterns of social interaction are probably reliable.

19. *Ibid.*, p. 37.

20. *Ibid.*

21. *The Air Officers Guide*, 1953 edition, p. 182.

IDENTITY AND IDEOLOGY:

THE PUBLIC SERVICE TRADITION

CHAPTER *11*

Military Honor Redefined

THE PROFESSIONAL BEHAVIOR of the military has profound political consequences. But, traditionally, officers have not fought primarily because of an explicit political ideology. On the contrary, the political interests of the typical officer have been intermittent at best. Only at the higher ranks and among its elite members is there a more sustained concern with the political purposes of the military establishment. "Honor" is the basis of its belief system.

Military honor is both a means and an end. The code of honor specifies how an officer ought to behave, but to be "honorable" is an objective to be achieved for its own right. When military honor is effective, its coercive power is considerable, since it persistently points to a single over-riding directive: The professional soldier always fights.

After the shock of the first successful Communist assaults in Korea had worn off, and military operations were stabilized, the United States *Army Combat Forces Journal* was able to repeat the military's essential definition of a professional soldier:

The Army can be proud that its regulars—whether three-year enlistees, reserve officers who volunteer for extended active duty, or the true professionals: the officers and non-commissioned officers who want no other life than army life—all fought and died as U.S. Regulars have always fought.[1]

In an age of skepticism such a dogmatic pronouncement—that regulars always fight—appears extremely old-fashioned. But the effectiveness of military honor operates precisely because it does not depend on elaborate moralistic justification.

Undoubtedly, military honor serves a variety of personal and social motives. For some, it is a rationalization for inertia; it permits others to operate somewhat beyond their personal capacities. However, the military profession is no different from other professions in that its performance is the result of the achievements of a small fraction of men. If the United States had better military leaders than it deserved in World War II, in view of its lack of interest and neglect of its military institution, military honor was responsible to a considerable degree.

Honor is supposed to be binding on the entire military profession. It is supposed to insure the unique characteristics of the officer, and to guarantee his career commitment. Yet, few military leaders are blind to the progressive inability of honor to resolve the strains within the profession. They are concerned that junior officers do not remain in the service long enough to assimilate the code. The broadening of the basis of social recruitment to include strata without service traditions, and the increased careerist motives of officer candidates, further weaken the importance of honor. The concept of military honor itself is subject to intense pressure by the values of contemporary society, and the services themselves engage in searching self-criticism over the "crisis":

There have been deviations from the code by individuals of high and low positions, in this and past periods, within the corps of officers. They have done much harm to their brother officers and the Army itself. Some have gained wide publicity, as the events are few and hence newsworthy. Others have been more minor. But as they have been more numerous, their cumulative effect has been large.[2]

The military forces of the United States had their origins in a revolutionary political movement—in an anti-colonial struggle. Yet, their code of honor derives from the aristocratic forms against which they struggled. Forms of officership and honor were transferred, if only because key officers in the Revolutionary forces had had direct contact with British military institutions, and there were no other directly available models.[3] At least four basic elements operated in the code derived from British aristocratic institutions, although these elements had to be adapted and modified to fit American conditions. Military honor meant, first, officers were gentlemen; second, fealty to the military commander was personal; third, officers were members of a cohesive brotherhood which claimed the right to extensive self-regulation; and fourth, officers fought for the preservation and enhancement of traditional glory.

Under feudalism, officers were gentlemen, not only because they came from aristocratic social backgrounds, but because they were concerned with the rules of chivalry. They hoped to keep the growing destructiveness of warfare in bounds, so that the pursuit of military honor would not become too costly and prohibitive. Personal fealty to immediate noble commanders, or to a royal head, was an expression of the personalized forms of authority that operated among the feudal nobility. Since impersonal bureaucracy had yet to take form, their oath of allegiance was to a person rather than to an office. The aristocratic officer corps was based on a sense of brotherhood and membership in a self-regulating fraternity. Alfred Vagts, in the *History of Militarism*, documents and analyzes the jealous group solidarity of the noblemen which helped make the officers' castes of European armies self-governing bodies, subject to their own traditions, dictates, and patterns of honor. The duel was a most dramatic index of the power of honor in solidifying the sense of brotherhood among aristocratic officers. By the time of the American Revolution, the aristocratic officer cadre was being systematically enlisted in the enhancement of national, rather than feudal, objectives. Nevertheless, the officer fought for glory as much as for concrete political objectives. He was both aware of the military history of his lineage and concerned with the beauty of his military uniform.

The Code of Honor

AFTER TWO CENTURIES, the United States officer corps has been transformed in the direction of a technical specialty, and military honor has had to be made compatible with skill and technical achievement despite the fact that honor is essentially ascriptive and traditional. Military honor has had to respond, likewise, to changes in the social values in the society at large.

In the modern scheme all four of the original components of military honor are still operative—gentlemanly conduct, personal fealty, self-regulating brotherhood, and the pursuit of glory. However, their individual importance has been altered, and their meaning has been modified. The three services vary in the degree to which they have moved away from traditional conceptions of aristocratic honor in military life. Traditional forms remain the most operative in the Navy, especially with regard to the struggle to maintain the gentleman concept. The almost exclusive reliance on Annapolis-trained personnel in the naval elite, its "upper class" self-image, its style of life, particularly aboard ship, and its greater detachment from political realities, all assist in the perpetuation of traditional military honor. The Army has been transformed by the problems of conducting large-scale land warfare, involving masses of civilian personnel, so that the gentleman concept has been strained. But the differences between the Army and Navy can easily be overstated; the sharper distinction is between the older services and the Air Force, where the concept of honor seems to rest heavily on the element of brotherhood.

1. *Gentlemanly Conduct.* The military in the United States have always been uneasy about the gentleman concept. The officer was originally formally defined as a gentleman; and in the earliest formulation of United States military law, the requirement that the officer be a gentleman in his personal conduct was explicitly stated.

Whatsoever commissioned officer shall be convicted, before a general courts martial, of behaving in a scandalous, infamous manner, such as is unbecoming the character of an officer and a gentleman, shall be discharged from the service.

From the heroic leader's point of view, the clearest indication of transformation of military honor is the reformulation of the gentleman concept in the 1951 Uniform Military Code of Justice, Article 133:

Any officer, cadet or midshipman who is convicted of conduct unbecoming an officer and a gentleman shall be punished as the courts martial may direct.

Conduct unbecoming a gentleman no longer automatically leads to dismissal, especially since it is so difficult to define such behavior. Thus, although the reformulation is more realistic, it represents a retreat from traditional dogma. The concept of a "gentleman" in the military setting is now derived from the responsibilities of the military manager as much as it is based on tradition. As of 1950, *The Armed Forces Officer* promulgated:

The military officer is considered a gentleman, not because Congress wills it, nor because it has been the custom of the people at all times to afford him that courtesy, but specifically because nothing less than a gentleman is truly suited for his particular set of responsibilities.[4]

Uneasiness about the gentleman concept has been linked to the decline in the importance of chivalry. The duel was never accepted, either by army or naval officers. The ever-increasing destructiveness of warfare made chivalry toward the enemy progressively less tenable, so that by the time of World War I, the theory of chivalry was relegated. The political objectives of totalitarian warfare shattered whatever illusions of chivalry remained, although the desert warfare carried out by the British against the Germans exemplified a unique historical hangover, and the Americans sought to make use of certain forms of chivalry in negotiating with the French officers in North Africa. The United States military establishment, however, developed a style of warfare which emphasized concern with the legalities of land warfare. The correct treatment of prisoners of war substituted for the heroic content of chivalry.

Of the aristocratic concept of gentlemanly conduct, there remains, besides the persistence of social manners, an enforced rejection of monetary pursuits as the highest personal value. Until the post-World War II inflation, the military profession was proudly arrogant in this respect. In 1895 Alfred Thayer Mahan wrote, of the advantages of a naval career, "In no event will there be money in it; but there may always be honor and quietness of mind and worthy occupation—which are better guarantees of happiness."[5]

By 1950, *The Armed Forces Officer* stated the case more defensively:

Indeed if love of money were the mainspring of all American action, the officer corps long since would have disintegrated.[6]

Despite the difficulties of adapting the gentleman concept to the American scene, it remains an essential part of military honor. As long as members of the military elite consider themselves to be special because they embody the martial spirit, it is indispensable that they consider themselves gentlemen.

2. *Personal Fealty.* Personal allegiance, as a component of honor, has had to be changed to fit the growth of bureaucratic organization. The American constitutional system, in order to insure civil supremacy, requires that the military swear allegiance to "support and defend the constitution." The organic law has transformed allegiance to a person to allegiance to a formal position—moreover, one filled by a civilian—the President, as Commander-in-Chief. Military officers make a point of their allegiance to the Commander-in-Chief, and this act embodies allegiance to a person as well as to an office. This image of personalized allegiance helps to make military honor compatible with civilian supremacy. An unanticipated consequence of the control of atomic weapons by legislation, which makes the president the sole authority, has been to enhance the importance of this image. Every operation involving atomic weapons is couched in the personalized authority of the Commander-in-Chief, because it is a responsibility which cannot be delegated.[7]

In the publications, both official and unofficial, of all three services, the explanation of civilian supremacy in the United States stresses that civilian supremacy is a traditional form.[8] There is more emphasis on precedent, and less on the argument that civilian supremacy produces a more efficient military establishment, or that it is required in order to insure the internal liberties of a democratic society, since such arguments would not re-enforce a military conception of personal allegiance. And in a large-scale armed force personal allegiance does not exclusively adhere to the Commander-in-Chief and highest ranking military officer. Just as military honor once meant a more immediate personal fealty, the contemporary officer often reserves part of this attachment for the commanding officer of his operational unit.

3. *Brotherhood.* In its contemporary form a major aspect of military honor comprises a sense of brotherhood and intense group loyalty. The organizational revolution and the decline in the exclusiveness of the military community have weakened the sense of fraternity among the military, but a sense of brotherhood can operate without regard to the values of civil society. With the shift from authority based on domination, the possibilities of group loyalty are not necessarily lessened. Here, professional realities are

highly compatible with official doctrine: "It will be seen that it is not primarily a cause which makes men loyal to each other, but the loyalty of men to each other which makes a cause."[9] The United States Army has not been able to maintain the historical continuity of its regimental units, so attachments to specific organizations do not develop. Brotherhood is a sense of fraternity to the men who are members of the unit at a particular time, unassisted by identification with historical achievements.

All professions and leadership groups require a sense of social solidarity, and the greater their solidarity, up to a point, the greater their effectiveness. But the sense of fraternity in the military is more than instrumental, it is an end in and of itself, and for this reason it becomes suspect to the outsider. Group loyalties are unfortunately narrow—to one's own service and branch—so that military honor exacerbates inter-service rivalries.

In interviews of potential military leaders, a dominant theme was the satisfaction derived merely from belonging to a group of "honorable" men. As one general officer stated the case, interpersonal relations in the military are superior to those in civilian life:

I have found it a life to be very honorable. You live with a select group and you never have to worry about a man's word because he is as good as his word and this is not true of civilian life.[10]

To the civilian outsider, one baffling element of the sense of military solidarity is the emphasis placed on the salute, for the salute requires all ranks in the hierarchy to acknowledge the presence of those in a higher-status position. In official policy, "the intent of the regulation concerning saluting is not that it embarrass or demean the individual, but that it serve as a signal of recognition and greeting between members of the military brotherhood." Managerial trends have not disturbed this practice; even in the Air Force, the salute is ever present. Since the wearing of civilian clothes off duty has become widespread, saluting is confined to the military base. Yet, one gets the impression that the salute has been selected as a symbol of opposition to civilianizing trends, and is therefore maintained with determination. While it has become almost automatic, and in a sense peripheral to consciousness, it is still laden with powerful meaning.[11]

Where military honor operates, it produces a group feeling which comprises more than nostalgia for past experiences and associations. Despite the endless dull routines which intrude into military life, the sense of honor propels the officer into an immediate and continual enthusiasm which is reminiscent of a "collegiate" sense of team spirit in athletics. Honor requires the officer to play the game without reservation; to do otherwise would be bad form:

The people you associate with are men of unquestionable integrity, the ideals are high, the enthusiasm with which they do their work is great to be around.[12]

Because the group fails to recognize the importance of privacy for its individual members, the group spirit of military honor does not necessarily contribute to individual creativity. It does, however, contribute to the military credo that the most honorable officer is the officer who never refuses combat assignment. To refuse combat assignment would be a breach of honor, a rupture of the sense of brotherhood, as well as a basis for court-martial. In fact, the profession must recognize conditions under which it is permissible to avoid combat. In Korea regulations permitted officers who served in Japanese prisoner-of-war camps during World War II to apply for reassignment. The elements of honor were still involved, in that such reassignment required the initiative of the officer, but some officers did apply for relief under the policy.

4. *The Pursuit of Glory.* The code of professional honor has had to be self-generating by drawing on its own historical achievement. Here again, aristocratic traditions have had to be adapted to the American setting. Given the pacifist outlook of a commercial society, there could be no veneration of the glories of war in and of itself. Since the turn of the century, only a handful of military leaders have publicly stated that war was a good thing. One must look hard for an utterance such as that issued by General Chafee, one of the old-style Indian fighters who rose to be an early chief-of-staff:

An occasional fight is a good thing for a nation. It strengthens the race. . . . Let war cease altogether and a nation will become effeminate.[13]

Probing the deeper psychological motives which propel men to devote their energies to the pursuit of military glory rests outside the scope of this book. But the military elite, or any elite, will never be adequately understood unless the question of whether there are important uniformities in their personality makeup is resolved. Social scientists are only in the process of learning how to systematically describe the psychodynamics of a professional or an elite group. Harold D. Lasswell, in his classic analysis of the psychological motives of politicians, offered the formulation that politics is the displacement of private motives on public objects and their rationalization in the public interest.[14] This formula would hold true for those men in the military profession who rise to the top, because of their sense of mission. The important difference is that for the officer, rationalizations about the public interest include the symbols of military honor.

The psychoanalyst would point out that aggressive impulses must be at work among many who select the military career and become heroic leaders. But for the military professional who is to rise in the hierarchy, the entire process of training and career development places a premium on the ability to curb, or at least repress, the direct exercise of aggression. The cult of manliness and toughness associated with junior officers is often a reaction against profound feelings of weakness. Such aggressive pressure can diminish as the officer develops actual competence, and as he advances in rank and organizational authority. The content and forms of military honor serve the officer in coming to terms with and managing his inner needs. Of course, curbed or repressed psychological pressures continue to direct a person's overt behavior. But there is still great truth in de Tocqueville's observation that in the army of a political democracy the most peaceful men are the generals.

As a result, military honor and the pursuit of glory are often a mixture of toughness and sentimentality. "Professional soldiers are sentimental men, for all the harsh realities of their calling. In their wallets and in their memories they carry bits of philosophy, fragments of poetry, quotations from the Scriptures, which, in times of stress and danger speak to them with great meaning."[15] The parallel with the professional journalist is most striking.[16] Both professions attract men who have rejected prosaic routines and who have strong motives which seem to them to be idealistic. The pressures of these professions require that personal idealism be submerged under a façade of realism. But the emotions which produced this idealism persist in the form of sentimentality.

Regardless of underlying motives, contemporary military honor repudiates the glory of war. Even before the development of thermo-nuclear weapons made the pursuit of glory by war ridiculous, the American military was forced to abandon the notion that war was honorable as an end in and of itself. Instead, military glory, like other American values, is based upon functional and pragmatic considerations. The redefinition of military honor, away from aristocratic forms, venerating the martial spirit to the practical justification of military ideals is perhaps most clearly set forth in the *The Armed Forces Officer*, issued in 1950 as a device for developing a common orientation among newly commissioned officers. This document is a reflection of the effort to maintain the validity of military honor in a democratic society. It was not prepared by a professional soldier, but by S. L. A. Marshall, a professional newspaper editor with extensive military experience, whose dual role equips him as a spokesman for military honor in a civilian setting.

According to *The Armed Forces Officer*, the glorification of war for war's sake is never ideal since "military ideals are not different than the ideals which make any man sound in himself and in his relations to others. They are called military ideals only because the proving ground is a little more rugged in the service than elsewhere." In fact:

Every normal man needs to have some sense of a contest, some feeling of a resistance to overcome, before he can make the best use of his faculties. Whatever experience serves to give him confidence that he can compete with other men helps to increase his solidarity with other men.[17]

Instead, the historical achievements of the armed forces are an essential ingredient of military honor. For these purposes military history is often not mere reality; it is not, for instance, the account of personal rivalries among competing generals, though accounts of the failures of the War of 1812, the Spanish-American War, and the breakdown of military management at the outset of World War I are studied by the armed forces. It is rather an idealized interpretation of past events designed to inspire the professional.[18] As to the teaching of history, military officials are openly critical of civilian instruction in college reserve officer training programs, since they feel that academic historians are indifferent to the use of history for the purpose of indoctrination of future officers.

With the exception of occasional references to German military traditions and German military history, the American military profession, even for its own consumption, does not express any sense of solidarity with military groups of other nations. In part, this represents the lack of interest and contact with other military formations which has prevailed until recently. Basically, the military in the United States have had to develop a sense of honor rooted in the practical contributions of the profession, rather than in the survival of feudal notions of military glory.

Self-Image

THE STRAIN on military honor has had a negative impact on the self-esteem of military leaders. Every profession assigns to itself a higher status than outsiders would be willing to concede, and every leadership group has a self-image which fails to correspond to the image the public holds. Yet, the "crisis" in the military profession is as much a crisis in self-esteem and self-image as it is a crisis in organization and purpose. Honor, which was a fundamental value of the aristocratic officer, and is a most important dimension of self-image among officers in the United States military today, has been strained.

In a democratic society it is highly inappropriate for honor to be the sole, or even the dominant, value of the professional military cadre. Honor comes to be combined with and dependent upon public prestige and popular recognition. The military must be afforded sufficient prestige and respect to insure a sense of self-esteem. But the rank and file professionals, and even many members of the elite, are not certain that this is evidenced in the attitudes of non-military society. Whether, in fact, the officer behaves as a heroic fighter or as a military manager, the anomalous position of the military professional in American social structure has literally deprived him of a consistent self-image. The simple-minded marine colonel who boasts that his profession is to kill is an anachronism. Even the most assault-minded officer does not consider himself a gunman; he wants to be esteemed for his patriotism, public service,

and judgment. The "cold war" has only served to further fracture
military self-esteem. It is true that the public is prepared to allocate
10 per cent of the national gross income for military expenditures
when confronted with the threat of war in international relations.
It is also true that military leaders have come to figure more
prominently in public life. However, there has been no general rise
in the prestige accorded the military officer; nor has there been any
greater willingness among young people to take on the responsibilities of military service. Selective service produces the same traditional negativism and opposition to governmental authority which
has so deeply characterized American history. After two decades of
selective service, civilian perspectives hardly operate to assist assimilation of recruits into the armed forces. Overt opposition to the
system, even political criticism of its injustices, is almost completely
absent. But even lacking adequate empirical studies, it is clear that
there is widespread confusion about military manpower systems,
depreciation of the administration of these programs, and a general
reluctance to serve.

In May 1952, during the Korean War, 83 per cent of a cross-
section sample of 2,975 university students were found by Cornell
University social scientists to be essentially negative toward their
military service obligations.[19] Personal needs, rather than military
or ideological factors, were at the root of many of the negative attitudes toward being called into the armed forces. Such public
attitudes serve to depreciate the image that the professional officer
holds of himself. As long as the military was relatively insulated
from civilian society, and comprised no more than a small homogeneous organization, prestige and self-esteem rested more on
internal standards. What the public thought mattered less. The
insulation of the profession protected it against indifferent and
hostile opinion by outsiders. Prior to 1939, those civilian contacts
which did take place operated to support and re-enforce the self-
esteem of the Army and Navy officer. Today's greater civilian contacts, and not necessarily more stable ones, mean that the military
man's self-esteem and self-image depends to a greater extent on
public attitudes and popular opinion. Generally, public employment
has risen in prestige in the United States over the last thirty years.[20]
Available public opinion research on the military officer, which
attests to his relatively low public prestige, unfortunately does not

distinguish between the rank and file and the top generals and admirals. Undoubtedly, there has been a long-term trend toward some increase in the prestige accorded leaders in the military, particularly Air Force generals, because of the public estimate of the importance of their mission in the cold war. The increased transferability of their skills and their greater presence in civilian government and business further contribute to this more favorable public image.

Table 27 presents the relative prestige of the officer in the armed forces and the enlisted man as based on attitudes of a 1955 national sampling. Unfortunately, this study, prepared by Dr. George Gallup, has not reported the basis of the prestige ranking in detail. Nevertheless, these data reveal that the officer has lower (and considerably lower by quantitative measures) prestige than the traditional

Table 27

Public Prestige of the Military Profession, 1955: Esteem Relative to Other Occupations[21]

National Adult Sample	Male Teen-Agers
1. Physician	Physician
2. Scientist	Scientist
3. College professor	Lawyer
4. Lawyer	College professor
5. Minister or Priest	OFFICER IN ARMED SERVICES
6. Public school teacher	Minister or Priest
7. OFFICER IN ARMED SERVICES	Radio or TV announcer
8. Farm owner	Public school teacher
9. Carpenter	Farm owner
10. Mail carrier	Owner of small store
11. Bookkeeper	Carpenter
12. Plumber	Garage mechanic
13. Radio or TV announcer	Bookkeeper
14. Owner of small store	ENLISTED MAN IN ARMED SERVICES
15. Garage mechanic	Mail carrier
16. ENLISTED MAN IN ARMED SERVICES	Plumber
17. Truck driver	

professions, including even the public school teacher, while the enlisted man is ranked between a garage mechanic and a truck driver. Teen-agers hold the officer in somewhat higher esteem. Of particular interest, they rate the officer above the school teacher. The military profession harbors the belief that they are not adequately recognized and, particularly, not sufficiently appreciated by civilian society. Such feelings are concentrated among officers in the middle ranks for whom career possibilities have come to an end, but this self-image is spread throughout the entire hierarchy.

Obviously, the military elite has no single common or unified self-image. Each general and admiral holds a self-image which is a product of his own personality and the impact of his own organizational experience; and it is formulated only after years of service. In any individual case it is difficult to separate the personal and the organizational components of the self-image. Thus, to speak of self-image is to run the risk of overgeneralization, but common patterns emerge in the way in which the profession views itself.

No person is fully articulate about his self-image, nor is his self-image a purely private matter. Still, while there are no simple tests by which to chart such self-images, and despite the real differences between the services and variations within each service, one basic theme emerges with clarity from the interviews and questionnaires. Whether these officers conformed to the model of the heroic fighter or of the military manager, few thought of themselves as technicians or mere military specialists, or even just professionals. The military was a profession, but it was also a group of "dedicated," "self-sacrificing" men who were actual and potential "leaders" of society. The deadly character of war permitted them—more secretly than openly—to defy the civilian definition that soldiers are military mechanics. The naval officers were the most emphatic and consistent in interviews, in their special claims as leaders. Army officers differed from naval personnel, not in the content of their self-image, but in their greater preoccupation with technological unemployment and shrinking fortunes for themselves and their service. Despite the ascendancy of air power, the typical Air Force colonel or general had the least consistent self-image. Air Force traditions are not powerful enough to offset the realization that, in the not too distant future, heroic fighters and military managers will be outnumbered by military engineers. Air Force officers were fully aware, but reluctant to admit, that more of a "leadership" role would reside in the Army and in the Navy.

Because, in the United States, business activities and business goals are highly valued, generals and admirals are keenly sensitive to the fact that the military establishment is "uneconomic," in that it produces nothing which can be sold in the marketplace. They believe that they, as "standard bearers," embody virtues which transcend "crass commercialism." The affairs of the world are intractable, unpredictable, and subject to profound instability. Toughness and tenacity are moral virtues which adhere to the officer, and which the officer must exemplify to civilian society. In the military profession it is often believed that urbanization weakens natural toughness and tenacity. The professional officer believes that he is equipped to counteract these effete tendencies and to serve as a barrier to the purely "materialistic" aspects of human nature. The military is frustrated because there is so little audience for such claims.

In a society in which both the myth and the reality of a "representative" elite operate, the military elite, like other leadership groups, is inhibited in proclaiming its special virtues. On the one hand, the officer's conceptions of honor, purpose, and human nature lead him to assume that he is a standard bearer, who embodies the superior virtues of men, yet, at the same time, he finds it expedient and necessary to present himself as a "representative man," no different from other men, and part of the mainstream of contemporary society. Few officers, including those of the highest rank, with the exception of an occasional isolated maverick, accept the self-image of a standard bearer without some degree of uneasiness. This uneasiness is not merely a way of expressing one's self to civilians. It has deeper significance, in that the military has learned to accept the political and cultural assumption that men are more alike than different. Despite the fact that they participate in the making of history, generals and admirals are as self-conscious as any other leadership group. They want to be both accepted as human beings and venerated for their official achievements. The ambiguous self-image of the military elite is partly due to the American character predisposition to be suspicious of self-appointed leaders. Only an American general could be expected, on leaving Austria at the end of the occupation, to burst into tears and to be photographed while exclaiming: "I hope we shall be remembered here by our human deeds rather than by our official actions."[22] In other words, General William Arnold was seeking to remind the Austrians, who had been freed from the Nazis and from the Russians, that American generals were human beings.

The military uniform is one of the most striking expressions of the uneasiness that complicates the military professional's sense of his being a special leader. As long as civilian society encourages the ceremonial function of the military, ceremonial uniforms are in order, although the long-term trend has been away from gaudy dress and toward more tailored uniforms.[23] However, the occupational uniform of both the Army and the Air Force, including that of the highest-ranking general, is in effect the mechanic's fatigue suit. The fatigue uniform which obscures the differences between ranks similarly obliterates the difference between the military and the industrial. It is a persistent expression of the thought that military men are not only representative men, but representatives of the technical contemporary society, rather than of a previous historical period.

Civilians who have infrequent contact with high military officials are usually impressed with the sense of self-assuredness they present. However, such self-assuredness may involve a defense against doubt and a lack of self-esteem. Only the most outstanding and exceptional military officer understands his own doubts, and can permit himself to express the ambiguities that beset those who have chosen a military career in the midst of the American social structure. General Robert E. Lee was the kind of man who could declare, when he returned to civilian life, "The greatest mistake of my life was taking a military education."[24] It was more than irony which led General Stilwell to exclaim: "It is common knowledge that an Army officer has a one-track mind, that he is personally interested in stirring up wars so that he can get promoted and be decorated, and that he has an extremely limited education, with no appreciation of the finer things of life."[25]

Most men suppress their uncertainties, and come to believe uncritically in their superior traits. Military men are no different; they develop an outlook which in a sense inverts civilian images of the military. Thus, many professional soldiers believe they are less war-like than their civilian counterparts:

Most senior military officers have had recent combat experience. As a result of their intimate knowledge of the horrors of modern warfare, they are in a better position than most civilians to appreciate the consequences of unpreparedness, or deficiencies in military capabilities as compared to the requirements generated by our international commitments.[26]

They feel that in view of their personal knowledge of the consequences of war, they are best equipped professionally with factual knowledge that can be counted on to avoid risky ventures. As exemplified by the comments of an army colonel who sought to define the differences between military and civilian values, a minority come to believe that military officers are the real national guardians:

The character of military leaders which transcends economic, political, and sociological pressures is expressed in dedicated service to the country based on the principles of duty, honor, country. I submit that few men, not early inculcated with these ideals and who have not lived their whole productive life in their expression, can learn, completely understand, or even comprehend this ideology which is the source of strength for the military leader in formulating his convictions and making his decisions. The military commander, who by this inner strength stands with clear conscience before his Maker and makes the decision to take away the most precious element in all the world—life—from his fellow man, can with understanding and unadulterated determination make the critical decisions on national security policy on which his nation's life depends. The greatest captain of industry can be but a comparative novice in this soul-searching undertaking.[27]

Notes

1. *United States Army Combat Forces Journal,* February 1951, p. 3.
2. *The Officer's Guide,* January 1956, p. 262.
3. Often, armies of national liberation have deep, although not necessarily overt, respect for the officers against whom they fight. As long as the imperial armies kept military hostilities within bounds, it was possible for the officers of the American Revolution to fashion themselves on the traditions of the British aristocratic officer. Nor were the experiences of the American Revolutionary Army unique; this pattern has repeated itself in contemporary history in new nations such as India and Israel, where the armed forces perpetuate British patterns.
4. Department of Defense, *The Armed Forces Officer.* Washington: Government Printing Office, 1950, p. 4.
5. Mahan, Captain Alfred Thayer, "The Navy as a Career." *The Forum,* 1895, *20,* 277–83.
6. Department of Defense, *op. cit.,* p. 7.
7. The Atomic Energy Act of 1954, Paragraph (2) Sub-section (b) authorizes the president from time to time to direct the Atomic Energy Commission "(1) to deliver such quantities of special nuclear material or atomic weapons to the Department of Defense for such use as *he deems necessary* in the interest of national defense." The phraseology of this clause is the basis for a personalized concept of authority in the use of atomic weapons.

8. For example, see *The Air Officer's Guide*, May 1952, p. 305.

9. Department of Defense, *op. cit.*, p. 104.

10. Interview No. 17.

11. The fraternal aspects of the code of honor seem to facilitate a capacity to interact intimately with fellow officers of even limited acquaintance. Officers will coach and criticize one another about personal mannerisms, style of speech, manner of presenting an oral briefing, or even posture, in a direct and casual manner which would strain even the most intimate civilian friendships.

12. Interview No. 18.

13. Chafee, General Adna R., "On War." *Army and Navy Journal*, 1902, 40, 298.

14. Lasswell, Harold D., *Psychopathology and Politics*. Chicago: University of Chicago Press, 1930.

15. Ridgway, Matthew, "My Battles in War and Peace." *Saturday Evening Post*, January 21, 1956, p. 17.

16. Rosten, Lee, *The Washington Correspondents*. New York: Harcourt, Brace, 1937.

17. Department of Defense, *op. cit.*, p. 142.

18. Yet, even American military historical writings of an official and semi-official nature have shown the influence of a pragmatic and skeptical approach to military achievement. Such American writings are more replete with self-criticism and analyses of shortcomings than are European materials.

19. Suchman, Edward A., Williams, Jr., Robin M., & Goldsen, Rose K., "Student Reaction to Impending Military Service." *American Sociological Review*, 1953, 18, 293–304.

20. Janowitz, Morris, & Wright, Deil S., "The Prestige of Public Employment." *Public Administration Review*, 1956, 16, 15–21.

21. Public Opinion Surveys, Inc., *Attitudes of Adult Civilians toward the Military Services as a Career*. Princeton: 1955.

22. *Life*, October 31, 1955, p. 33.

23. When the Air Force authorized its dress uniform, it was faced with the problem of differentiating itself from the other services, yet, at the same time, producing a traditional-type uniform. It solved the problem by contracting for the services of Cecil B. de Mille "because in his many years of producing motion pictures, he has studied and portrayed many past uniforms of the Armed Forces of this and many other countries."

24. Ekirch, Arthur A., Jr., *The Civilian and the Military*. New York: Oxford University Press, 1956.

25. White, Theodore H., *The Stilwell Papers*. New York: William Sloane Associates, Inc., 1948, p. 256.

26. Questionnaire No. 0045.

27. Questionnaire No. 0505.

CHAPTER *12*

Political Beliefs

ACCORDING TO the definitions of military honor, the professional soldier is "above politics" in domestic affairs. In an authoritarian society—monarchical or totalitarian—to be above politics means that the officer is committed to the status quo. Under democratic theory, the "above politics" formula requires that, in domestic politics, generals and admirals do not attach themselves to political parties or overtly display partisanship. Furthermore, military men are civil servants, so that elected leaders are assured of the military's partisan neutrality.

In practice, with only isolated exceptions, regulations and traditions have worked to enforce an essential absence of political partisanship. American experiences since the turn of the century are more in line with British politics than with those of either France or Germany, where many admirals and generals could readily be identified as monarchist or republican, conservative or liberal, socialist or fascist. The party neutrality of the military has been assisted by the social and political consensus of American society. Until the Korean conflict, generals and admirals had not been confronted with political conflicts in which they were either permitted, or required, to make alliances along partisan lines. On the contrary, military leaders have learned that in seeking to influence the fortunes of their services, in advising on strategic national defense policies, and in spending the bulk of the federal budget, a nonpartisan stance is essential.

But partisan neutrality does not mean being "above politics" to the point of being unpolitical. In analyzing the beliefs of the professional soldier, there is no advantage in assuming that they could or should be unpolitical. The British civil service is the classic example of a politically sophisticated leadership stratum, firm in its party neutrality, yet deeply committed to the parliamentary system of government. Civilian supremacy in the United States has operated because military officers function under rules which reduce or eliminate their ability to influence the electoral contests for national political leadership. Civilian supremacy also requires that military leaders operate under prescribed rules in offering advice and in stating dissenting opinions with regard to national defense policies. The strain on contemporary political institutions arises rather from the lack of clarity regarding rules for governing the behavior of the military as a "pressure group" in influencing both legislative and executive decisions about foreign affairs.

To declare that military leaders in the United States approached World War II without an orientation toward domestic political affairs is an intellectual, rather than an effective, definition of politics. First, it assumes that only those who are committed to change are political, while those who are committed to the status quo are unpolitical. Second, it assumes that men are only political when they have an explicit set of justifications for their behavior. Such a definition means that men are political only when they are ideological, or when they are doctrinaire.

The political beliefs of the military are not distinct from those that operate in civilian society. On the contrary, they are a refraction of civilian society wrought by the recruitment system, and by the education and military experiences of a professional career. War and hostilities increase political ferment, but changes in political thinking among the military elite are the result of a long-term process. The vast majority of officers are primarily concerned with purely professional and technical matters, yet, as they ascend in the hierarchy, they become increasingly conscious of their political loyalties and preferences. It is best to recognize that political beliefs are invariably sustained by a minority of men. Even within the elite, it has been those men whose unconventional careers have involved them in politico-military assignments who display the most sustained political consciousness. Finally, for all professional officers, there is a special gap between private and expressed beliefs because of the rules under which they operate.

While it is hazardous to reduce trends in political beliefs to propositions, two hypotheses emerge as important in describing the thinking of higher-echelon officers. First, during the initial half of the twentieth century, political attitudes among the military have become more representative of those of the larger society. This has been the result of changes in the social composition of the military profession, as well as increased contact between soldiers and civilians. Overwhelmingly, officers continue to describe themselves as conservative, yet the term has become an imprecise indicator of their beliefs. Second, political beliefs among the military have become more explicit, more elaborate, and more doctrinaire; in this sense, they have become more "ideological." Thus, it appears that political beliefs in the military have become more ideological during a period in which the political parties have weakened their ideological content.

The transformation of political beliefs from implicit commitments and loyalties to a more explicit ideology relates directly to the strain on military honor. To what extent have the growing limitations on the effectiveness of honor as an organizing concept of the military profession been accompanied by an increase in emphasis on explicit ideology? Ever since the writings of Max Weber, social research has stressed the theme that modern rationality and industrial efficiency weaken traditional authority. Since honor is an essential component of traditional authority, the growth of rationalism in the military establishment means the growth of a critical attitude, not only in technical and administrative matters, but toward the purposes and ends of one's profession. Each service, each weapons system, must consciously develop a "philosophy," because traditional assumptions about the efficacy of violence in the control of international relations no longer seem applicable.

The organizational revolution in the military establishment contributes heavily to the pressure for an ideological doctrine. Once authority has shifted from domination, the professional officer, not only at the highest ranks, but down to the tactical level, feels more and more obliged to have an answer to the question of why we fight. In short, the traditional answers of patriotic dogma and traditional authority are insufficient, and therefore a powerful concern has developed for an ideology and rationale of purpose.

Some social scientists, most conspicuously Edward A. Shils, contend that a decline in the importance of explicit ideology as a basis for political activity has begun to take effect in democratic societies and, for that matter, even in the Soviet Union.[1] In the long run, the argument goes, the rationality, skepticism, and civility that men develop in their scientific, economic, and professional pursuits may lead them to realize that ideological dogmas are neither essential for moral political behavior nor for the preservation of a democratic community. Without speculating about future trends, however, these hypotheses concerning the military profession contend that the political beliefs of the military have become more ideological, rather than less so.

The last fifty years have required greater and greater political expertise and vast amounts of political information in order for the United States military to operate on a world-wide basis. Yet, political expertise and a search for a political ideology are not the same. In tracing the political beliefs of the military since 1900, it is possible to demonstrate a growth of concern with ideology, both domestic and foreign. However, there is no evidence that those members of the military elite who have been most effective in politico-military assignments, or have demonstrated the greatest degree of political sophistication, have been or are the most ideological.

Conservative Identifications

MILITARY OFFICERS are willing to identify themselves as conservatives, if only because such an identification permits political perspectives without violation of nonpartisanship. Only a handful of officers (5 per cent) from the sample of 576 Army, Navy, and Air Force officers on staff duty in the Pentagon in 1954 identified themselves as liberals on an anonymous questionnaire (Table 28).[2] The question used to define political orientation was: "In domestic politics, do you regard yourself as: conservative, a little on the con-

Table 28

Political Identification—Conservative-Liberal:*
576 Officers Assigned to Pentagon Staff Duty, 1954

	ARMY			NAVY			AIR FORCE			Total
	Majors Lt. Cols. %	Cols. Gens. %	Total Army %	Lt. Comdrs. Comdrs. %	Capts. Adms. %	Total Navy %	Majors Lt. Cols. %	Cols. Gens. %	Total Air Force %	%
Conservative	20.0	31.3	25.1	15.7	31.3	23.0	10.9	17.2	14.7	
Somewhat conservative	48.7	39.6	44.5	47.8	42.4	45.2	46.9	46.2	46.5	
Somewhat liberal	21.7	20.8	21.3	24.9	11.1	18.3	31.2	32.2	31.8	
Liberal	7.0	3.1	5.3	8.4	4.1	6.3	4.7	2.2	3.2	
No answer	2.6	5.2	3.8	3.2	11.1	7.2	6.3	2.2	3.8	
Number	(117)	(96)	(211)	(109)	(99)	(208)	(64)	(93)	(157)	(576)

* Text of question: "In domestic politics, do you regard yourself as: conservative, a little on the conservative side, a little on the liberal side, liberal?"

servative side, a little on the liberal side, liberal?"* The extent of
conservative perspectives is documented by the full pattern of
responses: 21.6 per cent identify themselves as conservative, 45.3
per cent as a little on the conservative side, and 23.1 per cent as a
little on the liberal side.

To measure political attachment to the term "conservative"
leaves open the question of what specific content a person attributes to his political commitments. But precisely because these
data refer to general identification, they reflect basic orientations.
Unfortunately, comparable data do not exist for other professional
groups, or even for the political electorate at large.[3]

Herbert McClosky, a research political scientist, classified more
than 17 per cent of a representative sample of Minnesota residents
as liberals on the basis of an elaborate attitude scale.[4] Since Mc-
Closky did not ask the electorate to rate themselves as to whether
they were "conservatives" or "liberals," his data are not necessarily
comparable. However, from his findings, as well as other opinion
studies, it is clear that higher education is associated with a
greater concentration of liberal attitudes in the population at large.
Thus, the emphasis on conservative attachments among officers is
even more noteworthy, since they constitute a group in which
higher education does not weaken conservative orientations.

Comparison of political identifications among the three services
on the basis of these questionnaire data underlines the uniformity in
perspectives generated by membership in the military establishment. First, Army and Navy officers revealed a similar level of conservative commitment, contrary to the assumption that the Navy is
the most politically conservative. The percentage of men in each
service who thought themselves to be conservative, or a little on the
conservative side, was approximately 68 per cent. The only difference—and this was indeed a minor one—was that naval officers
refused to give an answer to the question of political perspective
more often than Army officers (7.2 per cent for the Navy, and 3.2
per cent for the Army).

Nor did the Air Force present a picture of decisive deviation
from the basic conservative orientation of the Army and Navy. The
percentage of officers in the Air Force sample who considered them-

* See the Methodological Appendix for the details of this questionnaire
survey.

selves conservative, or somewhat conservative, was not even 10 per
cent lower than the other two services (Army 69.6, Navy 68.2, Air
Force 61.2). The percentage of Air Force officers who fell in the un-
qualified liberal category was lower than that of either the Army or
the Navy. In short, the Air Force officer tended to be somewhat
more cautious in placing himself at either end of the political continuum. These data stand in marked contrast to the popular assumption that Air Force personnel are the most liberal.

No less important than the differences among the services is the
structure of conservative-liberal attitudes by rank (Table 28). For
the sample as a whole, conservative attitudes increased with higher
position in the military hierarchy, and this pattern held for each of
the three services. In fact, the link between political orientation and
rank is even sharper than shown in Table 28, for when the generals
and admirals are separated from the colonels and naval captains, the
former are characterized by the highest concentration of conservative attachments (39.1 per cent were conservative).[5] Higher rank
means longer organizational experience, greater commitment to the
organization, and more selecting out of deviant perspectives. A body
of evidence also indicates that older people in civilian society are
more conservative politically than younger people.[6] However, the
relationship between age, rank, and political identification in the
military profession is not a simple and direct one. In the case of the
Army and the Air Force, younger colonels are somewhat more conservative than older colonels. Those who rose most rapidly display
the greatest conformity to traditional patterns.

For a fuller understanding of these political preferences, academy graduates were compared with non-academy graduates, and
those who had attended higher military schools (war colleges) were
compared with those who had not. In all three services academy
graduates tended to fall into the unqualifiedly conservative category
more often than non-academy graduates (Table 29). For the Army,
the conservative difference was slight; it was greater for the Navy;
and it was the most pronounced for the Air Force. Interestingly
enough, in all three services the increased concentration of conservative thought among academy graduates was not the result of a decrease in unqualifiedly liberal attachments. Academy graduation
seemed to be associated with more clear-cut preferences—either

Table 29

Political Identification—Conservative-Liberal by Military Education*

Academy Graduates

	ARMY		NAVY		AIR FORCE		Total
	Academy Graduate	Non-academy Graduate	Academy Graduate	Non-academy Graduate	Academy Graduate	Non-academy Graduate	
	%	%	%	%	%	%	
Conservative	27.4	23.3	27.6	14.3	33.3	10.8	
Somewhat conservative	42.1	46.6	43.4	48.6	29.6	50.0	
Somewhat liberal	18.9	23.3	13.1	28.5	29.6	32.3	
Liberal	6.3	4.3	7.2	4.3	3.7	3.1	
No answer	5.3	2.5	8.7	4.3	3.8	3.8	
Number	(95)	(116)	(138)	(70)	(27)	(130)	(576)

War College Attendance

	ARMY		NAVY		AIR FORCE		Total
	War College	None	War College	None	War College	None	
	%	%	%	%	%	%	
Conservative	29.2	23.3	20.7	25.0	21.4	12.2	
Somewhat conservative	43.1	45.2	52.2	39.7	42.9	47.8	
Somewhat liberal	20.0	21.9	15.2	20.7	28.6	33.0	
Liberal	3.1	6.2	4.3	7.8	2.4	3.5	
No answer	4.6	3.4	7.6	6.8	4.8	3.5	
Number	(65)	(146)	(92)	(116)	(42)	(115)	(576)

* Five hundred and seventy-six officers assigned to Pentagon staff duty, 1954.

conservative or liberal. Among civilian groups, as well, more education usually produces clearer political commitments.

Attendance at a war college (or the National War College) was also linked to more conservative political preferences for Army and Air Force officers, but not for the Navy (Table 29). In all three services the non-war college graduate was clearly more liberal in outlook than was the graduate. Undoubtedly, at this point in an officer's career, who gets selected is more important than the actual impact of the course of study. These findings tie in directly with the previous observation that the higher the rank, the stronger the conservative attachment. Finally, combat officers tended to be more conservative than those in technical or non-combat service, but the differences were hardly pronounced. This difference could be accounted for by the fact that combat officers are more likely to be graduates of service academies.[7]

Admittedly, the conservative-liberal distinction is a crude one, but these data demonstrate that difference between the services in military doctrine and in political behavior have not been a direct expression of profound differences in political beliefs. A conservative orientation may be at the root of an Army or naval officer's critique of massive retaliation and preference for graduated deterrence; vice versa, in the Air Force, a liberal attachment may be linked to the same military philosophy. There is a political component to military doctrine, but there is no simple formula for translating political conservatism into military policy.* In order to understand the relationship between political ideology and the conduct of war in the American military establishment, it is first necessary to evolve a fuller definition of the content of conservatism, and to examine how the very nature of conservatism has undergone a change since the turn of the century.

The Content of Conservatism

How DIFFERENT are the political beliefs of the contemporary military elite from those held by the elite at the turn of the century, when it was less socially representative? It would have been most

* See Chapter 13, The Logic of War.

helpful if the questionnaire on political identifications had been administered to comparable samples in 1910, 1920, and 1935. On the basis of available evidence—military publications, memoirs, and interviews with informed persons—the conclusion emerges that the last fifty years have seen an increase in the concentration of officers who are willing to deviate from the traditional conservative identification. Up through 1920, it would have been most rare to find an officer who thought of himself as anything but conservative, although his conception of a conservative would have been more implicit than explicit. The growth of a "liberal" minority started during the great depression and reflected trends in civilian society. By the same token, a more socially representative military profession was certain to reflect the variety of political attachments in civilian society.

The fact that the symbol "conservative" is vague hardly detracts from its political utility. In its most general political usage, conservatism supports the belief in the moral desirability of maintaining the status quo. But in the military context, political conservatism must be reconciled with a preoccupation with technological change and, by implication, with change in other spheres of human behavior. Conservatism also implies that human nature is not highly perfectible. To the professional soldier, this aspect of conservatism asserts that violence is the final arbiter of human relations, and that, in fact, resort to violence is inevitable. Such an orientation is not easily reconciled with the growing destructiveness of modern weapons, a fact which increases the importance of other methods of regulating international relations.

Merely to label the military as conservative is a most incomplete political formulation, if nothing is said about which values are to be preserved. The noble officer of the late nineteenth century in Europe believed that he was an aristocratic conservative because he wanted to preserve feudal and landed forms. The successful businessman believes that he is a liberal conservative because he wants to conserve the free enterprise system. Some intellectuals believe that they are humanistic conservatives because they want to conserve human powers of creativity.

Political conservatism of the American military profession is perhaps more a conservatism of form than it is of content. The officer's social origins—his rural, non-cosmopolitan background—have predisposed him toward a provincial and status quo outlook. His education, in which military history is used as a source of inspiration, has particularly emphasized precedent and tradition. For all but the most venturesome and hardy members of the elite nucleus, the successful career has taught the virtues of playing the game according to the existing rules.

While military beliefs about politics remain heavily weighted on the conservative side, the content of conservatism itself has been transformed. The trends in political beliefs seem to range, not from less to greater political concern, but rather from implicit to more explicit orientations. As military conservatism has become more explicit, its internal paradoxes have not been eliminated. The necessity of adjusting formal conservatism to a rapidly altering economic and social setting means considerable flux. In the end military belief systems are as concerned with developing new solutions as they are conservative.

1. *Economic Assumptions.* Military conservatism predicates the indispensability of private property as the basis of a stable political order. At present, as in the past, the military professional can conceive of no other arrangement. The rules of war, as embodied in General Order 100, issued on April 24, 1863, and superseded by the rules of land warfare 27–10, issued in 1914, constitute a fundamental defense of private property, formulated simply enough to enable each officer to internalize the theses as an operating philosophy. But the indispensability of private property did not and still does not mean that the business enterprise system, and specifically the profit incentive, must be venerated. The residues of rural aristocratic-like traditions still operate to enhance the gentleman concept and the public service tradition. Until World War II, American businessmen, in the eyes of the American military elite, were too much concerned with the accumulation of money. The social attitudes of American generals, as inferred from publications and speeches up to 1940, reveal very little glorification of the private profit system.[8]

The military continue to be more attuned to the managerial aspects of American industrial organization than to its economic assumptions. Negative feelings have been manifested, not in any outspoken critique, but, rather, in mild criticism of the lack of a heroic attitude among American businessmen and their sons. The military

elite, particularly the ground forces, has been sensitive to the fact
that the ascendant upper class, whose social status is based upon
commerce and industry, has failed to send its sons into military
service:

Strange to say in America, those who by reason of accumulation of
property have assumed the roles of leisure class and have more or less
association with that British element which supplies the scions to the
Army, Navy and the Civil Service, seldom or never consider the propriety
of devoting themselves or their sons to the public service unless it be as
ambassadors or ministers at foreign courts.[9]

Similarly, until the outbreak of World War II, the military profession took for granted the persistent hostility of the business community. Political scientists, particularly Samuel Huntington, have
documented the pervasive capitalist negativism toward military values in the United States. World War I brought no more than a temporary cessation of business criticism of the military. By 1925, business "normalcy" was once more fully operative in American politics.
To some degree, the Navy escaped the direct hostility of the business community, for while business could not see its self-interest
served by an effective standing Army, its conception of commercial
interests abroad and of international trade was more compatible
with the needs of the naval establishment. From 1899 on, naval
expansionism met business acceptance, and was actively supported
by naval shipbuilding interests which were attracted by the prospect
of government contracts.[10]

But the extent of a "political" and "ideological" alliance between
the business community and the Navy before World War II can
easily be exaggerated. If the Navy escaped the scorn of the business
community, it was because of an effective relationship with Congress, and because it was obvious that the Navy had to exist as a
fleet in peacetime if it were to be mobilized for hostilities. Although
the Navy League came into being early in the 1920's as a channel
for mutual support between selected business interests and the
Navy, the dogged determination of the naval establishment to hold
onto and develop its own arsenal system indicated that it did not
accept the superiority of the private business enterprise system over
its own organizational arrangements.

If, until 1939, military leaders did not glorify the business community, neither did they express any profound sense of hostility.

They accepted the logic of the business community as inevitable and they sought to live in accord with its instructions, as expressed by the level of budget appropriations. The officer corps operated as if it were following the prescription of Gaetano Mosca, the Italian political scientist, that the military should reflect the economic and social balance in civilian society, and not seek to alter it. At the same time it sought to live within the confines of the dominant logic of the business community, the military profession also sought to accommodate itself to what it considered the realities of trade union organization.[11] The long-range planning of the military during the interwar years carefully avoided reference to a labor draft, and looked forward to the participation of the trade union movement in the mobilization plans. The military accepted the economic status quo, not only because of its conservative tradition, but because it believed that the economic system was compatible with its organizational needs in war time.

The latent elements of "military socialism" began to emerge with the great depression. The military, like the rest of society, could no longer take the economic system for granted. Military opinion was far less hostile to New Deal economic policies than might have been anticipated, in view of the professional officer's social origins and conservative political outlook. The expressed hostility of a few conspicuous Army leaders who opposed the "socialist" schemes of the Roosevelt administration was not typical. The military found its place quickly in the emerging scheme of economic change. Several military figures played prominent roles in the organization and administration of the New Deal.[12] A large number of Army officers were involved in the administration of the Civilian Conservation Corps. Although this was thought to be a low-status assignment, it fitted in well with the Army's self-conception that it was truly an educational institution. The military profession preferred to see governmental intervention in a crisis, even though they may not have understood, or may have had reservations about the tactics and policies employed.

The requirements of economic mobilization for World War II, and later the persistence of the cold war, deepened the political awareness of the military establishment which had been brought into play by the great depression. Few officers at the higher echelons were able to remain oblivious of the political issues involved in the role of government in the management of national economic affairs. Even the typical military professional, with a minimum of political commitments, developed a conception of what ought to be the economic budget for national defense, and of which economic controls and arrangements are essential to achieve allocation of resources. The military no longer took the economic system for granted.

If the military officer typically considers himself a conservative, it is hardly a "laissez faire" conservatism—with reverence for the automatic workings of the marketplace. The military approach to the economic system centers on the issue of the military budget, on what, theoretically, the nation needs and can afford for national security. "Military economics" has become an integral aspect of the curriculum of service academies and advanced military schools. While many officers are thoughtful, informed, and alert to the problems of economic organization, one consequence of the increased interest in economic matters has been a growth in criticism, implied and open, toward contemporary economic arrangements.

Increased knowledge about the mechanisms of the economic system means that the military manager is no longer content to rely completely on the judgment of civilian political authorities. In all three services conservative identifications have become compatible with a belief in the need for continuous and decisive governmental intervention in the economic order. But from the content of staff papers, the curriculum of the higher military schools, and the shop-talk of the more politically interested officers, it is clear that the military reject a managed economy. Contemporary "military socialism" is of the mixed variety. It is accepted that there is a point beyond which governmental taxation would weaken the political system and threaten the rate of economic growth. The main argument between the conservatives and the liberals focuses on the limit of taxation, with the more conservative-minded officer likely to set the limits at the lower level of 25 per cent of the gross national product (following Professor Colin Clark's formulation), while the liberal officer would raise the basic figure.

The Air Force, because its budgetary fortunes have met with the most success, is the least critical. But all the services, despite their political conservatism, are agreed that the budgetary level of military expenditure is inadequate. This is an inherent perspective of the profession. More privately than publicly, many military pro-

fessionals are convinced that the mechanisms of the marketplace
cannot bring about effective allocation of scarce resources and personnel required for national security. The rate of economic growth
also provokes dissatisfaction with the priorities that operate with
regard to consumer goods, capital investment, and social investment.
In short, military conservatism has become compatible with an intellectual and ideological critique of the economic system. Military
professionals are prepared to argue about the decisions of civilian
politicians in a way that would have been unthought of twenty-five
years ago.

But negativism in military circles toward economic practices goes
deeper than a rational calculation about the adequacy or inade-
quacy of specific policies. There is persistent resentment of the efforts of civilian administrators recruited from business corporations
for short appointment to evaluate military performance in the same
terms they would apply to an economic enterprise. As a military
manager, the professional officer is prepared to accept the philosophy of managerial efficiency, and, in fact, he believes that the military have pioneered in large-scale management devices. But he
rejects the notion that his organization can be evaluated in purely
economic or cost-accounting terms:

The military realizes that the armed forces will never show a dollar-and-
cents profit. The civilians, particularly the big business types, sometimes
fail to remember the foregoing fact.[13].

When *Fortune* magazine, the representative organ of businessmen's
thinking, analyzes the "U.S. military mind," and asks these questions
about expenditures in the military establishment: "How good is the
insurance? Will it deliver dollar-for-dollar value?," the typical military response is a mixture of amazement and resentment.[14] The experienced military manager is aware that cost-accounting has its
limitations in an arena where there is no salable product and no
profit criterion.[15] The heroic leader resents a concept which he believes reduces him to a mercenary.

But the symbols of big business are too powerful and too pervasive to permit underlying resentment to erupt into direct attack
or criticism. Negative attitudes toward business enterprise are inhibited and suppressed because of the desire and opportunity for

employment after retirement. As indicated earlier,* the retirement aspirations of military professionals, including the elite members, are indeed modest, and many retired officers prefer an institutional rather than a business career, in order to continue their public service traditions. But the prospect of employment in the aircraft and missile industry for many men in the Air Force, or the feeling that business may be the most feasible alternative, tends to curb overt hostility.

Instead, much of the discontent with contemporary economic arrangements expressed by military officers is directed toward the trade union movement. Trade union leaders are blamed for many of the shortcomings of our industrial system. In the past the military's desire to live within the socio-economic balance moderated its negativism toward trade unionism. However, the frustrations resulting from limitations on the military budget, and the rapid rate of industrial growth in the Soviet Union, have increased hostility toward the symbols of organized labor, especially among the middle and lower ranks of the profession.

2. *Social Relations.* Just as military conservatism does not revere laissez faire economics, so it does not subscribe to the belief that contemporary social relations embody the most desirable standards. Military ideology has maintained a disapproval of the lack of order and respect for authority which it feels characterizes civilian society. The military believe that the materialism and hedonism of American culture is blocking the essential military virtues of patriotism, duty, and self-sacrifice. In the past most professional soldiers even felt that the moral fibre of American manpower was "degenerating," and might not be able to withstand the rigors of battle. The professional soldier has been preoccupied with increased military training, not only for technical reasons, but to overcome the social and moral disabilities and weaknesses generated by civilian society.

Each sociological dimension of the military that has been analyzed—social origin, career lines, organizational experience—contributes to this strong belief that the military profession represents a distillate of superior social values. Since military professionals are deprived of the opportunity to accumulate material wealth in a commercial society, self-identity is directly tied to intense feelings of "national greatness." But, again, the civilian stereotype of the mili-

* In Chapter 9, Style of Life.

tary officer as a fanatical patriot, hostile to the main social and cultural trends and bitter about the moral assumptions of civilian society, can easily be overdrawn. Even before 1939, the military profession made it plain that it followed the social customs of civilian society, and was explicitly proud of its role as the "guardian" of society. This meant, among other things, that it adhered to the racial theories and racial practices which were the norms of civilian society.

As a result of World War II and its aftermath, the social values of the military are probably less at variance with civilian society than they have been at any period of American history. The greater social representativeness of the officer corps has resulted in fuller representation of religious and cultural values within the military profession. At the same time, many more Americans are employed in large-scale enterprises which have a managerial ethic similar to that of the military establishment. Civilian social values have undergone a great transformation with regard to minority groups. The military have participated extensively in the transformation in this area; the profession no longer follows social customs, but is in the forefront of social change.

To point out that the military profession now holds values more equivalent to those of civil society does not imply that the military is prepared to abandon its traditional outlook as to the inferiority of civilian social and moral standards. On the contrary, as in the case of economic beliefs, criticism seems to be intensified. Because generals and admirals are in closer contact with civilian social structure, they have learned that it is legitimate to criticize social practices, that it is not necessary to take them for granted.

In particular, military authorities are prepared to challenge the efficacy of American education more openly than they are prepared to criticize the economic system. The events of World War II have emboldened their criticism. An educational system which contributed to a greater than 20 per cent psychoneurotic rejection rate was, in the military view, a defective one. An educational system which failed to eliminate illiteracy was equally defective, especially as the armed forces could demonstrate that illiteracy can readily be eliminated by intensive effort. The behavior of troops in the Korean conflict gave military authorities what they considered additional justification for their critique of civilian educational institutions.

Some military leaders have asserted that civilian recruits in Korea were not indoctrinated properly with an ideological understanding of democracy or with sufficient patriotism; as a result, military performance was defective.* In the military conception, the educational system is not only inadequate in dealing with the mass of the student body, but it fails to cater to superior talent for national defense purposes. Figures such as Vice Admiral Hyman G. Rickover have become prominent spokesmen for educational reform, designed to produce a "split" system capable of challenging and training superior students.[16]

3. *Political Concepts.* The fundamental meaning of military conservatism rests in its purely political content. In particular, how does it judge the effectiveness of popular two-party government and the adequacy of civilian leadership produced by two-party government? During the years between World War I and II the concept of government held by military conservatives was little different from that of the "right wing" of the Republican Party. It is, of course, possible to extract from military writings of the 1920's quotations which appear anti-democratic. For example, the Army ROTC manual contained the following definition of democracy:

A government of the masses. Authority derived through mass meetings or any other forms of "direct" expression. Results in mobocracy. Attitude toward property is communistic—negating property rights. Attitude toward law is that the will of the majority shall regulate whether it be based upon deliberation or governed by passion, prejudice and impulse, without restraint or regards to consequences. Results in demagoguism, license, agitation, discontent and anarchy.[17]

However many or few officers may have held this political attitude, such rhetoric is now almost completely absent. In order to counter the claims of communist ideology, it has become obsolete to disparage the symbols of democracy, even in the military establishment.

Extremist political sentiment among the military has not been extensive. Throughout the turbulent response to the depression, only an occasional professional officer joined the native "lunatic" right. The most outspoken example was George Van Horn Mosely, who, after having served as an assistant chief of staff, was passed over by President Roosevelt for the post of chief of staff. He retired

* See Chapter 19, The New Public Relations.

from military duty to take an active role in extremist politics. Converts to the left were in effect nonexistent. Brigadier General Herbert Holdridge claimed for a time to be a socialist, but socialist party members were doubtful of his ideas and motives. Colonel (later General) Evans S. Carlson, a romantic Marine Corps figure, developed a vague attachment to Chinese communism,[18] but he was an isolate.*

From the point of view of democratic requirements, the important issue is not the extent of extremist thought, but rather the lack of understanding and respect for the creative role of the practical politician. A few conspicuous civilian leaders are seen as heroes, but the military shares the civilian image that politicians are an unworthy lot. There is, moreover, little sympathy for the particular qualities required to produce political compromise. There is little appreciation of the fact that a political democracy requires competing pressures. The endless struggles over the military budget only serve to re-enforce the conception that party politics and pressure group activities are nefarious. Military conservatism tends to overlook the advantages and safeguards of consensus arrived at by debating conflicting interests and pressures. In a mixture of realism and naiveté, the military is disposed to de-emphasize "politics" in national security matters. They want to improve the quality of the personnel involved, and especially the adequacy of the advice available to politicians. They see politics as being improved by the introduction of military staff techniques and even personnel with military experience, whose training they believe to be superior to that of the civilian:

The military officer in a policy advisory position becomes a capable generalist through a deliberately planned career pattern of variegated experience and schooling, starting with an experience in "shirt sleeve" positions. This approach is not at all easy and perhaps not practicable for the politically responsible civilian.[19]

Some even come to believe that the loyal dedication and technical competence of the civil servant—represented by the military profession—can substitute for the skill of political leadership.

Professional officers have always resented the intervention of politicians in military administration. But the quality of civilian

* See Chapter 18, Civilian Alliances, for military leaders' post-World War II partisan political activities.

direction cannot be judged by the opinions of professional officers alone. Civilian supremacy has operated effectively because political leaders select for key military assignments "unconventional" officers who are the least hostile to civilian intervention. But in the contemporary military establishment a large portion of military leaders, in the belief that they have sufficient political education and experience to justify their judgments, continuously scrutinize the behavior of civilian political leaders. In interviews these officers expressed marked reservations about the effectiveness of civilian political leadership of the military establishment.

Of what import is such criticism among the military elite? Clearly, the question does not involve the danger of Bonapartist sentiments, but, rather, it asks whether such criticism is reasonable and capable of creative results? Or is it of such character and intensity as to indicate frustration and resentment? To point to the reservations the military hold with regard to civilian political leaders, however, is not to overlook the trained capacity of the professional officer to subordinate personal convictions to the requirements imposed by his immediate assignments.

An indicator as to the nature of these convictions or sentiments can be found in the questionnaire responses of the 576 staff officers to the general question: "In the formulation of national security policy, military and civilian authorities sometimes find themselves taking different positions How does this happen?" The responses, although varying widely in content, focused on a few basic themes which sharply separated the officers. The most frequent response was that such differences arose out of differences of background, training, and responsibility; they were, so to speak, the result of situational factors. In all, approximately 35 per cent, or one-third, fell into this category. The officers who gave this response seemed to believe that such differences were inevitable, and, in general, were capable of reasonable adjustment. A small group of about 13 per cent believed that these differences resulted from deficiencies among both civilian and military authorities. Although a greater note of frustration was apparent in their attitude, they still seemed to imply that the differences were tolerable.

However, a third important group—approximately 30 per cent—was positive in the belief that differences in viewpoint between military and civilian authorities were due to the superior qualities of the military and/or to the deficiencies or handicaps of the civilians. Typical of this response was that of the naval captain who wrote:

Civilian authorities are subject to too many influences—elections, pressure groups, party policy, empire building, etc. It is my firm belief that, in spite of misconceptions to the contrary, the military are objective and to a greater extent dedicated to serving interests of country rather than self or own service.[20].

An Air Force colonel stated the same sentiment in more elaborate language:

On basic issues, military people will normally base their conclusions on a much firmer note of realism with respect to the world around them than will their civilian superiors. Civilian authorities are in my judgment woefully ill-informed on the facts of national security and the probabilities and means of maintaining it; and with the Department of Defense, civilian authorities are completely lacking in appreciation of what can and can't be done militarily and of the time element involved in gaining beneficial results from any selected policy. This lack of appreciation leads to termination, through disgust, of many ventures before they have a fair chance to run their course.[21]

Differences between the services were not pronounced, except that the Navy had the highest concentration of officers who believed that the military were superior to civilians and/or that civilians had more deficiencies than did military officers. Although there are no data to ascertain whether there has been an increase in such sentiments, or whether indeed they are traditional, they do operate and must be recognized by civilian leadership. The effectiveness of civilian political control over the military is dependent only to a small extent upon the political beliefs held by the military profession. Yet, a democratic political system assumes that its military officers are positively committed to, if not enthusiastic about, the merits of civilian supremacy and civilian leadership.

Most public administration experts in American academic life contend that it is essential that a political democracy have a civil and military service whose social origins and attitudes are broadly representative of the society at large. Experts, such as Paul P. Van Riper, are prone to speak of the need for a representative bureaucracy.[22] A civil or military service whose political beliefs were widely at variance with those of the electorate would present a danger to political democracy, for such a service could not be counted on to remain loyal to the concept of political neutrality. Yet, there is no reason to assume that by making a civil service more socially representative, it will automatically be more committed to the principle of partisan neutrality. Particularly in the case of the military, it is an open question as to whether permitting those of more humble origin to enter the profession necessarily recruits personnel which is more heavily committed to political neutrality.

Gaetano Mosca, in his search for the realistic components of political democracy, argued to the contrary in the nineteenth century. He believed that an officer corps drawn from aristocratic origins was most appropriate for a political democracy. His reasoning seemed to be that only an aristocratic officer corps—with effective social connections to the other members of the elite—could be counted on to act in terms of the social balance at work in society. Because of their sense of honor, these men could be counted on to be loyal to the government in power, and yet above the daily political strife. Contrariwise, the broadening of the social base of the officer corps, in his opinion, would only make active in the military establishment those social conflicts at work in society at large. The new social groups entering the military profession, unless adequately indoctrinated and controlled, could not be expected to continue to be subservient to the mandate of civilian authorities. The very fact that new groups in the military would not have stable connections with the civilian elite would tend to sharpen and heighten their political demands. The officer corps thereby would shift from its role as an instrument of national politics, and become deeply involved in national politics.

Mosca's interpretation is overdrawn because he assumes that only aristocratic-type officers can be made subject to democratic political control. But he was profoundly prophetic in his proposition that a broadening of the social base of the officer corps did not necessarily mean, particularly in Europe, a strengthening of political belief in the superiority and efficacy of political democracy. In the United States the trend toward a more socially representative officer corps has strained, but not weakened, nonpartisan traditions. Military honor also operates to inhibit such political attachments. But, fundamentally, the profession has never been fixated on a feudal myth, so that its attachment to the symbols of conservatism are compatible with flexible orientations toward domestic economic, social, and political issues. In fact, to date, military conservatism reveals a critical attitude toward contemporary institutions such as would be expected from any effective professional group.

Notes

1. Shils, Edward A., "Ideology and Civility: On the Politics of the Intellectual." *Sewanee Review*, 1958, *66*, 450–80.

2. It should be noted that only 5 per cent failed to give any political identification.

3. It is striking to note that social and political scientists have not investigated attachments to the symbol "conservative," although several efforts have been made in recent years to describe political attitudes in the United States. The term "conservative" is not even listed in the index of Hadley Cantril's compendium on public opinion, which contains a decade of sample survey research. See Cantril, Hadley, *Public Opinion, 1935–1946*. Princeton: Princeton University Press, 1951.

4. McClosky, Herbert, "Conservatism and Personality." *The American Political Science Review*, 1958, *52*, 27–45.

5. When the sample was grouped as to assignment to the office of the Secretary of Defense, the Joint Chiefs of Staff, or one of the three service headquarters, there was both a decline in firm liberal commitment and an increase in firm conservative ones, as one moved up the hierarchy, although the differences were not pronounced. The levels of the hierarchy seem to operate like the rank system in that the higher the stratum, the more apt one is to find political conservatism. Since, at the time of the survey, civilian political direction of the military establishment was in the hands of a "conservative" administration, undoubtedly the reciprocal effect of the officer on his assignment and assignment on officer was also at work.

6. For a summary of this research literature see Lipset, Seymour M., Lazarsfeld, Paul F., Barton, Allen H., & Linz, Juan, "The Psychology of Voting: An Analysis of Political Behavior," in *Handbook of Social Psychology*, edited by Gardner Lindzey. Cambridge: Addison-Wesley Publishing Co., 1954, Vol. II, pp. 1124–75.

7. Owing to the complexity of the military establishment, the simple distinction between combat officer and technician was not adequate to enable exploration of the impact of military role on political thinking. The 1954 sample of officers on staff duty was grouped by military assignment into strategic planning, logistical planning, and foreign aid. In 1954 foreign aid assignments were still viewed as outside the prescribed career pattern. In the field they were not considered real command assignments, and in Washington they were not considered as prestigeful as strategic planning. In the analysis, officers operating in foreign aid planning showed the most liberal attachments and the least conservative ones. This difference could not be ascribed to any tendency for liberal officers to select foreign aid assignments, since the factors of self-selection could be controlled. However, service in such assignments apparently had an impact on political orientations.

8. Brown, C. S., "The Social Attitudes of American Generals, 1898–1940."
Unpublished doctoral dissertation, University of Wisconsin, 1951.

9. Carter, General William H., "Army as a Career." *North American*, 1906, *183*, 871.

10. Ekirch, Arthur A., Jr., *The Civilian and the Military*. New York: Oxford University Press, 1956.

11. William Crozier, a technocratic-minded general, in an article published in 1920 on the positive contribution of a responsible trade union movement, commented favorably on the trade union movement and its positive attitude toward technological change. See Crozier, General William, "Labor's Interest in Administration." *Annals of the American Academy*, 1920, *91*, 157.

12. In addition to General Hugh S. Johnson, as organizer of the National Recovery Administration, conspicuous examples included: Major General Philip Fleming in P.W.A., and later as Federal Works Administrator; Colonel Francis C. Harrington, Works Projects Administration; and Major General Edmond H. Leary as Assistant Commissioner of the W.P.A.

13. Questionnaire No. 0516.

14. *Fortune*, vol. 45, February 1952, p. 91.

15. For a theoretical critique of cost-accounting in the military establishment, from the point of view of a professional economist, see Novick, David, & Fischer, G. H. "The Role of Management Tools in Making Military Decisions," Rand Report No. P-694. Santa Monica: The Rand Corporation, June 16, 1955.

16. Rickover, Admiral Hyman G., *Education and Freedom*. New York: E. P. Dutton, 1956.

17. *U.S. Army Training Manual*, No. 2000–25. Washington: 1928, p. 91.

18. Carlson, Evans S., *The Chinese Army; Its Organization and Military Efficiency*. New York: Institute of Pacific Relations, 1940.

19. Lincoln, Col. G. A., & Jordan, Jr., Lt. Col. A.A., "Leadership for The Common Defense." *Public Administration Review*, 1957, *19*, 264.

20. Questionnaire No. 0340.

21. Questionnaire No. 0747.

22. Van Riper, Paul P., "The Senior Civil Service and the Career System."
Public Administration Review, 1958, *18*, 196.

CHAPTER *13*

The Logic of War

GENERALS AND ADMIRALS stress the central importance of "doctrine." Military doctrine is the "logic" of their professional behavior.[1] As such, it is a synthesis of scientific knowledge and expertise on the one hand, and of traditions and political assumptions on the other. The military profession of each nation develops a military doctrine which reflects its social environment. In his volume on Soviet military doctrine, Raymond Garthoff demonstrates how Communist theories influence the military thinking of the Russian officer corps.[2] Since the United States is a pluralistic society, there is no reason to assume that the American military profession has been guided by a single unified philosophy, although it is heavily influenced by its particular form of political conservatism. On the contrary, its professional logic can best be understood as the outcome of competing doctrines of warfare.

There is something to be gained by describing the doctrine of the military elite as an "operational code." The term implies that professional thought has significant elements of historical continuity, but, at the same time, undergoes change as a result of experience and self-criticism. The importance of an operational code, or a doctrine, is that it supplies leaders with guide lines for estimating whether a particular set of policies is appropriate for achieving a desired goal. It is a mode of problem-solving, rather than a specific policy. To speak of an operational code is not to focus on the public statements of major leaders, but to analyze the changing pattern of thinking which penetrates an entire organization.[3] Invariably, there is a gap between the operational code and actual military policies, because doctrine tends to lag behind emerging pressures. For example, the operational code must adjust to the logic and limitations of the military budget, which is, in turn, contingent on the exigencies of international relations.

Military Means and Political Ends

INTERNATIONAL RELATIONS involves the use of economic resources, violence, and persuasion—diplomatic or mass—in order to achieve the aims of foreign policy. The military task of adjusting the instruments of violence to achieve foreign policy goals is based on a dilemma. It is a dilemma which has been growing since the beginning of the nineteenth century, when warfare began to rapidly develop its destructive power. The dilemma of the military profession is simply this: How is it possible to sustain conservative political commitments to the existing social order, while the instruments of warfare become more drastic devices of social change, with almost unpredictable and revolutionary consequences? Atomic and thermo-nuclear weapons are only the final stage in a process which seems to have made the dilemma almost impossible to resolve.

Before the advent of nuclear weapons, one response to this persistent dilemma was the effort of military managers to make the conduct of war increasingly scientific, and to achieve victory as quickly as possible. The quicker the war, the less destructive its consequences, and, by implication, the greater the possibility of containing the disruptive social and political aftermath. Another response prevalent in Western Europe, as Alfred Vagts has pointed out, was the growing reluctance of some military leaders to go to war. They saw the outcome of war—victory or defeat—as decimating their profession and destroying their social base. They became more concerned with planning war than with making war, and more involved in the ceremony of "militarism" than in rational military management. Civilian interference was essential, even to mobilize the professional German general staff into World War II.

This reluctance to go to war has had its adherents in the American military profession. For example, Major General Ethan Allen Hitchcock, one of the most intellectually creative generals of the nineteenth century, related in his diary his objection to a war with Spain which was threatening in the spring of 1854:

As to leaving the Army: I may do so if I choose at this time and no one notice me, for I am unknown except to a few friends. If I wait and a war with Spain be forced on us by the headlong ambition of false policy of the Cabinet at Washington it might be hazardous to retire, even though in principle opposed to the war, not only as unjustifiable towards Spain, but as impolitic and injurious as respects ourselves.[4]

Military criticism of civilian political leaders for their "reckless military adventurism" and "blind faith in the manifest destiny of the Republic" continued to recur until the Japanese attack on Pearl Harbor. These generals and admirals had been inclined to avoid actual war because they felt they did not have adequate resources at their disposal. Moreover, in the past, the reluctance to go to war has been grounded in a hemispheric concept of national defense and a desire to avoid "foreign alliances."

Members of the totalitarian elite, who rise to power by violence and force, seem even more sensitive than elected leaders to the revolutionary consequences of modern warfare. The professional military leaders they direct reflect these concerns. Moreover, when they have risen to power after periods of agitation and persecution, they are likely to plan far ahead. In particular, the Communist operational code assumes that the course of history is on its side and therefore their elite operate on the basis of a long-term definition of the future. This does not mean that totalitarian leaders are free from the dilemmas of the revolutionary and political consequences of modern warfare; they are merely more prepared to face them directly, and to utilize them for desired goals.

At the end of World War II the Russians assumed that extensive military operations and repressive occupational policies would weaken the old social structure, and therefore expedite a subsequent Communist reconstruction. In Poland, in particular, the Russians permitted the Germans to eliminate resistance groups, and thereby facilitated their military occupation.[5] Perhaps one of the most dramatic cases of exploiting the revolutionary consequences of warfare was the behavior of Japanese military forces during the period of their imminent defeat in World War II. The Japanese military elite had risen to power by the violent elimination of political opposition. When faced with defeat, its activist leaders developed the policy of deliberately arming nationalist groups in South Asia, partly in the hope that these groups would support the Japanese against the Allies. The result, as intended, was to confront the returning Allies with a series of effective political revolutions.

The American military establishment was founded to wage a national revolution, yet the operational code it had developed by 1910, the year used here as a baseline against which to chart contemporary trends, was hardly sensitive to the revolutionary consequences of warfare. This is not to say that military doctrine was unconcerned with political objectives. As demonstrated earlier,* the officer profession of this period and its elite members were not unpolitical; rather, they were implicitly conservative. They had developed a military doctrine which expressed their conservatism, and which was molded by the military assignments they had confronted. As of 1910, although the Navy was developing a mildly expansionistic philosophy, the military code of the United States was essentially an expression of the thinking of the ground forces: Doctrine still reflected the "heroic" roots of the profession, and could be labeled as a sort of "frontier" or punitive expedition doctrine. The military problems of the expanding frontier had fashioned the operational code. It had three basic elements, which, in essence, assumed that the tasks of adjusting military means to political goals presented no special problems.

First, war was inevitable. To assume that war was inevitable did not mean that war was desirable, but that the nature of human nature was such that organized violence was the final arbiter among nations. The intellectual justification for this thesis, if any was required, was a mixture of religious zeal and crude social Darwinism, adapted to the military setting. If war was inevitable, the highest technical and organizational efficiency was justified and, in fact, morally required. Since war was inevitable, to be prepared was the lesser evil.

Second, war was essentially a punitive action. The purpose of war was, in effect, to bring people who lived outside the rules of law and order within the orbit of civilization. The military opera-

* See Chapter 12, Political Beliefs.

tional code at the outbreak of World War I was, in crucial respects, no more than the concept of the pacification of the Indians writ large. There was little concern with the philosophy of the use of organized violence to achieve a specific political settlement or a new balance of power. Military action was designed to facilitate total political incorporation, or merely to "punish" the lawless.

American military traditions have been extremely varied and have included the use of force to achieve specific political objectives. Contrary to popular assumptions, American military history is replete with experiences in which military actions were coordinated with political negotiations—sometimes successfully, sometimes unsuccessfully. The major armed conflicts of the Revolutionary War, the War of 1812, and the Mexican War were of this nature. Yet, it is not baffling to account for the emergence of the punitive expedition philosophy. The way in which wars are fought is a function of the civilian social structure and political leadership. The Civil War started as a political military operation, though political leaders may have been hazy as to the strategy for achieving their objectives. It ended as a total war, fought along the lines of a punitive expedition. The logic that developed in the Civil War seems to have been kept alive and perpetuated by descendants—familial and professional— on both sides. The Civil War was followed by a continuation of the wars against the Indians, in the style of no political settlement. From 1865 to 1898 the Army fought 943 engagements of varying intensity and duration against Indian tribes.

Until the Spanish-American War, the military did not have to face the intricate workings of a political balance of power, or the political dilemmas involved in applying force. It did not have to deal with superior numbers of foreign troops and populations. It did not even have to confront problems of colonialism, since the native populations could be subjugated without a political settlement. Successful military action produced national expansion, and introduced law and order rather than social disruption. In short, the military was spared the experiences of Western Europe, where the aftermath of war often produced popular and armed revolutions.

Even the Navy, relieved of strategic tasks by the supremacy of the British naval forces, could operate on a theory of punitive expeditions. It operated mainly to suppress the slave trade and piracy and to protect American commerce, although, to some degree, these limited tasks made it more sensitive to the limitations of force than an army whose training consisted of successful punitive expeditions against the Indians. The Spanish-American War was conducted by the Army with little more preparation than if it were engaged in a traditional expedition against the Indians. But after the easy defeat of a weak opponent, the Army faced the stubborn task of subjugating the defiant native Moros in the Philippines. In administering its new possessions, the Army learned the limitations of its operational code and the necessity of political compromise. In the aftermath of the Spanish-American War, the military profession had to deal with the full range of modern politico-military problems: political intelligence, control of guerilla forces, military government, the arming of indigenous forces, and the terms of political settlement. If the experiences in Cuba and in the Philippines had little influence on the conduct of subsequent military operations, it was because the military had not yet developed techniques of self-evaluation and indoctrination of officers in the complexities of modern warfare.

Third, at the turn of the century the military considered the national purposes of war as self-evident; they did not require explicit ideological justification. A small group of officers, mainly naval personnel, sought an ideology of manifest destiny by which to justify overseas military action, and such jingoistic thinking helped to force involvement in the Spanish-American War. But at that time the military profession was not sufficiently detached from its provincial background to feel the need for ideological guide lines. It sufficed to operate on the self-evident principle of common defense, and on the implicit moral crusade to enforce American-type law and order. The touchstones of the moral crusade were Christian principles and private property. Thus, in the Indian wars each Indian had to be made law-abiding, and, implicitly, for him to become a Christian was the most appropriate indication of his having become civilized.[6] And because military conservatism in the United States was linked to the concept of private property, even where territorial ambitions were not present, the implicit objective of war, as seen by the military, was to spread American economic influence.

The differences in military doctrine between the United States and Great Britain in the period before World War I were basic, even though the officer ·orps in both nations operated under civilian democratic political control. For the United States, because its "colonial" areas were capable of political integration, and because its boundaries kept expanding, the military tasks of internal security and foreign policy were entwined. The military forces believed they were imposing law and order, internally and externally. The fact that federal troops were repeatedly used during the nineteenth century to enforce the authority of the central government contributed to this self-conception. The twentieth century has witnessed a distinct separation of the internal police function from the national military function in the United States, but this was not always the case.

In England the military was exempted from internal security or police functions at an earlier date. The Navy was exempted by its very nature. After Cromwell, the Army found itself relatively free from the task of enforcing internal peace, the last Jacobin uprising taking place in 1745. England had no active frontiers in the nineteenth century, except for the pacification of Ireland, and this problem interjected the military into internal politics with almost disastrous results. Relieved of an internal police function, the British Army did not hold to the assumption that its primary task was to force British standards of behavior on unfriendly states. Instead, it was able to implement a variety of political objectives. Whether in Continental Europe, in colonial expeditions, or in policing sea lanes, the British military was charged with the task of limited objectives.

In the aftermath of the Spanish-American War, the United States military had to prepare for the possibility that they might one day have to fight a major war. The frontier function had disappeared, and the internal police function was in effect, separated from the strategic military one. Progressively, military leaders had to discover that the heroic and frontier operational code was not applicable to their tasks. The rise of military managers meant that the military elite and those who aspired to enter that elite must become concerned with questions of "policy." The operational code and the professional self-image were no longer universally based on a "philosophy" which considered war inevitable, implicitly punitive, and fought for self-evident objectives.

The Rise of Policy

As of 1960, after fifty years of professional ferment, it is not possible to identify an American military doctrine; instead, it is more revealing to speak of two competing theories of how military forces should be used to achieve political objectives. Each theory has its own philosophy of long-range political goals, a conception of politico-military strategy, an image of enemy intentions, and an estimate of the uncommitted nations. Both theories claim to be grounded in a scientific and professional understanding of war-making, but, in actuality, they give expression to the fundamental social and political values inherent in American society.

One school of thought, the "absolute," is a direct outgrowth of the frontier and punitive expedition tradition. Warfare—actual or threatened—is the most fundamental basis of international relations. Since the political objectives of war are gained by victory, the more complete the victory, the greater the possibility of achieving political goals. In short, there is no substitute for "total victory." Contrariwise, the other is the "pragmatic" school. Warfare is but one instrument of international relations, along with ideological and economic struggle. The political objectives of warfare are gained by adapting the use or the threat of violence to the objectives to be achieved. To use too much or too little is self-defeating.

The "absolute" doctrine, while it has had to adapt itself to the implications of atomic destruction, emphasizes the permanency of the rules of warfare and continues to be concerned with victory. It tends to think of atomic wars as relatively short wars. By contrast, the "pragmatic" doctrine emphasizes the revolutionary character of atomic energy, and the discontinuity of the military past with the future. As formulated by General Maxwell D. Taylor, in a hearing before the Senate Preparedness Committee in the spring of 1959, the pragmatic doctrine assumes that the decisive part of a nuclear war could take place quickly, but "it might take 100 years to end the desolation and to restore some form of order." In this view, the term victory loses its meaning. "In my judgment," General Taylor declared, "any dogmatic prediction of what will take place after an initial nuclear exchange is beyond human capability. However, there is no reason to believe that peace is going to ensue at once, except, perhaps, the peace of the dead."[7]

Both theories—absolute and pragmatic—are expressions of a managerial outlook. In both cases there is an effort to adjust means and ends, but the calculus is markedly different. The "absolutists" assume the end as given—total victory; the means must be adjusted in order to achieve it. The "pragmatists" are concerned not only with adapting military means to achieve desired political ends, but insist that the end must be conditioned by what military technology is capable of achieving.[8] In short, some ends cannot be achieved.

Lieutenant General James M. Gavin describes the two aspects of United States military doctrine as conservative or liberal.[9] His analysis is of special importance, for it represents the first attempt by a major professional military thinker in the United States to formulate the elements of military doctrine in general terms, rather than on the basis of technical details. In essence, his standpoint is that of the social analyst who seeks to identify underlying patterns in human thinking and behavior. His distinction between conservative and liberal military doctrine is not explicitly linked to political ideology. These terms are used because he believes that it is possible to place any military leader on a continuum, ranging from conservative to liberal. However, the distinction between "absolute" and "pragmatic" codes is roughly equivalent to that which obtains between conservative and liberal doctrine, as defined by Gavin. The meaning of these terms—absolute-pragmatic, or conservative-liberal—is clarified by reference to the issue of the inevitability of war, and the political objectives of military action.

1. *The Inevitability of War.* Even though there has been a decline in belief in the inevitability of war, this question still remains highly relevant for distinguishing between the absolute and the pragmatic military manager. Traditionally, when an officer asserted that war was inevitable, he was expressing a simple and unreflected sentiment. It was not the result of rational skepticism or sophisticated thinking about history, but rather a subjective feeling about human nature and the struggle for survival. Nor is it strange that a strong belief in the inevitability of violence should go hand and hand with a strong acceptance of orthodox religion. To believe in the necessity of violence requires strong prescriptions for sanctioning its use.

Each increase in the destructive power of weapons has raised grave questions about the inevitability of war in the minds of the military profession. The most revolutionary step—thermo-nuclear weapons—seriously weakened the principle.[10] With the introduction of intercontinental ballistic missiles, the operational code of the military is no longer based on a belief in the inevitability of general war. The military profession must now recognize the fact that the power of destruction is so great that it is dangerous to generalize from past experience. Nevertheless, it is still possible to maintain implicit faith in the necessity of war by shifting the definition or scope of war. Wars will be limited wars. Or, what is inevitable is a continuation of the struggle between nation states—by means other than total war. Or, what is inevitable is a continuation of the struggle for superior military potentials. Thus, an Air Force general can appear before Congress and argue that the arms race will continue indefinitely, since after the intercontinental missile, the struggle will be transferred to control of the moon, Venus, and other planets.

The intensive interviews with the sample of potential members of the military elite—colonels, brigadier generals, and their naval equivalents marked for continued promotion—are most revealing. Public statements by top officers and their writings in service journals are, in a sense, political warfare, directed either to the civilian home population or to the potential enemy. The opinions expressed in these informal interviews indicate the professional outlook in the three services. They reflect the consequences of organizational pressures and higher military education, and they confirm the observations of other civilian observers who have had prolonged contact with United States military planners. When probed about the chances of a major atomic war, a majority of the sample of more than one hundred staff officers rejected its inevitability:

Sixty-five per cent believed that there would be no major atomic war, or that the probability was very low.

Twenty-five per cent believed that there would be a major atomic war, or that the chances were more than very low.*

Ten per cent stated that they did not know, or could not make an estimate.

The 65 per cent who believed there would be no major atomic war fell into two groups: A minority believed that atomic weapons

* Of this group, one out of five believed that a major atomic war would be the outgrowth of limited warfare.

were such a deterrent that there was not a high probability of even limited nuclear warfare. The majority, however, believed that limited nuclear warfare was a definite possibility. The degree to which the inevitability of major war, as a professional assumption, has weakened can even be seen from a closer examination of the 25 per cent who believed that atomic war was a real possibility. Many of these officers thought that atomic warfare would not be the result of deliberate policy, but of a miscalculation (not an isolated accident). In short, even for them, professional rationality qualified belief in the inevitability of major atomic warfare. On the other hand, the likelihood of limited warfare was taken for granted by all those interviewed.

From this sample, and from all available evidence, we can conclude that officers with an "absolute" viewpoint are more prone than are the "pragmatic" ones to believe in the likelihood of major atomic warfare. Thus, belief in the inevitability of war becomes transformed into a political matter, with strong ideological overtones. As an issue of doctrine, the question is posed: Must the United States be limited in its strategy to the principle that the enemy will be permitted to strike the first blow? There is almost universal acceptance among the military of the principle that the enemy will strike first, either because this principle is enforced by civilian policy, and/or because it is recognized as an essential ingredient of American political values. But the "absolutists" differ from the "pragmatists" in their estimate of the consequences of this assumption. The "absolutists" are more likely to see the principle as a serious limitation on day-to-day military practice and as a long-term weakness; contrariwise, the "pragmatists" are much less likely to see it as a military liability, and, in fact, tend to consider it an immediate political asset.

2. *Punitive versus Political Objectives.* The operational code has been gradually modified, away from the punitive concept of war toward the pursuit of political objectives. Even before the advent of atomic weapons, the military elite had become increasingly prone to define victory as something short of total military subjugation. There has been a growing recognition that the objective of military action is not necessarily to impose American moral standards and economic institutions.

In effect, the United States fought World War I under the "absolute" doctrine, as if it were again engaged in a punitive expedition. We entered the war with a mixture of goals: idealistic beliefs about national self-determination, economic self-interest, and vague notions of the political conditions for national and international security. There was an underlying desire to transform Western Europe into the image of America. The political and the military formula converged, since both assumed that nations living outside the realm of law and order had to be punished, and military defeat was the necessary form of punishment.

In order that the defeat be thorough, and that Americans get their due reward, General Pershing insisted that United States military forces be kept intact and deployed as an integrated unit. In 1917, when the final German offensive failed, and while Allied forces were developing their counteroffensive, negotiations for an armistice were started.

To achieve what he thought were United States political goals, Pershing did not favor an armistice, and pressed for "unconditional surrender." The desire for glory undoubtedly operated; he ordered his troops to attack right up to the moment of the armistice. Since, in his opinion, the political aim of the war would be frustrated without complete military defeat, Pershing wrote to his superiors in the United States:

Finally, I believe that complete victory can only be obtained by continuing the war until we force unconditional surrender from Germany; but if the Allied Governments decide to grant an armistice, the terms should be so rigid that under no circumstances could Germany again take up arms.[11]

Pershing never spelled out the political conditions of such a settlement. From his insistence on following the rules of land warfare and of military occupation, it is also evident that ne was expressing a romantic, rather than a political, concept of total victory. The armistice was signed, and the military made few positive contributions to the peace negotiations.

By World War II, the operational code had been transformed to the extent that the American military in Western Europe pressed for a revision of the unconditional surrender formula, which had been promulgated, in part, both for the home front and for the politics of the alliance with Russia. Whether in its effect the unconditional surrender formula prolonged military hostilities in Europe, or whether a viable political settlement could have been obtained by altering this strategy permits of no simple answer. The bulk of evidence and the evaluation of disinterested analysts indicates the "unconditional surrender" formula had little or no effect on German military resistance in the field.[12] The German military establishment was relatively impervious to political appeals from the Allies. In retrospect, the direct encouragement of resistance elements would probably have had little practical effect on military operations, although the question will supply permanent employment for academic historians.

Yet, the sheer scope of military operations was so demanding of resources that there was great pressure for political settlement with secondary Axis allies or ex-Axis powers (Vichy France in North Africa, and the Badoglio regime in Italy). In Western Europe a pragmatic outlook among top commanders was extremely strong.[13] Military commanders of the ground forces in North Africa also welcomed those arrangements, which relieved them of military government responsibilities, even though these tasks were of high political importance. In part, field commanders were primarily concerned with achieving "victory" over the Germans. But they were also displaying a political preference to deal with constituted authorities in the area, since they implicitly assumed that such arrangements would maintain the status quo and prevent social unrest. General George Patton reported in his diary that he called on the Grand Vizier of Morocco as part of the protocol of the military occupation. But he took the occasion to tell the chieftain that he had no intention of disturbing local political arrangements.[14] At the same time, his politico-military officers were forced to intervene continuously, for example, by controlling Radio Maroc, censoring the local French press, and forcing the release of De Gaullists who were retained in French prisons. In his on-the-spot report Colonel Charles R. Codman, aide-de-camp to General Patton, testified to the conflict which the military believed to exist between combat efficiency and political objectives:

Casablanca is teeming with O.W.I. boys, journalists, and assorted visiting firemen, clamoring for immediate solution of the Jewish question, the democratization of the Arabs, and the turning over of North Africa to DeGaulle. The hearts of these enthusiasts are doubtless in the right

place, and in the long run they are likely to get their way, though the
wisdom of prematurely forcing their objectives remains to be seen. For
the moment their demands appear impractical to, and will be resisted by
the military.[15]

Even in regard to Nazi Germany, military commanders in Western Europe resisted the application of unconditional surrender and
pressed for its modification. SHAEF headquarters repeatedly requested civilian review of the policy, even though its political warfare staff experts were convinced that its modification would have
little practical effect on military operations.[16] It was not because
of profound political insight that the military pressed to relieve
Germany from unconditional surrender; rather, it was an expression
of pragmatic managerialism, which was continuously seeking to
fight the war in the most rational and efficient way.

The "absolutist" doctrine had much greater force in the war
against Japan. The Far East campaign showed more overtones of
a punitive expedition, not only because of the attack on Pearl
Harbor, but because of a strong sense of racial and traditional
hostility toward the Japanese armed forces. Military planners were
mainly concerned with the question of whether Japan could be
defeated by naval forces or whether a land invasion was required.
Military leaders operating in the Far East in the pursuit of glory
did not resist the idea of unconditional surrender. Nor were they
concerned with negotiations with opposition groups in Japan, although the possibility of successful political settlement has in
retrospect been judged more likely in Japan than in Nazi Germany.
Admiral William Leahy was the one military leader who claimed
that he considered a political approach, rather than actual invasion,
preferable for achieving United States strategic objectives.

I was unable to see any justification, from a national detense point of
view, for an invasion of an already thoroughly defeated Japan. I feared
that the cost would be enormous in both lives and treasures.

It was my opinion at that time [June 1945] that a surrender could be
arranged with terms acceptable to Japan that would make fully satisfactory provisions for America's defense against any future trans-Pacific
aggression.[17]

But pressure was exerted for a political settlement by civilian
leadership. Ambassador Joseph C. Grew was persistent in asserting
that the United States would have to permit the Japanese to retain

their Emperor in post-war Japan.[18] Ultimately, a decision was reached at a White House conference on June 18, 1945, under President Harry S. Truman. Despite the reluctance of a majority of the Joint Chiefs of Staff, the decision for political action to hasten the final surrender of the Japanese was taken.[19] Once the decision was made, the military energetically sought to implement these political warfare objectives, but they were hampered by the absence of a unified political and military command operation in the Far East. The use of two atomic bombs, instead, occasioned the surrender. Less than a decade l~ter, the Korean conflict again provoked a clash between "absolutist" and "pragmatic" doctrines about military operations.[*]

3. *Self-Evident versus Explicit Objectives.* If the heroic leader was content to wage war for self-evident objectives, contemporary military planners—both "absolute" and "pragmatic"—use the political phrase "national objectives" as often as they use any technical military term. Much of the higher education of the military, when not centered on technical matters, is an expression of the concern that "we should know what we are for, as well as what we are against," that the most conspicuous lack of our war and post-war policies has been the absence of realistic and "worthwhile" national aims. Men who are bent on the accumulation of power do not conscientiously search for policy. They are likely to have fixed notions of what needs to be done. The constant concern with policy directives of the military is a testament to the reserve with which it exercises its influence.

Because generals and admirals have spent most of their lives in a large bureaucracy which seeks to avoid partisan attachments, they are indifferent to and even suspicious of the efforts of party politicians to formulate national goals. National objectives, in their opinion, must be rooted in the common values of American society. They envision these values being formalized into objectives by super-staff work, unencumbered by the passions of political man and detached from daily routine. In a sense, this is truly the expression of the politics of those who "stand above" politics. General A. C. Wedemeyer presents his formula for such a policy-making body, which has the appearance of a military staff planning group, rather

* See Chapter 15, Total versus Limited Warfare.

than a political organ. He sees the group as expert, nonpartisan, and with lifetime tenure:

Such a foreign policy group, or Grand Strategy Board, would be comprised of carefully selected members representing collective knowledge and experience in the political, economic, psychological, and military fields. In order that they could recommend appropriate aims and sound courses of action in each country—friendly, neutral, or hostile—they would have access to all information available to the government as provided by the Central Intelligence Agency and other intelligence sources so that their determinations would not be made in a vacuum but would be attuned to developments in all parts of the world. To give continuity and to insure non-partisan evaluations, members of the foreign policy group, or Grand Strategy Board, should be appointed for life.[20]

Military literature is replete with self-generated efforts to ascertain the consensus of American society, as a basis for long-range planning. In general, these efforts are not the work of "militarists" who wish to modify American society. Instead, as efforts to reflect and enhance ideological consensus, they produce a middle-of-the-road concept which speaks of a private enterprise economy with governmental intervention, of individual liberties and social responsibility, and the like. Typical of the political consensus that the armed forces have come to find congenial is the textbook entitled *Democracy versus Communism*, prepared by Kenneth Colegrove for the Institute of Political Education, and distributed by the Office of Information and Education as a basis of service indoctrination.[21] Although Colegrove, a political scientist who served as an adviser on General Douglas MacArthur's military government staff, would identify himself as a "confirmed right-wing" Republican, the volume is hardly doctrinaire, let alone extremist. The author acknowledges suggestions and criticisms from political theorists as diverse in their views as Merle Fainsod, of Harvard University, with a "Fair Deal" outlook, to Willmore Kendall of Yale University, who has served as an editor of the "ultra-conservative" *National Review*. Colegrove presents a compromise doctrine which the professional officer is prepared to accept in the "national interest," and which, correspondingly, is so generalized that military planners with differing conceptions of the logic of war are able to accept it.

"Absolutists" are distinguishable from "pragmatists," not primarily because their assumptions about American values differ, but because they have developed differing conceptions of international relations. The "absolutists" have their political roots in the traditions of continental or Gibraltar ("Fortress America") theories of national security; the "pragmatists" assume commitments to a system of international alliance. Both viewpoints, of course, have had to be radically adapted to modern military technology, and both doctrines involve estimates, though differing, of the viability of the Soviet Union and its long-term goals.

It is still possible for a ranking Air Force general, in an off-the-record briefing, to recommend that American policy be based on sheer brute force: "Let's start killing people. People need to respect the United States and when we start killing people, then there will be more respect for the United States. . . ." It is more likely, however, that the exponent of the "absolutist" doctrine will state United States long-range goals in terms of the necessity of world ideological supremacy. (See Table 30, paradigm for a comparison of the "absolute" and "pragmatic" operational code.) Thus, Admiral Felix B. Stump told the Freedom Foundation that "communist nations and free nations cannot survive indefinitely in the same world." In the long-term process the intermediate political goals are to maintain the status quo in the "free world" and to "liberate" Communist-dominated political systems.

Table 30

Paradigm: Contemporary Operational Codes in the Military Profession

	"Absolute" Doctrine	"Pragmatic" Doctrine
U.S. long-term political goals	Total supremacy	Active competition
U.S. political-military strategy	Gibraltar defense	Mutual security
U.S. military strategy	Show of strength (massive deterrence)	Measured violence (graduated deterrence)
Soviet long-term political goals	World domination	Expansionist
Uncommitted nations	Potential enemies	Potential allies

By contrast, the "pragmatic" military manager is committed to a long-range political goal of active competition with the Soviet

Union, and a belief in the intermediate goal of gradual social change, since the continued existence of both sides cannot be denied. In 1947 General Eisenhower established a three-man committee, designated as the Advanced Study Group, to make a long-term estimate of the role of military operations in American foreign policy. The conclusions of this group can be taken as an articulate statement of the pragmatic view of the logic of war. The punitive concept of military action is abandoned, and there are no purely ideological goals:

> We should emphasize over and over that we desire friendly relations with all nations. We should have no objection to any nation's internal government so long as it learns to live peacefully in the world. We should clearly state that we are not fighting communism as such but are opposed to the imposition of communism upon nations. We should take the position that democracy can exist peacefully and progressively in the same world with communism, socialism and other ideologies.[22]

Under this operational code, war is no longer inevitable. In fact, it recommends, "we should stress our abhorrence of war and our faith that war is not inevitable." Even the traditional military commitment to the status quo is no longer operative: "We encourage peaceful progress and change, since change will occur despite efforts to stop it."

The "absolute" and "pragmatic" doctrines show differing conceptions of Soviet intentions. The "pragmatist" sees Soviet plans as expansionist, and based on the combined use of political, ideological, economic, and military force. The "absolutist" describes Soviet intentions as centering basically on world domination and as fundamentally military, supported by an unchanging ideology. Each doctrine formulates a military strategy. For "pragmatists," there is no single solution to the threat of permanent expansionism, only graduated deterrence. This means the precise ability to reply with military efforts equal to the military threat, ranging from strategic atomic retaliation to limited warfare, as well as the ability to control indirect aggression through powers which are uncommitted to either bloc. The "pragmatic" school is forced, therefore, to emphasize a system of alliances and mutual security arrangements. The control of indirect aggression requires political and economic support for uncommitted nations, which are seen as potential allies.

The theory of graduated deterrence, which became the object of intense civilian debate in the period around 1955, had already been formulated by "pragmatic" planners of the Advanced Study Group in 1947:

As war develops, we should emphasize that our military forces are being used to stop the war as soon as possible, in order to prevent further destruction and allow remaining conflicts to be settled peacefully.

The "absolute" doctrine is based on the primary necessity of maximum ability to retaliate. Although it has its origins in a hemispheric concept of security, it had to face the requirements of overseas bases. Requisite alliances, however, are thought of, mainly, as military arrangements to supply bases for massive retaliation, rather than as political devices for developing resources for conventional warfare.

Both doctrines are modes of military thinking that have their counterparts among the civilian population. Some military leaders are as "pragmatic" as any civilian political leader, while some civilians are as "absolute" as any military officer. All of the observations about the changing military profession—from the changing nature of military authority to its broadening social composition— point to narrowed differences between civilians and the military. Yet, these differences are not obliterated, since the military, as a profession, maintains its distinctive combat-mindedness because of its operational responsibilities.

Consequently, military leaders, whether of the "absolutist" or "pragmatic" school, tend to place great emphasis on military factors in international politics. Because of the tremendous ambiguities they face in planning military operations, they seek to develop elaborate and specific plans to cover alternative contingencies, and they demand of their civilian political counterparts the same type of explicit planning. Yet, because of professional background training and immediate responsibilities, diplomats and politicians place much less emphasis on explicit and formal planning procedures. The problems of military command and administration require definitive solutions. Therefore, the military operational code seeks to reduce ambiguity. International political negotiation and communication between political leaders requires the ability to balance ambiguities, while exploring areas of compromise and agreement. Political success involves the ability to tolerate uncertainty, or, in the language of the diplomat, to "live with insoluble problems." The military officer who can serve as an effective diplomat owes a great deal to his previous military training which perpared him to shift from one role to another. The shift from a military to a diplomatic role may be more feasible in the contemporary scene than it was four or five decades ago, but this does not imply that the operational code of diplomacy is the same as the operational code of combat preparation.

The application of the game theory and mathematical studies of risk-taking have yet to demonstrate their practical utility for the conduct of international relations, although they may have some relevance in training potential policy makers and diplomats.[23] Interestingly enough, these research efforts have produced some suggestive evidence that military personnel select more high pay-off, low-probability solution than comparable civilian groups; in short, these experiments point to a lower tolerance for ambiguity in military thinking.[24]

In interviews, and in responses to questionnaires, a typical version of the impatience with the political process would erupt at times. These eruptions reflect the professional military environment, and indicate the extent to which, even with the growth of military managers, the effective military diplomat is an unconventional type. For example, one rear admiral in a responsible policy post declared:

Space and time permits only an over-simplified discussion and, therefore, one which, I fear, will sound ill-tempered. The military mind is more direct than the civilian. It prefers a reasonably good answer to a philosophical discussion which becomes lost in its own logic (the last is precisely my criticism of the average NSC document). We need both types of minds but the military mind needs to be leaned more heavily upon at this time than is being done. The NSC [National Security Council] is turning out documents which may cover all the angles but this is war and, in my opinion, the NSC documents are establishing an excellent pattern for losing the war by fighting it purely on an intellectual plane. Such literature as they contain may have its value, but, in dealing with war, we must grasp the nettle; we must throw away these learned treatises and produce something which can be understood and remembered, not only by intellectuals, but also by the man in the street.[25]

While civilian commitments to military doctrine have a different origin, and therefore a different character, within the military profession it does seem possible to account for absolute and pragmatic doctrines as expressions of a type-of-service point of view. The Air Force, because its primary mission is the delivery of strategic atomic weapons, tends to be committed to an absolutist outlook. By contrast, the Army has become pragmatic, since it has lost its primary mission of strategic destruction of the enemy's military forces. The Navy's mixed orientation can be attributed to its effort to maintain a strategic mission and, at the same time, to expand its limited warfare role. Still, such an explanation does not account for the evolution of military doctrine, nor for substantial minority positions within particular services.

Lieutenant General James Gavin's analysis of military codes, referred to earlier, is highly relevant, because it seeks to distinguish between a service point of view and a professional point of view. Professional background and experience explain how military doctrine evolves, why some officers deviate from the dominant service viewpoint, and how doctrine actually influences the political behavior of each service. The social backgrounds of the military profession are of declining importance in explaining the adherence of an officer to one doctrine or another. Instead, professional experience, including the special impact of the military faction in which an officer finds himself, has become of increasing importance.

As long as military thinking was limited to a frontier—land or sea—doctrine, its heroic stance and social exclusiveness were highly appropriate and served the needs of both the profession and political democracy. The officer was prepared to fight because it was a gentlemanly way of life, and the political system did not require much of him by way of political expertise. As the officer corps became more and more socially representative, it simultaneously found itself confronted with tasks which required it to become more policy-oriented. The heroic leader has been, and remains, relatively indifferent to politico-military affairs. But the military manager, because he is policy-oriented, develops either an absolute or pragmatic outlook, depending on his military education and professional experience. The conflict between the two orientations was originally manifested in the Army, because of its earlier and more extensive involvement in politico-military affairs.

Notes

1. Hanson W. Baldwin, military analyst, uses the term "military philosophy": "A military philosophy and that somewhat more tangible thing—a military policy—are the product of many factors. A philosophy grows from the minds and hearts, social mores and customs, traditions and environment of a people. It is the product of national and racial attributes, geography, the nature of a potential enemy threat, standards of living and national traditions, influenced and modified by great military philosophers, like Clausewitz and Mahan, and by great national leaders like Napoleon." *New York Times,* Magazine Section, November 3, 1957, p. 13.

2. Garthoff, Raymond, *Soviet Military Doctrine.* Glencoe: The Free Press, 1953.

3. See Leites, Nathan, *The Operational Code of the Politburo.* New York: McGraw-Hill, 1951, for an analysis of Soviet theories of political conduct. Leites has been criticized for relying exclusively on the published texts of major Soviet theorists, and for assuming that the operational conduct of the Soviets has not undergone a change. However, he does point out that more than such writings are required to account for Politburo action: "The historical record reveals unverbalized, but equally important, rules of conduct" (p. xiii).

4. Croffut, W. A., *Fifty Years in Camp and Field: The Diary of Major-General Ethan Allen Hitchcock, USA.* New York: G. P. Putnam's Sons, 1909, p. 411.

5. However, the Communists did not divert their resources from what they believed to be primary military objectives in order to create social disruption, which might at some future date be exploited by political means. The most conspicuous case was the total absence of long-range bombardment of Nazi Germany by the Russians, as compared with the practices of the Allies. Allied strategy was dictated by military considerations, namely, that strategic bombardment was the most immediate and direct approach to bringing the war to Germany. The Russians, in turn, calculated that their military resources could best be used in tactical aircraft to support their land forces. They did not believe it necessary to disrupt German home-front morale by aerial bombardment, as did many Allied military leaders. See, for example, Brereton, Lewis H., *The Brereton Diaries; The War in the Pacific, Middle East and Europe, 30 October 1941—8 May 1945.* New York: Morrow, 1946, p. 289. Where it is reported that a "strong air attack was ordered on Berlin at a meeting on June 20, 1944, in order to counteract Nazi propaganda about V-1 weapons."

6. A parallel could be drawn between the efforts of the military to support the mass Christianization of the Indians and the bureaucratic processes of denazification instituted in post-war Germany, since both were expressions of a moral crusade.

7. *New York Times,* March 14, 1959, p. 6.

8. The heroic leader and the two types of military managers, absolute and pragmatic, can be related to Max Weber's types of authority and rationality. The heroic leader operates under a traditional orientation; he takes the relationship between means and ends for granted. The pragmatic doctrine is an expression of "zweckrational," or an orientation to a system of discreet individual ends. Absolute doctrine is an expression of "wertrational," or an orientation to an absolute value. The keynote to the distinction lies, as

Talcott Parsons points out, in the absoluteness with which the values involved in "Wertrationitet" are held. See Weber, Max, *The Theory of Social and Economic Organization*, translated by A. R. Henderson and Talcott Parsons. London: William Hodge & Co., 1947, pp. 104–05.

9. Gavin, James M., *War and Peace in the Space Age*. New York: Harper & Bros., 1948, pp. 248ff.

10. However, diminished belief in the inevitability of war is more than a response to the increased destructiveness of weapons. In the military profession, as in other scientifically-oriented specialties, a minority has become increasingly skeptical and rational, and this rationality resists overdeterministic formulations.

11. Quoted in Mott, Colonel T. Bentley, *Twenty Years as a Military Attache*. New York: Oxford University Press, 1937, p. 266.

12. Speier, Hans, "War Aims in Political Warfare." *Social Research*, 1945, 12, 157–80.

13. It is difficult to accept Dr. Paul Kecskemeti's evaluation of Allied efforts to produce a politcal settlement with Badoglio. Kecskemeti, a student of political ideology and propaganda, concluded that the Allies used the wrong strategy, because they were captured by their unconditional surrender formula and therefore refused to give the Italians a face-saving formula. See Kecskemeti, Paul, *Strategic Surrender: The Politics of Victory and Defeat*. Stanford: Stanford University Press, 1958, pp. 71ff. Closer examination of the military situation indicates, however, that the Badoglio group did not have effective control of Italian ground forces. They could not guarantee minimum assistance for the Allied air-borne troops earmarked to seize Rome as part of the surrender plan.

14. Patton, George S., Jr., *War as I Knew It*. Boston: Houghton, Mifflin, 1947, p. 23.

15. Codman Charles R., *Drive*. Boston: Little, Brown & Co., 1957, pp. 48–49.

16. It should also be noted that the Allied propagandists did not feel unduly inhibited by the unconditional surrender concept. In particular, see Crossman, Richard H. S., "Supplementary Essay," in *Sykewar: Psychological Warfare against Germany, D-Day to VE-Day*, edited by Daniel Lerner. New York: George W. Stewart, 1949.

17. Leahy, William, *I Was There*. New York: Whittlesey House, 1950, p. 384.

18. Grew, Joseph C., *Turbulent Era II: A Diplomatic Record of Forty Years, 1904–1945*. Boston: Houghton Mifflin, 1952, pp. 406–11.

19. See, in particular, McCloy, John J., *The Challenge to American Foreign Policy*. Cambridge: Harvard University Press, 1953.

20. Wedemeyer, A. C., *Wedemeyer Reports*. New York: Henry Holt, 1958, p. 437.

21. Colegrove, Kenneth, *Democracy versus Communism*. Princeton: D. Van Nostrand, 1957.

22. Norman Lloyd, "Operation Future." *Combat Forces Journal*, 1950, 1, 30.

23. Kaplan, Morton A., *System and Process in International Politics*. New York: John Wiley, 1953.

24. Scoldel, Alvin, Ratoosh, Philburn, & Minas, J. Aayer, "Some Personality Correlates of Decision Making under Conditions of Risk." *Behavioral Science*, 1959, 4, 19–27.

25. Personal communication.

VI

POLITICAL BEHAVIOR:
PRAGMATIC VERSUS ABSOLUTIST

CHAPTER *14*

Coalition Warfare

INEVITABLY, a gap exists between doctrine and practice in politico-military affairs. The political behavior of military leaders is a reaction to actual and immediate military experience, as well as an expression of explicit doctrine. The impact of conducting a war of coalition on a world-wide basis against the Axis "matured" the American military elite as much as did years of professional training. If, by 1950, key military managers could be judged either as absolutists or as pragmatists in their thinking, the career experiences of World War II had much to do with molding their outlook.

An understanding of contemporary military politics must take into account the judgments which officers have come to hold about the conduct of World War II. Most officers who served either in Europe or in the Far East became convinced that the United States did not fully exploit the political potentials of the military resources mobilized during World War II. An important theme in contemporary military thinking centers precisely on the necessity of preventing such a repetition of events in international relations.

Considerable thought has been devoted by military staff officers and by study groups at higher military schools as to how military resources available to the United States could have been used for more satisfactory political settlements in central Europe and in China after 1945. Although the intellectual clarity of such studies varies considerably, on the whole, they are not characterized by political realism. One such study, Project Control, sponsored by the Air War College under the direction of Colonel Raymond Sleeper, went so far as to conclude that air power alone could have prevented the rise of Nazi expansionism and simultaneously contained the Soviet Union. These war games in retrospect generally fail to take into consideration the domestic political factors which placed limitations on United States foreign policy, and which produced such rapid demobilization of military resources after 1945.

While, in general, the military profession feels that the United States could have been more successful politically, its ranks are sharply divided in assessing the role of military strategy in the final political outcome. Did the United States employ correct military strategy for defeating the Axis? Would a different strategy have produced greater political returns? These questions have developed into polemics almost equivalent to the arguments that plagued the German general staff as to why Germany lost World War I. The issue is debated by means of the rhetoric of military operations—namely, the relative priority of the theaters of war: Europe versus the Far East. In its baldest form, the question is: What would have been the political outcome of the war if the Far East had been given first priority instead of Europe? In more sophisticated form the question is posed: Did the United States place an imbalance of emphasis on Europe as against the Far East?

An officer's participation in the Far East or in Europe strongly conditioned his views on this question of strategy. Consequently, World War II produced two groups of leaders, who by experience or by conviction, or both, were either Europe-oriented or Asia oriented. While neither group was oblivious of the global dimensions of modern warfare, in retrospect each reflected a different concept of the struggle, and each placed a different emphasis on post-war problems. For more than a decade, as new members entered the military elite, they still could be classified in terms of theater affiliations.

One source of these differences was a system of personal alliances, centering around loyalties to strong leaders. The military establishment, like any large-scale organization, produces personal alliances which play a role in fashioning attitudes and influencing decisions. In the military these pre-war alliances were essentially unpolitical in origin, since they arose out of personal associations during peacetime. But the hypothesis is offered that in the course of World War II, and thereafter, these personal alliances became the focal points of politico-military thinking.

Although personal and career experiences in time of war influence their political behavior, military leaders are also profoundly concerned with maintaining the prerogatives of their organization and their branch of service. From this point of view, doctrine is irrelevant, or at best a rationale for the pursuit of personal glory or organizational success. For example, when during the defense of the Philippines, General Douglas MacArthur asked General Wainwright what command he wanted, Wainwright answered, without reference to the complexities of military strategy: "The place where some distinction can be gained."[1] Often, a military operation can be viewed as both contributing to the strategy for victory and enhancing the future of a particular service. Secretary of the Navy Forrestal, a civilian with a deep understanding of military affairs, was aboard a naval vessel off Iwo Jima when the island was being assaulted. Surrounded by a group of ranking officers, he is reported to have said while the American flag was being raised: "The raising of the flag on Suribachi means a Marine Corps for the next 500 years."[2]

Clearly, the political behavior of the military, like that of any large organization, is grounded in strong elements of personal and organizational self-interest; this can be taken for granted. What invites analysis is the way these interests and sporadic rivalries have influenced military policy and political behavior.

Strategic Priorities

BEFORE 1939, military planners in both the Army and the Navy were more concerned professionally with the Far East than with Europe, if only because the United States had important military installations in the Far East. When the Navy thought of military operations, it envisioned its organizational commitments in the Far East, where it believed it would have major responsibility. The geopolitical writings of Captain Alfred Thayer Mahan were used to supply an intellectual basis for such an orientation. Naval conflict would conform to the classic pattern of a struggle between opposing fleets, and would involve prestigeful weapons—the battleship and the heavy cruiser. After World War I, the Navy ruled out the possibility of operations against the British fleet, and came to assume that, for the Navy, to fight in Europe would be a secondary operation of escorting convoys and engaging in anti-submarine warfare, activities hardly suited to strategic planning.

Officers involved in Army planning, perhaps the majority, also looked toward the Far East. These included men who had been stationed in Hawaii, the Philippines, and China. The troops stationed in the Far East provided at least some basis for planning during a period in which all other military elements were imponderable and continuously in flux. As part of the mechanics of a peacetime army, alternate plans, including operations in Europe were prepared for the files, but few officers foresaw a global conflict. Even after the rise of national socialism, Army thinking was limited to passive defense and, up to 1938, to hemispheric resistance. Officers working on the development of air power were involved almost exclusively with the technology of their weapons, rather than the theaters of war.

Beyond these service commitmerts, the implicit cultural bias defined Japan as the traditional enemy of the United States. As for political interests, Europe had had its centuries of national wars, which seemed merely to shift the balance of power back and forth. American intervention would not be likely to alter drastically the course of events.* Even though the United States had, in effect, renounced territorial aspirations, the Far East provided the more likely arena for war and a locale for enhancing the prestige and influence of the country.

Yet, if there was a Far East orientation in the military before 1939, it was at best a vague and generalized feeling rather than an explicit doctrine. When World War I ended, the military did not prepare requirements as to what might be considered strategic positions for national security. During the inter-war years, War Plan Orange—military operations in the event of an attack by Japan—was repeatedly revised and with much more concern than

* And, indeed, why should military leaders have anticipated the consequences of totalitarian movements on international relations before civilian political leaders did?

were the Blue plans for Europe. Nevertheless, Louis Morton, the military historian, has concluded that the available military resources were so limited as to reduce these plans to fragile exercises.[3]

The military leaders, like the elected political leaders, lagged in the development of political expertise and confidence to deal with the vastly increased foreign responsibilities of the United States since the turn of the century. However, it is misleading to claim that the source of the difficulty was an unpolitical attitude on the part of the military; it is more accurate to point out that their political horizons were limited, and reflected the interests of civilian society. The armed forces, especially the Army, had been so constrained by Congressional action and by their self-imposed professional isolation, that even the elite members hardly thought in strategic terms. Mark S. Watson has characterized the period as one in which "Army chiefs, discouraged by rejections of their recommendations year after year, were reduced to asking not for what was needed but for what they thought they could get."[4]

However, once confronted with global war, professional expertise over-ruled service preferences, and military leaders unanimously endorsed priority for the European theater. Apparently, the military necessity of first defeating Germany, the more powerful enemy, was so basic and so obvious that, at the time, the question of military strategy could not produce professional differences.

Because of the immense scale of military operations, the residue of autonomous power in each service, as well as the power of each regional commander to redirect policy, was considerable. An excerpt from General Truscott's memoirs, recounting the lack of cooperation between the Navy and the Army in the use of landing craft for the European theater, helps to recall that military coordination had to cope with a strong element of service preference which weakened command decisions:

Our Navy, General Eisenhower went on to say, was cold toward this plan. They favored operations in the Pacific where the Navy would have the dominant role. Our naval authorities thought that commitments in the Pacific would absorb all of their resources, and they were unwilling to undertake to provide the landing craft and to organize and train the crews to operate the craft which would be required in large number. There, Army Ground Forces itself would organize special engineer units to operate and maintain landing craft, establish bases and the like. . . .[5]

The strategic decision of Europe first had to face the "human fact that no general in his right mind wants to be downgraded to a secondary role."[6] Every general and admiral operating outside of the number-one target pushed continuously for a greater share of available military resources. And, in the end, the defeat of Japan followed very shortly after the destruction of Nazi Germany.

Ten years after the end of World War II, professional officers who had participated in military operations had had time to reflect on their war-time experiences and the outcome of the post-war settlement. On the basis of their expressed attitudes, either in interviews or in public pronouncements, it was still possible to classify the more articulate ones as either Europe-oriented or Asia-oriented. Social scientists have long pointed out that a person's political attitudes and behavior are not composed of separate and disparate elements, but, instead, fall into some sort of consistent pattern. The theater-orientation distinction, while admittedly oversimplified, nevertheless is a partial key to an officer's attitude toward such questions as responsibility for the Pearl Harbor disaster, the reliability of the British as allies, and a host of other policy issues. In other words, the distinction is one that seems to keynote fundamental differences between military managers.

The "Europeans" not only accept the priority of war against the Nazis as having been correct, although they pressed for an early opening of a second front in Northwest Europe, in retrospect, they believe that shortages of ground troops and anti-submarine devices, and especially a shortage of landing craft, probably precluded an earlier invasion of the continent. They believe that the strategy employed was essentially sound, and that a quicker defeat of Germany, which would have placed the Allies in a stronger bargaining position vis-à-vis the Russians in central Europe, was most doubtful because of military limitations. Some might argue that there was an over-allocation of resources to the strategic air offensive, or that General Eisenhower's command direction after the breakthrough at Normandy was defective, but they agree that these factors could have altered the course of the war only by some few months at most. In their opinion, if Allied military power was not used effectively to contain the Soviet Union in Central Europe, this was the result of decisions made in the closing weeks of the war, not of basic strategy. These were decisions in which the military participated, influenced to some degree by their concern for avoiding casualties rather than solely for the exploitation of political objectives in Central Europe. Moreover, the "Europeans" do not believe that the war in Europe was fought to weaken United States efforts in China.

If the "Far Easterns" accept the wisdom of first priority in Europe, in retrospect they believe it was implemented in such fashion as to weaken or prevent the achievement of United States objectives in both Europe and the Far East, particularly in China. General Albert C. Wedemeyer, a truly unconventional military manager, has become the most articulate exponent of the Asia theory of World War II, as revealed in his memoirs.[7]

Wedemeyer holds that it would have been to the advantage of the United States not to have entered the war, or at least to have waited until Germany and Russia had exhausted each other. Once in the war, the strategy of the United States played into the hands of the Communists. Although the correct strategy was to fight the war in Europe first, it should have been done more quickly and directly, so as to deny the Communists access to central Europe. In his view, this could have been accomplished if, according to the strategy which he and General Marshall had developed, a direct cross-Channel assault had been launched in 1943. Instead, he feels, the peripheral campaigns in North Africa and Italy actually weakened the Allied effort, and permitted the Russians to take over central Europe.

Similarly, the "Far Easterners" argue that, once the Axis had been defeated in Western Europe, it was still within the power of the United States to prosecute the war in the Far East in such a way as not to have assisted the Chinese Communists. The "intrigue" of General Stilwell; the limitations of Department of State representatives in China; plus the actions of President Roosevelt and his civilian advisers, particularly Harry Hopkins, were to blame, not the professional military. An all-out strategy could have been developed which would have assisted in the reconstruction of the Chinese Nationalist Army. General Marshall, in his role as President Truman's special envoy to China in 1947, seeking a coalition between the Communists and the Nationalists, was responsible for blocking a military aid policy which would have permitted the Chinese Nationalists to defeat the Communists.[8]

The question as to how the war started and who was responsible for Pearl Harbor helps clarify the different political orientations of the two groups. Among those officers with extreme commitments to the "Far Eastern" point of view, some believe that the
politicians, especially Franklin D. Roosevelt, were responsible. This
point of view is embodied in a book by Admiral Robert A.
Theobald.[9] Theobald, who was directly involved in the disaster
as commander of the destroyer forces, asserts that President Roosevelt forced Japan into war by unrelenting diplomatic and economic
pressure, and enticed it to initiate hostilities with a suprise attack
by holding the Pacific fleet in Hawaiian waters as an invitation to
attack. Admiral "Bull" Halsey's introduction to the volume, which
endorses these conclusions, reflects the appeal of this argument to
a number of military officers.[10]

A similar pattern of differences emerges on a variety of other
political-military issues. The "Far Easterners" are prone to see the
British as unreliable allies, reluctant to fight, except in defense of
narrow self-interest. The "Europeans," although critical of British
procedures, are more sympathetic to their contributions and their
intentions.

Over-all, the Asia-oriented group is convinced, in retrospect
that even within the framework of a "Europe first" strategy, a strong
anti-Communist China could have been created. As professional
officers, they tend to place the bulk of the blame for political
losses on the civilian direction of war, rather than the military
establishment. They consider the outcome of World War II a failure,
mainly because of strategic political decisions. The Europe-oriented
group, while admitting the shortcomings of both the military establishment and civilians in World War II, considers the strategy and
its implementation to have been basically sound, and a measured
success, in the sense that other outcomes could have been disastrous.

Moreover, our interviews revealed a strong continuity between
an officer's estimate of the conduct of World War II and his contemporary adherence to pragmatic or absolute doctrine. Those officers who believe that the coalition warfare against the Axis was an
unsuccessful war expressed an absolutist conception of warfare.
They are not inclined to acknowledge any limitations in the pursuit
of total victory. By contrast, the Europe-oriented group, who hold

that World War II was a measured success, tends to adhere to a pragmatic doctrine. In the politics of the cold war there is a line of continuity, ranging from the issues of Asia versus Europe to those of massive, versus graduated, deterrence.* The link is supplied by the activities of the leading spokesmen of each group. This continuity is so powerful that, for example, Army officers of the Asia orientation, such as General Albert Wedemeyer, who hold the extreme absolutist view, have emerged as advocates of massive and strategic air power at the expense of reliance on ground forces.

Year by year, the military elite recruits new officers whose direct involvement in World War II came at an earlier stage in their military career. For these officers, especially those in the Air Force, concern with the strategic issues of World War II has declined. But for all members of the military elite who were studied, including those interviewed as a sample of the future, a pattern could be found which linked their views of World War II and their contemporary conceptions of the military operational code. Young officers, although less concerned with the details of the strategy of World War II, were concerned with its political outcome. Almost invariably, the stronger the criticism of the political outcome, the greater the commitment to absolutist doctrine for the cold war.

The Emergence of Personal Alliances

No SIMPLE EXPLANATIONS can account for the evolution of a military leader's attitude toward the strategic questions of World War II. The data that were assembled permit analysis of only the elite nucleus, and mainly of those officers who were involved in politico-military assignments. But these are precisely the key decision-makers in each service and in each theater of operations.

The analytical task is parallel to that involved in investigating the split between the Nazi and the anti-Nazi factions in the German *Wehrmacht*. Which dimensions of the military profession influenced these political perspectives? In a detailed study of the top eighty-five *Wehrmacht* generals of World War II, Kurt Lang found that social background, as well as military experiences, were at work in

* See Chapter 15, Total Versus Limited Warfare.

giving rise to the twentieth *Putsch* against Hitler.[11] Lang divided
the group of officers in his sample into the pro-Nazi praetorians,
the uncommitted, and the anti-Nazi conspirators, on the basis of
their demonstrated opposition to Hitler. The pro-Nazi praetorians
tended to display those social traits which generally identified
Nazi party leaders. More of them came from southern Germany,
and from lower middle-class backgrounds. On the other hand, the
opposition was not a monopoly of the aristocratic Junker group.
While the anti-Nazi conspirators tended to come somewhat disproportionately from upper middle-class backgrounds, they could not
be distinguished from the uncommitted on the basis of social background. Instead, their military careers, personal alliances, and
civilian contacts were more important. Both conspirators and
praetorians had many more quasi-political assignments than had the
uncommitted, and their careers more often deviated from institutionalized army patterns. In all military organizations the most
politically conscious are often characterized by unconventional
career lines. The uncommitted officers were older, had the most
traditional careers, conformed to the ideals of the purely technical
officer, and were most isolated from the larger society.

In the United States, to an even greater extent, differences in
political behavior between services or within services cannot be
accounted for by social background. In the past, the military profession has recruited those whose social backgrounds have inclined
them toward conservative commitments. Yet, analysis of social
origins of the military elite demonstrates that there has been a
progressive decline in the importance of social heritage and a rise
in the importance of organizational experiences. The general or
admiral who conforms to the heroic model demonstrates real or
acquired ties to the "upper class," while the modern military
manager is a more representative social type.

Undoubtedly, the political behavior of a military leader reflects
his personality and his underlying motives to some degree. The
efforts of social research to link political behavior to personality are
revealing, but hardly definitive. In the study of any elite group,
personality and motivational factors remain remote, and are available only from inference. On *a priori* grounds, it could be argued
that the most "authoritarian" personality would be the most inclined
to adopt an absolutist conception of warfare. While this assertion

remains an untested hypothesis, personality factors clearly seem to re-enforce career experiences.

The following analysis focuses on the combined impact of the service and the theater in which an officer fought, and the elite alliance into which he was recruited. As already shown, each general and admiral displayed an obvious tendency to judge the outcome of the war from the point of view of his own service and theater. Those who had fought in the Far East, particularly in China, came to believe that their theater had been neglected.* They came to believe that a more decisive political victory could have been achieved by a higher priority to their own operations. This pattern applies most strongly to the ground force, which was involved in both theaters; to a lesser extent to the Navy, whose prestigeful operations were mostly in the Far East; and least to the Air Force, whose officers revealed the least identification with a particular theater of war.

In the military, as in any organization, the "big issues" are personified by outstanding men and the factions that develop around them. Within the elite nucleus the hypothesis is also relevant that an officer's perspectives are influenced by his network of personal alliances and contacts. Many an officer has served in a particular command without developing the point of view of the commander. More often he has found himself directly involved and personally committed to leading personalities and their points of view.

Intimate alliances are essential aspects of career success in a closed institution which places high emphasis on personal characteristics. The hierarchical structure of the military establishment, and the fact that organized factions are not permitted within the military bureaucracy, require that factionalism in doctrine and political behavior be expressed in the clash of alliances around outstanding personalities. In time of war, because of the pressures and strains of responsibility, intense interpersonal loyalties and antipathies develop within the nucleus of leaders.[12]

It is neither feasible nor necessary to inventory all the personal networks within the military establishment during World War II. But it is possible to speak of the natural history of leadership group-

* The same feeling was apparent among those officers who had fought on the Italian front

ings which persist over long periods of time and which mold the
orientation of its members, and which in the long run, have important political consequences. Of the variety of personal networks
that existed in the military establishment during World War II,
alliances centering around George C. Marshall and Douglas Mac-
Arthur and their followers were the most dramatic, and in the end
could be linked most clearly to differences between pragmatic and
absolute conceptions of warfare, respectively. Like all organizational alliances their boundaries are difficult to determine, and their
importance and pervasiveness can be overstated by the outsider.
Because all organizational factions are amorphous, many officers
remained indifferent, some shifted their attachments, while others
sought to remain in contact with both leaders.

During World War II, this personality-doctrinal struggle originated in the Army, but at the very highest echelons it cut across
service lines. The Marshall group was centered in the War Department and among those leaders involved in the war in Western
Europe, although there were Marshall associates in important commands in the Far East. The MacArthur alliance, on the other hand,
was based among those who fought against the Japanese in the Far
East and in China. In fact, the rivalry has been described as a
clash of opinion between MacArthur, as commander in the Far
East, and the War Department in Washington. Moreover, during
the decade after 1945 the pragmatic group recruited many of its
leaders from among those who had managed the European theater
of operations, while some of the most vocal exponents of the
absolutist group came from the Far Eastern theater.

The factional divide between the Europe-first and the Asia-first
groups was primarily a difference between managerial perspectives.
The military careers of MacArthur and Marshall, the two key
opinion leaders, were intertwined for more than forty years. Both
served as junior officers in the Philippines before World War I, and
both achieved prominence in France in 1917. Douglas MacArthur
became a brigade commander; George Marshall was a staff operations officer. During the inter-war years, MacArthur, although only
a year older, was Marshall's senior in rank and close to the center
of power.

As Superintendent of the United States Military Academy, and
later as Chief of Staff under Herbert Hoover, MacArthur had the

widest network of personal contacts. But the leading members of the MacArthur group were not recruited from among the important associates who had served under him while he was Chief of Staff. Older-type officers who dominated the Army, such as Generals Hugh Drum and Ben Lear, were friends of MacArthur, but not his associates. The core of the MacArthur group were loyal and devoted staff officers whom he recruited while in the Far East. In the service these officers were known as the "Bataan crowd," since some had served continuously with MacArthur from Pearl Harbor through the occupation of Japan. Among the most conspicuous were Major General Charles A. Willoughby, chief intelligence officer, Bonner F. Fellers, public relations officer, and Courtney Whitney, legal officer and chief of civil affairs matters. Whitney was a Manila lawyer, who had been acquainted with MacArthur since the early 1920's. This closely knit staff nucleus reflected Mac-Arthur's thinking and operated to extend his influence.

Secondly, the MacArthur group included operational and field officers whom he retained in his command. Because MacArthur was such a strong personality, some of his subordinate commanders became close associates; others did not. One of his chief ground force commanders, General Robert L. Eichelberger, had served in Washington while MacArthur was Chief of Staff, but his more personal attachment was to General Marshall and others of the Marshall group. By contrast, General George Kenney, MacArthur's air commander, became one of his most vocal supporters.

The Korean conflict brought additional officers into direct contact with MacArthur. Of special note was General Edward M. Almond, who had served on MacArthur's staff since 1946, and who held the crucial 20th Corps command during the Chinese intervention in Korea. Equally important was the enlargement of the MacArthur circle in Korea by other Far Easterners who had served in China during World War II. Among such officers was, for example, General George D. Stratemeyer, Commander of Army air forces in the India-Burma sector in 1943 and in the China theater in 1945. General Albert Wedemeyer was another; Wedemeyer had served in the Far East before 1941 and, ultimately, as Army commander in China during World War II. Although he had not been under MacArthur's command in World War II, the issues of Korea put the men into close political contact.

Until he went to the Far East, MacArthur had been a leading figure in Army affairs. But the entourage which he created during World War II was regional in scope and, in fact, limited to the Far East. His "discipleship" was much less clear-cut than that created by the leadership of Marshall. With the events of Korea, Mac-Arthur's policy demands had ramifications throughout the entire military establishment. However, by that time, the Air Force had become the ascendant arm. Many followers of MacArthur had retired without leaving a direct line of descent, and the main advocates of an absolutist doctrine came to be found in the Air Force.

By contrast, although Marshall occupied a more marginal position for part of his career, during World War II his influence became central, and it continued to have consequences in the ground forces in the post-war period. At one point during the inter-war years while MacArthur was Chief of Staff, Marshall was given a minor National Guard training assignment in Illinois. His appointment as brigadier general, as preparation for the Chief of Staff appointment was in part the work of civilian political leaders, who were searching for vigorous leadership which could modernize the Army. In 1936 Secretary of War George H. Dern was surveying potential officers for higher command. Dern was advised by General Frank McCoy, a close associate of General Pershing, who had known Marshall personally since World War I. Mrs. Marshall reports in her autobiography that General and Mrs. McCoy arranged a dinner in Chicago for Secretary of War Dern and Marshall during his period of "exile" to National Guard training duty.[18] Dern discovered that in many Army quarters Marshall had a reputation as an outstanding organizer and a man of considerable energy. Many individuals take credit for, and, indeed, were probably involved, in bringing Marshall to the attention of President Roosevelt; the influence of General Pershing was no doubt highly relevant. However, his appointment represents the efforts of civilian leaders to select from among the widest list of eligibles, rather than from among the most senior in rank and position.

Just as Marshall's appointment represented a departure from seniority appointment, so he, in turn, was vigorous in recruiting officers for higher command. His personnel appointments filled central staff positions in Washington and manned key posts in the military structure for the European theater, which it was presumed he might command one day. Many of these officers were deeply influenced by Marshall's leadership, and came to reflect his sentiments. For years, Marshall, like other aspiring officers, had been keeping lists of officers whose talents had impressed him, and whom he intended to select as commanders, if he were appointed Chief of Staff, or in a position to influence the selection of commanders. Being an innovator, he selected for his list men who were energetic and who had demonstrated ability at problem-solving by his standards.

Many of the key Marshall appointments were men who had come to his personal attention while he was commanding officer of the Infantry School at Fort Benning, Georgia. For Marshall, the assignment at Fort Benning was not a routine one, but provided an opportunity to develop infantry tactics and to continue the talent search. While there, he first became acquainted with Omar Bradley in 1929, and in 1931 he met Walter Bedell Smith, two men who were to become key figures in Europe. The central figure in the European command, Dwight Eisenhower, although he did not have a history of long personal acquaintance with General Marshall, considered himself a disciple. Eisenhower was probably known to Marshall as a result of his service on the American Battle Monuments Commission with General Pershing. (A competent officer who came to the attention of Pershing, was usually known by Marshall, in turn.) After his successful participation in the Louisiana field exercises in 1940 Eisenhower came into more direct contact with Marshall. Prior to that time, Eisenhower had served under MacArthur, first in Washington and later as a personal assistant on public relations and political matters when MacArthur went to the Philippines in 1935.

The men Omar Bradley had as his key commanders—Courtney Hodges, Lawton Collins, and Leonard Gerow—had also become personally acquainted with either Marshall or Bradley at the Fort Benning Infantry School. The same was true for Jacob Devers, the other Army group commander in the campaign in France. General George Patton was not a close personal associate of Marshall. Patton was the commandant at Fort Myer when General Marshall was assigned to Washington in 1938–39. However, by reputation, he was high on General Marshall's personal list, even before he went to

North Africa. In addition, Patton had a personal link to Eisenhower which dated back to their association in the tank corps in 1919.

Marshall's professional "family tree" can be traced in various directions. H. H. Arnold, Chief of the Air Force, was a close associate, and their personal relation expedited the arrangement by which Marshall gave the Air Force organizational autonomy within the Army command structure. Marshall was generally recognized by air officers as inclined to support the development of air power. MacArthur did not have this reputation while he served as Chief of Staff; indeed he was resented for his alleged role in the court-martial of Billy Mitchell. The inner core of top planners and logistical specialists included Lesley McNair, commander of the United States Army Field Forces, and Brehon Somervell, in charge of supply services, who were Marshall's associates, but did not serve in Europe.

The striking aspect of the Marshall alliance is its direct and indirect line of descent, because each field commander is permitted wide discretion in the selection of his subordinates. One of the most conspicuous example is General Alfred Gruenther, who had an extensive war-time career in Europe, who rose to be Eisenhower's Chief of Staff at SHAPE, and, later, commander of SHAPE. The line of second-generation descendants includes Generals Matthew Ridgway, Maxwell Taylor, and James M. Gavin. All of these officers, who served in the same division in Europe, were deeply influenced by Marshall and his direct followers, such as Omar Bradley. Ridgway, for example, served with Marshall at Fort Benning, accompanied him on a mission to Brazil, and was secretary of the general staff in 1940–41, while Marshall was Chief of Staff. The third level of association, where the link begins to run out, is with officers such as General Lemnitzer. Lemnitzer served under Eisenhower in North Africa, and became Chief of Staff after having served as Commander of United States and United Nations forces in the Far East.

Personal alliances can break down under pressure and defections can occur. General Joseph W. Stilwell served with Marshall in China in the 1930's and was vigorously supported by him. Marshall esteemed Stilwell because he did not take the Army for granted. Stilwell also was the recognized expert on China in the War Department. The reversals of the China theater and the political demands of the Chinese Nationalists dissolved this association.

General Mark Clark was marked for higher command by Marshall when they both served in the 3rd Division at Vancouver Barracks in Washington in 1937. In 1944-45 he found himself in the isolated Italian theater of war. He was embittered by public attacks on his handling of American troops at the Rapido River crossing, and disappointed by the collapse of President Truman's effort to make him ambassador to the Vatican. After his duty in Korea, he became critical of General Marshall, and began to associate himself ideologically with the Wedemeyer conception of World War II. Another outspoken figure was General James A. Van Fleet. Apparently, Van Fleet was not known to Marshall before 1941 as an officer with potentials for strategic command.[14] He distinguished himself as a regimental and divisional commander in combat, and was given higher commands on the recommendations of Eisenhower and Bradley. Ultimately, he became associated with MacArthur during the Korean conflict and found expression for his politico-military sympathies in the outlook of MacArthur.

But military operations influence military leaders in turn. The war in Europe, far more costly in lives and material, was cast more in terms of liberation than were operations in the Far East. From the top general to the lowest private, the end of hostilities brought more than a sense of personal relief. Americans sensed that their military efforts had produced some positive accomplishment, along with the destruction of the enemy. Because of relatively limited cultural and social differences, American forces were able to develop some sense of community, rudimentary though it may have been, with Western Europe.

By contrast, in military operations in the Far East, the enemy was satanized to a greater degree. Conflicts between isolated American and Japanese units were often fought to a bitter end. With the exception of the Philippines, there was no sense of liberation on the part of the native population of the occupied southwest Pacific islands. While Japan acquiesced with formal ritualism, a deep gulf remained between the population and the occupying military forces, who found themselves in a completely alien world.

Military leaders in Europe who were charged with military government and occupational duties, recognized the powerful impulses of Western Europe to remain part of the non-communist world as the pressure of Soviet forces increased. American forces developed a real attachment to their immediate surroundings. The task of military defense seemed geo-politically feasible, even though the mechanics remained problematic. American military leaders, because of their experiences as "liberators," and because of their sense of community, became convinced that Western Europe had to be defended, and not used merely as a base of military operations. By contrast, as the cold war developed, the military forces in the Far East felt themselves in a much more isolated social setting. In addition to bitterness over the loss of China, an awareness of the immensity of the geo-political task was ever present. If, after 1945, military forces in Europe became fused into the social structure to some extent, in the Far East they remained relatively detached. Asia seemed more of an outpost than part of a political community.

Thus, in summary, professional experiences and personal attachments become deeply intertwined in fashioning an officer's outlook. To point out that policy orientations are conditionel by personal factors does not mean that officers are insincere in their beliefs about military policy, but that they are human beings. If historians broaden their efforts beyond the analysis of official records and collect essential data by the techniques of oral history, they will be able to document in greater and greater detail the interpersonal relations generated by two such strong leaders as Marshall and MacArthur, among others. The political behavior of the military elite, like that of any leadership group, cannot be understood without reference to the natural history of these rivalries and loyalties. In the case of the military, these personal attachments were tied, during World War II, to the issues of the European versus the Far Eastern theater.

After 1945, the importance of air power shifted the world-wide dimensions of the military establishment. Strategic questions were less theater-based and more concerned with the preparation for total versus limited warfare. With military unification and the creation of three services, the politico-military issues were no longer anchored within the War Department. New strategic issues submerged the personal associations created by World War II, although these associations persisted. The Korean conflict tended to perpetuate and transform them, especially within the ground forces. American military policy has come to be formulated at the political center of the nation. But, clearly, the military and personal experiences of World War II in the different theaters of war contributed to the strategic outlook—pragmatic or absolute—of the ranking officers.

Notes

1. Wainwright, Jonathan, *General Wainwright's Story*. Garden City Doubleday, 1946, p. 11.
2. Smith, Holland, *Coral and Brass*. New York: Scribner's 1949, p. 261.
3. Morton, Louis, "War Plan Orange: Evolution of a Strategy." *World Politics*, 1959, *11*, 221–50.
4. Watson, Mark S., *Chief of Staff: Prewar Plans and Preparations*. Washington: Historical Division, Department of the Army, 1950, p. 37. Watson points out that once the planning machinery of the War Department was geared to plan for a global war, it produced a vastly overexpanded set of military requirements. The victory program in which General Albert Wedemeyer was centrally involved was "far fom the actual composition of the 1945 Army—a conspicuous variation being the conjectured total of 215 divisions, including 61 armored, which compared with the ultimate 91 divisions, of which 16 were armored" p. 344).
5. Truscott, Lieutenant General L. K., Jr., *Comman Missions: A Personal Story*. New York: E. P. Dutton, 1954, p. 20.
6. Marshall, S. L. A., "*Memoirs of a Military Meteor*." *Saturday Review*, December 12, 1958, p. 21.
7. Wedemeyer, Albert C., *Wedemeyer Reports*. New York: Henry Holt, 1958.
8. Our analysis is concerned with the patterns of political behavior among military leaders that resulted from World War II, and not with the activities and responsibilities of specific officers during hostilities. Nevertheless, it is historically important to note that General Wedemeyer, while commander of United States forces in China, repeatedly recommended military assistance to the Chinese Communists, and as late as January 27, 1945, suggested to General Marshall that United States policy regarding China should coerce the Nationalists and the Communists into a coalition. (See Sunderland, Riley, *Army*, February 1959, pp. 94–95.) The retrospective estimates and claims of Wedemeyer are crucial aspects in analyzing the post-war political behavior of the military.
9. Theobald, Rear Admiral Robert A., *The Final Secret of Pearl Harbor: The Washington Contribution to the Japanese Attack*. New York: Devin-Adair, 1954.
10. The more typical concept accepts a measure of military responsibility, and is devoid of belief in political conspiracy. In particular, self-critical naval officers emphasize that "battleship-minded officers little appreciated the terrible destructive power of a mass air attack." Sherman, Admiral Frederick C., *Combat Command: The American Aircraft Carriers in the Pacific War*. New York: E. P. Dutton, 1950, pp. 29–30.

11. Lang, Kurt, "Tradition, Skill, and Politics in the German Army." Unpublished manuscript.

12. The clash of personalities in the high command of the French Army at the time of the fall of France is brilliantly portrayed by the British general, Sir Edward Spears. Spears, who served as Churchill's personal representative to Paul Reynaud, French defense minister, explicity states that "female" intrigue made its contribution to the tensions and rivalries among top French generals. Spears, Edward L., *Assignment to Catastrophe*. New York: A. A. Wyn, 1954, Vol. I, *Prelude to Dunkirk, July 1939–May 1940*.

13. Marshall, Katherine Tupper, *Together, Annals of an Army Wife*. New York: Tupper & Love, 1946, p. 20.

14. It is widely believed in Army circles that General Van Fleet was held back for promotion by General Marshall because Marshall had confused him with another officer—Van Vliet (also pronounced Van Fleet). Van Vliet was on Marshall's list as an officer who had earned a reputation that he should not be promoted. Apparently, it was not until Van Fleet showed great ability as a regimental commander on D-Day that Marshall learned of his mistake; thereafter, Van Fleet was promoted with suitable rapidity.

CHAPTER *15*

Total versus Limited Warfare

THE DEFEAT of the Axis powers ended a war-time coalition, and required the United States to participate in a new world-wide coalition, supported by the new military technology. The emergence of a managerial outlook in the military insured that there would be a step-by-step, if not a revolutionary, incorporation of new weapons. But complex policy issues tend to be defined as over-simplified alternatives, given the basis on which decisions must be made. Within the military establishment, the issue of the military's contribution to the new coalition rapidly came to be defined as a struggle over the proper balance of forces: What was the relative weight to be assigned to massive versus graduated deterrence?

The military is required to translate "policies" into priorities which will have consequences on international relations five to ten years in the future. Since combat—real or threatened—is the primary purpose of the military professional, priority was given to adapting military organization to drastic technological innovation. In both the short and the long run, the new weapons systems would be basic determinants in the international balance of power.

However, the new international coalition required immediate involvement of the military establishment in many quasi-military operations, and in direct political administration as well. The military establishment had become a multi-purpose organization in

which "ancillary" functions—military government, military assistance programs, political propaganda, and police functions—assumed great importance. Since political parties in a democracy do
not have overseas organizations, and because of the limited resources available to the foreign service in 1945, the military establishment had to broaden the definition of its role in the direction
and administration of foreign policy. Yet, crucial though these new
functions were in erecting a new coalition, they were never and
could never be given the same priority as the incorporation of new
weapons.

Each service continued to exercise traditional pressure-group
tactics in order to maintain and expand its resources and missions.
The new ingredient was that the struggle was fiercer, more complex,
and more extensive, since the stakes were so high.[1] But the political
behavior of the military elite over "defense policy" is more than a
struggle to accumulate resources. The elite is conscious of the fact
that the military is no longer accumulating a potential for future
engagements. The new term, "military posture," reflects the sensitivity of the military to the "cold war." They are aware that the
size, location, and disposition of military forces have become active
and immediate ingredients in international relations, rather than a
potential element.

In theory, decision-making in military affairs must deal with a
series of basic alternatives. However, ultimately, the actions taken
are not the expression of the demands of a single service or of any
particular professional perspective. The military establishment,
despite the military character of its structure, is still a bureaucratic
organization, operating under democratic political control.

Professional rivalries, therefore, have come to reflect two sets
of issues: first, differences among officers as to what is the "correct"
military posture to support American foreign policy; second, bureaucratic struggles among the three services as to their responsibilities
in implementing military policy. The first type of rivalry may contribute to clarifying policy alternatives, but the second is more
likely to be wasteful and disruptive. While struggles over the allocation of tasks and responsibilities take place along service lines,
the clash of perspectives during the 1945–60 period as to military
posture cannot be analyzed as merely a clash of Air Force, Army,
and Navy doctrines. The issue of massive versus graduated deter-

rence is an expression of differing professional perspectives—absolute and pragmatic. No service was monolithic in its outlook toward doctrine during this period, although the minority point of view in a particular service may have been without effective influence.

Policy Alternatives

SINCE THE DEVELOPMENT of nuclear weapons, military professionals—both absolutists and pragmatists—have come to believe that "national security" rests on creating and maintaining an effective organization for the long-range delivery of strategic weapons of retaliation. But there are sharp differences as to its size and composition. Moreover, similar differences exist as to the military limitations of such an organization, and how it could be used to have maximum political effectiveness.

The rapid development of the Strategic Air Command and the more limited, yet highly destructive, naval air element, were accomplishments of military management. The responsible officers were primarily concerned with the technical and organizational problems of creating a strategic retaliatory force, not with politico-military affairs. In fact, the Strategic Air Command broke with the military tradition that its officers should be generalists, and assumed long-run control over their careers, so as to permit extreme specialization. It also developed a most elaborate communications network in order to maintain a constant state of readiness and, at the same time prevent accidents and miscalculations. One technique for maintaining combat readiness is to require continuous competition between operational units. By means of complicated simulated exercises, including mock bombing runs numerically scored by radar, each combat crew is rated for its operational efficiency.

To be a member of SAC, living apart from the rest of the military community, entrusted with the most important mission, and rotating through a cycle of alerts, is something special for each officer. The resulting pressures pervade the entire organization, up to the highest commander, and condition its outlook. Living with these tensions, the men retain the fighter spirit, even though the element of personal combat has disappeared. Strong and intimate

personal attachments develop among officers, and there is a deep
sense of fraternity, since elaborate technology, *per se*, does not
depersonalize men. On the contrary, the gravity of the mission
enhances the value of each officer as a human being, responsible
for keeping a vital part of the organization in a state of readiness.

At a public relations briefing, the author was informed step by
step of the elaborate procedures which the Strategic Air Command
would follow during the six-hour period following the warning of
a Soviet attack launched by manned bombers. Devices were
described by which the most complex radar communications and
computational systems would be utilized, and by which erroneous
messages would be screened out and appropriate counter-measures
launched. After the formal presentation, the ranking officer, who
did not take part in the briefing, added that in all probability no
irreversible counter-measures would be launched without a direct
effort by SAC commanders to communicate with their Soviet
equivalents by telephone or radio channels. Time and again, in
interviews, SAC officers expressed pride in the fact that the system
of manned bombers provided an element of flexibility in the strategic retaliatory forces of the United States; defensive action could
be launched and, if necessary, recalled. But the imminence of missile warfare, which requires only fifteen minutes from the point of
launching for an attack, and has no features of flexibility, trans-
forms even these operational assumptions and self-images.

Thus, it is understandable that the military doctrine of Strategic
Air Command should express a purely absolutist formula. Career
advancement in the Air Force, especially in the Strategic Air Command, has generally been more rapid than in other services. Com-
paratively younger men with outstanding leadership and administrative ability, but without a background of assignment experience
which would sensitize them to the complex political aspects of
warfare, rise to leadership positions. The tensions and pressures of
life in SAC are so great that these men, although, in their own
conceptions, they are completely subservient to civilian authority,
remain unconcerned with the knotty problems of military means
and political ends. For them, "optimum efficiency" and "readiness
for instant action" are the solutions to problems of international
politics. Even organizational dominance of the air forces becomes
an end in itself.[2]

But even the most technical-minded Air Force general wants to make some contribution to resolving the question, "How can the machinery of the Air Force have its maximum effect politically?" The necessity of answering the advocates of "limited warfare" alone requires that the managerial Air Force officer have at his command a theory of air power. Thus, the absolutists speak of a "counter-force" strategy which requires that the United States maintain a strategic atomic force which, in quantity and diversity of delivery systems, is equal to that of the Soviet Union.

Critics of massive retaliation and the counter-force theory speak, at the operational level, of a "finite strategy." The finite strategy is not designed to match the Russian effort, but to achieve the goal of deterring Soviet expansionism. Such a strategy claims that, since it requires less resources, more effort should be allocated to the forces for "limited war." The size and type of force required is not an equal force, but one that represents a qualitative balance. The finite strategy has been formulated as:

The really important thing about a deterrent force is not numbers but invulnerability; not total numbers built, but numbers we will be able to use. In making our retaliatory forces secure from enemy attack, we do not need great numbers of missiles and bombers.[3]

Strategic deterrence involves a range of additional political questions—negotiations with the Russians for a mutual warning system to prevent surprise attack and for atomic test suspensions, sharing of atomic weapons with allies, and even the importance of civil defense in the continental United States.[4] The absolutists and the pragmatists advocate different policies for each of these issues, although the political issues are often complicated by considerations of technical feasibility. For the absolutist, a mutual warning system which would prevent missiles from being fired on the basis of erroneous information might be desirable, but there is little point in pursuing negotiations with the Soviets because of their political unreliability. (Some SAC officers even believe that professional air force officers—American and Russian—have a better chance of agreement and trust on these matters than do professional politicians.) For the pragmatist, mutual warning systems are desirable, and every effort ought to be made to press negotiations with the Soviets, if only because of the political advantage that would accrue to the United States by demonstrating its desire to prevent general war.

In regard to the problem of the suspension of nuclear tests, both schools of thought have been doubtful about the Russians accepting a workable system of inspection. Moreover, there has been widespread concern in the military that test suspension might deprive the United States of weapons essential to strengthening its strategic position; for example, the development of anti-missile devices, or of small yield weapons for tactical nuclear warfare. But while the absolutists express their preoccupation with the importance of technical feasibility, the pragmatists emphasize the necessity of demonstrating United States political intentions.

The sharing of atomic weapons with Allied nations becomes a complex problem which defies clear-cut policies for both schools. Both are aware of the political and technical dangers involved in sharing nuclear weapons with the Allies in Western Europe. Since the absolutist position is a form of "fortress America" strategy, the sharing of nuclear weapons is resisted because of the military and political commitments it creates and the corresponding loss of "freedom of action" for the United States. The pragmatist school emphasizes that military planning must reflect alliances with overseas allies and must seek to strengthen them. On the one hand, the sharing of nuclear weapons may hinder a political settlement in Central Europe. Yet, to deny the Allies the right to participate in decisions about atomic weapons, or even some type of direct involvement, is to reduce their will to resist and to invite political pressure (atomic blackmail) from the Soviet Union.[5] Finally, for the absolutist, civil defense has at best a low priority, and is essentially a military function; while for the pragmatist, civil defense has higher importance as part of the self-protective posture, and, to be effective, should be a civilian responsibility, in which military resources would assist.

Since all professionals acknowledge the possibility of limited warfare, disagreements between the advocates of opposing doctrines center also on the size and composition of limited warfare forces, and on their appropriate political utilization. The argument offered by the pragmatists is that the ability to deal with Soviet aggression in any but the most extreme terms decreases as military policy becomes more and more dependent on the most powerful weapons.[6]

The military establishment must maintain a capacity to respond in kind to every form of Soviet military intervention.

Because limited warfare, either with or without nuclear weapons, runs the risk of becoming total nuclear war, there are gradations in the spectrum of viewpoints about limited warfare. At one end of the continuum professional opinion holds that limitations on nuclear weapons are most difficult, if not impossible, to sustain in the battle-field. Therefore, limited warfare must be conducted along conventional lines for technical as well as political reasons. This policy was formulated by Admiral Charles R. "Cat" Brown, when he served as commander of the atomic-equipped sixth fleet in the Mediterranean:

We've got to make up our minds that if we have to go to war at all, we do so with conventional weapons only. You can't decide to use this kind of atomic weapon and not that. One leads to the other. It's like being pregnant: you can't be a little bit pregnant, you know.[7]

In the middle of the spectrum is the view that, although the feasibility of tactical nuclear war may be problematic, the strategy of limited warfare is to display to the Soviet Union the intention of the United States to respond with whatever weapons are required. At the other end of the spectrum, it is assumed that tactical nuclear weapons should be used to counterbalance any Soviet efforts based on conventional weapons, since such efforts would be an advantage over manpower superiority.

The variety of possible forms of limited warfare raises a host of complex technical problems in the allocation of resources. Perhaps the most crucial problem is whether it is possible to organize and equip a military force, so that it can perform in conventional limited war operations, as well as in nuclear warfare—limited or total. Each technical military issue reflects underlying political assumptions. For the pragmatist, because he sees Soviet intentions as essentially expansionist, limited wars would be fought to contain the Russians, and to maintain the alliance system required for mutual security Military forces should be tailored to specific objectives, to defend the political independence of coalition partners. The stationing of troops abroad is an essential political token of guarantee that the United States is prepared to fight a limited war with forces in being. The use of limited war is a military device which would make it possible for long-term political and economic policies to operate successfully in behalf of United States interests.

For the absolutist, limited wars, should they occur, would represent a weakness in United States foreign policy. If they do occur, they should be fought to thwart Soviet military intentions by decisive military effort, so as to achieve rapid victory. Victory in limited war should be used as a psychological device to demonstrate United States intentions to achieve total victory. Coalitions are necessary, in the conduct of limited warfare, but, again, it must be recognized that such arrangements represent dangers by limiting United States freedom of action.

In actuality, conducting a limited war under a military alliance with an unstable authoritarian political system, such as that of South Korea, presents complex problems for the United States. The danger that it might launch risky and irresponsible military operations is ever present. Yet, at the level of military organization, General MacArthur and General Ridgway revealed two different conceptions of implementing such an alliance. MacArthur, in the name of military realism, was primarily concerned with the security of United States troops and with maintaining freedom of action for the United States; Ridgway, in the name of political objectives, was concerned with strengthening the system of mutual alliance. Before the arrival of Ridgway in Korea, South Korean troops, as well as those from other United Nations countries, were segregated at the front. Under Ridgway, a more integrated international formation was created in which Korean units were interspersed among other United Nations units. Ridgway undertook this reform for tactical reasons, that is, to create a more effective and cohesive fighting force. Nevertheless, it was also an expression of political solidarity and of a positive expectation about the alliance. MacArthur was oriented toward direct negotiation with President Syngman Rhee, while the Ridgway type of administration, through more extensive contact, sought to win a measure of consent from the South Korean officer corps.

In interviews regarding the Korean conflict, officers offered their views of the political functions of limited warfare. Those who held the most extreme absolutist concepts of contemporary strategic problems were those who believed that General MacArthur should have been permitted to bomb North China with atomic bombs. The more typical absolutist believed that conventional strategic bombing would have been feasible and successful. (Neither seemed particularly concerned with the possibility that, in return, the Chinese could have bombed United States ports and supply installations in the Far East.)

The question of the use of nuclear weapons in Korea served in itself to distinguish degrees of commitment to the pragmatic conception. Some held that nuclear weapons could have been used as substitutes for traditional high explosives without expanding the scope of the conflict, and without undue political liability. However, leaders most heavily committed to the pragmatic conception of limited warfare opposed the idea that either strategic or tactical nuclear weapons should have been used. Their opposition was grounded not only in their belief in the unsuitability of atomic weapons for the Korean terrain, but also in the belief that these weapons would have thwarted the political objectives of the campaign, particularly alienating allies and neutrals. On the whole, the concepts of limited warfare involve more than a well-defined conflict between opposing schools; as with most politico-military issues, a range of alternatives pose the real problem.

The Pattern of Decision

FROM 1945 to 1960, there has been a decline in the influence of those members of the military elite committed to the pragmatic school and, conversely, a rise in the power of the absolutists. But the pattern of policy-making has never been monolithic. In the military establishment, as in the marketplace, decisions are not commands; the outcome is arrived at by bargaining and negotiation and by a balancing of factions. From 1945 to 1952, the pragmatic elements within the military establishment were dominant, although even at that time the trend toward greater authority for the absolutists was present. The reorganization of the Joint Chiefs of Staff under President Eisenhower in 1953 was the crucial turning point in giving greater weight to the absolutist doctrine.

In that year, with profound historical irony, President Eisenhower, a disciple of Marshall and a man whose career epitomized a measured and pragmatic approach to war, ended the reign of the

"Europeans," with his appointment of the chairman of the Joint
Chiefs of Staff. According to Robert J. Donovan, official reporter
of the policy decisions in the Eisenhower cabinet, the President "felt
that the new chairman [of the Joint Chiefs of Staff] should be an
officer who was in sympathy with the notion of a broadened strategy
in Asia, which Radford surely was."[8] Eisenhower was looking "for a
chairman of the JCS whose record would indicate an urgent interest
in the Far East." Admiral Radford has had extensive experience in
the Far East, having been on duty in the Pacific in 1943–44. In 1949
he became commander-in-chief of the United States Pacific fleet,
and was in command of the strategic Philippine-Formosa area in
1952. In the course of these duties he was recalled temporarily to
Washington during the Congressional investigation of the Navy-
Air Force dispute over the B-36 bomber program. As part of the
struggle to maintain a naval responsibility for atomic retaliation, he
expressed some criticism of the absolutist doctrine of the Air Force.
The events of Korea, and his contacts with the MacArthur group in
the Far East had apparently modified his strategic thinking, and
made him available to take over the chairmanship of the reoriented
Joint Chiefs of Staff.

Despite the shift in policy, the most basic military decision of
the first years of the Eisenhower administration—nonintervention in
Indo-China—represented the strategy of the pragmatists, carried out
under the decision of civilian leadership. After the Geneva conference in 1955, the absolutist emphasis of the Eisenhower regime
began to display signs of its own gradual transformation. By the
end of the decade, the pragmatic elements within the military were
more prominent, but they had not regained dominance, or even
parity.

Historians will undoubtedly record the transformations of American military posture as a pattern of response to prolonged crisis. As
the crisis deepened, the behavior of both protagonists—the United
States and the Soviet Union—became more and more extreme.
Then, slow reversals began to operate, as the two superpowers
recognized their limitations in any attempt to dominate the world
arena. Although American foreign policy decisions are the outcome
of a political test of strength, involving the agents of civilian control,
the military establishment, and an array of pressure groups on the
government, the internal political balance in the military establish-

ment has had a discernible consequence in stabilizing trends in foreign policy. Implementation of the massive retaliation doctrine was crucially resisted and modified by the persistence and effectiveness of opposition groups within the military establishment. The element of stability and balance was supplied mainly by the "European" group in the ground forces, who were subsequently joined by elements in the Navy and by segments of the younger officers in the Air Force. Thus, the military contribution to the national security "posture" since 1945 is an end result of the balance of organizational interests and professional perspectives in each of the three services.

1. Decision-Making in The Army. While land warfare predisposes the ground forces to a conception of coalition warfare, the responsibilities of World War II sensitized Army leaders to the political implications of military action. The loss of its strategic mission to the Air Force also produced extensive self-criticism, the search for new functions, and an interest in civilian points of view. Moreover, the Army's system of higher education had produced a cadre of higher officers who had broad intellectual concerns about military affairs, and who did not confine their interest to military technology.[9]

The post-World War II ground force leadership maintained continuity of pragmatic policy, despite the pressures generated by General MacArthur and others during the Korean conflict. The succession of chiefs of staff, including Eisenhower, Bradley, Collins, Ridgway, and Taylor—men whose careers formed an intimate personal network around the person of Marshall— were all "Europeans," not only in the sense that they had gained their crucial military experiences in Europe during World War II, but insofar as they rejected the thesis that the conduct of the war in Europe was the cause of the "loss" of China. Their orientation to military policy reflected the influence of civilian political control. However, they were able to remain in power as a result of their own organizational strength. Even the events of Korea did not bring into dominance advocates of absolutist policy in the ground forces. [10]

The line did not come to an end with the retirement of Taylor in 1959, for his successor, General Lyman Lemnitzer fitted into the model. Even though Lemnitzer was a younger man, he had had higher staff duty in the European theater, and his service as commander of the United States and United Nations forces in Korea came after the end of the MacArthur regime. Among the indirect heirs was General Clyde Eddelman, a critic of massive retaliation, who made his reputation as a junior planning officer in the War Department while Marshall was Chief of Staff, and who served subsequently as commander of the United States Army in Europe.

These officers constituted the main military spokesmen in development of the North Atlantic Treaty Organization and the military aid program. They supplied leadership for the military strategy of the "containment" foreign policy. In particular, Ridgway was available to assume the top command position in the Far East after the removal of MacArthur. They operated as counterweights to the absolutist policies advocated for the Korean conflict before Congress and in domestic public debate.

Although American foreign policy shifted to a progressively greater reliance on massive retaliation, it was still necessary that military alliances be maintained, that overseas bases be politically guaranteed, military aid continued, and exploratory negotiations launched with the Soviet Union on the suspension of nuclear testing. The Eisenhower administration had at its disposal a pool of top Army leaders, supported by lesser ranking staff officers whose careers and public reputations permitted them to be used effectively in these negotiations. One of the most successful of these was General Alfred M. Gruenther, who served as Supreme Commander of the NATO forces. During the period in which United States policy was emphasizing massive retaliation, his task included convincing the German *Bundestag*, notably by his personal representation in 1956, that conscription of German troops was meaningful and related to United States military intentions in Europe.

The assignment of advocating and developing political support for military assistance programs also fell heavily on Army officers of the pragmatic school, especially on retired officers who could be less inhibited in their activities. In 1958, for example, General Joseph T. McNarney, Major General Gerald Higgins, and Brigadier General S. L. A. Marshall, military commentator for the *Detroit News*, helped to prepare a special report for the Senate which concluded that the United States was getting a "good return" on its military assistance program.

The same pattern operated in the selection of military personnel to deal with political aspects of international arms control. In 1958 Secretary of State John Foster Dulles chose two military officers to advise James J. Wadsworth; the men were Alfred M. Gruenther and Walter Bedell Smith, elder statesmen of the Army and key figures in the "European" group. When, in the fall of that year, Wadsworth met with the Russian delegation in Geneva on the suspension of nuclear tests, his military adviser was Lieutenant General Alonzo P. Fox, an Army officer with extensive political-military experience, who was then serving as Deputy Assistant Secretary of Defense for International Security Affairs. Within the military establishment, the Army was making initial efforts at staff planning for nuclear disarmament and disengagement while official policy was still in general opposition to such a program. The first public statement by a military officer in support of the strategic and tactical feasibility of a withdrawal of western military forces to the Rhine and a Soviet army withdrawal from Germany was issued on the eve of the 1959 Geneva conference by General Clyde Eddelman, commander of the United States Army in Europe.[11] The limitations he saw were essentially political and administrative.

Yet, as of 1959, Army officers are not unanimously in support of the pragmatic position. At the highest levels there are few exceptions, but these exceptions are important because they include officers whose technical expertise permit them to exercise considerable veto power.[12] Opposition to the dominant outlook in the Army —more latent than manifest—is mostly to be found among younger officers who have not had full higher education or extensive experience in politico-military affairs. These include officers who served as company and field grade commanders in Korea, and for whom these experiences were a deep personal frustration. While these young officers reject the proposition of massive retaliation, they are inclined to seek absolutist solutions within the context of Army doctrine.

2. *Decision-Making in The Air Force.* In contrast to the internal political balance in the Army, decision-making in the Air Force has been dominated by a more homogeneous outlook. Since the earliest organization of the Air Corps within the structure of the United States Army, disciples of "Billy" Mitchell, who have advocated strategic bombardment, have formed the inner elite. During World War II, most top Air Force planners fully accepted the

Europe-first strategy, because it gave them suitable targets on which to test their theories, and because they were essentially unconcerned with politico-military details. The development of atomic and thermo-nuclear weapons supplied the final step in the dominance of specialists in long-range aerial bombardment. The most prominent and most outspoken advocate has been General Curtis Le May. Le May saw service in the air raid on Schweinfurt, Germany, but first came to public attention as a result of his service in the Far East during World War II.[13] He was responsible for directing much of the long-range bombing of Japan and for instituting, on his own initiative, low-level fire bomb raids. Le May assumed command of the Strategic Air Command in 1948, at a time when it was rapidly being expanded. When, in 1953, President Eisenhower reorganized the military establishment, he appointed General Nathan Twining, who had served in the Far East and who was committed to the massive retaliation outlook, as Chief of Staff of the Air Force.[14]

Yet, among the highest ranks of the Air Force, there have been officers who have had strong reservations concerning absolutist concepts and massive retaliation. While these generals do not form a clear personal alliance, their career experiences and personal associations help to explain their minority point of view. The Air Force has recruited its top leaders from the Army, and these minority-view officers developed their politico-military concerns as a result of early association with the ground forces during World War II. One group of Air Force officers whose outlook conforms more to the pragmatic school are those who had service with the fighter and ground support forces, and who, therefore, had contact with other services and arms. In particular, they had a combination of service in the tactical air commands and in the European theater.

One of the most conspicuous of these was General Elwood Quesada, whose career was hardly a prescribed one. Quesada entered the military profession as a private in the United States Army, and advanced through the ranks to become one of the youngest generals without attendance at West Point; his career was replete with a variety of assignments, including politico-military assignments as air attache and as a member of a military mission in Argentina. During World War II, he held fighter commands in North Africa, England, and on the continent which put him in close contact with General Eisenhower. Since he retired in 1951, however, he did not remain a central figure in the debates within the Air Force. Three other Air Force officers supplied the minority continuity—Generals Hoyt Vandenberg, Lauris Norstad, and Otto Weyland—all of whom had interconnected careers in Europe during World War II and had direct contact with the Army "Europeans."

Even before 1939, Hoyt Vandenberg had achieved a reputation in the Air Corps as an attack pilot, the term for fighter pilots of that period. During World War II, he was extensively involved in planning and developing air-ground cooperation in North Africa and in Europe, and served as Commander of the 9th Air Force, which was the major tactical air support command in Northwest Europe. Subsequently, Vandenberg served as Director of the Central Intelligence Agency; and then, in 1948, he became Chief of Staff for the Air Force. Norstad rose to strategic command by route of staff assignments in Europe and Washington. In 1945 he was the Army representative to the Senate subcommittee preparing legislation on the unification of the armed forces. His career has been directly tied to NATO assignments, since he has served successively as Commander-in-Chief of the Allied Air Forces in Central Europe, Air Deputy for SHAPE, and Commander-in-Chief of SHAPE. In executing these assignments, Norstad demonstrated interest in the concept of limited warfare, and was at variance with the "pure" massive retaliation posture. At a press conference in April 1959, he declared that if the Russians started hostilities in Europe and a crisis developed over Berlin, the "Western powers did not plan to resort automatically to strategic nuclear weapons."[15] He said that, first, the "Western forces would attempt to 'compel a pause' in the military action by using ready forces," and, second, the Western objective would be to "compel the aggressor to make a conscious decision that he is either going to war or he is not going to war," not through miscalculation, but by design. In short, he announced his intention to rely on graduated deterrence.

General Otto Weyland also had a career in the tactical command in Europe, commanding the air forces that supported General Patton's breakthrough in Normandy. He has been an exponent of the use of tactical nuclear weapons in limited warfare. Weyland, rather than an officer of the Strategic Air Command, was chosen as military representative at the Geneva conference on surprise attack in 1958. He is typical of the interest in graduated deterrence found in the Tactical Air Command. Some officers in the Air Transport Command, including those who received their political education in the operation of the Berlin Airlift, also deviate from the doctrine of massive retaliation. For them, the possibility of the airlift for limited warfare and for specific political objectives is both a technical and a strategic concern. But such officers, even at the general officer level, hold peripheral positions in the Air Force hierarchy.

Yet, the greatest source of potential deviation comes not from a continuity with past experience, but from the emergence of independent thinking among younger officers—colonels and brigadier generals—who have not been associated with efforts to establish the independence of strategic air power. Many younger officers in the Air Force are developing secondary careers as engineers or technologists and remain unconcerned with political goals. A minority, however, are more oriented to politico-military issues. Some of these officers have held responsible positions overseas, managing air bases or participating in international military organizations. Some have had extensive higher education in military and civilian schools. As these officers gain organizational prominence, they are likely to express their views in terms similar to those of the pragmatists. For example, Brigadier General Sidney F. Giffin, Vice Commandant of the Air War College, while he still insists on the necessity of victory, expressed his acceptance of the pragmatic argument:

A nuclear stalemate is coming to exist because, as nuclear weapons in a struggle for survival will ravage both sides, the awfulness of the mutual threat will postpone or eliminate a final test of strength.

Meanwhile, the real danger may lie in piecemeal defeat through infiltration and through local war launched by an aggressive enemy.[16]

3. *Decision-Making in The Navy.* The political behavior of naval leadership during the period from 1945 to 1960 with respect to strategic doctrine has been a step away from an absolutist conception toward a pragmatic approach. Because the naval elite places a much greater emphasis on organizational solidarity, differences as to strategic doctrine remain more within the establishment and do not present themselves as struggles between organized

personal alliances. Personal alliances, of course, exist, and are grounded in common experiences with particular weapons or types of ships. These factions engage mainly in struggles of organizational survival; only in recent years have they developed overtones of doctrinal and political goals.

During the immediate post-World War II period, naval air officers engaged in a bitter inter-service feud with the Air Force over the responsibilities for strategic air warfare. This struggle led the Navy to establish special section "Op-23," which produced propaganda against the Air Force, and in support of its own claims that aircraft carriers were superior to the B-36 as a means of delivering atomic weapons. This dispute led to a series of investigations by the House Armed Services Committee and a vindication of the military adequacy of the Air Force B-36 program. In opposing the Air Force, naval authorities were not primarily concerned with a critique of Air Force doctrine. They were concerned with maintaining an organizational prerogative for the Navy. They were pressing their claim for an important stake in the strategic retaliatory mission.

However, in the course of the hearings, which revealed organized efforts of naval officers to discredit the Air Force, more basic issues of United States military doctrine emerged. The extent of reliance on strategic retaliation was revealed, and, in the course of defending its own position, the Navy began to criticize the concept of massive retaliation. One of the key spokesmen for the Navy was Admiral Radford, who, in the process of attacking the B-36 program, was in effect criticizing massive retaliation. However, when he became Chairman of the Joint Chiefs of Staff, Radford actively supported massive retaliation policies.

Naval interest in limited warfare and pragmatic doctrine was slow to develop, and came as the outgrowth of a gradual process of self-criticism. After the negative outcome of the B-36 investigations, official naval opinion avoided public involvement in the basic issues of total versus limited warfare. During the crucial period of 1952–55, high-ranking naval officers did not engage in public discussion of massive retaliation, although there was considerable unofficial ferment. Open criticism of massive retaliation among naval circles began only after the Navy had devolped a new role in strategic deterrence via the Polaris undersea missile. After the

congressional election of 1958, when Secretary of State Dulles began
to modify his approach to the Soviet Union, naval leaders began to
publicly express criticism of massive retaliation policies. Admiral
Arleigh Burke, Chief of Naval Operations, Admiral Charles R.
Brown, Commander of the 6th fleet, and Admiral Harry D. Felt
emerged as leading spokesmen for pragmatic naval policies. At this
point the doctrine of limited warfare had become an organizational
stand, rather than an expression of a minority faction.

A clash of service and professional perspectives has prevented
the military from emerging as a unified elite. Social scientists who
have asserted that the growth of governmental bureaucracy is
certain to produce a monolithic element in the political process will
find little support for this thesis in the political behavior of the
military establishment. The process of "bureaucratic bargaining"
operates, not only in regard to the basic issue of total versus limited
warfare, but in decision-making as to political warfare, by which
military intentions are communicated and alliances with other
nations strengthened or weakened.

Notes

1. Millis, Walter, *Arms and the State*. New York: The Twentieth Century
Fund, 1958.
2. Such behavior is exemplified by an RAF marshal, who, on his retirement from a NATO post in 1957, limited himself to the recommendation that:
"This [atomic attack] demands some drastic changes in organization, the setting
up of a chain of air command, the creation of air defense commands and the
handling of Air Forces by airmen who have made the study of three-dimen-
sional war their life profession." Embry, Basil, *Mission Completed*. London:
Methuen, 1957, p. 331.
3. Report by Hanson W. Baldwin of Admiral Arleigh A. Burke's speech,
delivered to the Charleston (S. C.) Chamber of Commerce on February 20,
1959. *New York Times*, March 6, 1959.
4. See Wohlstetter, Albert, "The Delicate Balance of Terror," *Foreign
Affairs*, January 1959, for a discussion of the technical problems of maintaining
atomic deterrence as guided missiles augment and replace manned bombers.
5. Differences in military doctrine pervade every technical problem in the
military establishment. For example, air defense planning has led outspoken
pragmatists to question the military advisability of the extensive Air Force and
Army expenditures on ground-to-air missiles. Rear Admiral John T. Haywood,
Assistant Chief of Naval Operations, has described them as a "Maginot Line."
"We are members of a free alliance. There are forty-five nations allied with

us. We swim or sink with this alliance and if we go fortress America, and just forget it, we are going to die." *New York Times*, May 26, 1959.

6. See, in particular, Kaufmann, William W., ed., *Military Policy and National Security.* Princeton: Princeton University Press, 1956.

7. Morris, James, "The Sixth Fleet in a Total War," *Manchester Guardian*, April 21, 1958, p. 7.

8. Donovan, Robert J., *Eisenhower: The Inside Story.* New York: Harper & Bros., 1956, p. 19.

9. As reflected in free-time reading habits, the Army general is clearly the most widely read, and the Air Force general the least, with the Navy admiral conforming more closely to the Army pattern. In future generations the differences will undoubtedly diminish as the educational program of the Air Force has its impact. But these differences reflect differences in tradition, career responsibilities, and professional milieu.

10. Both General Mark Clark and General Van Fleet had come to assume they were candidates for the post of Chief of Staff of the Army when Eisenhower was elected President. They assumed that the President would break the line of succession and install an officer who was critical of the Truman administration's direction of the Korean conflict, and who would complement Admiral Radford as Chief of the Joint Chiefs of Staff. Instead, Eisenhower selected General Ridgway, who had executed the Truman limited war policies in Korea. Ridgway, and subsequently Taylor, were "Europeans" and pragmatists who had sufficient service in the Far East to make them available for the post of Chief of Staff under the Eisenhower administration.

11. *New York Times*, May 8, 1959, p. 1.

12. Representative of absolutist thinking is Lieutenant General Arthur G. Trudeau, a former chief of the Office of Military Intelligence, and later director of research and development. In a speech to the American Society for Industrial Security in 1958, Trudeau declared, "The advanced state of Soviet technology today is due more to Soviet espionage and subversion than it is to their scientific apparatus, good as it is." (*New York Times*, October 10, 1958.) His viewpoint reflects one aspect of the intelligence community, which, because of its professional responsibilities, as well as its personal attitudes, emphasizes the problems of enforcing international arrangements.

13. General Le May served during World War II as commanding general of the 20th Bomber Command; of the 21st Bomber Command, Marianas; and, finally, of the 20th Air Force, Guam.

14. General Twining was chief of staff to the Commanding General, South Pacific, 1942–43, and Commanding General, 13th Air Force, Solomon Islands, 1943.

15. *New York Times*, April 6, 1959.

16. Giffin, Brigadier General Sidney F., "Relationships among Military Forces." *Air University Quarterly Review*, 1957–58, 9, 31.

CHAPTER *16*

Political Warfare

SINCE THE PUBLICATION OF Sun Tzu's *The Book of War*, written in fifth-century B.C. China, it has been a continuing assumption of military leaders that success in war is best achieved by destruction of the enemy's will to resist, with a minimum annihilation of fighting resources. However, the formula for proper balance between violence and persuasion in a crisis is elusive and ever-changing. Generals and admirals are invariably caught between opposing tendencies. One is their own tendency to overemphasize the specific potency of the particular weapons with which they are associated. The other is to subordinate the instruments of warfare to a larger political plan in which their weapons may be economized and their contributions diminished in importance.

Each phase in the growth of the destructive power of weapons produces greater concern with techniques of economizing in warfare so as to avoid needless slaughter and enhance the prospects of political success. The contemporary term, "political warfare," of British origin, is merely a modern phrase for the traditional use of persuasion in a political setting where military force—actual or threatened—is involved. It focuses on the symbolic aspects of military strategy. How can the strategy and tactics of military operations be managed so as to maximize political impact? How can the operations of the military establishment be effectively coordinated with the techniques of diplomacy and mass persuasion?

When war was conducted on a limited and periodic scale, the military commander and his immediate staff viewed these tasks as integral parts of military strategy. Whereas, historically, political warfare could be managed in periods of crisis by key figures—military or civilian—today vast staffs, elaborate organizations, and highly specialized personnel are required. The task of coordination of efforts is great. The targets of persuasion are no longer merely the leaders of opposing nations in war-time. The targets have become the total populations, not only of unfriendly states, but of allies, neutrals, and of one's own nation as well.

In the Soviet Union coordination of efforts of military, para-military, diplomatic, and propaganda personnel falls to the organs of the Communist party. Party control over instruments of foreign affairs is highly centralized. Moreover, among its assets, the Communist party has the indigenous Communist groups which operate abroad. As a result, the Soviet Union appears to have less difficulty in directing the activities of political warfare than do the political democracies, whose control system is much more diffuse and whose political parties have no external or overseas elements.

Along with the new requirements of coordinating persuasion and violence in the United States, new phrases have appeared to describe traditional functions. The term "propaganda" came into vogue in World War I to refer to the importance of destroying the enemy's will to fight. The term was not limited to publicity, or to the printing of leaflets and newspapers for circulation to enemy troops and civilians. It included "propaganda of the deed," a concept borrowed from leftist revolutionaries, which stressed the importance of political acts—from assassinations to the formation of "front" organizations. In World War II the phrase "psychological warfare" was used to mean propaganda. This term originated in Germany, where Nazi political and military authorities sought to learn from their experiences of 1914–18, when, in their belief, Germany was defeated by propaganda and not by military operations. As a term, "psychological warfare" enjoyed a vogue in the United States because of the rapid increase in the use of psychologists in civilian society, especially in mass communications and advertising. It acquired unfortunate and confusing connotations, however, since it came to mean publicity and propaganda in the narrowest sense, rather than coordination of military operations with techniques of diplomacy and mass persuasion.

As the major function of the military establishment becomes increasingly that of deterring war, rather than conducting hostilities, the term "psychological warfare" becomes progressively obsolete. In coordinating diplomacy and military force, the focus is less on weakening the potential enemy's will to resist in the event of war, and more on strengthening the "morale" of allied and neutral nations. Accordingly, in military circles political and psychological "warfare" has given way to such terms as "national strategy," "international security," and "politico-military affairs." A major political task of the military is to demonstrate to allies and neutrals that the policies of a military alliance are compatible with their own self-interest.

The debate that has arisen over terms such as propaganda, psychological warfare, and international information reflects the difficulties of organizing foreign affairs in a political democracy, and, especially, of defining the appropriate role of the military. Civilian leaders in a political democracy, especially in the United States, tend to function in limited, short-range time spans, and often their behavior is a reaction to that of other nations, rather than initiatory. Coordination of military and political policy is facilitated if longer time spans are used as the basis for planning, but the domestic political system works against long-term planning and long-range programs.

In a political democracy the notion that the government is engaged in propaganda and publicity is repulsive to wide segments of the public. The United States government seems able to justify its international information activities only as emergency measures of the cold war, with the result that its efforts are handicapped in the struggle to exploit symbols of peaceful intention. Civilian control of politico-military policy, especially in the supervision of organs of "political warfare," has been inadequate because of the absence of effective mechanisms of legislative oversight.* There is no equivalent in this area to the Joint Committee on Atomic Energy, which operates on a continuous basis. Wide areas of political warfare require secret preparations, and secrecy is disruptive of democratic political control. Moreover, the Department of State has, in the

---

* See Chapter 17, Pressures of Civilian Control.

past, lacked the requisite prestige and personnel for enforcing coordination of military and diplomatic policy. The extensive machinery of the National Security Council is deemed by experts to be more elaborate than effective.

Effective political warfare assumes adequate intelligence, and American officials—civilian and military—are prone to ascribe political reversals to a "failure of intelligence." Undoubtedly, numerous cases of inadequate intelligence on which to base decisions can be cited. However, analysis of the intelligence process in both the military establishment and the Department of State indicates organizational defects in the utilization of available research and intelligence.[1] On the one hand, there is a tendency to exaggerate the importance of intelligence by seeking specific predictions or policy recommendations in intelligence. On the other hand, there is a neglect of detailed contents of intelligence findings by policy-makers who are limited in their own reading and intellectual reflection.

Finally, the traditions of the Department of State have emphasized a code of international relations which is essentially concerned with negotiations between heads of nations and their official representatives. The negotiations of diplomats remain the regulating mechanisms of international relations when nations are not at war. But in Soviet diplomacy, threats of coercion and appeals of persuasion issued directly to foreign audiences have become a mass undertaking. Mass appeals based on reason and on traditions of enlightenment, which pervade official United States information, are not necessarily appropriate for influencing audiences caught up in the new wave of revolutionary nationalism and rising economic expectations.

The inherent difficulties in managing foreign affairs have given rise to a widespread belief among professional officers that the United States has little tradition and skill in the use of mass communications and diplomacy to support its military objectives. Yet, on the contrary, American history, from the Revolutionary War to World War II, is replete with examples of imaginative and successful "political warfare."[2] For example, by offering free land to Hessian troops, and by careful treatment after capture, the Continental Congress produced desertion and disaffection among British mercenaries.[3] During the Civil War, Confederate agents in Great Britain were successful in mobilizing British opinion for the South and against "northern imperialism," mainly by manipulating newspaper editorials.[4] But, in turn, the federal government initiated a campaign of public speeches which slowly converted British political opinion to its side, despite the adverse effect of the cotton blockade. Perhaps the high point of American international propaganda was the "Fourteen Points," written by President Woodrow Wilson. At the request of Edgar Sisson, American representative in Russia, Wilson stated United States war aims in less than a thousand words, in short "placard paragraphs," so that they could be used for mass propaganda.[5] More often than not, these instances were the result of energetic leadership and represented the assets of a nation with no or few international responsibilities. The growth of international political commitments has decreased the ability of the United States to stress themes of national liberation, while the Soviet Union has gained this prerogative and advantage.

But the military elite's interest in and understanding of "psychological warfare" is not grounded in a historical perspective. It is much more an aspect of managerialism. As specialists in violence, both absolutists and pragmatists, but absolutists more so, have come to overestimate the potentialities of propaganda and mass communications as instruments of international relations. Only a minority maintain traditional contempt and hostility. In American society mass communications, especially advertising, have come to have extrinsic power beyond their demonstrated effectiveness. Moreover, the military have been influenced by accounts of the political history of national socialism and Soviet communism which tend to exaggerate the importance of mass persuasion.

Independent of these considerations, members of the military elite have come to demonstrate greater preoccupation with "psychological warfare" as the destructive power of weapons has increased, particularly with the advent of atomic weapons. And they have progressively pressed for more extensive efforts in order to match Soviet activities. In their concern for "modernizing" the mechanics of foreign policy, they have more often been concerned with organizational forms, than with substantive policy. Their managerial expertise orients them to questions of collection and the evaluation of intelligence, to the mechanics of staff planning, and to the establishment of firm directives. While they have sharpened their attention to symbolic aspects of international relations, they are not necessarily more aware of their own specific contributions

and roles in creating an image of the United States in the world community.

Since political warfare involves balancing force and persuasion,
the military has a two-fold role: First, its behavior and pronouncements must maintain the credibility of United States military intentions. Second, the military must operate to assist in strengthening
alliance systems and in consolidating political assets among neutrals. As absolutist doctrine increases and wanes in importance, the
emphasis on threats over persuasion grows and declines, and the
world image of the United States is influenced accordingly.

Credibility of Intentions

POLITICAL WARFARE is more likely to be effective if the official
declarations of politicians and military leaders about their intentions are realistically based on the military resources at their command. The United States has best maintained the credibility of its
military intentions in the "old-fashioned" type of war which had an
official outbreak and a definitive conclusion. Before both World
War I and World War II, civilian political leadership remained
vague and inconsistent regarding intentions. Once war was declared, the image of the vast technological resources of the United
States gave authenticity to the expressed intention to defeat the
enemy. Therefore, in both World War I and World War II efforts
at mass persuasion directed to neutrals, allies, and even to the
enemy, had great impact during military hostilities, precisely because pronouncements of military intentions appeared both genuine and realistic.

With the development of atomic weapons, maintaining credibility of intentions becomes much more difficult, because the risks
of using such weapons are so great. Repeated threats of massive
retaliation can lose their effectiveness in containing adversaries,
and, contrariwise, can unduly alarm neutrals and allies. Once the
United States lost its monopoly of atomic weapons, absolutists and
pragmatists were sharply divided on the appropriate political warfare strategy for maintaining credibility of military intentions. In
the absolutist perspective every possible occasion had to be utilized
to display initiative and to maximize the political impact of the

threat of atomic retaliation. Vice-President Richard Nixon gave the clearest statement of these principles in 1954:

We found that economically their [the Soviet] plan, apparently, was to force the United States to stay armed to the teeth, to be prepared to fight—anywhere in the world—that they, the men in the Kremlin, chose. Why? Because they knew that this would force us into bankruptcy; that we would destroy our freedom in attempting to defend it. Well, we decided we would not fall into these traps. And so we adopted a new principle. And the new principle summed up is this: Rather than let communism nibble us to death all over the world in little wars, we would rely in the future primarily on our massive mobile retaliatory power which we would use in our discretion against the major source of aggression at times and places we chose.[6]

To support the public relations of massive retaliation, absolutists believe that repeated statements of intentions by military leaders, disclosure of new weapons, military demonstrations, publicity about military routines, and even tactical deployment designed to highlight these potentialities, are all required. For example, the Strategic Air Command gave extensive publicity to long-distance refueling flights of B-52's and enhanced their newsworthiness by having the commanding officer, General Curtis LeMay, act as pilot.

As an adjunct tactic, it is essential to commit the opposition to objectives which the United States assumes cannot be achieved. Thus, General Laurence Kuter, while air commander in the Pacific, proclaimed, in an interview in Tokyo in October 1958, that the reason Communist China instituted a seven-day cease fire in the Formosa Straits was "the failure of the announced and boasted Chinese Communist intent to take the offshore islands."[7]

Pragmatic advocates are critical of the political consequences of such a military posture. They assume that Russia is fully informed of United States military resources for strategic retaliation, and that repeated political pronouncements about massive retaliation, therefore, depreciate the credibility of United States intentions. In their view, the best techniques for informing the Russians of military intention are diplomatic messages, authoritative statements, and public pronouncements limited to the kind of formulation made by General Maxwell Taylor before the Senate Preparedness Committee in 1959: "We must be willing to go all the way down the road. We cannot turn back at any point."[8]

Exaggerated and diffuse threats become mere sabre rattling which weakens the ability of the United States to demonstrate its peaceful goals and, instead, increases the possibility of general war. Strategic retaliation, in their opinion, can operate successfully only if the United States demonstrates to the world community, including the Soviet Union, its peaceful intentions. Otherwise, the threat of a Russian preventive attack is increased. A "military realist," such as General Leslie Groves, war-time director of the Manhattan Project, which engineered the atomic bomb, stated that "our reluctance to strike first is a military disadvantage to us; but it is also, paradoxically, a factor in preventing a world conflict."⁹ The traditional policy of the United States, "long established and so firmly supported by the American people that we must never strike the first blow," was, in his opinion, a powerful deterrent to war, since the Russians can assume that there does not have to be war unless they start it.

The handling of strategic threats by Soviet political leaders is markedly different from that of frequently repeating general intentions of strategic deterrence. The Soviets are not reticent in describing the existence and power of their atomic weapons. On the eve of the Geneva conference in May 1959, a visiting delegation of West German newspapermen were reminded that eight hydrogen bombs were enough to neutralize West Germany. At the same time, Russian leaders limit generalized threats, and utilize atomic blackmail by fixing their intentions to specific objectives—for example, the successful threat to use "new" weapons against the Israeli at the time of the Sinai campaign. Pronouncements by military leaders of the pragmatic school, although important within the military establishment after 1953, were clearly not accepted abroad as authoritative statements of United States intentions and policy. The image of the United States was based on the impact of massive retaliation and the absolutist doctrine.

How the Soviet Union has interpreted United States military intentions during the period 1953–59 is the kind of fundamental question which almost defies explication. Experts on Soviet military strategy, relying on the same sources, come to different conclusions which support different schools of United States military doctrine. R. S. Dinerstein of the Rand Corporation, an independent research affiliate of the Air Force, concluded, in his evaluation published in 1959, that the Soviet Union is not prepared to believe that the United States will limit itself to retaliation, that is, to striking only after having been attacked. Instead, he asserted that Soviet strategists believe they must be prepared to launch a "pre-emptive" attack to counter in advance a United States atomic thrust.[10] Such an estimate of Soviet intentions, in effect, justifies a vigorous policy of massive retaliation, and, ultimately, a counter "pre-emptive" strategy by the United States. By contrast, Raymond L. Garthoff, a former Rand employee and subsequently an expert in the Department of the Army, concluded that the Russians are not committed to such fixed strategy, but, rather, operate on the basis of a fuller range of alternatives, depending on the development of United States policies.[11] If the United States relies on graduated deterrence, the Soviet Union is prepared to respond with similar strategy, whereas greater United States reliance on massive retaliation would push the Soviets unreservedly toward the pre-emptive attack approach.

The political warfare consequences of the massive retaliation posture on allied and neutral countries is much more discernible. Public opinion in Western Europe, as measured by systematic opinion surveys, reveals an increase in the proportion of opinion leaders and among the mass population who believe that, if a third world war were to occur, the United States might start it. Such are the public perceptions of absolutist doctrine in a period of nuclear weapons. In the Middle East and in South Asian countries, the same opinion trends have been demonstrated to an even greater degree. Although systematic surveys are limited, editorial comments and the attitudes of opinion leaders in the area reveal widespread belief that the Soviet Union is as much interested in avoiding World War III as is the United States.

Pragmatic advocates of limited warfare argue that graduated deterrence would erase the "aggressive" image of the United States and, at the same time, maintain the credibility of her strategic intentions. Since 1955, in the Army, and since 1958, in the Navy, pragmatic elements have been more and more outspoken in the budgetary struggle for resources to maintain a limited war potential. They can argue for such resources without becoming directly involved in the more complex issues of suspension of nuclear weapons tests or nuclear arms control. Yet, in pressing for such budgetary support, they have had to de-emphasize existing resources for limited war operations. The short-run result has been to strengthen the image abroad that the United States is, in fact, completely committed to massive retaliation policies. Thus, in order to argue domestically for what they essentially believe, they have tended to weaken the intention they sought to communicate abroad.

Moreover, the actual conduct of limited warfare operations is as important as is public debate in communicating United States military intentions and in creating world images. As pointed out earlier,* in the Korean conflict, the original strategic concept was pragmatic, and the removal of General MacArthur confirmed that intention. Yet, the management of limited warfare for a political democracy is a difficult task, for the tendency in battle is to describe military intentions in all-out terms. As a result, it was no simple matter to maintain a political warfare strategy appropriate for the limited United States intentions. Military leaders resisted any formal statement of the limitations of United States goals as an undue military liability, likely to have adverse effect on United States troops' morale.

After the stabilization of the front, the political warfare arena of the Korean conflict was in effect transferred to truce negotiations and to prisoner-of-war camps. The United States truce negotiators, approaching their tasks as if they were engaged in a test of personal strength, pressed for, and achieved, the principle that repatriation would be voluntary.[12] Despite the experiences of World War II, prisoner-of-war camps were handled as a military police operation, rather than as a political task. The immediate result was that Communist elements were prepared, by internal organization of the camps, to thwart expression by those who did not wish to be repatriated. The military, under the direction of Colonel Kenneth K. Hansen, Chief of Psychological Warfare in Korea and a former advertising and public relations expert, was able to improvise an effective system of political support for anti-Communist elements in the prisoner-of-war camps.[18]

Since the Americans found themselves with limited personnel who had the necessary language skills for making contact with Korean and Chinese anti-Communists, the task of counteracting the use of terror in the camps was most difficult. Because it was a limited war and not a fuller mobilization, civilian and reserve military talent was not extensively utilized. Yet, in the end, the efforts of American personnel made it possible for anti-Communist sentiment in the camps to emerge, and the overwhelming bulk of prisoners elected not to be repatriated. The prisoners were realistically in-

* See Chapter 15, Total versus Limited Warfare.

formed of their future fate, and the fair treatment by American personnel, who demonstrated genuine interest in their welfare, had its effect. As a by-product, the India Custodial Forces, under Lieutenant General K. S. Thimayya, which were originally hostile to United States presence in Asia, were favorably impressed by the behavior of Americans involved in the repatriation.

After Korea, reorganization of the Joint Chiefs of Staff to implement the "rollback," and the massive retaliation policy under Secretary of State John Foster Dulles, modified the direction of political warfare operations. To conform to the format of absolutist doctrine, the new policies required changes in personnel within the military establishment. Major General Robert A. McClure was replaced by Brigadier General William C. Bullock as Army Chief of Psychological Warfare. McClure was a long-time associate of Eisenhower, and had held numerous political-military assignments which identified him with the "Europeans." Bullock was an officer who, though not directly associated with MacArthur, had had extensive experience in the Far East. McClure was transferred because he had become too closely associated with the containment foreign policy. However, the importance of the shift was more symbolic than real, since the Army psychological warfare branch subsequently declined in importance.

Instead, the Central Intelligence Agency increased its dominance in these matters. The struggle between the professional military and secret operational intelligence agencies in political warfare can only be studied by reference to historical examples, and not by contemporary analysis.[14] For this period, the line between the Central Intelligence Agency and the armed forces becomes difficult to draw, as a variety of secret and semi-secret operations were launched in the Far East. "Limited warfare" became more and more a device for subjecting the Communist bloc to symbolic military pressure. Chinese Nationalist forces were stationed on the off-shore islands and a variety of propaganda and commando-type operations were instituted against the mainland. In Burma, Chinese Nationalist troops were supplied with arms. In Europe the Logan Act, which encouraged the recruitment of Iron Curtain refugees into the United States armed forces, was put into effect, without much success, while the scope and intensity of Radio Free Europe increased. It was a period in which political warfare appeals and claims tended to become detached from military intentions.

However, even after the crescendo of "rollback" strategy was past, the absolutist doctrine continued to have impact on the management of military demonstrations and operations. In July 1958, United States marines and infantry troops were landed in Lebanon at the request of the legitimate government, under the Eisenhower doctrine of preventing aggression in the Middle East. While the United States troops were invited to intervene by a pro-Western government, the rebels were not acting directly on behalf of the Soviet Union, although they were assisted by Soviet arms. This limited action was transformed into a military demonstration of strength. Instead of landing a small mobile force which would have been tactically and militarily appropriate, fifteen thousand troops were landed, a general build-up of naval forces in the area was ordered, and air-borne troops were flown into Turkish bases. The size and armament of the troops were well beyond the security and political requirements for the limited and specific objective of supporting the legitimate government. This action was interpreted by neutral observers as a political warfare action, presumably directed against the Soviet Union. In effect, a limited police action had been used as a full-scale rehearsal to test the mechanics of limited war. The immediate outcome was to weaken further the pro-Western Lebanese government, and to produce outspoken criticism among Western allies. Although the intervention, in retrospect, appears to have been a partial success, the actual military contribution, because it was not measured, apparently did not enhance the credibility of United States intentions.

Strengthening Alliance Systems

FUNDAMENTALLY, mutual alliances depend for their viability on the security they offer their members. Political leaders adjust these alliances to changing factors in the international balance of power. If either political or military leaders are preoccupied with maintaining the status quo, their behavior is likely to strain relations with their allies. Military leaders are also required to administer alliances so as to enhance the internal strength of the members.

As generals and admirals have broadened their intellectual and cultural horizons, United States military practices have become more and more modified to conform to the social and political re-

quirements of allied nations. Yet, the barriers to effective political
conduct of military alliances among sovereign nation states are considerable. Military managers are necessarily oriented toward conducting military alliance systems so that they will be effective in
the event of hostilities—limited or total. The day-to-day concern
with the political and psychological consequences of their behavior,
especially on their allies, has much lower priority. While officers at
headquarters may well be alert to the issues of political management of military coalitions, the behavior of the entire military establishment is involved. Given American traditions, military commanders find it more feasible to launch a "public relations" program to the host population, than to modify administrative practices which lie at the root of inter-allied tensions. They must show
considerable initiative in order to overcome the tendency of their
lower commanders and their troops to define tasks as purely technical and military. Every act involved in maintaining and operating
a military establishment, especially its overseas elements, can result in strengthening or weakening mutual alliance systems. "International security affairs" includes the political consequences of
military government, the conduct of United States troops abroad,
the behavior of military assistance missions, the military protocol of
interallied headquarters, and even the format of military parades
and demonstrations. They are all aspects of maintaining a system
of military alliances.

In the period immediately after the close of World War II, the
military establishment displayed considerable sensitivity to the
pressures of social and political change. The war-time spirit of improvisation operated to increase flexibility in policy and organization, particularly in the area of military government. The initial,
and perhaps the most effective, contributions of the armed forces to
the new balance of world power after World War II were the military governments of Germany and Japan. It was assumed that if
these countries became economically viable and had relatively free
and stable governments, they would be committed to the West. Yet,
few, if any, civilian or military officials foresaw the eventuality that
these defeated nations, particularly Germany, would in a few years
make a positive military contribution to the mutual security system.

In both countries military government was hampered because
its organization had to conform to tactical military organization,
rather than to a political format. In Germany particular localities

were successively managed by as many as four different military government units as tactical units passed through and were relieved of their responsibilities by higher headquarters. Each shift in organization produced confusion and the necessity to rebuild contacts with German personnel. Moreover, in Germany, and even more so in Japan, after the cessation of hostilities military government units were placed under the jurisdiction of tactical commanders, so that communication with higher headquarters and with other military government units was greatly impeded. The lack of linguistic skill and the weaknesses in the interpretation of intelligence, plus the personnel turnover, were extensive and often disruptive.[15]

The effectiveness of military government in Germany was based on the dedication of key military men, and on military policies of employing expert civilian personnel. The conservatism of higher military officials was appropriate for the political tasks they faced. Trained in comprehensive planning, they created an organization which was sufficiently large and elaborate to cope with every aspect of organized society under military rule. Logistical and engineering problems of the occupation were handled most effectively. This was "good politics" for a population which had become temporarily apathetic about politics under the impact of prolonged war and defeat.

Although military government operated on principles designed to strengthen private property and free enterprise, occupational authorities, because of their public service tradition and respect for the role of government, supported wide state intervention in economic and social affairs. These attitudes reflected more than a willingness to follow political directives; they were an expression of military managerialism, with its problem-solving orientation and its resistance to ideological dogmas. It was this orientation which caused the military government in Germany to oppose and hasten the elimination of directives which sought to de-industrialize Germany.

Civilian political directives led to mass de-nazification programs, which have been criticized as ineffective, because they were too general, and unjust, and because many of the decisions were later reversed. A statistical analysis of the purges in Germany and Japan, prepared by John D. Montgomery, would seem to support this conclusion.[16] However, as pointed out by many analysts, Allied purges created a "clear field for non-totalitarian political leaders, in Germany as well as in Japan, during the critical years when new political habits were formed and the politics of both countries [fifteen years later] still bear the marks of this achievement."[17]

No doubt, the military occupation of West Germany was assisted by the repressive tactics of the Russians in the eastern zone. Yet, the clear-cut intentions of military government to reconstruct West Germany without new political experiments had a positive appeal to most Germans—of the right and of the left—who had experienced two military defeats and a Nazi revolution. Direct contacts with United States personnel, down to the lowest level of organization, presented to the Germans new models of behavior and new sources of encouragement which were as important as political policies.

While the Japanese occupation followed the same pattern as that in Germany, the social and cultural setting made personal and political communication more difficult. In the initial phase the mystique of General MacArthur was ubiquitous, and occupational authorities capitalized on traditional Japanese subservience to constituted authority. The most profound and lasting contribution was perhaps the system of land reform. The occupation was managed mainly through cooperation between top United States officials and top Japanese officials of the constituted government. Because of more limited contacts and the language barrier, the extensive penetration that resulted in Germany did not take place in Japan. Therefore, in both Japan and Korea, military occupation entailed a program of economic reconstruction with limited political objectives.[18]

Since the national strategy that evolved after 1948 called for a system of mutual security pacts around the perimeter of the Soviet Union, the tasks of military government became enmeshed with the management of military alliances. For the first time in United States history, it was necessary to station large numbers of troops and equipment abroad in allied countries, and to develop military assistance programs for these nations. The major former enemies— Germany and Japan—were recruited into the mutual defense system. West Germany, because of its crucial strategic position and its manpower, was more fully integrated into the alliance system than was Japan. The "no war" clause in the military government constitution of Japan complicated its rearmament. Among the new nations of the Middle and Far East, continuous efforts were made, mainly through military assistance programs, to extend the alliance system. Where the United States had stable governments to deal with, as in Western Europe, these new types of "international security" arrangements were much more feasible than they were under the conditions of political instability of the Far East and the Middle East.

In Europe, the experiences of World War II set the pattern for post-war integration of top command and higher headquarters into an Allied military force. The influence of military protocol and the sense of official duty operated to contain national rivalries and personal preferences. While theorists of international relations generally claimed that economic integration in Western Europe would have to precede political forms, in actuality, the reverse took place. Military and political institutions of NATO have been the basis of a greater European integration, including economic cooperation. The mechanics of an international military establishment—integrated higher headquarters, multi-lingual staffs, and even NATO symbolism—have contributed to the political integration of Western Europe.

The stationing of United States military forces in Western Europe presented elaborate political problems, especially since no nation looks favorably upon foreign troops on its soil, even though they are allies. The decision to deploy atomic weapons in Western Europe served to make the tasks of a "permanent occupation" even more complex. Thus, it is understandable that the first response of the military establishment was to segregate itself from the host populations in order to avoid social and political tensions. But segregation, whether self-generated or imposed, could not be an effective long-term solution. Instead, the military learned painfully, but with considerable initiative, that selective involvement in community and social welfare activities, plus correct personal conduct in host countries, is the basis of a politically desirable solution. Significant of the contact, many more Europeans listen to the news and music of the Armed Forces Network than to the Voice of America. Experience in contact varied from country to country, of course. During the occupation of Austria, since the number of troops was limited and their counter-pressure to the Russians was obvious, even the ordinary G.I. became an integral part of Austrian society. In France, the country with the greatest organized opposition to the NATO alliance, United States troops became targets of political attack for a time. But even in France the attacks eventually were neutralized and spent themselves.

The pattern of successful integration is demonstrated by the Southern European Task Force, operating in northwest Italy. Although relatively small, this task force, armed with atomic weapons, and located in an environment having the largest Communist party outside the Soviet Union, has become a political asset by refusing to segregate itself from Italian society. An extensive language-training program prepares officers and soldiers for joint Italo-American maneuvers, and assists in integrating them into their immediate surroundings. Company commanders indoctrinate their troops merely by presenting them with Communist propaganda distortions of their behavior. As would be expected, Americans have launched extensive athletic programs with Italian youth and a variety of community service programs. At headquarters, in Verona, there is no "Little America" which would elicit the hostility of the population. Instead, American officers and married enlisted men live in the Italian community. Because of the relative sensitivity of military managers to the political and social setting of Western Europe, the strains on NATO do not derive from its internal organization, but rather from adapting the alliance to the changing military and security needs of Western Europe.

The case of Spain, however, is markedly different, because of the special problems of cooperation with an authoritarian government. The United States has erected an air base system and a major naval installation in Spain without integrating the country into the NATO structure. Military commanders have developed these installations with a minimum of social disruption and interpersonal friction. The Air Force has instituted the full range of managerial devices for handling such problems, including courses in Spanish for key personnel and instruction in local customs. However, the program has been accompanied by some rise in anti-American feeling, with political overtones. The economic impact of the construction program has caused local dislocation and tension. But, more fundamental, the Franco regime has come under heavy internal political pressure, and is unprepared to compromise with the political opposition. The military base program itself is interpreted within Spain as a political commitment to Franco, despite the on-the-spot political neutrality of United States military commanders. Yet, while American officials like to think of themselves as "outside" of Spanish politics, they are, in fact, heavily committed, especially since diplomatic personnel maintain only limited contacts with even the mildest opposition to Franco.

While the Western European military alliance system has been managed so as to minimize social tension and immediate political liabilities, this has not been possible in the Far East, where there has been increasing frustration and tension. Military commanders have not been able to bridge the cultural and racial gap. In the spring of 1957 extensive civilian rioting broke out on Taiwan when a United States Marine master sergeant, having shot a Chinese file clerk whom his wife claimed was a "peeping Tom," was freed unconditionally. Indicative of the mutual distrust and tension, the Americans in the courtroom cheered wildly when the acquittal was read.[19] The rioting came as a shock to American officials, who seemed to have assumed that extensive military and civilian aid programs had produced pro-American sentiments. Racial prejudice, antagonisms about different standards of living, and the fact that United States military leaders, partly due to the misguided efforts of Chinese officials, were relatively uninformed of Chinese local opinion were at the root.

In the Far East, the United States has been most reluctant to permit allied powers to exercise legal control over civilian crimes by United States forces, as has been the arrangement in Western Europe. This issue has been a source of major political tension in the Philippines. In Okinawa the military occupation was so disruptive of the social structure that local Communists assumed considerable political power. The only type of counter-measure available was the drastic one of incorporating Okinawa into the dollar economy.

Military alliances and military assistance programs in new nations of the Middle East and southeast Asia, having to operate through unstable governments, have had varied political consequences. In these areas the clash between absolutists and pragmatists is at work. The absolutists have emphasized the immediate military potentials for resisting communism, while the pragmatists have been more interested in strengthening the internal political stability of new nations. Outright frustration of United States objectives has resulted where military efforts have been strongly identified with the perpetuation of the elite who were adjuncts to the older colonial system, as in the case of Iraq.

At times, the first phase of the military assistance program was conceived as a military demonstration, "a display of the flag," when such tactics were no longer effective. In 1950, when the United States announced a $20 million program for Vietnam, carrier-based planes flew over the country as a "psychological warfare" strategem, and two United States destroyers were anchored in the harbor of Saigon. Communist elements used their arrival to provoke a major riot, which caused the destroyers to be withdrawn after the Navy issued a statement that their presence was a gesture of friendship to Bao Dai, a gesture made at the suggestion of the Department of State.[20]

It is difficult to estimate the amount of military aid an under-developed country can absorb without creating economic disloca-tion. As a result of absolutist policies, military assistance programs have tended to become overextended. Laos is an example of a country that suffered extensive temporary disruption for this rea-son. Organizationally, these programs have tended to be more con-cerned with material than with the training of military cadres, although the trend has been toward more effective personnel in-struction. After 1955, in countries such as South Korea and South Vietnam, where the programs have been a reaction to direct Com-munist military action, the United States has been able to produce fighting forces in a very short period of time by mass production techniques.

Strategically, the programs have been oriented toward develop-ing a national military force, especially infantry units, for opposing the Soviet Union. In Turkey the equipping of infantry divisions has strengthened regional stability, but in Pakistan the military assist-ance program has served mainly to increase tension between Pak-istan and India. United States military leaders have been slow to develop military assistance programs which are appropriate for the internal security needs of underdeveloped countries. The sharp American distinction between the civilian police function and the military function is not applicable to these nations. Their new armies are required as an effective frontier force, but they cannot be thought of as highly relevant in the event of a direct Soviet at-tack. Thus, the creation of a national military force is an essential aspect of military assistance to a new nation, not because such a force could fight Russian troops, but because it is a symbol of national sovereignty and self-identity.

An effective military assistance program to a new nation requires developing the army as a reliable and law-abiding internal police force, and as an instrument against internal subversion and guerilla forces. The model would not be the infantry division, but the constabulary and military police unit, neither of which has been at the center of United States thinking about military assistance. Often, these new armies are modelled in the image of United States forces, and not in terms of the new nation's own needs. United States forces have not had an extensive tradition in the tactics of guerilla or counter-guerilla warfare.[21] The experiences of the British in Malaya and Kenya, and of the French in North Africa, are more relevant.

Two notable cases where United States military assistance programs have been adapted to local requirements are Iran and the Philippines. In Iran, Major General H. N. Schwarzkopf developed a military force to cope with internal subversion and indirect aggression. Schwarzkopf was a West Point graduate who did not conform to the conventional model. He resigned from the service at the age of twenty-six to organize the newly formed state police of New Jersey, and returned to active military duty via the National Guard. Because of his training, he did not share the belief of the profession that police work has lower prestige than soldiering. Since he was not committed to a prescribed career, he was prepared and permitted to spend five and one-half years in Iran without rotation in order to accomplish the task.

In the Philippine Islands the initiative of Ramon Magsaysay, while he was Secretary General of National Defense, directed American military assistance into an effective instrument against the Communist Huks. Magsaysay's experience as a guerilla fighter under the Japanese occupation provided him with his "strategy." While the military assistance program supplied essential materials, such as light vehicles and communications equipment, he was aware of the economic dimension of anti-guerilla warfare. The success of his strategy demonstrates that the role of military assistance in anti-guerilla warfare mainly involves engineering, logistics, and economics. Within the Philippine Army, an economic development corps was established and supplied with United States engineering equipment. It built an extensive roadway system in guerilla area, transported the population to new and more suitable land, and served as a kind of economic TVA, all in the name of military assistance.[22]

In general, assistance programs in underdeveloped countries have potential side-effects, since the new military cadres constitute an important source of technically trained and public-spirited personnel, whose engineering outlook makes them valuable in the tasks of modernizing their countries. In Indonesia, after the disaster of launching military assistance by demanding a political commitment to the United States, the program was reconstituted with a view to strengthening internal stability. Not only were the officers trained in the United States crucial in suppressing the internal rebellion, they have also increased the cadres of military personnel available to manage government enterprises, especially those nationalized from Dutch ownership.

As part of the politics of strengthening alliances, the United States forces are engaged in programs of military assistance to South American countries. These programs have important consequences on the internal politics of these countries. After the fall of the Peron regime in 1956, the Argentine Army broke its tradition of emulating the German military, and took steps to model itself after the United States. On November 10, 1956, Brigadier General Raul Tassi announced that a mission would be sent to the United States with the full support and approval of the new President, General Pedro Eugenio Aramburu, as part of his program of "democratizing" the Argentine Army.[23] After Arturo Frondizi became President and visited the United States, a plan was announced for sending United States military instructors to the Argentine War College to assist the Argentine Army in its program of controlling Communist subversion. Military training and assistance activities are extensive in other South American nations as well.

In summary, a "political warfare" dimension has come to permeate almost every type of military operation in a "no-war—no peace" period. Military managers can be judged on the basis of whether they are sensitive to these political consequences. The more technical-minded officers are a hazard to the conduct of foreign policy; the more political-minded require more elaborate direction than is supplied by traditional forms of civilian supremacy.

In the United States, where political leadership is diffuse, civilian politicians have come to assume that the military will be an active ingredient in decision-making about national security. Samuel Huntington, in his study on *The Soldier and The State*, submitted the recommendation that the military should operate only as professionals, in the sense of responsible specialists.[24] But while the original contributions of his analysis are generally recognized, many liberals and conservaties alike seem to reject such a concept. Conservatives believe that his philosophy is not conservative. One military intellectual said privately, "I suspect that his dramatic neoconservatism is really the same old liberal desire to suppress the soldier dressed up in a new form." Liberals feel that the positive leadership of men like Marshall, as soldiers, cannot be written off. Moreover, in their view, the military can only be controlled by being effectively integrated into the larger society, not merely by being professional.

But the military are not a unified elite. Since the profession has no unified perspective toward military strategy or political warfare, or national security, and since internal differences over doctrine reflect civilian dilemmas, the political system is geared to accommodate an active role for the military in policymaking. Under these circumstances, to judge whether military professionals are behaving with responsibility, by examining the policies they have recommended and their administrative successes and failures, is not sufficient. It is equally important to examine the political techniques they use in making their recommendations and in pressing for their objectives. Their activities as a pressure group, if responsible, circumscribed, and responsive to civilian authority are a part of the decision-making process of a political democracy. Yet, at a point, knowingly or unknowingly, efforts to act as a leadership group can transcend the limits of civilian supremacy.

Notes

1. See Hilsman, Roger, *Strategic Intelligence and National Decisions*. Glencoe: The Free Press, 1956.

2. Daugherty, William, & Janowitz, Morris, *A Case Book in Psychological Warfare*. Baltimore: Johns Hopkins Press, 1958.

3. See Butterfield, Lyman H., *Proceedings of the American Philosophical Society*, 1950, 94, 233–41. It was in the Mexican War, not the Korean conflict, that the United States Army had to face political defection for the first time. Irish Catholic recruits deserted when they became convinced that they were

on the wrong side of a religious war. They formed the San Patricio Battalion and fought effectively for Mexico until routed at Chapultepec. Most of them were subsequently hanged.

4. Hendrick, Burton J., *Statesman of the Lost Cause*. New York: Literary Guild of America, Inc., 1939, pp. 389–99.

5. Sisson, Edgar, *One Hundred Red Days: A Personal Chronicle of the Bolshevik Revolution*. New Haven: Yale University Press, 1931.

6. *New York Times*, March 14, 1954, p. 44.

7. *New York Herald Tribune*, October 9, 1958.

8. *New York Times*, March 19, 1959, p. 1.

9. *New York Times*, December 29, 1957, p. 20.

10. Dinerstein, H. S., *War and the Soviet Union*. New York: Praeger,, 1959.

11. Garthoff, Raymond, *Soviet Strategy in the Nuclear Age*. New York: Praeger, 1958.

12. Vatcher, William H., *Panmunjon*. New York: Praeger, 1958.

13. Hansen, Kenneth K., *Heroes Behind Barbed Wires*. Princeton: D. Van Nostrand Co., 1957.

14. Ransom, Harry Howe, *Central Intelligence and National Security*. Cambridge: Harvard University Press, 1958. This book contains no mention of the role of the Central Intelligence Agency in political warfare.

15. Brigadier General Frank Howley, Commandant of Berlin, reports that by December 1, 1947, he was the only top-ranking official left of the group which had originally entered the city two and one-half years before. Key personnel had changed three or four times more frequently than had the Russian. *Berlin Command*, New York: G. P. Putnam's, 1950, p. 154.

16. Montgomery, John D., *Forced To Be Free: The Artificial Revolution in Germany and Japan*. Chicago: University of Chicago Press, 1957.

17. Deutsch, Karl, Review of John D. Montgomery's *Forced To Be Free*. *American Sociological Review*, 1959, 24, 265.

18. See Meade, Grant E., *American Military Government*. New York: Columbia University Press, 1951. This study is an excellent report of the actual functioning of military government as a social and political process. It presents a detailed account of the mechanics of administration, of the personnel involved, and of the problems of translating directives into practice.

19. *New York Times*, June 2, 1957.

20. *New York Times*, March 19, 1950, p. 14.

21. For an analysis of the problems and limitations of counter-guerilla warfare, see Paret, Peter, "The French Army and La Guerre Revolutionnaire." *Survival*, 1959, I, 25–32.

22. When Magsaysay launched his Community Development Program of rural reform, many Philippine Army officers, including some who had been active in the anti-Huk campaigns, played important roles. As part of the internal security program for political stability, in the 1949 election Magsaysay supported a movement called the National Movement for Free Elections, and directed the Army to insure a free election. The Philippine Army's psychological warfare unit, organized by the United States Army, popularized the mission of the Army as guardian of the election system.

23. *New York Times*, November 11, 1956, p. 15.

24. Huntington, Samuel, *The Soldier and the State*. Cambridge: Harvard University Press, 1957.

VII

POLITICAL TECHNIQUE:

PRESSURE GROUP TACTICS

CHAPTER *17*

Pressures of Civilian Control

PROLIFERATION in the size and functions of the military profession has produced a corresponding organizational revolution in the mechanics of civilian control. Except for the continuous efforts of the Truman committee, which investigated the administrative procedures of the military establishment, World War II was conducted with only limited congressional oversight.[1] A small group of civilian executives operated at the top levels of the War and Navy Departments, with considerable influence in fashioning organizational and procurement decisions. Strategic decisions were formulated by the President, his immediate trusted advisors, and major figures of the Joint Chiefs of Staff.

Continuously, since the end of World War II, both the legislative and the executive branches of government have sought to strengthen the machinery of political control over the armed forces The number of congressmen on committees dealing with military affairs, as well as the staff personnel for these committees, has grown. At the same time, there has been a marked development of the activities of the office of the Secretary of Defense: in 1958 the Secretary of Defense had more than a dozen principal assistants and a staff of more than one thousand professionals. At the time of the reorganization of the Department of Defense in 1958–59, the Army Chief of Staff observed that he had nineteen civilian layers between himself and the President. In addition, the President has been equipped with an expanded personal staff, and has at his disposal the elaborate structure of the National Security Council as the central means for political direction of the military establishment.

Formulating policy and maintaining civilian oversight cannot be reduced to questions of the number of civilians involved or of the administrative format, however, although these are essential preconditions. The machinery evolved is the decisive framework within which military leaders press their conflicting policy recommendations. A permanent military establishment which consumes more than half of the federal budget requires extensive political support, and, in turn, the machinery of civilian control is required to mobilize this political support. As a result, the trends from 1945 to the time of the Reorganization Act of 1958 have had a cumulative effect of producing greater organizational balance between military and civilian administrators.[2]

Two main trends can be discerned in the pattern of decision-making. First, much of the effort at civilian control has been oriented toward questions of administrative structure, rather than performance or policy.[3] Because so much of civilian control is oriented toward management forms, the military has developed greater sensitivity to these problems than to the political consequences of their policies. In many fields—cost budgeting, work measurement, statistical controls, automation—officials in the military establishment are "out in front," in the professional judgment of administrative experts. Second, the pressure of civilian control since the end of World War II has had the effect of producing a more sophisticated capacity on the part of segments of the military elite to intervene in the complex process by which national security decisions are made. Students of government have been preoccupied with analyzing and documenting the specific decisions which have "been made" because of military pressure.[4] Frequently, however, to focus on specific decisions is to overlook the pattern "in depth."

If the conduct of World War II led the military to assume, almost reluctantly, wide political responsibilities, the pattern repeated itself in the period after 1945. In 1945 the military expected to be greatly reduced in both size and responsibility, and was fully prepared for such a political directive. Military planners hoped for and pressed for universal military training. Yet, they looked forward to budgets of perhaps three, or, at the most, $4 billion.[5] However, the impasse of international relations and limitations on civilian political leadership again forced the military to a broader definition of their role than their self-conceptions, traditions, and logic would have suggested.

Military managers of either pragmatic or absolutist outlook viewed the foreign policy produced by civilian leadership as essentially reactive to Soviet intentions, short range, and in many respects highly optimistic. Such a foreign policy, in fact, reflected civilian values and the lack of stability in the mechanisms for administering foreign affairs. Under these circumstances, it was almost inevitable that tension would be created and maintained between civilian and military leaders.

From this point of view, the tension in formulating national defense policy is deeper than a political struggle of one group of civilian political and military leaders against another alliance of civilians and military officers. The tension is that of the military response to the structure of civilian control. The pressure of civilian control points to three propositions which, in ways unanticipated, appear to have increased, rather than decreased, the involvement of the military profession as a pressure group in the domestic political arena.

First, civilian management, both legislative and administrative, despite its concern for administrative efficiency, has not produced effective arrangements for realistic unification of the military establishment. On the contrary, the long-term impact of civilian control since 1945 has increased inter-service rivalries and rivalries between officers of the three services. Second, the forms of congressional supervision have been essentially budgetary and mainly negative. Therefore, the role of Congress as a forum for debating and reviewing national security policy remains limited. While military leaders are sensitive to the few key persons in Congress who are involved in national security policy, Congress as a whole is approached as an object of public relations, whose inquiries on behalf of its constituents require priority service. Historically, congressional influence in military affairs has been limited, and it is difficult to judge whether there has been any actual decline in its power. While Congress has been limited in its influences, wars in the past have been of relatively short duration. The contemporary issues center around the prolonged nature of the military crisis and the traditional congressional difficulties in intervening in military affairs. Nevertheless, Congress and its committee system remain fundamental sources of information on which public discussion of military affairs must be based. Third, as the locus of civilian control rests in the executve branch of government, and since, simultaneously, the structure of civilian controls has increased in complexity, military response to executive control has been an intensified struggle to gain access to the pinnacle—to the chief executive and to the National Security Council.

Intensification of Inter-Service Rivalries

EACH SERVICE has an official position on unification, which only partially reflects its success in the budgetary struggle. The Air Force, having fared best, has been least opposed to the trend toward managing the military establishment as a unified whole. The Army has fared the worst budget-wise, yet, it is heavily committed to increased unification, because it believes that by such means it has the best chance of implementing a pragmatic doctrine and containing the pressures of the Air Force. The reluctance of the Navy to press for unification is also an expression of opposition to Air Force strategy. It is as well a reflection of naval traditionalism, a desire to maintan organizational unity, and an awareness of its special access to congressional leaders.

Behind these offical service positions, the professional and personal attitudes of ranking officers operate to influence day-to-day decision-making and to supply the matrix through which civilian control must operate. Data reported by Henry, Masland, and Radway on attitudes of 576 staff officers on duty in the Pentagon make it possible to evaluate the extent to which members of the military profession were personally committed to the "broad non-service" point of view.[6] Results indicate that an officer's position in the military hierarchy, rather than his service affiliation, is relevant to his commitment to unification. The higher the position of an officer in the command structure, the more likely it is that he had the "broad non-service" point of view.

In order to probe this "broad non-service" point of view, officers were asked the question: "In a job like yours, which of these two officers would contribute more to the fulfillment of the mission of this organization: one who vigorously supports the view of his own service, or one who is receptive to views of other services, even to the extent of sometimes compromising the viewpoint of his own service?" Roughly one-half of all officers on duty at the three service headquarters in the sample asserted that the officer who is "receptive to the views of other services" would contribute more than the officer who "vigorously supports the view of his own service." In the Air Force headquarters, the percentage who favored a broad non-service approach reached 60, while in the Army and the Navy it was lower (47 per cent and 41 per cent respectively).

The notable difference, however, was between those officers who were assigned to service headquarters and those who were on duty with the Joint Chiefs of Staff or the office of the Secretary of Defense. The concentration of officers receptive to the views of other services varied as follows: Service headquarters, 49 per cent; Joint Chiefs of Staff, 96 per cent; office of the Secretary of Defense, 97 per cent.[7] How meaningful are these findings; what do such expressed opinions reflect? On the basis of these data, Henry, Masland, and Radway conclude that "officers assigned to the Joint Staff and to the Office of the Secretary of Defense share broad non-service ideals required by joint national planning of defense policy." However, such attitudes are, in part, official ideology, for Henry, Masland, and Radway are quick to add to their conclusions, "The supporting institutional arrangements are not believed to be wholly in keeping with the required values."[8] Their evidence, supported by the interviews collected in this study, emphasizes that a broad non-service orientation is not considered by most officers to be a concrete basis for developing one's career. Or, at least, that is the perspective of most officers, except for the very unconventional.

The officers in the Pentagon sample were also asked the question: "In a job like yours, which of these two officers would stand the better chance for promotion: one who vigorously supports the viewpoint of his own service, or one who is receptive to the views of other services, even to the extent of sometimes compromising his own service?" This question probed beyond official viewpoints, since it involved the crucial question of personal promotion. On this more concrete question, only half of those on duty with the Office of the Secretary of Defense believed that the officer with "joint values" stands a better chance of promotion. At each lower level of the military hierarchy, the question of promotion opportunities produced a corresponding and marked decrease in commitment to pro-unificaton values.[9] Moreover, officer attitudes on chances for promotion did not sustain the image of the Air Force as the most committed to a broad non-service point of view; the Air Force officer was no more unification-oriented than the Army or Navy officer.

Tension between a "joint" orientation and recognition of where career rewards rest is of particular importance for the staff of the Joint Chiefs, because all of these officers must operate with an essentially impartial point of view. Yet, nearly half of them believed that the officer who "vigorously supports the point of view of his own service" stands a better chance of promotion. At the root of the belief that performance dedicated to unification may not be the best basis for career success lies a realistic understanding of the mechanisms of promotion.

Whether or not an officer believed in "joint" orientation was heavily conditioned by the factor of who would recommend him for promotion. Sixty per cent of those staff officers with an immediate superior from their own service, who would be responsible for rating them for promotion, believed that the officer who "vigorously supports the view of his own service" stands the better chance of promotion. However, the percentage drops to 30 among those reporting to an officer from a different service. The Pentagon, large as it may be, is not so vast that the performance of staff officers of the Joint Chiefs of Staff does not become known to their immediate service headquarters and their service chiefs.

The task of converting the military format into one that would support and encourage a "broad non-service" orientation is a responsibility of civilian political authorities. Establishment of the Air Force as a third service, as part of the process of unification, was justified on the basis of the ascendancy of air power. However, it exacerbated rivalries between air and ground force officers, who consequently thought of themselves less as members of the same organization.

Civilian authorities have not succeeded in creating an educational system within the military establishment which would dampen inter-service rivalries. In 1948 the Ferdinand Eberstadt Task Mission on National Security Organization, of the Hoover Commission, recommended that "efforts be made throughout the entire educational process to instill a stronger sense of inter-service unity." It proposed a thorough examination of "possible means of securing a period of joint education and training at the undergraduate level for prospective officers of the Army, Navy, Air Force, and Marine Corps, as well as a survey of possible alternatives to the establishment of an air academy."[10]

Secretary of Defense Louis Johnson held up legislation for an Air Force academy on the grounds that he preferred a common basic education for all officers, at the same school, followed by specialized training. In the end, Air Force representations to Congress, the limited possibilities for expanding the older academies, plus long-standing traditions, forced the establishment of a third academy. Instead of a unified undergraduate educational system, there are some token exchange visits among students during their third year. Similarly, the efforts of the National War College to become the apex of military education, and to supply a focal point for unification, have failed because each service considers attendance at the War College an alternative for attendance at its own war college.

Modification of the system of promotions, a crucial lever of civilian control, has not been undertaken for the purpose of enhancing unification. The Department of Defense has been reluctant to interfere with the selection of higher officers, and Congress has been inhibited on the grounds of "playing politics." Consequently, there has been no effort to guarantee that the officer with a broad non-service point of view would be rewarded. Arrangements, such as a single unified promotion system for general officers, or creation of establishment-wide rather than service-wide promotion boards, have not been explored by civilian authorities. As the fortunes of the Air Force increase, at the expense of the Army and the Navy, career opportunities are curtailed in the declining services. A comprehensive system of transfer for mid-level officers has not emerged. Service officers at the highest echelons learn that it is essential to create the impression that their service is committed to unification. But, like all military battles, the war is continued at lower units, where it is recognized that career advancements are tied to the fortunes of one's service.

Congressional Negativism

ONE of the means by which the legislative branch of government exercises civilian control over the military is congressional control of expenditures. Because the size of the military budget is so vast, the annual budget review by Congress becomes an elaborate undertaking. A parliamentary form of government—such as that in Great Britain—permits the political opposition to question the government's ministers about on-going policies and budgetary programs by means of direct inquiry and formal debate. In the absence of these parliamentary devices, the importance of the annual budgetary review by a congressional committee is enhanced. Yet, it is the uniform conclusion of various researches into the congressional review of the military budget that it is an outmoded technique of rather limited consequence.[11] Its effect on the military profession seems to be that of generating hostility and tension, rather than effective control and political consent.

In operation, the basic objective of congressional budgetary review focuses on elimination of waste, rather than on evaluation of military performance. The procedure of the House of Representatives subcommittee on defense appropriations consists of a detailed, grand-jury type "item by item" review. After clearance by the Bureau of the Budget, requests for funds submitted by the Department of Defense, are broken down by services, and each service is assigned to a small group, each of which consists in all of three representatives and a few clerks to review a budget which exceeds tens of billions of dollars.

Congressmen are typically suspicious of military budgets, and witnesses from the armed forces are generally interrogated on the presumption that the military is in error. In a typical year, for example, in 1954, some five hundred witnesses were examined, a quarter of whom were civilian workers at the Department of

Defense. The line of questioning was extremely detailed in an effort to eliminate waste or duplication. The following exchange is typical:

Congressman: "As I recall it, the principal changes [in the armored vest program] under discussion a year ago were to give more protection to the neck and groin. Have there been changes to accomplish this?"

Colonel: "The groin part and the neck part have not yet been standardized."

When, in 1952, the armed forces, particularly the Air Force, sought to submit performance-oriented budgets which were being developed for internal management within the military establishment, Congressman John Taber protested because he considered the technique to be an administrative cover-up. Such practices in budget review have, in effect, prevented the subcommittees from any consideration of basic military policy, such as the adequacy of air-lift resources or the size of atomic weapon stockpiles. Moreover, congressional efforts at reducing the military budget in the years since World War II have resulted in a reduction of less than 5 per cent from the recommended levels, and this has generally been accomplished by suggestions volunteered by the military and effected by bookkeeping changes. When, on occasion, congressional leadership has reversed its usual position and sought to increase specific aspects of the military budget, it has usually found itself thwarted by the decision of the executive to ignore its recommendations.

In the few limited efforts to evaluate the adequacy of specific weapon systems, particularly anti-aircraft devices, congressional committees have found themselves unequal to the technical problems, and have essentially depended upon technical information from military and industrial sources. In March 1959, a House subcommittee investigated the complex question of "excessive" nuclear retaliatory power. After listening to conflicting testimony, Representative George H. Mahon, subcommittee chairman, told the press: "Upon whom can we rely? There is no one to whom the Congress can turn with complete assurance that we can get the right story."[12]

Negativism has also pervaded congressional attitudes toward issues of military organization. At the turn of the century Congress was reluctant to accept recommendations for modernizing the ground forces. Following the reorganization of the Army during the Root regime, the National Defense Act of 1916 was passed with a crippling amendment which limited the number of general officers to nineteen, compared to six hundred fifty in the German organization of that period. Repeatedly, Congress has asserted its opposition to unification of the armed forces, because it felt that excessive unification would weaken the balance between the executive and legislative branches of government. It has feared overconcentration of military power, and has looked to inter-service rivalry as a source of information and as a basis for civilian intervention in military affairs.

Congressional contributions to military personnel policy have also frequently been essentially negative in overtone, or concerned with minor details. Congress has not extensively debated basic questions of the adequacy of the system of recruiting officers, or the effectiveness of the Reserve Officer Training Corps training programs. Instead, it has been preoccupied with issues such as the efforts of the Air Force to promote James Stewart, a movie star, from colonel to brigadier general in the reserve. The Air Force was aware of the public relations advantages of such a promotion; senatorial leaders, particularly Margaret Chase Smith, were seeking a guarantee that success in big business and entertainment enterprises would not be placed above military training.

The review of military policy that does take place in Congress is mainly the result of the efforts of the extremely powerful chairmen of the Senate and House Armed Services Committees. Within Congress, internal organization of these committees gives each considerable autonomy, and the seniority system confers extensive power on committee chairmen. Two southern legislators, as a result of guaranteed re-election, have come into positions of commanding authority. They are Representative Carl Vinson of Georgia, a Democrat, Chairman of the Armed Services Committee in the House of Representatives, who has been in Congress for over forty years and who has held a commanding position continuously since 1945 when he served as chairman of the House Naval Affairs Committee; and in the Senate, Richard D. Russell, a Democrat from Georgia, who is Chairman of the Armed Services Committee.

Questions of military contributions to foreign policy have also been raised by the Preparedness Investigating Subcommittee of the Senate Armed Forces Committee, under Senator Lyndon Johnson, and by the Subcommittee on Disarmament of the Senate Foreign Affairs Committee, under Senator Hubert Humphrey. Since 1958, the Senate Foreign Affairs Committee has displayed considerable initiative in the area of military aid, particularly to South America. From the activities of these committees comes a flow of information which is indispensable for informing the press and the electorate on military affairs.

By contrast, most legislators have limited involvement in matters of strategic military affairs. On the basis of interviews with selected senators and congressmen, Lewis Dexter came to the extreme conclusion that "no one with whom I talked ever maintained that Congress had any significant role in the formulation of military policies."[13] Dexter found the "rank and file" attitude of legislators to be essentially, "who am I to say 'NO' to the military?" This attitude pervades even top congressional leaders, when it comes to the operation of the Central Intelligence Agency as it relates to military affairs. Mike Mansfield is the only senator who has openly discussed the problems of congressional control of the Central Intelligence Agency.[14]

Aside from the propensity of legislators to tackle simpler problems than those of military affairs, congressional behavior is a result of the very limited audience for questions of military policy. Congress responds to the direct and immediate pressures of its constituents. Only on the issue of selective service do senators and congressmen hear from their constituents. When, in 1959, the extension of Selective Service was up for debate, members of both houses displayed considerable interest in the issue. Nevertheless, only twenty-four senators voted for an amendment which would have required thorough study of the adequacy of contemporary selective service procedures.

Legislators become involved in military affairs in expediting contacts of their constituents with the military bureaucracy. In obtaining defense contracts, in procurement matters, in the acquisition of land, and even in obtaining emergency leave for enlisted personnel, members of Congress are continually servicing the electorate. Much of the work of the staffs of the Armed Services

Committees deals with these details, and many senators and congressmen have a person familiar with the routines of the military establishment on their staff.

In turn, the three services maintain extensive staffs for congressional liaison, not only to deal with major legislation, but to assist legislators who submit inquiries or requests to the defense establishment. In 1958 the Department of the Air Force Office of Congressional Liaison, under the direction of a major general, had 137 persons (55 officers and 82 civilians) or more than the number of personnel on the congressional staff used in civilian control. On the average, this group "monitored" 3,000 congressional contacts each month, in addition to the personal contacts of the three Senate and four House liaison officers who were on full-time duty in the Capitol and the House and Senate office buildings.[15] These service staffs, developed in response to the pressures of Congress, have become a major link between the military and the national legislature, although they operate, not in terms of basic policies, but in seeking to create good will and informal contacts. However, the service activities which senators and congressmen perform for their clients make a broad positive contribution. On a day-to-day basis they mitigate against individual injustices or administrative errors. Cumulatively, they operate as a form of legislative control. They substitute for the question period in the British parliamentary system, and supply a basis for developing new legislation.

Congressional perspectives toward the military are built on the legislator's prior military experience. To be a professional officer is an almost insurmountable barrier against election to the national legislature, whereas a war-time veteran's status is a useful political asset.* In the 86th Congress, 62.2 per cent of the senators were veterans, as were approximately the same percentage (59.9 per cent) of the members of the House of Representatives. The overwhelming bulk had served either as enlisted men or as junior grade officers. Legislators who have either had distinguished war-time careers or held relatively important staff positions have come to serve as unofficial spokesmen for one or another of the services: for example, Senator Paul Douglas, Democrat

* See Chapter 18, Civilian Alliances.

of Illinois—lieutenant colonel in the Marine Corps; Representative James Van Zandt, Republican of Pennsylvania—captain in the Navy; and Senator Barry Goldwater, Republican of Arizona—Air Force colonel. Aside from such men, the perspective of the typical legislator who served in the armed forces is deeply colored by his war-time experiences, in which he saw the military establishment in the participant-observer role of a low-level actor. It is often a highly personalized perspective, fraught with personal frustrations, and not conducive to an overview of the military establishment.

One effective and positive link between Congress and the military profession is the testimony of the chiefs of staff before congressional committees. The military establishment has supported the insistence of Congress that the chief of staff of each service have direct access to Congress and the right to present a dissent from executive policy. As opposed to detailed testimony on budget items, the presentation of the "chiefs" on Capitol Hill is a matter of great importance. In turn, the chiefs of staff have shown considerable political responsibility in seeking to develop a formula for expressing their opinions to Congress, while at the same time demonstrating their loyalty to the Secretary of Defense and the executive branch of the government. Both General Matthew Ridgway and General Maxwell Taylor have resisted urging by members of congressional subcommittees to continue their opposition to executive policy in public debate. With the attitude, "I have had my day in court, and I am now prepared to carry out my orders," they have left the task of political opposition to professional politicians.

The pattern of congressional-military establishment relations produces mutually re-enforcing tensions, and compounds the task of political control. Congress fully recognizes its dependency on the expertise of the military professional, and feelings of distrust thrive because members feel they are inadequately "informed" on military affairs. Despite efforts of the Legislative Reference Service to build up its capacities and facilities for assisting Congress, legislators often feel that they do not have sufficient basis for evaluating the testimony of the military establishment.

In turn, negative pressures of congressional control produce resentful reactions to his congressional contacts in the professional

officer. In particular, the McCarthy investigations of the Army
were interpreted as unwarranted and excessive outbursts of hostility. While many military leaders had strong sympathies for the
objectives of the McCarthy investigations, the impact of the hearings was to re-enforce skepticism about the quality of congressional leadership. Officers in charge of congressional liaison remain constantly on the alert to present a pose of "good public
relations." But managerially-oriented generals and admirals see
the system of budgetary review as outmoded, and consider the
whole process a formality to be circumvented. They have considerable respect for the few powerful figures who manage the fate
of the military establishment in the halls of Congress, but they do
not see these men as part of the political process, but rather as
individual leaders.

If the actions of Congress in preserving democratic political
control must often be negative, the necessity is not recognized as
such by the professional officer. If Congress is preoccupied with
making "contacts" on behalf of its constituents, the services are
prepared to be obliging, with the hope that thereby they will be
able in the long run to influence military policy. But if it is legitimate for congressional members to service inquiries on behalf of
their constituents, the military, in turn, believe themselves to be on
safe ground in considering legislators as objects of public relations.
Special efforts are made to invite senators and congressmen to observe military demonstrations, where the mechanics of warfare
are displayed and competing doctrines of the various services are
propounded. Often the line becomes difficult to draw between
genuine efforts to inform, and attempts to impress, overawe, and
court favor.

Again and again in interviews, ranking professional soldiers
seemed unconvinced, with a kind of political naiveté, that the "politicians" were doing all in their power to develop public support
for national security policies. Advocates of absolutist doctrines are
particularly prone to emphasize the limitations of congressional
leaders and their vulnerability to pressures of public opinion. As
an actor in the midst of a complex political process, it is difficult
for the professional officer to maintain a sense of balance and
detachment.

Access to Executive Authority

SINCE THE EFFECTIVE LOCUS of civilian control rests in the executive branch, military leaders must accommodate themselves to a set of pressures different from those of congressional controls. Supervision by the executive branch is continuous, rather than sporadic, and is deeply conditioned by the rate of turnover of key personnel—both military and civilian. Military personnel rotate continuously, generally on three-year terms of duty at service headquarters, the Joint Staff, or the Department of Defense. Because rotation is essential to the military concept of career development, by the time the officer reaches the rank of general or admiral he has served at least two tours of duty in the Pentagon. Service personnel integrate themselves very rapidly into the higher headquarters structure, and quickly reflect the perspective of the organization or professional group they have entered.

Key civilian appointees have a higher rate of turnover than do military officers, and have greater difficulty in integrating themselves into the establishment because of the diversity of their backgrounds. The most exceptional has been Assistant Secretary of Defense Wilfred McNeil, who has held his position as "virtually indispensable man" since 1947. A naval reserve officer who rose to become a rear admiral in charge of the fiscal operation of the Navy, he was given his key post by Secretary of Defense James Forrestal, and has functioned in fiscal matters as the equivalent of a permanent under-secretary of the Department of Defense. Under the Truman administration, appointees to the secretarial and assistant secretarial levels of the Department of Defense during the years from 1948 to 1952 had an average tenure of office of 1.3 years. During the same period, in the three services, length of tenure for equivalent posts was not much longer: Department of the Army, 1.5 years; Department of the Air Force, 1.7; and Department of the Navy, 1.7. During its first 6 years, the Eisenhower administration was not able to recruit and maintain a more stable group of political appointees for these top managerial positions. The length of tenure increased only slightly: Department of Defense, 1.9 years; Department of the Army, 1.8; Department of the Air Force, 2.1; and Department of the Navy, 1.6.

Continuity is given to the civilian structure by a group of

long-tenure, dedicated, and relatively anonymous civil servants who have come into prominence since 1945. Their task, since they have long-term career commitments, is to maintain the organization through their technical expertise and fund of knowledge, rather than to give it policy direction. In recent years, young recruits into the permanent civil service have considered a career in the Department of Defense to be highly prestigeful.[16] Such a career is viewed as offering an opportunity for rapid advancement and the acquisition of administrative skills.

Over the past fifty years, the basic trend in executive control of the military has been toward a greater centralization of authority at the top of each service, and in the last decade there has been a trend toward more centralization in the civilian superstructure of the Department of Defense. Yet, centralization of policy-making is compatible with, and in fact requires, greater decentralization in implementation of decisions. Military leaders often talk about the vertical aspects of civilian control, but the downward penetration of civilian control over the military hierarchy has not been extensive as compared with the military establishments of other nations. The growth of the Department of Defense gives the impression of downward penetration. But below the top departmental level, there is little or no direct organization of civilian political control. Civilians have been spread vertically throughout the military establishment, but they are employed mainly as scientific experts or auxiliaries, and not as part of the administrative and political control apparatus. For example, there are no equivalents to British political officers who have been given considerable power over operational units to handle political matters in the field.

Reorganization of the military establishment in 1959 was one additional step in a long series of changes in the direction of increased centralization of authority.[17] By the new legislation, presidential powers to abolish, merge, and transfer functions of the military establishment were strengthened, although still subject to congressional review. The size of the Joint Staff was increased, both for strategic planning and for operational purposes, and the role of the Department of Defense in administering research and development was expanded. The position of the Secretary of Defense was strengthened, although the chiefs of staff of the three services still retain some direct access to Congress. The Joint Chiefs, under the direction of the Secretary of Defense, were given operational control over unified overseas commands, while the individual departments correspondingly dropped from the chain of command. Instead, the secretaries of the three departments were limited to training and logistic functions.

Centralization of authority in the hands of top civilian executives and in the Joint Staff in part reflects the increasing difficulty in maintaining the separate identities of the three services. But, essentially, increased civilian authority derives from the fact that the bulk of the energies of the military establishment is involved in weapons research and development. These are matters which, it is argued, lend themselves to more centralized control by civilian executives and civilian scientists. As a result, the formal powers of civilians to coordinate the management of the military establishment have become extensive. Yet, civilian political authorities show a reluctance to utilize the full powers at their disposal. The complexity of the problems, the absence of clear-cut alternatives, and the strength of outside industrial contractors influence civilian authorities to operate by balancing competing interests.

Three major devices of control are at the disposal of the civilian administrative authorities. First, like congressional oversight, are the mechanisms of budget control, but the decisions of civilian executives are more important than those of Congress, since they have more immediate consequence, are based upon more adequate knowledge and have greater flexibility. The level of defense expenditure is an executive decision, involving an endless process of political and technical adjustment. Except during periods of actual hostilities, administrations, whether Democrat or Republican, have set the upper limits on the basis of a balance of presumed economic capabilities and political feasibility. Once the budget level has been set and accepted, with whatever limited modification by Congress, civilian administrative control means civilian guidance of the struggle among the three services for allocation of available funds. The machinery of fiscal management is formidable and gives the civilian officials a firm sense of control over the vast military establishment.

Planning is carried out in terms of what specific programs will cost in budget dollars. Civilian executives, especially those with business experience, are convinced that such cost-accounting gives them indispensable tools for executive decisions. Yet a considerable amount of the budget-making process is a façade behind which the real mechanics of planning must be accomplished. The mechanics of budget-making lag behind the day-to-day realities of organizational decisions: The budget does not lead; it follows. Cost-accounting procedures are relevant mainly when it is possible to compare costs of military operations with civilian operations, and these comparisons are limited. The task of comparing the military need for one aircraft carrier versus a number of submarines is a comparison which cannot be completely reduced to cost-accounting procedures.

Therefore, budgetary control becomes crucial because of the second device of civilian executive authority, namely, wide discretion in allocating missions and responsibilities among the three services, even though the main outlines are defined by Congress. Allocation of missions and responsibilities tends to be defined by civilians as administrative decisions, though in effect they are the mechanics by which military strategy is developed and implemented.

After World War II, one basic issue of civilian control centered on allocation of responsibility for strategic atomic retaliation, as between the Air Force and the Navy. Subsequently, it was necessary to decide on crucial issues between the Air Force and the Army in three areas: operational control over aircraft in support of ground force missions, type of intermediate-range ballistic missiles, and responsibilities for air defense. All of these decisions were mainly within the power and jurisdiction of the Secretary of Defense.

Civilian political appointees to the military establishment speak of the necessity for clear-cut decisions in assigning responsibility for missions and weapons development. But, in fact, they tend to take over the same pattern of routinized innovation* that characterizes the military profession. Their contributions to decision-making are cautious, concerned with gradual innovation, and oriented toward limited compromises. Typical is the de facto compromise reached by Secretary McElroy in the dispute between the Army's Jupiter and the Air Force's Thor as intermediate ballistic

* Described in Chapter 2, Technology and Decision-Making.

missiles. The decision reached was to allow both of them to be produced.

Despite the growth in size of the Department of Defense and the development of semi-independent research groups, such as the Rand Corporation, Operations Research Office, and the Institute of Defense Analysis, civilian executives find it very difficult to interpose themselves on the basic issues of weapons development. The permanent civil servants are not able to contribute to the solution of these issues, mainly because they operate as specialists on procedure. Weapons development remains primarily the responsibility of military officers assigned to the Pentagon, since they set the technical terms of reference within which the decisions are made. Because they speak of military necessity, they retain a wide residue of veto power. In recent years, however, there has been a growth in emphasis, mainly by the Air Force, on contracts with private industry for research and development, as opposed to the older government-operated arsenals and proving grounds. This trend has increased the influence of industrial contractors in setting the pace and direction of military technology. Department secretaries and their immediate staffs encounter the full weight of business interests, assisted by retired generals and admirals in their employ. Public criticism by President Eisenhower in June 1959 of the practices of industrial contractors who seek to intervene in decisions about anti-aircraft missiles reflects the intensity of these pressures.

Third, civilian authority in the military establishment has the responsibility of advising the President and the Department of State on military aspects of international relations, and in turn, of implementing directives which deal with politico-military affairs. The administration of foreign affairs involves not only the declaration of high principles by top statesmen, but also an endless stream of specific decisions about economic, political, and military affairs. The type of civilians appointed in recent years to the top levels of the military establishment tends to define their task as a form of industrial management. They are only reluctantly drawn into the implications of the political dimensions of day-to-day military operations. While full analysis of the social background of these men remains to be undertaken, the trend seems to have been away from corporation lawyers, investment bankers, and political figures and toward industrial managers. The older types, especially the investment bankers and corporation lawyers with strong international political interests, were more concerned with the implications of their actions on foreign affairs.

Professional officers have thus come to carry the burden of administering the politico-military responsibilities of the armed forces. They represent the armed forces on the elaborate committee machinery of inter-department coordination, where professional foreign service career officers and the ever-present, but obscure, members of the intelligence community, are to be found. There is a wide gap between the working levels in this machinery and the top political personnel. Yet, since representatives from both the armed forces and the Department of State assume that their opposite numbers are "career" men with lifetime commitments, the system has a strong element of continuity and stability.

All activities involving joint responsibility of the military establishment and the Department of State require, in theory, a directive by the National Security Council. But the time involved in operating its elaborate machinery is so great that there is a constant lag, and much of the coordination of political direction is conducted informally. The handling of the political implications of German rearmament may serve as a typical case of the informal coordination supplied by professional career officers. Although negotiations on German rearmament had been underway since 1950, by 1954, when the pace began to accelerate, no official directive had been issued outlining a plan for dealing with the impact of rearmament on German institutions. Many career officers, aware of the problem, took steps independently to insure that the program would be carried out in such a way as to minimize disruption of German democratic institutions. Yet, it was almost another year before the machinery of government cranked out "a piece of paper" which authorized action by the agencies involved.

In the meantime, in the absence of an official directive from political leaders, self-generated efforts by responsible officers had long been under way. In the military agencies, especially in the Department of the Army, which had the bulk of the responsibility, it was first necessary for planners to alert the various commanders about the existence of a political problem. In particular, strong emphasis was placed on the necessity of communicating to German officers and to Western European nations that the United States had no intentions of unilateral collaboration with the Germans, but was committed to integrating German rearmament within the NATO structure. Such a directive ran counter to the predispositions of many United States officers involved in implementing the program. However, such directives and the skill of top commanders eliminated any possible conception of unilateral action. The military also developed a program of visits by key German officials, especially those involved in planning internal organization of the new German Army, to the United States. Technical assistance to the new German Army included assistance in training personnel and formulating doctrine appropriate to civilian supremacy.[18] Because of the political discretion required, these efforts involved elaborate informal coordination with the Department of State. Nevertheless, as in many similar circumstances, the professional officers were not operating under rigid and detailed civilian control, but had to exercise considerable initiative.

Analysis of the pressures of civilian control over the military establishment leads ultimately to the full complexity of the American federal and pluralistic system of government. In the conduct of foreign affairs, the United States system of government has its own distinctive balance: highly centralized power in the executive branch, matched by diffusion in the responsibility of the political opposition. The professional officer thrives in this setting only if he has the strongest positive commitments to the system of civilian control. Fundamentally, this means that civilian supremacy is effective because the professional soldier believes that his political superiors are dedicated men who are prepared to weigh his professional advice with great care. At a minimum, military leaders want to be assured that they will have effective access to the seats of power.

The ability of top military officers to act as a pressure group in the formulation of national security policy is based in part on America's high respect for the professional specialist. The traditional dogmas of the military profession—honor, public service, and career commitment—have in the past predisposed the officer to nonpartisan alignments and limited the scope of his pressure group activities. But it is no simple matter to evaluate the impact of increased civilian control on the perpetuation of these traditions and on potential sources of professional frustration. Up to the present, the mechanics of promotion and selection have operated to place in military power those who would conform and be in rapport with the system of civilian control. Admirals and generals who have achieved personal success within the system are not very likely to challenge or tamper with the basic rules of the game. The sense of frustration falls heaviest on the rising generation of military leaders who have yet to achieve their mark. If frustration leads to increased political activities, it is the rising generation of colonels and brigadier generals who will carry the burden of agitation.*

All the available evidence underlines the conclusion that the officer's sense of professional and service frustration increases as one moves down the military hierarchy. Earlier in this volume,† it was reported that one-third of the sample of staff officers held the attitude that the military profession had skills superior to those of civilians in the formulation of national security policy. Such an attitude, which cannot be judged as working to strengthen civilian supremacy, tended to be more pronounced among younger and lower-ranking officers. Such officers also showed a distinct preference for compromising their service point of view with those of other services over compromising with "civilian points of view." In short, the lower the rank, the greater was the opposition to civilian points of view.[19]

One response of military leaders to their sense of frustration is an intensified struggle to gain access to the centralized civilian control structure and to influence its decisions. The constant rotation of civilian appointees only increases the efforts of military officers to influence the political dimensions of policy. Yet, it is striking to observe that the demands for recognition and participation in the decision-making process by the highest-ranking officers remain circumscribed and delimited. In their day-to-day activities they live according to the self-conception that they are public servants, and according to their own formulation of civilian-military relations, namely, that "there is no question about who is in control."

---

* This seems to be the case in circumstances as varied as those of the French Army in Algeria and the revolutionary movements of new nations.
† In Chapter 12, Political Beliefs.

Because of professional commitments to the civilian commander in chief, the chief executive must respond effectively to the military pressure for political access. President Franklin D. Roosevelt was well known for the semi-formal lines of communication from the military establishment to his office. Each major military element had its representative or its personal spokesman on the staff of the President. While these arrangements gave the impression of chaotic control, they did serve to reassure military professionals that their points of view were being considered by the President himself. President Eisenhower has imposed the outer forms of military staff organization as the device for controlling access to himself. Regardless of the forms of presidential intervention, only the behavior of the President can guarantee to the professional officer that strategic decisions have been reached after full deliberation of his expert advice.

Along with the increased struggle for administrative access, military pressure group activities on Congress and on the public at large have been expanded. The absence of a parliamentary form of government and the rivalries between Congress and the President increase the opportunities for such tactics. But as a pressure group the military establishment is not a voluntary association, acting on the organs of government; on the contrary, it is an organ of government, seeking to develop new techniques for intervening in domestic politics.

Notes

1. See *Hearings and Reports of the Senate Special Committee Investigating the National Defense Program*, 76th and 77th Congresses.
2. Radway, Laurence, "Uniforms and Mufti: What Place in Policy?" *Public Administration Review*, 1958, *18*, 182.
3. Paul Y. Hammond, a political scientist who has devoted his energies to appraising the impact of administrative forms on military policy, concludes that "continuing disposition of the Department of Defense and the [civilian] administration to seek the solution to major policy problems in reorganization is disquieting." (Hammond, Paul Y., "Effects of Structure on Policy." *Public Administration Review*, 1958, *18*, 179.) His research into the offices of the Secretary of the Navy and the Secretary of War led him to the conclusion that, despite differences in the organizational charts, civilian direction in both departments operated along similar lines. (Hammond, Paul Y., "The Secretary-

ships of War, and of the Navy: A Study of the Civilian Control of the Military." Ph.D. thesis, Harvard University, 1953.)

4. For an exposition of this point of view, see Sapin, Burton, & Snyder, Richard C., *The Role of the Military in American Foreign Policy*. Garden City: Doubleday, 1954.

5. General Otto Nelson wrote in 1946, "Taking $330,000,000 as the average pre-World War II annual expenditure and applying the trend factor of three, it is doubtful if the War Department can expect in the post-World War II era funds in excess of a billion dollars annually. . . . it seems very optimistic to hope for annual government expenditures in excess of eighteen or twenty billion dollars. If this represents the to-be-hoped for government take, then at best the War and Navy Departments cannot expect more than a total of three or four billion dollars for all ground, air and sea defense needs." (*National Security and the General Staff*. Washington: Infantry Journal Press, 1946, pp. 594–95.)

6. Henry, Andrew F., John W. Masland & Radway, Laurence I., "Armed Forces Unification and the Pentagon Officer." *Public Administration Review*, 1955, *15*, 178–80. This is the same body of data which was re-analyzed for political preferences and reported in Chapter 12, Political Beliefs. These data were collected in 1954 and there is no reason to believe that in the interim individual officer commitment to unification has increased; because of intensified rivalries, the reverse has probably been the case. See Methodological Appendix.

7. *Ibid.*, p. 177.

8. *Ibid.*, p. 179.

9. Two-fifths of the Joint Staff officers felt that an officer who had a joint orientation had the better chance for promotion, while only one-fourth of headquarters service officers were of this opinion.

10. Task Force Report on National Security Organization (Appendix G), Prepared for the Commission on the Organization of the Executive Branch of the Government, January 1949.

11. A number of detailed administrative studies have been made of the congressional budget control of the armed forces and its efficiency. See Smithies, Arthur, *The Budgetary Process in the United States*. New York: McGraw-Hill, 1955; Mosher, Frederick C., *Program Budgeting, Theory and Practice with Particular Reference to the United States*. Chicago: U.S. Department of the Army, Public Administration Service, 1954; Huzar, Elias, *The Purse and the Sword: Control of the Army by Congress Through Military Appropriations, 1933–1950*. Ithaca: Cornell University Press, 1950; Katzenbach, Edward L., Jr., *The Pentagon and the Hill*, forthcoming.

12. *New York Times*, March 31, 1959, p. 19.

13. Dexter, Lewis, *Congress, Social Science and The Formulation of Military Policy*. Washington: American Association for the Advancement of Science, December 31, 1958, Section K.

14. See, in particular, Brogan, D. W., "United States: Civil and Military Power," in *Soldiers and Government*, edited by Michael Howard. London: Eyre and Spottiswoode, 1957, pp. 169–85. Brogan presents a historical analysis of the decline of the role of Congress in the direction of military affairs.

15. Data supplied by Professor Morton Grodzins, University of Chicago.

16. The relative "prestige" of federal agencies among civil servants appointed via the Junior Management Assistant Program is as follows: Bureau

of the Budget, Office of the Secretary of Defense, Navy Department, Treasury Department, Air Force, Agriculture, Public Health Service, Civil Service Commission, Commerce, Labor, Interior, and Army. (Based on the responses of 368 civil servants, as collected by Jonathan Slesinger, Institute of Public Administration, University of Michigan, 1959.)

17. For a detailed history of organizational changes in the control structure of the United States Army, see Nelson, Otto, *op. cit.* The evolution of the Department of Defense and its consequences for the three services are described in Kintner, William R., *Forging a Sword: A Study of the Department of Defense* New York: Harper & Bros., 1958.

18. The staff of the American embassy prepared for the ambassador and top political representatives a series of speeches on American concern for civilian supremacy in Germany, with frank admission of the problems the United States had faced in its own history. The United States Information Service launched a mass media program which sought to stimulate discussion of the political problems of civilian control among German opinion leaders.

19. The question was asked, "Which of these two officers would contribute most to the fulfillment of the mission of this organization: one who vigorously supports the views of his own service, or one who is receptive to the views of civilian government, even to the extent of sometimes compromising the viewpoint of his own service?" For the group of officers as a whole, 61 per cent believed that the officers receptive to civilian viewpoints contributed the most. The range of responses varied from 56 per cent, from majors and lieutenant colonels, and their naval equivalents, to 79 per cent for generals and admirals.

CHAPTER 18

Civilian Alliances

THE EFFECTIVENESS of the military as a pressure group depends on the network of its civilian alliances and contracts. Since the politics of the military in the domestic political arena are not the politics of a distinct social stratum, the more elaborate the linkage—formal and informal—of the military officer with civilian leadership groups and institutions, the greater is its potential influence. Of the variety of civilian alliances which professional officers develop, three are crucial: civilian employment of retired officers, activities in professional associations, and direct participation in partisan politics.

Traditionally, the officer of the heroic model lived, while on duty, within the confines of the military establishment and its circumscribed patterns of civilian social contacts. On retirement, he sought for a life style of leisure and sociability. The contemporary military manager, if he ascends into the military elite, has had a career which has put him into contact, although interrupted contact, with a variety of civilian enterprises and organizations. The officer engaged in research and development, or in procurement, has had extensive contact with civilian industries. On retirement, the contemporary officer is more likely to desire a prestigeful civilian assignment, not only because his skills are transferable and new opportunities are available to him; he also wants to continue to do something which he considers worthwhile. Moreover, the terms of his retirement benefits permit continued employment outside of the government.

The post-retirement employment of generals and admirals became conspicuous with the growth in the size of the officer corps. In the years immediately after World War II, some four to five hundred high-ranking officers became available for civilian employment. In subsequent years, the number becoming available annually has varied from twenty-five to fifty. Has the concentration of their employment in particular governmental agencies or sectors of industry been so great as to indicate significant mutual penetration? Is there any evidence that retired generals and admirals are developing an interlocking directorate with other leadership groups? And, contrariwise, how many retired officers believe that they cannot find satisfactory employment for their skills?

For many years, the military have supported a variety of voluntary and professional associations. Each service has a "mutual aid" society, and a single organization has been established for the retired officer's interests. The graduates of the service academies have their own associations, as do the reserve officers of each of the services. Technical and professional groups have been formed along skill lines, such as ordnance, military engineering, communications, etc. But, as pressure group devices, the three services have developed "front" organizations which combine regular officers on active duty, reserve officers on active duty, inactive reserve officers, and civilians. As inter-service rivalries have intensified, these associations have broadened their efforts as lobbyists for the separate services. While it is difficult to evaluate the effectiveness of these groups—the Navy League, the Air Force Association, and the Army Association—their enlarged activities represent a new pattern in the military.

The most direct form of political intervention for a professional officer is to enter partisan politics. In taking such a step, the officer acts on his own, for such action is in opposition to the concept of military honor and the traditions of a nonpartisan stance. The military hero as president is generally considered as exceptional within the profession; that is, the general who runs for president on the basis of his war-time record, and presents himself as "above politics," has been exempt from the rule. In the military view, it is desirable that he not actively seek the candidacy, but that the politicians seek him. But, aside from the presidency, the taboo against the regular officer entering partisan politics on retirement remains powerful and essentially effective. Yet, since the end of World War II, there have been important exceptions. For the most part, these officers have been advocates of the absolutist doctrine, and have affiliated themselves with the extreme right wing of the Republican party. They give voice to the underlying sentiments which can become manifest during periods of extreme political frustration. On the other hand, the pragmatic members of the military elite are more likely to be committed to the civil service concept of neutrality after retirement.

In reacting to the pressures of civilian control, generals and admirals avail themselves of the channels at their disposal to press their demands. These types of civilian alliance—post-retirement employment, professional association activities, direct partisan participation—are, therefore, essential dimensions of the power position of the military in American society. The hypothesis is offered that by means of its professional organizations, more than by post-retirement employment activities, the military elite operate as a pressure group and place strains on the traditional formula of civil-military relations.

Post-Retirement Employment

THE TREND toward a second career for generals and admirals when they leave active duty has developed rapidly since the end of World War II. Among the 1950 military leadership sample, 40 per cent of the Army generals held post-retirement assignments which could be classified as full-time.[1] Among the admirals, a smaller percentage took civilian employment, although many undertook part-time or local community activities.

Of officers who rise to the rank of major general or rear admiral, and higher, only a minority are employed on the basis of specific technical skill. In general, their second occupations are based on administrative, negotiating, and representational skills. Often these officers are persons who have specialized knowledge of the processes of government, and who have personal access to governmental agencies. Of 222 Army generals who held post-retirement jobs in 1954, about 40 per cent had had training as engineers, doctors, lawyers, dentists, ministers, or teachers.[2] Analysis of the jobs held by men with such training indicates that they tended to function as administrative and management personnel and not as technical specialists, although their technical background assisted them in obtaining employment.

Since retired military personnel are employed in civilian occupations on the basis of their general administrative skills, the range of employment has been wide. The personal contacts the officer has made, and the connections between the military establishment and civilian organizations—business and other—create these opportunities. Employment has most frequently been with industrial corporations, followed by government service. The range includes educational institutions; voluntary associations, especially welfare agencies, trade associations; communications and transportation corporations; finance and banking. Among the one hundred sixty major generals and above who were on active duty in the Army in 1950, nineteen held business assignments by 1959, three had major governmental posts, three served as ambassadors, eight had civil service posts of varying importance, and seven were connected with educational institutions. The movement into industry is a direct result of the Dual Compensation Act which permits the retired officer to receive his retirement pay if he is not hired by a government agency.

More than four hundred high-ranking military officers have been employed in the field of industrial enterprise and finance since the end of World War II. Less than a score of military managers have made prominent careers in industry and banking, which would place them at the center of the interlocking directorates which dominate American economic life. Floyd Hunter, in his informal list of the national leaders of the United States, cites approximately four hundred seventy-five persons from various functional groupings, but mainly from business.[3] His list includes only four military names; in addition to President Eisenhower, they are Carl Spaatz, contributing editor of *Newsweek*; Lucius D Clay, and James H. Doolittle. Lucius Clay is the outstanding example of a professional officer turned key industrialist. In addition

to being chairman of the board and chief executive officer of the
Continental Can Corporation, he holds numerous corporate assignments. He is a member of the financial policy committee of
General Motors, a director of the Marine Midland Trust Corporation, the American Express Company, the Lehman Corporation,
the Newmont Mining Corporation, and the Metropolitan Life
Insurance Company.

Within the defense contract industries—particularly aircraft,
missiles, shipbuilding, and, to a lesser extent, electronics—the presence of retired military officers is widespread and indicates a new
type of interlocking directorate between industry and the military
establishment. All of the major aircraft and missile companies
employ retired admirals and generals in key management posts;
their duties involve both internal management and liaison in
Washington. In June 1959, Senator Paul Douglas made public a list
of 768 former military officers of the rank of colonel, naval captain,
and above who were in the employ of the 100 companies and their
153 subsidiaries which in the period from July 1, 1957 to June 30,
1958 received 74.2 per cent of all military prime contract awards.
Breakdown of the group indicates that 218 were generals or
admirals. The retired admiral was more successful than the retired
general in obtaining such employment, in that among the high-
ranking officers, over 60 per cent were naval personnel.[4] This reflects
not so much the technical training of naval officers as the wider
contacts in general between the Navy and industry.

While it was rare for an officer to be employed by more than one
company, there was, of course, a considerable concentration of
hiring of military personnel by a small group of the largest corporations. Ten companies reported that they employed a total of 372 of
these ranking officers, and an industry breakdown showed that
seven aircraft companies employed a total of 177.[5] Among the more
conspicuous names are Lieutenant General Ira C. Eaker, vice-
president of Douglas Aircraft; Lieutenant General Donald L. Putt,
president of United Research Corporation, a subsidiary of the
United Aircraft Corporation; and Lieutenant General Clarence S.
Irvine, vice-president and director of planning for Arco Corporation. General Orval Cook serves as managing director of Aero Space
Industries (formerly the Aircraft Industries Association of America),

which is the influential trade association of aircraft and missile manufacturers.

In the spring of 1959 the presence of retired officers in such posts brought forth congressional demands for an amendment to the defense appropriation bill that would bar their employment by contractors for five years after retirement. A House of Representatives subcommittee held a number of investigating sessions which produced no dramatic revelations. Private industry was hiring some officers whose sole official duty was to preside over annual meetings of the board of directors. Both civilian and military officials in the Department of Defense testified to the contribution these officers made in handling military procurement problems and warned of the adverse effect on recruitment into the military profession if post-retirement employment was unduly restricted. The influence of the prospect of civilian employment on the behavior of military personnel still on duty was not investigated.

In addition to defense contract industries, retired military officers were found in transportation, shipping, and engineering concerns. Even at the rank of general and admiral, more than half of the 1950 leadership sample had employment in local or regional com panies, and typical assignments were as administrative officers. Sometimes, they were hired in order that they might be placed on the board of directors for public relations and representational purposes.

In federal government employment, appointment has been so diffuse that the impact of military personnel is limited, with some notable exceptions. The recruitment and retaining of superior talent for the federal government is a perennial and difficult problem in the United States. The movement of military personnel into high appointive federal agency posts was a deliberate post-war policy to meet the personnel shortage of an expanded bureaucracy, especially in foreign affairs and defense-related agencies. The high point probably was reached around 1948–50 when, it has been estimated, one hundred fifty military men occupied important policy-making posts in civilian government. The Hoover Commission estimated in 1955 that there were about three thousand top management career positions in the federal government, so that in terms of numbers the influx of military personnel was slight. The rigidity of the United States higher civil service has prevented any systematic program of transfer of military personnel into the civilian establishment, and the practice of appointing military personnel to politically responsible posts, although it continues, has declined sharply since 1950.

Much of the political debate about military personnel in government policy positions centers on a few conspicuous cases where civilian leadership sought to make use of prestigeful military officers to deal with difficult political problems. In 1946 General George C. Marshall was sent to China as the President's special representative as a reaction to the political "crisis" which developed when Ambassador Patrick Hurley unexpectedly resigned in protest to the "pro-communist elements" in the Department of State whom he accused of sabotaging his efforts to reunite China. At a cabinet meeting, Secretary of Agriculture Clinton Anderson recommended that Marshall be sent as special ambassador, because "he believed the appointment of George Marshall would take the headlines away from Hurley's resignation. . . ."[6] President Truman proposed the appointment of General Mark Clark as ambassador to the Vatican because he thought it advisable to assign a Protestant to the post, and because he believed that a soldier in this role would be more acceptable to the Congress. But he misjudged political sentiment, and the proposal was promptly dropped. Truman also sought to deal with the political problems of internal security by nominating Admiral Chester W. Nimitz as chairman of a presidential commission on internal security and individual rights.

In the case of his effort to appoint Major General Lawrence S. Kuter as chairman of the Civil Aeronautics Board, President Truman reportedly had formerly offered the CAB chairmanship to six civilians. After all of them declined, he nominated General Kuter, who failed to be confirmed. When President Eisenhower appointed General Elwood R. Quesada as administrator of the Federal Aviation Agency, there was civilian opposition to a military figure in that post. Quesada had to resign his commission because congressional-enabling legislation required a civilian appointee, but political opposition weakened as many congressional leaders recognized that there were few prestigeful civilians not connected with the airlines who were prepared to accept this important, but controversial, post. Opposition to the appointment by President Eisenhower of General Herbert D. Vogel to the Tennessee Valley Authority was based on the belief that Vogel was not sufficiently in favor of public power, rather than the fact that he was a professional soldier. However, military-civilian alliances in the federal government are not only a result of such conspicuous cases, but depend on the concentration of military personnel in specific agencies. How extensive have military appointments been to the Department of State, to the Atomic Energy Commission, and to defense-related and security-type agencies?

After the end of World War II, the Department of State was searching for competent personnel to serve as ambassadors, particularly men with some public reputation. Military personnel were by profession prepared for overseas duties, they often knew foreign languages, and had personal contacts abroad; most important, they were prepared to follow directives from Washington. Henry L. Stimson attributed to Theodore Roosevelt the statement, "The great thing about an Army officer is that he does what you tell him to do." In addition to General George Marshall's secretaryship, from 1947 to 1949, ten military officers served as principal departmental officers and ambassadors under the Truman administration; the number dropped to but a few after 1952 as the foreign service began to produce more suitable career personnel, and as the Eisenhower regime reverted to political appointees as ambassadors.[7] These officers were predominantly Army generals with extensive politico-military experience. Yet, the suspicion against military influence was so great that the appointments produced considerable criticism. In practice, they adhered closely to the Truman foreign policy, and their military prestige was in large degree used to support these political objectives.

Since 1945, military officers have held posts as civilians in policy positions dealing with selective service, defense mobilization, manpower planning, the liquidation of war assets, and veterans' affairs, but even in these areas there has been a gradual decrease.[8] The presence of military personnel in the Atomic Energy Commission has not attracted public attention, although the agency was set up so as to insure civilian control. However, a special section was established to develop military applications, and military personnel were authorized to staff this division. In addition, a succession of military officers have held the position of general manager: Major General Kenneth Nichols, 1953–55; Rear Admiral Paul Frederick Foster, 1955–58; and Major General Alvin R. Ludecke, 1958–.

The Central Intelligence Agency was never designed to be a "civilian" agency, since its operation must be completely integrated with the military establishment. The directorship of the CIA had been held by two military officers—Rear Admiral Roscoe H. Hillenkoeter, 1947–50, and Lieutenant General Walter Bedell Smith, 1950–53—until it was turned over to Allen Dulles.

A notable case involving a "security" agency was the selection of General Joseph M. Swing for the post of Commissioner of Immigration and Naturalization, Department of Justice, in 1945. After his appointment two additional professional officers joined the agency: General Edwin R. Howard, as special assistant to General Swing, and General Frank H. Partridge. In the wake of the McCarthy investigation, these appointments were designed to tighten up "internal security," but they produced extensive congressional criticism as representing excessive military influence in a particular agency.

At the state and metropolitan levels, high-ranking personnel enter civil defense work and police-type operations, occasionally, as, for example, Lieutenant General George P. Hays, who served as a member of the New York-New Jersey Waterfront Commission, an agency for controlling racketeering in the Port of New York. As state and municipal governments search for administrative talent who will accept public service salaries, retired generals and admirals become a new source of personnel. For example, in 1959 Major General Roger James Browne became Deputy Chief Administrator of New York City at a yearly salary of $20,000, after having had an extensive career as a military manager, including service as United States planner for NATO.

Since many retired officers want to continue the public service tradition, they prefer to enter the field of education. Either because of their prior experience as teachers in the military service, or, more likely, because of their administrative ability, education is the third most frequent post-retirement occupation among generals and admirals, after industry and business and government service. Except for the teaching of mathematics and engineering by lower-ranking officers, appointments to both military and civilian schools tend to be concentrated in the southern states. About half the retired generals and admirals who have gone into education have become presidents or deans of military academies and military schools.[9] In addition to the temporary tenure of General Eisenhower as president at Columbia University, the list of important military figures who have accepted university posts includes, as presidents, Lieutenant General Troy Middleton, Louisiana State University; Lieutenant General Andrew B. Bruce, University of Houston; Admiral Richard L. Connolly, Long Island University; Rear Admiral Chandler, William and Mary College; and as dean of faculties of George Washington University, Vice Admiral Oswald C. Colcough, formerly Judge Advocate General of the Navy. But, as with ambassadorships, the demand for generals and admirals as university presidents has declined and retired officers are more likely to serve as administrators in the field of education, or on engineering faculties, or to become involved in research supported by government contracts.

Retired officers are often recruited for "semi-military" posts which involve emergency, disaster, or public welfare work. These jobs appeal to the military officer, and there are instances where officers, having found business dull and routine, subsequently sought more "dramatic" activities. Lieutenant General John B. Coulter served as agent general of the United Nations Reconstruction Agency in Korea, and Lieutenant General Raymond A. Wheeler, who was Chief of Engineers until 1949, organized the United Nations operations to clear the Suez Canal after the Egyptian-Israeli war. Wheeler was subsequently nominated as head of the United Nations Relief and Works Agency for Palestine Refugees, since the Eisenhower administration wanted an officer for this post who was not closely identified with the Roosevelt and Truman administrations in the Middle East. When General Alfred Gruenther became head of the American Red Cross, there was no civilian opposition; not only was he a "civilian" type, but a soldier in charge of emergency relief work seemed entirely appropriate.

Civilian voluntary associations in community affairs and social work specifically recruit retired generals and admirals for their boards of directors, because the military tend to be nonpartisan figures with a strong interest in the administration of social welfare. Just as military leaders have been pressed to assume wider political responsibilities in international affairs, so the retired general and admiral is coopted for public relations support in the management of community activities. Examples are numerous and varied. On the letterhead of the Osborne Association, a prison reform group, appears the name of Major General William F. Dean, who was a prisoner-of-war in Korea; the International Rescue Committee lists Rear Admiral Ellis M. Zacharias, who made a reputation by his radio broadcasts to the Japanese during World War II. General Omar Bradley has become a spokesman for the 166 members of the Health for Peace Committee, lobbying for the National Institute of International Health. One of the most active in public life and "good causes" has been Major General Otto Nelson, vice-president in charge of housing for the New York Life Insurance Company. His military career included extensive teaching experience at West Point and service as Assistant Deputy Chief of the Army under George C. Marshall, a post which he held after his work on the reorganization of the War Department in the spring of 1942. In addition to serving as government consultant on civil defense, he has an extensive portfolio of public service assignments.[10]

If there is a pattern in the post-retirement occupations and activities of the military elite it is one of extreme diversity. Moreover, ample retirement benefits and an abundance of employment opportunities, plus the ease of starting a second career, have prevented any profound sense of frustration. Since the number of ex-general grade officers will increase very slowly, their position in civilian society is not likely to alter. However, after 1962, a large number of officers, ranging in rank from major to colonel, will be released after twenty years of service, and they will be actively seeking civilian employment.[11]

Professional Associations

IF POST-RETIREMENT EMPLOYMENT tends to disperse the professional officer and assimilate him into civilian society, his professional associations operate in the opposite direction. They are very important in strengthening the social solidarity of the regular officer both during active duty and after retirement. The military has a long tradition of societies concerned with the professional and technical aspects of warfare and the publication of professional journals. Before the Civil War there were short-lived military associations with scientific and professional aspirations, such as the West Point Philosophical Society and the United States Naval Lyceum. As early as 1873, the United States Naval Institute was founded by a group of officers at Annapolis in conscious parallel to the British Royal United Service Institution. The *Proceedings* of the Institute have been published continuously, with increasing focus on the political aspects of war. In 1879 Army officers organized the Military Service Institution, which, along with its journal, became extinct during World War I. In the main, the professional associations and journals in the Army were organized along specialist lines, with the United States Infantry Association and its *Infantry Journal* being the most influential until the outbreak of World War II.

After 1945, the associational life of the military officer underwent a change. Much of the technical and scientific activities were channeled into civilian societies, where military officers who had advanced training found common interests with civilians. At the same time, each of the services created or transformed one of its professional associations into a general organization, designed to present the service's point of view to the public. In response to the pressure of civilian controls, the services became aware that they could influence the legislative and executive process by influencing public opinion.

The largest and most influential of these service organizations is the Air Force Association, founded in 1946, which was organized without the traditional inhibitions of the professional association in the other services. Its membership in 1958 was estimated at 52,000 persons with 125 community organizations, and included retired Air Force officers, reservists, and regular Air Force officers on active duty. According to one news source the Air Force Association had some 300 "affiliates" in the form of industrial firms, each of which paid $350 in annual dues.[12] Approximately forty persons were employed on its staff in the Washington, D.C. office in 1958.

Like the Navy League and the Army Association, the Air Force Association is a private organization in form, and, therefore, is not directly subject to the control of the Secretary of Defense or the Secretary of the Air Force. However, in effect, it is a semi-official organ of the Air Force. Its directorate in any year represents a balance of the various elements being mobilized by the Association. In 1958 there were six Air Force officers, including Generals James Doolittle, Carl Spaatz, George Kenney, plus representatives of the reserve officers. The president was Peter J. Schenk, a former official of General Electric and subsequently president of the Ray-

theon Corporation, a supplier of electronics and communications
equipment for the military establishment. Civilian members were
executives in the aircraft and air transport field, publicists, and
lawyers; there was a wide geographical distribution and no overtones of political partisanship. The directorate contained few important financial figures or socially prominent leaders. They were
mainly men linked to the aviation industry, whose reputations were
confined to their own circles and were not nationally based. The
"intellectual" and academic spokesman was Professor W. Barton
Leach, a professor of law at Harvard University and a brigadier
general in the Air Force Reserve, who served as the Air Force
counsel at the congressional investigation of the Air Force-Navy
rivalries concerning strategic bombing missions.

While the Air Force Association does not maintain registered
lobbyists in Washington, one of its functions is to supply "information" to senators and congressmen. As one of the publications of the
Association states, "AFA has the information that legislators and
policymakers need. . . . They turn naturally to AFA for this help
because the ideas that AFA backs have won national recognition."
Its major task is to act as a public relations outlet for the concept
of air power, beyond the official publicity of the Department of
the Air Force. The Association publishes a lavish monthly magazine,
Air Force, with extensive advertising from Air Force contractors.
It holds a variety of meetings and conferences on Air Force
problems and disseminates material for the mass media. Because
the bulk of the Air Force contract funds go into the aircraft industry, the aviation manufacturers' association, Aero Space Industries Association, with its annual budget of $1,500,000 and staff
of sixty, including registered lobbyists and specialists in public
relations, augments the Air Force Association. Each year the Association holds a national convention at which resolutions are passed
on legislation affecting the Department of the Air Force. On March
30, 1959, General Thomas D. White, Chief of Staff of the Air
Force, testified before the House Defense Appropriations Subcommittee that the Air Force had used 127 planes to fly civilians and
military men to the Air Force Association convention that year at
Dallas, Texas. He told the committee, "I can only say we endeavor
to hold it down."[13]

The propaganda technique of the Air Force Association, as
reflected by analysis of its output, is mainly concerned with "selling"

the importance of air power. The basic theme is the central importance of strategic retaliatory air power, although the organization does not engage in elaborate discussion of military doctrine or politico-military matters. In particular, it does not comment on nuclear test suspension and disarmament, beyond declaring its suspicion of dealing with the Soviet Union.

On matters of unification, the Air Force Association expresses more openly the position of top Air Force commanders who are inhibited in speaking personally by official administrative pressures. While the Air Force Association has been nominally committed to an extreme position on unification—namely, a single military service—it took objection to the basic features of President Eisenhower's reorganization bill of 1958 which increased the power of the Secretary of Defense. The Association's hostility helped to defeat the features of the bill, which would have centralized the public information and legislative liaison functions of the three services.

While the Navy League is the oldest of the service organizations, having been established shortly after World War I, its activities are much more limited. Although originally linked to the steel and shipbuilding corporations, its interests have broadened since Navy contracts have become distributed over a variety of industries, including aircraft.[14] It has not received the same kind of unified support as the Air Force Association has received from an industry wholly dependent on government contracts. Naval traditions operate to set the forms of its activities, so that its public relations program is not as well deveolped. The Navy League is more a pressure group which believes that its personal contacts are still effective, especially in lobbying before Congress, since key congressional leaders are proud of their personal affiliations with the U.S. Navy.

The composition of the Navy League reflects the position of the naval officer in American social structure and the style of naval politics. Retired naval officers are not prominent on the board. There is a complete absence of professional publicists, and, instead, the board is composed mainly of important investment bankers, industrialists of considerable reputation, and men of upper-class social background. The board is predominantly Republican, with a sufficient number of Democrats to enable it to appear bipartisan. But there are no elected government officials or persons who would be designated party people as such.

The Navy League cultivates, much more carefully than does the Air Force Association, the image that it is an independent civilian organization. Its monthly publication regularly contains a statement to the effect that its contents do not have the official sanction or approval of the Navy Department. But by means of its annual convention, its press releases, and its public relations program, the Navy League is more likely than the Air Force Association to comment on strategic political-military issues. The contents of its publications articulate the Navy's critique of massive retaliation, and the Navy is represented as being an effective instrument of diplomacy. Another basic theme is its defense of the organizational autonomy of the Navy.[15]

The Army was the last of the three services to develop a semi-official public relations organization when, in 1957–58, it converted the Combat Forces Association into the Army Association. Army leadership felt it was being "outgunned" by the Air Force Association and the Navy League, and the break with the old tradition was rationalized as an act of self-defense. The shift in the composition of the board of directors and the conversion of *Combat Forces Journal* to the new magazine, *Army*, was the shift from a mainly professional association to a combined professional society and pressure group.

As late as 1950, the Combat Forces Association's major activity was the publication of a journal for the professional soldier. Its executive council listed Harry Truman as honorary president, and its council, as well as all of its membership, were regular officers, plus a scattering of reservists. By 1958, the Association had taken on the format of the Air Force Association. It had developed a central executive under Lieutenant General Walter L. Weible, a nation-wide organization with local chapters, an active recruiting program, and redesigned its journal—under the title *Army*—to attract advertisements from military contractors.

The new council, trustees, and advisory board of directors constitute the Army's device for civilian alliances and its means for developing political support for its limited war doctrine. Among the officers of the Association in 1958, thirteen were retired Army generals, including Matthew B. Ridgway, while the civilians represented a wider range of social and functional groups than found among the leaders of either the Air Force Association or the Navy

League. Affiliations with the older eastern upper social stratum were symbolized by men, such as the president of the Association, Anthony J. D. Biddle of Philadelphia, who during World War II served as Eisenhower's military diplomat to the European governments in exile at SHAEF headquarters; Henry Cabot Lodge, Jr. of Boston, who holds the reserve rank of brigadier general; and Ogden R. Reid of New York City.

Investment bankers and men of corporate finance who had been educated at West Point, or who served in the Army during World War II, included Major General Charles E. Saltzman and William Paley of the Columbia Broadcasting Corporation. Industrial enterprise and Army contractors were represented by Robert L. Biggers, vice president of the Chrysler Motors Corporation, and Harry Bullis, chairman of the board of General Mills. For the foundations and education, there were Dean Rusk of the Rockefeller Foundation, and Reverend Robert Gannon, president of Georgetown University; and for the university intellectuals, Professor Henry A. Kissinger, theoretician of limited nuclear warfare. Senators and congressmen were included and carefully balanced as to region and political affiliation. When the list first appeared one public relations officer commented to the author that "a colonel in the chief of staff's office must have read C. W. Mills' *The Power Elite* and thought it was a good idea to have one." While these men are undoubtedly concerned about the future of the ground forces and the doctrine of limited warfare, the list hardly reflects a unity of interest such as is prevalent among the Air Force Association's leaders.

The composition of this group, as well as the intellectual tone of *Army*, indicates the public relations problem of the ground forces. In the language of public relations, limited warfare is a more difficult "package to sell." Articles in *Army* contain elaborate doctrinal analysis, and there is an extensive review section of current books on world affairs, features almost wholly absent in *Air Force*. Massive retaliation is criticized, and some discussion of the problems involved in nuclear test suspension and international control of armament is included. Yet, the primary goal, as in the case of the other two organizations, is to create a favorable climate for budgetary requests to Congress and to support the administrative politics of the Department of the Army.

Partisan Politics

FOR SOME PROFESSIONAL OFFICERS, after retirement, nonpartisan pressure group politics is an inadequate expression of their domestic political interests. Yet, officers who stand for elected office are so few as to constitute almost special cases, for the barriers against their entering professional politics are immense. A lifetime in a specialized career which weakens geographic affiliations renders access to organized party politics very difficult. Professional honor has inhibited direct involvement in politics. It is typical for generals to advise one another that "the best service a retired general can perform is to turn in his tongue along with his suit and mothball his opinions."[16]

The exclusion of the military professional from organized party politics is a result of the two-way struggle between generals and politicians; historically, the military have fought against the appointment of political generals, and the politicians have been opposed to the use of military service as a device for building a public reputation that could be used in politics. Since the Civil War, the military profession has struggled to assert the necessity of an academy education and a lifetime career commitment as the basis for higher command. It has fought against politically appointed National Guard officers, and even against the use of professional politicians for top political-military assignments. Patrick Hurley, an organization Republican, whose appointment as major general was sponsored by President Franklin D. Roosevelt, was the last of the political generals. Although Hurley was not given command of troops, he performed a variety of diplomatic and political-military assignments, and in part represented Roosevelt's conscious efforts to demonstrate bipartisanism in the conduct of the war.

The decline of the political general has also been hastened by the suspicions of each political party regarding any efforts by the other to use military office as a launching platform for potential candidates. Newton D. Baker told Henry Stimson that he had removed his name from a list of officers to be sent to France because he did not want the Army to be used as a source of glory for politicians.[17] When Major Fiorello LaGuardia was proposed as brigadier general for military government operations in Italy, not only did the military professionals object to his appointment, but

Republicans were opposed to giving a Democrat such a political advantage.

While military service during war-time is a political asset, especially military service as an enlisted man, it is a rare event when an academy-trained regular officer stands for election to the House of Representatives or the Senate, and even rarer when he succeeds in getting elected. In the 86th Congress, 1959–60, Representative Frank Kowalski, a Democrat from Bridgeport, Connecticut, was the only regular officer—a retired Army colonel—and the first in many years. Kowalski apparently was sought out and given the nomination because the Democratic Party needed a Polish name to balance its slate. One of his first actions in Congress, as a member of the newly created House Armed Services Subcommittee on Manpower, was to issue an attack on the armed services for wasting expensive manpower by using "thousands" of enlisted men as houseboys, domestic servants, and chauffeurs for senior officers. Another military figure who attracted national attention in the political arena, in his efforts to obtain the governorship of Alabama on a segregationist ticket, was Rear Admiral John Crommelin, leader of "Op. 23," the naval group which opposed the Air Force B-36 program.

The exclusion of retired professional officers from political life in the United States stands in marked contrast to the practice in Great Britain, where the regular officer is an important source of personnel for the Conservative party. Regular officers seldom become important political members of Parliament, but they are acceptable candidates to the electorate. Between World War I and World War II, regular officers were, after lawyers, the second most frequent occupational group in the House of Commons, and although their number declined somewhat from 1945 to 1951, they still held the same relative position.[18] In 1951 there were eighty-four lawyers and forty-eight regular officers in Parliament, not including men who held temporary or territorial commissions.

All but two of the regular Army officers were Conservatives. Most were officers of the rank of major to colonel who had retired after twenty years or more of service. Typically, generals seldom felt disposed to offer themselves to the uncertainties of election; if they were conspicuously important, they were made members of the House of Lords. In England this concentration of regular officers in Parliament is not taken as a threat to democratic institutions. In fact, a careful study of British parliamentary institutions by J. F. S. Ross does not even comment on their presence.[19] The British officer, compared to the American, is more fully integrated into the fabric of society. As a retired officer he can be active in conservative politics, and such activity is compatible with civilian supremacy.

In the United States a step between nonpartisan pressure group activities and direct entrance into the political arena is activity in voluntary associations designed to influence political opinion. Professional officers do not become centrally involved in the major veterans' associations, since these groups often have an anti-"big brass" bias. The great number of smaller associations organized for the veterans of specific military units include professional officers, but these associations are avowedly unpolitical.

The major organizational effort to mobilize the extreme right wing of the military leaders was the formation of Pro-America by Colonel Robert R. McCormick and ex-Representative Hamilton Fish of New York, after the election of President Eisenhower. Many of the figures involved—both military and civilian—had been active in the Citizens for Taft Committee, under the national chairmanship of Lieutenant General Albert C. Wedemeyer, which sought to obtain the Republican presidential nomination for Senator Robert Taft. After the failure of these efforts, the more extreme partisans organized Pro-America.

Among the central figures were five military officers, all of whom were advocates of absolutist military doctrine and "Far Easterners" or MacArthur's associates. Brigadier General Bonner Fellers, who had been General MacArthur's public relations expert in Japan, was the national chairman. Two other MacArthur subordinates were on the central policy committee—Lieutenant General George D. Stratemeyer and General James A. Van Fleet, as well as General Mark Clark and General Albert C. Wedemeyer. Among the civilian members were such political figures as Dean Clarence Manion of Notre Dame Law School, ex-Senator A. W. Hawkes, of New Jersey, and Frank E. Gannett. The political objectives of the organization included passing the Bricker amendment and the Reed-Dirksen amendment to limit congressional taxing power, safeguarding states' rights, upholding the McCarren-Walter Immigration Act, abolishing the withholding tax and guar-

anteeing the "right to work." For national security, these retired
military professionals, most of whom had been Army officers, were
committed to a program of maintaining air superiority and abolishing conscription. The ideological requirements of victory led them
to a political position completely at variance with the majority of
their professional associates. With the political decline of Senator
McCarthy, and the reassertion of a politics of compromise within
the Republican Party, Pro-America lost its prominence.

Such patriotic groups attract retired regular officers whose conservative partisanship ranges from right-wing Republican to implied criticism of the two-party system. The Coalition of Patriotic
Societies of America, which claims to represent 112 patriotic associations, supplies a focal point for these activities. Its annual speakers
include such men as Major General Charles A. Willoughby, former
staff member for General Douglas MacArthur. At its 1959 annual
Washington Seminar, the theme was developed that both former
and present United States leaders have been unable to understand
the communist menace and have permitted it to develop in this
country.[20]

In contrast to these forms of "right wing" political behavior,
there has been a complete absence of even a mild "fellow travel-
ing" equivalent since the end of World War II. The conservative
bias of the profession and internal American politics have combined to prevent such a response. Only the unknown Brigadier
General Hugh B. S. Hester, quartermaster specialist, emerged as a
lone critic of the militarization of American foreign policy. In a
1957 speech before the National Lawyers' Guild program for
peace, the most he could offer his audience was the statement that
he believed that the Russians wanted peace just as much as Americans want peace.[21]

In summary, as a pressure group, the military profession has a
unique relation to Congress and to the President because of the
vital functions it performs. Yet, in many respects it conforms to
the pattern typical of other pressure groups which represent professional and occupational specialists. Its activities are highly decentralized, the services and individual officers compete among
themselves. None of the three forms of civilian alliance—post-
retirement employment, professional association activities, and
direct participation in politics—serves to integrate the military
into a unified political force. With few exceptions, post-retirement

employment does not link the military professional into the older and well-established financial elite groups; most frequently, he follows in the pattern of the public servant, or the organizational specialist, or the salesman for an industry seeking to expand its government defense contracts. The direct involvement of the military in partisan politics has been too limited to be significant, except to indicate the direction of sentiment and the style of politics that frustration might produce.

The conflicting interests among the military profession are perpetuated in associational life. Each faction, as it bids for public and political support, can best be described as exercising a veto. This negative power reflects the different sources of public support; the Air Force advantage in support by industrial contractors is counterbalanced by the support of the Army's pragmatic point of view by news commentators and specialized opinion leaders; the Navy draws on its special alliances with key congressional leaders.

In the short run, the pressure group activities of the military are still very much the expression of a public position, behind which professional expertise and administrative compromise operate. In the long run, it is not the civilian alliances of the military establishment, but the new public relations of the military service which has the potentiality for threatening the system of political balance. An organ of government lobbying on its own behalf—especially one which deals with such a vital function—is difficult to contain. One danger is that the new public relations, because it reflects military estimates of international relations, might in the long run distort public discussion of national defense policy, and thereby increase rigidity in international relations. More fundamentally, the proposition that requires investigation is the extent to which the new public relations is transforming the debate on national security from one of questioning alternative policies of national self-interest to a debate based on rigid ideological claims.

Notes

1. Leonard Reissman, on the basis of material reported in *Who's Who in America*, found only 23.4 per cent post-retirement occupations for the 945

retired Army generals, as of 1954. Reissman, Leonard, "Life Careers, Power and the Professions: The Retired Army General." *American Sociological Review*, 1956, 21, 215–21. However, because of his reliance on this single source, there was no definite information on 455, or 48.1 per cent of his sample. The no-information group seems to be composed mainly of officers who retired after 1950, and whose post-retirement information was not yet listed in *Who's Who*. If this group is eliminated, the percentage who had a second career is 45.3, approximately the same as found in the 1950 military leadership sample investigated for this study.

2. *Ibid.*, p. 218.

3. Hunter, Floyd, *Top Leadership, U.S.A.* Chapel Hill: University of North Carolina Press, 1959, pp. 17–28.

4. *Congressional Record*, Vol. 105, June 17, 1959, pp. 10055–59.

5. The ten companies with the largest number of retired military personnel were: Lockheed Aircraft, 60; General Dynamics, 54; Westinghouse Air Brake Co., 42; Radio Corporation of America, 39; General Electric, 35; Westinghouse Electric, 33; Boeing Aircraft, 30; General Tire and Rubber Company, 28; North American Aviation, 27; International Telephone and Telegraph, 24. In addition to these listed above, four other aircraft companies and their figures are: Northrop Aircraft, 16; Douglas Aircraft, 15; Martin Company, 15; and Bendix Aviation Corp., 14.

6. Millis, Walter, ed., *The Forrestal Diaries*. New York: Viking Press, 1951, p. 113.

7. General George C. Marshall, Special Representative of the President to China, 1946, Secretary of State, 1947–49; Brig. Gen. Henry C. Byroade, Director, Bureau of German Affairs, 1949–52, Assistant Secretary of State, 1952–55; Maj. Gen. John H. Hilldring, Assistant Secretary of State, 1946–47; Rear Adm. John W. Bays, Chief, Division of Foreign Service Administration, 1947–49; Lt. Gen. Albert C. Wedemeyer, Special Representative of the President to China and Korea, 1947. Ambassadors: Maj. Gen. Thomas Holcomb, USMC, South Africa, 1944–48; Lt. Gen. Walter Bedell Smith, Russia, 1946–49; Adm. Alan G. Kirk, Belgium, 1946, Russia, 1949–52; Brig. Gen. Frank T. Hines, Panama, 1945–48; Maj. Gen. Philip Fleming, Costa Rica, 1951–53; Rear Adm. Arthur Ageton, Paraguay, 1954–57. Under the Eisenhower administration, three professional soldiers were given major appointments in the Department of State: Lt. Gen. Walter Bedell Smith, Under-Secretary of State, 1953–55. Ambassadors: Adm. Raymond A. Spruance, Philippines, 1952–55; Brig. Gen. Henry C. Byroade, Egypt, 1955–56. Lt. Gen. William E. Riley was named Deputy Director of the Foreign Operations Administration in 1958. (Based on data presented by Samuel Huntington, *The Soldier and the State*. Cambridge: Harvard University Press, 1957, p. 360.)

8. For example, Maj. Gen. Lewis Hershey has served as Director of Selective Service continuously since 1941; General Omar Bradley as Administrator, Veterans' Administration, 1945–47; Lt. Gen. Raymond S. McLain as member of the National Security Training Commission, 1951–54; Admiral Thomas C. Kinkaid as member of the National Security Training Commission, 1951–57; General of the Army George C. Marshall as Secretary of Defense, 1950–51; Lt. Gen. W. S. Paul as Assistant to the Director, Office of Defense Mobilization, 1954–56; Maj. Gen. Edmund B. Gregory as Administrator, War Assets Administration, 1946; Maj. Gen. Robert M. Littlejohn as Administrator, War Assets Administration, 1946–47.

9. For example, Gen. Mark Clark became president of The Citadel, a South Carolina military college, and Lt. Gen. Milton G. Baker, superintendent of Valley Forge Military Academy. Under Gen. Clark's management the enrollment has risen rapidly, as football activities were strengthened. Although a "spit and polish" atmosphere was introduced, Gen. Clark also inaugurated bi-weekly meetings with cadet leaders to "allow cadets to air their gripes and make suggestions."

10. Nelson's appointments include: Vice President of the Regional Plan Association (New York metropolitan area), a director of the Governmental Affairs Institute, a non-profit organization in administering cultural exchange programs; Vice-Chairman of the board of the Institute of Public Administration, a trustee of the Carnegie Endowment for International Peace; and Executive Director for Construction for the Lincoln Center for Performing Arts.

11. See Biderman, Albert, & Croker, George W., "The Prospective Impact of Large Scale Military Retirement." *Social Problems* (in press, 1959). The authors point out that retired officers concentrate in five states: California, Florida, New York, Texas, and Virginia. The localities that are favored include San Antonio, Texas; San Francisco-Oakland (particularly the Lower Peninsula); San Diego, California; the northern Virginia suburbs of Washington, and Norfolk, Virginia; the upper half of the east coast of Florida; and the New York metropolitan area. Newly popular localities include Phoenix, Arizona; Colorado Springs and Denver, Colorado; Montgomery, Alabama; Honolulu, Hawaii; and Seattle, Washington.

12. Fairfield, William S., "PR for the Services—in Uniform and in Mufti." *The Reporter,* May 15, 1958, p. 22.

13. *New York Times,* March 31, 1959, p. 7.

14. The original founders of the Navy League included: Charles M. Schwab, Bethlehem Steel Corp.; J. Pierpont Morgan, U.S. Steel Corp.; Colonel R. N. Thompson, International Nickel; B. F. Tracy, attorney, Carnegie Steel; Harvey Steel, Director, Tennessee Coal and Iron; and George Westinghouse, Westinghouse Electric Corporation.

15. The Navy League has created a field organization called Advisory Council of Naval Affairs, whose duties at the local level have been announced to include: (a) resolving differences between the local community and naval authorities on personnel, (b) encouraging adoption of constructive personnel and employment practices so that employees who are reserves will receive credit rather than be handicapped, (c) disseminating factual information, as a result of which desirable men will be encouraged to seek entrance to the naval academy and other naval programs, (d) assisting in securing employment for officers and enlisted men retiring and returning to civil life. The Navy League operates an extensive "buddy" program for recruiting career personnel.

16. Bradley, General Omar, *New York Times,* May 7, 1957, p. 44.

17. Stimson, Henry, and McGeorge, Bundy, *On Active Service.* New York: Harper & Bros., 1948, p. 93.

18. Ross, J. F. S., *Elections and Electors.* London: Eyre and Spottiswoode, 1955, p. 433.

19. *Ibid.*

20. *New York Times,* February 4, 1959, p. 8.

21. *New York Times,* February 24, 1957, p. 62.

CHAPTER *19*

The New Public Relations

DESPITE CONGRESSIONAL OPPOSITION, the military establishment has been able to develop and maintain extensive "public relations"—or, in official terminology, public information programs. The gravity of military affairs, the spectacle of new weapons, and the visibility of military heroes make the military "newsworthy." While the bulk of this mass media content is either human interest or popular science, the pressure group activities of the military in domestic politics are facilitated by the pervasiveness of its public information efforts.

At one time, military leaders had a long-standing tradition of hostility to the press because of their dislike of contradiction. They saw journalists as particularly obnoxious sources of public criticism. But by World War I, American generals and admirals had learned that their place in history depended in no small part on their ability to project themselves into the headlines of the mass media. Because of the extensive mobilization of military and civilian personnel required in modern warfare, civilian political leaders, particularly in democratic nations, came to believe that the maintenance of "morale" was important. Therefore, in time of war the military was forced to accept the public relations principle. A steady flow of news was required, both for the troops and for the home front, in order to keep popular expectations from wavering between extremes of undue pessimism and exaggerated optimism.

In periods of military operations, news released to the civilian population seeps back to combat formations. During World War II, there was constant friction between the various services as to who was getting the headlines at home. Troops on the stalemated front in Italy came to believe they had been forgotten at home, since correspondents found little that was newsworthy to report in the day-to-day grinding war. When a special program of press releases was prepared glorifying individual soldiers and small units, and published by home-town newspapers, the result was a flow of personal mail back to the Italian front, which helped overcome the sense of isolation.

Especially for the American "home front," with its insatiable consumption of the products of mass media, generals and admirals abroad had to learn how to face the correspondents' corps. General Douglas MacArthur came to be considered by friendly and critical correspondents alike as a "master" in the handling of his press relations. Like most ranking officers, he employed a staff of press relations experts to manage the mechanics of his public relations. Only such "old-fashioned" and personally reticent soldiers as General Walton H. Walker, who bore the brunt of early fighting in the Korean conflict, did not employ the services of a public information officer.

General Omar Bradley spoke thus of the difference between old and new conceptions of public relations: "Thirty-two years in the peacetime army had taught me to do my job, hold my tongue, and keep my name out of the papers."[1] But he soon learned that commanding eighty thousand troops made him front-page news. In meeting the new conception, he was delicately assisted by Lieutenant Colonel Chester B. Hansen, with the result that the press created the sympathetic image of Bradley as the soldier's soldier.

In the effort to conform to civilian control, the military establishment makes a sharp separation between public information activities and the previously described "psychological warfare" operations against the enemy. Such a distinction is designed to give greater freedom of action to political warfare services and to enforce the requirement of "objectivity" on public information officers. But the whole spectrum of public relations activities, internal and external, tends to become diffuse. What generals and admirals say to the home population becomes matter for dissemination in neutral and hostile territories, and vice versa.

The Mechanics of Persuasion

THE PUBLIC RELATIONS EFFORTS of the three services are organized to make use of the domestic mass media, and to reach so-called "opinion leaders" by direct "face-to-face" contact. Early in 1915, President Woodrow Wilson issued an order which was circulated through the War Department, prohibiting officers from giving out for publication any interview statement, discussion, or article on the military situation in the United States or abroad.[2] Such an order was unrealistic, if only because of the prerogative of the press to reward the reporter who is most enterprising in extracting statements from reluctant public officials. It is also impossible to bar the press completely from access to military officers, since the flow of news from these sources is indispensable to civilian control. Yet, in 1922, when General Pershing released a counter-order permitting and encouraging soldiers to express their "personal views on the day," the military was expanding its public relations activities, without explicit regard for appropriate standards of behavior.

In the cold war the main and most conspicuous source of public statements by military leaders for domestic consumption consists of the testimony that service chiefs are called upon to present before congressional committees. These statements are part of the indispensable mechanics of civilian control and public discussion. Because the Chairman of the Joint Chiefs of Staff and the three service chiefs are such prominent figures, they tend to be held in high demand as public speakers. Although systematic data could not be compiled, there does not seem to be evidence of an increase in the frequency of such public speeches since 1945. If anything, the trend seems to be toward a curtailment of this activity by the military chiefs, but not because of any explicit policy about civil-military relations. Under the Eisenhower administration, the chief executive, being a professional soldier, saw himself as the authoritative spokesman on military affairs.

Since elaborate public statements on military doctrine do not produce headlines, the three services seek to exploit military demonstrations, especially of new weapons. Military doctrine is debated by means of "propaganda stunts." General "Billy" Mitchell's famous boast that the airplane could sink a battleship led to a trial demonstration, in which evaluation of the effectiveness of air power in repelling a sea-borne invasion became hopelessly entangled in press reports about the dramatic spectacle. The publicity war has been intense in seeking to influence the allocation of responsibilities for guided missiles. Civilian officials in the Department of Defense have sought to develop public information policies which would at least control the flow of information about new weapons, so as to minimize confusion and loss of prestige abroad. The difficulties of enforcing security rules, the desire of the services to achieve publicity, but, most of all, the prerogatives of the press, have negated these civilian controls. Alistair Cooke, correspondent for the *Manchester Guardian,* is one of the few journalists who have pointed out that the public relations activities of the military establishment are not only a product of the services themselves, but also the result of newspaper pressure to produce news. If the mass media coverage of the development and testing of guided missiles lacks balance, this is the consequence of "a free country which is stubbornly dedicated to the view that the freedom of the press means a wild freedom of untested assertion."[3]

Propaganda of the deed does not necessarily have to be staged, nor does it have to deal with basic strategic issues. When seven enlisted men were "bumped" from their California-bound airplane flight at the Tachikawa Air Force base near Tokyo to make room for a lieutenant colonel and his family who were going to vacation in Hawaii, Lieutenant General Robert W. Burns, informed of the incident, personally went to the air base. By radio, he ordered the plane at sea to return to the base, and stood by while it was reloaded according to official priorities. The result was a flow of publicity in the United States press, confirming the Air Force image of itself as an organization devoid of arbitrary authoritarian practices.

Along with major policy speeches and dramatic military demonstrations, the public information apparatus produces quantities of material about personalities and "background" information to feed the demand for copy by the mass media. With managerial efficiency, public information officers are located at every level of the military establishment down to the smallest isolated Air Force base. Activities range from preparing full-length features for television to writing news releases for home-town newspapers about changes of station of enlisted personnel.

Inter-service rivalries are reflected even in the battle to make the comic strips. The Air Force has paid special tribute to Milton Caniff, originator of "Terry and the Pirates" and producer of "Steve Canyon," for effective Air Force presentations. The Navy has been able to project itself through "Buzz Sawyer," whose hero is a naval aviation officer of considerable dash. But the fortunes of the Army have been much less successful, with only the production of such unglamorous heroes as "Beetle Bailey" and "Sergeant Bilko."

Public information has become a specialized military career. The services use their own internal training programs, as well as civilian schools of journalism and public relations, to develop professional competence. The number of persons engaged in such work is difficult to ascertain, because job definitions are hardly clear-cut. According to an Air Force source, the Air Force, in 1959, had the largest number of officers engaged in information activities —650; the Army had 600, while the Navy reported 212.[4] In addition, 100 persons in the Department of Defense were engaged in information service. These 1,462 officers were supported by larger staffs of enlisted and civilian personnel, which number in the thousands.[5] About one-third of these personnel are employed mainly on internal information programs within the military establishment, but even these internal programs furnish material for public relations activities.

It is difficult to make meaningful comparisons between military public relations efforts and those of private industry or voluntary associations. On the basis of dollars spent or number of personnel employed, the ratio for the military establishment is probably not much greater. A great deal of public information work in the armed forces involves routines of reviewing material for military security. But it could be estimated that, on the average, armed forces public relations personnel produce many more column inches and minutes on the air than do their privately employed colleagues.

Professional "public relations" requires a balance between mass appeals and efforts to reach opinion leaders. The three services, especially the Air Force, hold special demonstrations and briefings to reach men who "count" in molding public opinion.[6] A Defense Orientation Conference Association has been established, as a unified service effort, which is made up of business, industry, labor, and other national leaders who regularly receive briefings on national defense. Specialized associations, such as the American Society for Industrial Security, supply additional channels for such activities. While these briefings disseminate basic background information, they place heavy emphasis on service points of view. One civilian "opinion leader," with extensive combat experience during World War II, reported in a personal communication his impressions of such "briefings" in the following skeptical fashion:

You wouldn't believe it, but the Marine Corps won the orientation battle. First we visited an Air Force base and we were shown a B-52 with a mock up of an H-bomb. Most of the rest of the time with the Air Force was spent demonstrating that there was no possibility of an atomic accident. The Army's demonstration of the atomic tactical warfare problem was theoretical as hell, although staged by guys who had been doing a lot of scientific homework. The Navy demonstrated an anti-aircraft missile at sea, but something went wrong during the first demonstration. The Marines looked really good. They paraded around with great precision, then a couple of squads did a well-timed amphibious problem. In the evening, the Marines served the best meal and ran their entertainment without wives. This made it a lot easier on the civilians who didn't have to make social conversation but could really enjoy themselves.

In a different vein, the United States Army War College sponsors annually a "national strategy seminar" to which approximately one hundred outsiders are invited for an intensive review of American military and diplomatic strategy. In addition to a sample of "opinion leaders" from civilian life, the participants include government and university specialists, plus well-known advocates of "limited war doctrine." Although the major speeches have a strong public relations overtone, the intellectual level is comparable to, if not above, that of a university seminar on foreign policy.

The new public relations requires converting all personnel of the military establishment into informal spokesmen, for military managers are aware that the behavior and manners of military personnel lie at the root of public images of the services. The 1955 survey of public attitudes toward military service as a career concluded, "The civilian public bases its attitudes toward the military service more on reports from people who have been in the service than on any other source of information. The next most often mentioned source is personal experience in the service."[7]

The tactics of interpersonal and "face-to-face" public relations are no different in the military from those of any industrial corporation, and they are supported and enhanced by the military's preoccupation with protocol and good manners. Public inspections of Air Force bases, Army installations, and the fleet in port are regular and routine events. Military installations run "open houses" to which civilians are invited for informal inspections. Twenty thousand mothers and fathers attend the annual Mother's Day operation at Fort Dix, where they see first-hand the modernized type of training which, while not pampering recruits, offers a tolerable existence.

Officers are encouraged to write for national magazines about military affairs. The formula is that of commercial advertising: Stress the advantages of your own service, and avoid criticism of other services. Even wives are mobilized. The manual for Army wives points out that "the Army today is making a bid for civilian favor as the Navy has done. It is important that we merit the respect of taxpayers and that all Army wives do their utmost in promoting cordial relations."[8]

The Search for Ideology

It is most important to assess the impact of the new public relations, both on civilian society and on the military profession itself. One of the hazards of public relations is that the producers come to accept their own output uncritically. The effort to convince an audience is simultaneously an effort to convince oneself. Explicitly, the new public relations is part of the struggle of inter-service rivalries and budget justifications and, indirectly, a contribution to the international image of the United States. Implicitly, these activities reflect the changing functions of the military manager and his search for an appropriate self-conception.

It remains outside the capacity of social research—even with the most elaborate field techniques available—to give a clear answer to the question: What are the consequences of these public information programs on public attitudes and political decisions? Available research knowledge suggests that mass communications can be decisive in moments of crisis and tension, but that, in general, their influence is limited and has effect gradually, over a long period of time.[9] The influence of the mass media, supported by networks of interpersonal contacts among opinion leaders, is not in dramatic conversion of public opinion, but rather in setting the limits within which public debate on controversial issues takes place. To this end, the public information programs of the military establishment are important, even though it is impossible to say how important.

Assessing the impact of the new public relations on military leaders themselves and on the profession as a whole is a more manageable task. While the heroic model fought because of honor and tradition, the military manager insists on policy and ideological directives. The American military profession has always had individual men who spoke of the purposes and meaning of war in religious and nationalist terms, but, traditionally, they were at best tolerated by their fellow officers. The organizational revolution which has transformed military authority requires greater professional expertise. As soon as military authority comes to rest on group discipline, military leaders tend to press for ideological indoctrination. The tasks of managing more complex and more destructive machinery of warfare has led the professional soldier to become more interested in a set of ideological principles as to "why we fight." Self-evident objectives no longer suffice.

All of these pressures fuse internal communications and public relations activities The search for a "philosophy" goes hand in hand with the need to develop an image and a "line" for public relations. The reactions of the military are similar to those of American business leaders after the depression, when they consciously sought a philosophy, although in effect their public acceptance depended on their performance. William H. Whyte, Jr., in his reportage of business public relations, reveals the extent to which the business community itself is one of the major audiences of its own public relations.[10] A parallel pattern operates in the military profession.

During World War II, the need to assimilate large numbers of civilian recruits brought increased interest in ideological indoctrination. Could films, pamphlets, and speeches by company commanders speed up the processes of converting civilians into soldiers? Civilians continuously prodded the military to explain to troops "why we fight." Military authorities were fully prepared to create an organization to educate the newly inducted officers and enlisted men about United States "war aims," and to indoctrinate them as to the moral superiority of the Allied cause. While the response of the Navy was much more limited than that of the Army or the Air Force, an elaborate system of internal communications was erected in the haste of war which was considered by both professional officers and citizen soldiers as irrelevant. If the Information and Education efforts proved to have any function, it was not to indoctrinate the troops, but, contrariwise, to serve as an informal channel to communicate the enlisted men's attitudes and sentiments to higher command levels.[11] Public opinion polling by Information and Education officers assisted in this task.

If the Information and Education function was seen by most military leaders as a war-time device that had to be accepted, it was not possible to dispense with this machinery at the end of hostilities. The profession emerged from World War II with a sense of competence about its command and organizational ability, yet, military leaders had to recognize that widespread hostility had been generated against the privileges and authority of officers. The military establishment was planning for universal military training and expanded reserve programs, which meant that the profession could not revert to its pre-war self-containment. To meet the strains of handling the new type of personnel, the top military managers were prepared to enlist the services of communications specialists. Officers at the highest echelons are more likely than those of lower or middle rank to emphasize the importance of ideology and troop indoctrination, because of their longer separation from the direct involvement of personal leadership on which tactical units depend.[12]

The issues of the Korean conflict, including the behavior of American soldiers in Communist prisoner-of-war camps, served to heighten the concern with ideological indoctrination. Rather than being unique, American military personnel displayed the essential characteristics of human behavior in extreme situations. Soldiers in prisoner-of-war camps respond, in varying degrees, with personal

regression, collaboration, and betrayal. The degree of their response
depends on the brutality and positive efforts of their captors. The
Russian troops captured by the Germans in 1941 and the Germans
captured by the Soviets after Stalingrad experienced extreme treatment. The United States armed forces had a limited exposure to
such treatment after Bataan at the hands of the Japanese, but the
scale of brutality during the first months of the Korean war was
unprecedented in American experience.

In Korea, American prisoners were also subjected to extensive
pressure to collaborate with the enemy, because the political objectives of Communist powers require them to treat prisoners as
potential recruits. Officers and enlisted men reacted to Communist
pressure and indoctrination with great variation, but the differences
could not be related to membership in one or another of the services. To a limited degree, differences were due to the backgrounds
of the prisoners and to their previous training, but more important
was the kind of treatment they received at the hands of the Communists. Since the largest number of prisoners were from the Army,
the kind of information released tended to exaggerate the difference
between Army personnel and those of the Air Force and the
Marines. The ground force personnel captured in the early months
of the fighting came from garrison-type units which had not developed high social cohesion, and which also suffered the most
extensive mistreatment. These units supplied the bulk of the collab-
orators. Army personnel captured in later months behaved much
like those of the other services, as conditions in the camps became
more routinized.

The events of the Korean conflict would indicate that the troops
were not trained or prepared for the type of prisoner-of-war situation to which they were exposed. The defects in training were such
that, once corrected, they would have been better soldiers, but
whether their resistance to Communist indoctrination would have
been markedly different is problematic. When a complete evaluation
of this episode is undertaken, it will analyze the difficulties which
confront a political democracy in fighting a limited war. The military
action in Korea was not a "popular" crusade, and was at variance
with the notion that the United States always fights to achieve a
decisive victory. In the end, the number of men who went over to
the Communists when presented with an alternative was very

limited, while the Communists suffered extensively in this regard.

The belief that the Chinese Communists had perfected revolutionary techniques of indoctrination was disproved by two independent studies, supported by the military service.[13] The techniques used were well known, but in Korea they were applied with great intensity, although not always with great expertness or forethought. Significantly, there was a lack of correspondence between the degree to which prisoners were favorably impressed by the ideological doctrines of their captors and the extent to which they would go along in active collaboration. Albert Biderman, the author of one of these two studies, concludes that characteristic American tendencies, including a distrust of political dogma in general, and an aversion to Communist dogma in particular, formed a basis for resistance to Communist indoctrination. In fact, in a later paper, he inferred, on the basis of his study of Air Force personnel, that political education might have had negative consequences if it either undermined the distrust most Americans have for any dogma, or made men feel guilty about being apolitical.[14]

The shock to service pride, particularly in the ground forces, and to the American public was immense when it was learned that fellow Americans had turned traitor in Chinese prison camps. Popular reaction was highly emotional, and even responsible journalists failed to appreciate the complex military realities. The belief developed, and it has been hard to dispel, that American behavior was the result of moral and ideological weakness.[15] The report of the United States Senate Committee on Government Operations which investigated the conduct of military personnel in Korean prisoner-of-war camps was representative of civilian viewpoints.[16] The group paid no attention to the extensive defections the Communists experienced when voluntary repatriation took place. It overlooked the inherent limitations of resistance to Communist tactics by a partially mobilized armed force of a political democracy, and understated the actual extent of correct behavior by American troops. The subcommittee acknowledged that the armed forces were not solely responsible for the moral character of American youth, but it recommended ideological indoctrination, rather than suggesting changes in administrative and training procedures which would produce more effective military forces. The effect of civilian and congressional criticism was to strengthen those elements in the military profession who held that the armed forces should have a broad educational function.

For the professional officer the aftermath of Korea involved more than standards of personal conduct in military operations against Communist nations. Korea represents a case study in limited warfare and a demonstration by the United States that it was not pursuing a military conflict to the point of decisive outcome. Thus, it is understandable that elements in the military profession, particularly the absolutists, paralleling civilian political developments, would emphasize that, as a result of the Korea stalemate, the ideological struggle with the Soviet Union had become intensified. After 1952, the foreign policy pronouncements of Secretary of State John Foster Dulles stressed the importance of the ideological conflict. In the armed forces there was increased agitation to accept the assumption that the profession had greater responsibility for the ideological "toughening" of its members, and of civilian society as well.

One main focus in the search for content of the new ideology was at the very top of the military hierarchy, in the office of the Chairman of the Joint Chiefs of Staff, when that post was occupied by Admiral Arthur Radford. As part of the absolutist orientation of the reorganized Joint Chiefs of Staff, Radford authorized, in 1954, the "implementation" of a "program of Evaluation and Assessment of Freedom," entitled "Militant Liberty." John Broger, president of the Far East Broadcasting Company, was the central figure and formulator of this indoctrination program. Broger, educated at the Southern California Bible College, had served in the Navy as a warrant officer in the intelligence branch on the aircraft carrier, Bonhomme Richard. Appropriately, after demobilization he remained in the Far East and organized a broadcasting station in the Philippines, with funds from Protestant denominations, to disseminate Christian messages to the peoples of Asia. "Militant Liberty" supplied the basis for a conference held that year under the leadership of Chancellor Raymond Allen of the University of California at Los Angeles, at which Brigadier General Millard Young represented Admiral Radford.

The main principles of Militant Liberty were set forth in a pamphlet, issued with a foreword by Charles E. Wilson, Secretary of Defense, in 1955, and promulgated to provide "unified and purposeful guiding precepts for all members of the Armed Forces and the Department of Defense." The document speaks of "the ideological necessity" and postulates that "Communist ideology can only be defeated by a stronger dynamic ideology." "Free World Ideology is the sensitive individual conscience which stands opposed to the annihilated individual conscience of the Communists." As an alleged "theoretical" foundation for this ideology, any nation could be measured on a scale of one to one hundred by the extent to which it moves toward a "sensitive conscience," on the basis of six categories: discipline, religion, civics, education, social order, and economic order.

Despite its "top level" endorsement, plus extensive dissemination of its contents, organizational resistance frustrated the implementation of Militant Liberty. An interview by a professional journalist of a colonel on staff duty in the Pentagon reflected the widespread opposition, or rather inertia, in the armed forces to planned ideology:

You want to know what the G.I. is going to say when they hand him this stuff about how the Free World objective must be to develop tactics and plans . . . that will draw the Free World nations toward a consolidated position based on sensitive conscientious individuals versus the imposed class conscience of the authoritarian state? I can tell you what he'll say if it ever gets down to him.

But don't worry, it won't. This is just another front-office boondoggle. The Admiral says we need an ideology, so they hire a guy and appoint a committee that unanimously agrees we're all for clean living and American Motherhood and the rest of it. So the fellow writes up a lot of stuff that was said better in the Boy Scout Handbook, wraps it up into a capsule, and now they think they've got something like ideological little liver pills.[17]

From 1952 to 1957, military managers in the three services continued to debate the question of ideology in the profession. As indicated above,* the ideological consensus of the professional officer operates within the framework of administrative nonpartisanship. The search for ideology produced no more than a vague and undifferentiated middle-of-the-road political consensus. The impact of directives and discussions at top levels resulted in the most intensified professional uneasiness about not having an adequate ideology.

Yet, the search for a comprehensive ideology—to guide the

* See Chapter 12, Political Beliefs.

profession and for public relations—became part of the larger issues of military strategy and doctrine. During this period, advocates of absolutist doctrine were more preoccupied with the need for an ideology or a philosophy than were the pragmatists. In its extreme form, the absolutists' objective of ideological supremacy over communism led them to argue that an explicit political content is necessary for military life. The pragmatic officers resisted any effort to create an arbitrary philosophy. They recognized the necessity of drawing on historical and moral traditions, and they were less critical of the implicit principles governing the military profession. The most sophisticated among them felt that any effort to construct an ideology was artificial and might in effect interfere with the scientific and technical basis of the military profession. For them, realistic training, improved organization, and intellectual investigation of the problems of foreign affairs are of first importance.

The Air Force, with its commitment to absolutist military doctrine and its sensitivity toward public relations activities, reacted most ambitiously in the search for an ideology, while the older services were more resistant to such efforts. It instituted a variety of programs, almost devoid of historical reference and centering mainly on the glorification of air power. The Air Force official directive for its Information Services Program for the year 1956–57 came to public attention in the course of the investigations of the Moss Committee on secrecy in government information. Although the program had very little by way of philosophic content, it demonstrates the extent to which the search for an ideology and public relations have become fused:

This program has a philosophy. It has no intention of merely passing out information. Flooding the public with facts is very helpful. But facts, facts and more facts are quite useless unless they implant logical conclusions. Facts must be convincing, demonstrated, living salesmen of practical benefits. These are the only kinds of facts that mold public opinion and channel the vibrant tensions of public thinking, always deciding issues, in the end altering military policy as surely as defeat in war —they make public opinion the most powerful tool of all, more powerful even than war itself. . . .

. . . The following facts must be clearly understood and forcefully brought home to the American citizen as well as to our own Air Force personnel.[18]

In the body of the directive, there is no political content or ideology other than the assertion that air power "gives the United States the initiative in developing a climate of freedom in areas that might be enslaved morally, politically or economically." Congressional distaste caused it to be withdrawn and a new one was issued, more compatible with the rules of the game. Instead of trying to convince the public, Air Force public information was to seek "by all proper means to merit public esteem," and to enhance the reputation of the Air Force with the accuracy and truthfulness of its information. It was directed that the slogan, "the supremacy of air power," be fitted into the team concept of the military establishment.[19]

Air Force programs to modernize college campus reserve officer training corps programs revealed this same search for a philosophy. In the effort to make the curriculum more attractive, and in order to emphasize general education while leaving technical education to in-service training, the AFROTC developed the avowed objective of educating the college students of the nation for "air age citizenship." The content of "air age citizenship" training was a mixture of history, political science, and international geography as seen from the cockpit of a heavy bomber, and in support of Air Force doctrine.

These "educational programs" came under sharp criticism within the Air Force itself: Was it the responsibility of the Air Force to engage in such types of "air age citizenship" training on college campuses? A report by the Inspector General of the Air Force—the highly professional core of the service—dated July 1956, found that an intensive training program was required after AFROTC-trained officers were commissioned, because the AFROTC program itself failed to provide them with a good grounding in the fundamentals of military organization and procedures. According to Lyons and Masland, the report "quite candidly questioned the necessity and indeed the propriety of the Air Force's indulging in a broad program of educating the general citizenry, and suggested that the program be brought down to first things first—the provision of rated officers for the career service."[20] Nevertheless, as late as March 1959, the Air Force issued regulations directing itself to "the difficult task of trying to build back the true sense of values the country once had." The Air Force decreed that "in this immediate aim of reeducating the country in its basic beliefs, the military services had an opportunity to make a significant contribution—reeducation of the serviceman."[21]

The Navy has displayed much less receptivity to ideological indoctrination. The Navy, unlike the Army, did not face the problem of the conduct of its personnel in prisoner-of-war camps and, unlike the Air Force, was not confronted with reservists who were reluctant to perform flight duty when recalled. The absence of selective service personnel in its ranks simplified its tasks. Top naval officers were of the opinion that indoctrination of its personnel was a traditional function, and one which it was able to accomplish with great effectiveness mainly by personal example. Nor did the naval profession develop the belief that it had to contribute to the re-education of the civilian population. Its emphasis on tradition and the gentleman concept decreased the necessity of an explicit, politically-based ideology.

Nevertheless, there has been a gradual increase in formal indoctrination in the Navy, since indoctrination has become part of the managerial equipment of the armed forces. In May 1958, Secretary of the Navy Gates signed an order establishing a special staff to develop a program of moral leadership in the Navy.[22] He described the program as follows: "Each person in the naval service will be called on to review his own behavior, his precepts, his example and his sense of moral responsibility." The order directed all naval commanders to teach and enforce the principle of moral leadership, and Gates stated that the program would have repercussions in other services and civilian life. The materials for the program were essentially unpolitical, and stressed a generalized religious and moral ethic.

Although the impact of Korea was greatest on the ground forces, the Army made no declaration in which it assumed responsibility for a contribution to the re-education of civilian society. Internally, informational programs are considered something that the professional officer has to tolerate. Because civilian soldiers, inducted by selective service, pass so rapidly through military training, Army officials have come to consider the "information and education" programs of only limited consequence. In the Army the issue of personal conduct, which the Korean conflict created, has been defined as one of military authority and discipline, not primarily of ideology. After the Korean armistice, there were widespread demands in the Army for more formal discipline in order to maintain the fighter spirit. The Army took the most traditionalist and "old fashioned" line when the services revised the rules of conduct for prisoners-of-war so as to take into account the experiences of Korea. Army representatives believed that after capture military personnel should be bound to a strict code of behavior. While such a position was considered unrealistic in some quarters, Army commanders believed they were perpetuating the educative efforts of military law.[23] As discussed earlier,* despite the agitation for "stricter" discipline, the ground forces responded mainly with more realistic and improved training methods, since the older style of authority cannot be reimposed, except as a form of ritualism. To increase combat effectiveness, the ground forces also sought to enlarge the percentage of volunteers and regulars in the alert units of the Strategic Army Corps, rather than to engage in any massive indoctrination of selective service personnel. In its public relations Army spokesmen are still prepared to speak of the moral weakness of a nation which is unprepared to fight with its human resources. But the pragmatists in the ground forces tend to rely on symbols of patriotism, religion, and personal ethics, rather than political content, for their philosophy.

By 1957, the agitation for ideological clarification within the armed forces began to subside. United States foreign policy was de-emphasizing massive retaliation and "psychological warfare," and entering a phase of direct negotiations with the Soviet Union. The military establishment itself wearied of the endless debate as to the basis of military ideology. In 1957 the Joint Chiefs of Staff reviewed military public information and "cold war activities," and in fact accepted a set of delimited military responsibilities, which were being practiced officially, but about which there had been considerable ambiguity and disagreement.

The Joint Chiefs of Staff recognized that the military establishment was engaged in an educational program for its own personnel. It recognized that the armed forces were also engaged in community relations programs, in military assistance programs, in the stationing of troops abroad, and in a host of other politico-military functions which had political content. Responsible officers had come to feel

* See Chapter 3, Discipline and Combat Goals.

that the informational aspects of these programs required more explicit direction and coordination. Interestingly enough, the pressure for these new directives did not come from officers concerned directly with troop indoctrination, or from public relations officers operating with the American media, but from the officers responsible for strategic planning and military operations.

These directives were explicit in reaffirming that international information was the responsibility of civilian agencies, and that one of the major military responsibilities abroad was to give logistical support to efforts of the Department of State and the United States Information Agency. Yet, under civilian political directives, the role of the military in "creating favorable attitudes abroad toward the United States" was acknowledged, and the "public relations" mechanics spelled out in detail. What is important in these directives is the official philosophy which the armed forces have accepted as the basis of both their internal educational programs and their public relations.

In contrast to the political ruggedness of early efforts, such as Militant Liberty, the later objectives reflect considerable sophistication. In general, rather than attempts to create slogans to toughen the American population, these efforts represent a detached evaluation of the strength and weakness of American values in the world community. For example, the new guide lines inform military personnel that freedom and free enterprise are not synonymous, although they may be closely connected. The directives realistically point out that in many of the underdeveloped areas of the world, there exists a favorable image of Russians because they are seen as having modernized their society with great speed. Religion and education are cited as two fundamental sources of American values, but the limits of the applicability of United States educational and religious values are pointed up in a manner which eliminates any sense of crude nationalism. Officers and enlisted men are fully reminded of the liabilities of race prejudice and discrimination. In the attempt to state the "positive" aspects of ideology, equality and freedom are seen as central, to which is added brotherhood. Much stress is placed on the foreign resentment of any implication of the superiority of American behavior; while, as to personal qualities, Americans are described as strong and attractive.

Like so many contemporay intellectual formulations of American values, the result of this search for an ideology tends at times to become overly self-critical and negative. Yet, if the military profession has come to feel, in part because of civilian criticism, that it must have an ideology, what it has eventually produced is undoubtedly acceptable to most of its civilian political leadership. However, its efforts in this direction underline the fact that the military, like other leadership groups in the United States, could become doctrinaire and rigid under the pressures of prolonged frustration and crisis.

Notes

1. Bradley, Omar, *A Soldier's Story*. New York: Henry Holt, 1951, p. 147.
2. General Order No. 10–1915, Adjutant General's Office, 1915.
3. Cooke, Alistair, *Manchester Guardian*, December 8, 1957, p. 3.
4. Communication from Albert D. Biderman, May 20, 1959. The low figure for the Navy is due, in part, to a narrowed definition.
5. For the Air Force, 1,400 enlisted personnel and 230 civilians; for the Army, 2,150 enlisted personnel and 200–300 civilians; for the Navy, 500 enlisted personnel and no available figure for civilians.
6. Senator Paul Douglas criticized the Air Force for spending $626,074 in 1959 to fly 1,617 civilian and 774 military passengers to two aerial demonstrations, one at Eglin Air Force base, Florida, the other at Nellis Air Force base near Las Vegas. He said most of the civilians were influential "individuals of some means" on whom the Air Force was counting "to help build up a body of permanent lobbyists for its appropriations." Senator Douglas did not recommend that these demonstrations be eliminated, but that the Air Force institute a "pay-as-you-go plan" for flying civilians to such events, with rates based on commercial airline charges. (*New York Times*, July 17, 1959.)
7. Public Opinion Surveys, Inc., *Attitudes of Adult Civilians Toward the Military Services as a Career*. Princeton: 1955.
8. Shea, Nancy, *The Army Wife*. New York: Harper & Bros., 1954, p. 107.
9. For a summary of this literature, see Hovland, Carl I., "Effects of the Mass Media of Communication," in *Handbook of Social Psychology*, edited by Gardner Lindzey. Cambridge: Addison-Wesley Publishing Co., 1954, Vol. II, pp. 1062–1103.
10. Whyte, William H., Jr., *Is Anybody Listening?* New York: Simon and Schuster, 1952.
11. See Alex Inkeles' analysis of the oral agitator, in *Public Opinion in Soviet Russia, A Study in Mass Persuasion*. (Cambridge: Harvard University Press, 1950.) In the Soviet Union the oral propagandist, during the Stalinist period, also served as a channel of communications upward from the population to the party hierarchy.
12. Military leaders' concern with ideological indoctrination results in part from a misunderstanding of the control structure of totalitarian states. Like other leadership groups in the United States, they have tended to overemphasize the importance of propaganda in the dynamics of these states.

While mass communications is one of the crucial instruments of social control in the Soviet Union, and was particularly important in the rise to power of the Communist Party, the significance of mass persuasion depends on fundamental economic policy, as well as on police and administrative controls.

13. Biderman, Albert D., *Effects of Communist Indoctrination Attempts: Some Comments Based on an Air Force Prisoner of War Study*, Air Force Personnel and Training Research Center, Development Report TN-56-72. Texas: Lackland Air Force Base, September 1947; Segal, J., *Factors Related to the Collaboration and Resistance Behavior of U.S. Army PW's in Korea*, Human Resources Research Office, Technical Report No. 33. Washington, D.C.: George Washington University, December 1956.

14. Biderman, Albert, "Communist Indoctrination Attempts." *Social Problems*, 1959, 6, 312.

15. See, in particular, Kinkead, Eugene, *In Every War but One*. New York: Norton, 1959. Kinkead displayed considerable initiative in obtaining from military authorities access to the official investigations of the released prisoners-of-war and the record of their treatment after return to the United States. The series of articles he prepared for the *New Yorker* magazine were highly dramatic and helped develop public interest, but they did not focus on the underlying situational and organizational factors in the prisoner-of-war camps.

16. U.S. Congress Senate Report No. 2832, 84th Congress, *Communist Interrogation, Indoctrination and Exploitation of American Military and Civilian Prisoners*, Report of Committee on Government Operations Made by Its Permanent Subcommittee on Investigations, December 31, 1956.

17. Hale, William Harlan, *The Reporter*, February 9, 1956, p. 31.

18. Twenty-seventh Report by the Committee on Government Operations, *Availability of Information from Federal Departments and Agencies, Department of Defense, 85th Congress*, 2nd Session, House Report No. 1884, XIII-A.

19. *Ibid.*, Exhibit III-C.

20. Lyons, Gene M., & Masland, John W., *Education and Military Leadership*. Princeton: Princeton University Press, 1959, p. 227.

21. Department of the Air Force, AFR 55-11A, March 5, 1959, Air Force Psychological Operations, p. 26.

22. *New York Times*, May 17, 1958.

23. Hugh Milton has been active in these matters within the Department of the Army. He was a reserve general, who, before he was called back to active duty in 1951, was President of New Mexico Military College in Roswell, New Mexico. In 1951 he was recalled to active duty as a major general as Executive for reserve and ROTC affairs. In November 1953 he was appointed as a civilian as Assistant Secretary of the Army for Manpower and Personnel, and in August 1958 as Under-secretary of the Army. In 1955 he served on the Department of Defense Committee on Prisoners-of-War.

VIII

EPILOGUE:

TOWARD THE CONSTABULARY CONCEPT

CHAPTER *20*

The Future of the Military Profession

AS IN THE PAST, the future of the military profession rests on a balance between organizational stability and adaptation to rapid technological and political change. Military leaders must be prepared to solve, or perhaps more accurately, to live with a series of dilemmas. First, they must strive for an appropriate balance between conventional and modern weapons. New types of warfare do not eliminate older and even primitive forms. During the period in which the super-powers have developed atomic mass destructive weapons, the tempo of limited warfare, irregular warfare, and armed revolutionary uprisings in politically unstable areas has been intense. Perhaps the deepest dilemma is whether conventional military formations can be armed with tactical atomic weapons, and still operate without employing them.

Second, military leaders must be prepared to assist in accurately estimating the consequences of the threat or use of force against the potentials for persuasion and conflict resolution. The industrialized nations of the West cannot take for granted that mutual security systems against Soviet expansionism will receive mass political support, if these systems are viewed as increasing the threat of mass destruction. Moreover, as a basis for their national security, many political leadership groups in the new nations prefer "neutrality," to military alliance with the West. Historically, the

threat and use of violence to influence international relations has
operated within definite limits, and the development of mass weapons of destruction has drastically narrowed these limits.

Third, military leaders must make the management of an effective military force compatible with participation in political and
administrative schemes for arms inspection and control that may
emerge in the future. Any system of nuclear arms control would
probably enhance the importance of conventional arms. In fact,
some analysts have urged a return to a mass militia system in areas
of Western and Central Europe, as part of the process of de-nuclear-
izing these zones. Finally, dilemmas of the military profession include the assumption that in the event of an unthinkable general
atomic war—the so-called "broken-back war"—the final military
decision might well rest with the side which is prepared and committed to continuing the struggle with very primitive methods of
warfare.

Professional Requirements

To MEET these continuing dilemmas, the officer corps has been
seeking to redefine its professional requirements. The military profession, however, also requires a new set of self-conceptions. The
use of force in international relations has been so altered that it
seems appropriate to speak of constabulary forces, rather than of
military forces. The constabulary concept provides a continuity
with past military experiences and traditions, but it also offers a
basis for the radical adaptation of the profession. The military establishment becomes a constabulary force when it is continuously prepared to act, committed to the minimum use of force, and seeks
viable international relations, rather than victory, because it has
incorporated a protective military posture. The constabulary outlook is grounded in, and extends, pragmatic doctrine.

The constabulary force concept encompasses the entire range of
military power and organization. At the upper end are the weapons
of mass destruction; those of flexible and specialized capacity are
at the lower end, including the specialists in military aid programs,
in para-military operations, in guerilla and counter-guerilla warfare. To equate the management of mass destructive weapons with

strategy, and the management of low destructive weapons with tactics, has been and remains a source of professional and public confusion. The constabulary concept recognizes that there are strategic and tactical dimensions at each end of the range. For example, the tactics of strategic deterrence require day-to-day decisions from the management of community relations at overseas bases, to the timing of political-military pronouncements by national leaders. On the other hand, strategic decisions regarding limited warfare involve far-reaching policies about the size, control, and allocations of military units.

No longer is it feasible for the officer corps, if it is to be organized effectively for strategic deterrence and for limited war, to operate on a double standard of "peacetime" and "wartime" premises. Since the constabulary force concept eliminates the distinction between the peacetime and the wartime military establishment, it draws on the police concept. The professional soldier resists identifying himself with the "police," and the military profession has struggled to distinguish itself from the internal police force. In this sense, civilian supremacy in the United States has rested on the assumption that its national military forces were organized and controlled separately from the local and more decentralized police forces. The military tends to think of police activities as less prestigeful and less honorable tasks, and within the military establishment the military police have had relatively low status.

In the early history of the United States, the Army, as an internal police force, was called on to enforce the authority of the central government. As the authority of the central government became paramount, after the Civil War, the internal police activity of the Army was required to enforce laws strained by opposing social and economic groups—strikes and race tension, in particular. In modern times, the Army has been reluctant to become involved in such disputes, except as the ultimate source of sanctions. Such intervention, which often involves the Army in short-run political conflict, is seen as detracting from its ability to perform as a guardian of the nation. When called on to intervene in support of the Supreme Court decisions on desegregation of the public school system, the Army found itself relatively unprepared for such police work. While, as a public servant, the military automatically and vigorously complied with orders, such duty ran counter to their self-

conceptions.[1] The constabulary concept does not refer to police functions in this historical role. On the contrary, extensive involvement
of the military as an internal police force—except as the reserve
instrument of ultimate legitimate force—would hinder the development of the constabulary concept in international relations.

The officer in the constabulary force is particularly attuned to
withstand the pressures of constant alerts and tension. He is sensitive to the political and social impact of the military establishment
on international security affairs. He is subject to civilian control,
not only because of the "rule of law" and tradition, but also because
of self-imposed professional standards and meaningful integration
with civilian values. Moreover, civilian control over the military, as
it moves in the direction of a constabulary force, cannot be based
on outmoded assumptions that it must merely prod the military
into modernization or prevent a Bonapartist uprising.

Instead, the problems of civilian control consist of a variety of
managerial and political tasks. As a requisite for adequate civilian
control, the legislature and the executive must have at their disposal
both criteria and information for judging the state of readiness and
effectiveness of the military establishment in its constabulary role.
The formulation of the standards of performance the military are
expected to achieve are civilian responsibilities, although these
standards cannot be evolved independent of professional military
judgment.[2] In this respect, the conventional aspects of warfare and
military activities at the lower end of the destructive range present
difficult problems for civilian leaders. The adequacy of forces for
strategic deterrence and the conditions for atomic inspection and
control have come to be posed as scientific questions over which the
military have no monopoly of professional expertise, a fact which
they recognize. The adequacy of limited war forces facilities, the
management of military assistance, and the conduct of irregular
warfare are questions over which segments of the military seek to
perpetuate an exclusive professional jurisdiction.

Until the constabulary concept is firmly established, civilian
authorities must also be prepared to respond to the pressures
generated by the military definition of international relations. In
varying degree, military responsibility for combat predisposes officers toward low tolerance for the ambiguities of international
politics, and leads to high concern for definitive solutions of politi-

co-military problems. Military management—of strategic deterrence or limited war—involves risk-taking according to one set of premises; conflict resolution, nuclear test suspension, and arms inspection involve risk-taking based on another calculus.

Finally, civilian control of the constabulary must be fashioned in terms of the kind of military service required of the citizen population. Three alternatives are available: First, citizen service could be eliminated by relying on a complete professional and voluntarily recruited military force. Second, a system of universal public service could be enacted in which military service was but one alternative to civilian defense, community service, or human and natural resource conservation duty. Third, the present mixed system of a predominately professional armed force and a limited system of selective service, which must necessarily operate without equality or clarity, could be continued. All three arrangements are compatible with the constabulary force conception, although each presents different problems of political supervision.

While one may argue that a system of universal public service is most appropriate for the consensus of a political democracy, there is no reason to assume that a completely professionalized constabulary force would necessarily be incompatible with democratic political institutions. The technological necessities of warfare weaken the citizen-soldier concept, at least in its traditional form. The constabulary officer corps must be composed of highly-trained personnel, ready for immediate operations. Citizen reservists must be organized on a stand-by basis. Short-term, active-duty officers will be more and more replaced by men who are available for periods of five to ten years of professional service. Longer and more continuous service will be required for enlisted personnel as well. The trend is toward a military force of career professionals, although strong arguments, both military and political, can still be offered against such a development.

In considering the development of a voluntary career service, political leaders tend to pose the question of professional officer motivation more and more in economic terms. How much money will be required to raise the necessary officer and enlisted personnel? Studies have been launched by defense-supported research groups to determine the price and costs of converting the military establishment into an occupation competitive with civilian occupations. What will it cost to make a military pilot competitive with the pilot of a commercial air line? In the short run, the military profession, like other public service careers, becomes more and more effective as salaries are raised. Yet it remains an open question whether a political democracy should have a constabulary force motivated purely by monetary incentives. In the long run, it is doubtful whether the military establishment, like other public agencies, could maintain its organizational effectiveness merely by raising monetary rewards, and by making the conditions of employment approach those found in civilian enterprise. Monetary rewards might work most effectively for those officers engaged as military technologists. Even if salaries were to become truly competitive, the incentive system would not necessarily produce the required perspectives and professional commitments. Men can be motivated by money to undertake dangerous and irksome tasks, but the result would be to weaken essential heroic traditions. In a private enterprise society, the military establishment could not hold its most creative talents without the binding force of service traditions, professional identifications, and honor.

The shift from the contemporary partial selective service system to a fully voluntarily recruited and professional military establishment is likely to be a slow process. Although selective service operates only to supply directly the manpower needs of the military establishment, military leaders see the system as essential because young men become short-term duty officers and reservists in all services as an alternative to meeting the obligations of selective service. Political leaders are reluctant to increase military appropriations to the point of making military salaries more attractive, if not fully competitive. Thus, the constabulary force concept in the United States will have to be built on the contemporary system of citizen military service, although in the long run a completely professional service is likely to emerge.

The initial hypotheses of this study concerning military authority, skill structure, officer recruitment, career patterns, and political indoctrination were designed to highlight the characteristics unique to the military profession. Each of these dimensions is crucial in assessing the potentials of the military to modify itself. The technological and organizational revolution narrowed the gap between the "military" and the "civilian" so that it appears to be less than

in any other period in modern history. But the over-riding conclusion points in the very opposite direction. In the end, it is still
necessary to return to the original point of departure; namely, the
military establishment has a special environment because it alone
has the organizational responsibility for preparing and managing
war and combat.

First is the problem of military authority. The long-term trend
has been a shift from military authority based on domination toward
a greater reliance on techniques of group control and consensus.
The complexity of military technology prevents a return to older
forms if initiative is to be maintained. But there must be limits on
the newer forms of indirect control if military organization is to be
effective. What these limits should be remains an area of controversy. When military leaders operate successfully, they use their
organizational skills to produce stable and purposeful participation
at each level in the hierarchy of ranks. This is true for all managerial
leaders, except that in the military the threat of danger and the need
to endure the tensions of constant alert complicate the tasks of
managerial authority. As a result, the military profession is vulnerable to organizational rigidity, ceremonialism, and overprofession-
alization.

Although it can draw on the experiences of other organizations,
the military establishment must find its own authority equilibrium.
The style of management offered by university schools of business
which emphasizes cost-accounting, budgeting, and "human relations," and which has considerable vogue in military circles, is
probably not adequate for the combat formations of the constabulary forces But it is possible to assess whether the military are
evolving a form of 'fraternal authority"—the recognized equality
of unequals—which, theoretically, would permit initiative and
creativity within a hierarchical command structure. Such a fraternal-
type authority would be characterized by two elements: One, the
formal superordinate and subordinate roles, with little or no attempt
to hide the facts of power and authority. Two, from the highest to
the lowest levels, technical and interpersonal skill plus group loyalty
qualify subordinate personnel for effective but circumscribed participation in the decision-making process.

Human beings cannot operate effectively if they find themselves
under the pressures of conflicting authority. Therefore, the constabu-

lary forces must function as an integrated whole under unified com·
mand. The great divide in styles of authority is between the logis·
tical support formations and the constabulary forces. The military
profession has been slow to learn that the accumulation of those
logistic and engineering functions which can be performed by a
civilian Department of Supply weaken the effectiveness of military
styles of management. The profession seems only dimly aware that
the elimination of many of these research and supply operations
would, in effect, unify the military establishment and reduce the
strains on authority. However, it is evident that military authority, in
the most combat-oriented units at both the lower and higher end of
the destructive range, has become compatible with the values of a
civilian society which emphasizeѕ technical achievement, rationality, and pragmatic ethics.

The second problem in transforming the military profession into
a constabulary force is its skill structure. Skill changes in the military
profession have narrowed the difference between military and
civilian occupations. The professional soldier must develop more and
more skills and orientations common to civilian administrators. Yet,
the effectiveness of the military establishment depends on maintaining a proper balance between military technologists, heroic leaders,
and military managers.

The constabulary force will depend on the military manager to
maintain this appropriate balance. He is better equipped today
to participate in the management of international security affairs
than in the past, not only because of the improved quality of military
education, but also because his day-to-day tasks develop broader
administrative skills. He will have to demonstrate considerable skill
in segregating the constabulary functions from those of logistical
and engineering support, although they are obviously interde-
pendent. Even more important, military managers will have to
prevent the constabulary from being dominated or defined by either
the military technologist or the heroic leader. The military technologists tend to thwart the constabulary concept because of their
essential preoccupation with the upper end of the destructive
continuum and their pressure to perfect weapons without regard to
issues of international politics. The heroic leaders, in turn, tend
to thwart the constabulary concept because of their desire to maintain conventional military doctrine and their resistance to assessing

the political consequences of limited military actions which do not produce "victory."

Because the military establishment is managerially oriented, the gap between the heroic leader and the military manager has also narrowed. At the lower levels, to be a company commander, an aircraft commander, or an officer in command of a small vessel requires administrative expertise. At the middle and upper levels, the same officer must often fuse both roles, as the most routine operations become enmeshed in political-military tasks. By contrast, the greatest gap in the skill structure of the contemporary military establishment rests between the military technologist and the military manager. The technologist is likely to be most concerned with means, the manager with the purposes of military policy.

The contents of a military career for the multiple tasks of the constabulary force becomes a third problem. The military profession has traditionally placed heavy emphasis on a prescribed career involving a rotation through various assignments in order to train for top-ranking leadership posts. In the future it will require more extensive general competence from its military managers and more intensive scientific specialization from its military technologists.

Many military technologists will be drawn from civilian universities; even now the purpose of university-based ROTC programs is changing from that of supplying reserve officers to that of recruiting technical career officers. The extensive programs of sending officers to civilian technical graduate schools operate in the same direction. Higher technical specialization will result as the undergraduate curriculum of the military academies becomes more differentiated and permits some students to engage in more extensive scientific specialization. The academies will learn that liberal education is compatible with some degree of professional specialization, if students have adequate secondary education.

But the education and career development of future military managers also present the crucial problem of redefinition. Presently, the military academies are deeply concerned with whether they can adequately present an image of a "whole man," who, realistically, is both a modern heroic leader and a military manager. Can the curriculum infuse into the potential candidates for the military elite the skills of military organization and, at the same time, emphasize the traditions required for the fighter spirit?

Moreover, one of the basic findings of this study is that the strategic leaders of the past often prepared themselves for emerging tasks, not merely by following closely the prescribed career, but by their own initiative and efforts. Therefore, the problem of future career development is two-fold: adaptation of the prescribed career line to the needs of the constabulary force, especially in fusing the roles of heroic leader and military managers; and maintaining and increasing professional tolerance for those who seek to develop innovating careers by their own initiative.

The prescribed career of the future is one that will sensitize the military officer to the political and social consequences of military action. It is not true that all officers need to be broadly educated in political-military affairs, although this is a desirable objective. However, all officers must be trained in the meaning of civilian supremacy. Under the constabulary concept, even the most junior officer, depending on his assignment, may be acting as a political agent. Political-military education cannot be delayed until the middle of the officer's career, when he enters the war college. Officer education in politico-military affairs should start in the military academy where tactical training must be related to the requirements of international relations, and continue at higher levels of education and professional experience.

To develop a broad, detached, and strategic perspective, career rotation cannot be limited to any single service, if the officer is to gain understanding, by actual experience or observation, with the full range of the military spectrum. Unification of the armed forces realistically involes creating career lines which will permit selected officers to familiarize themselves with a greater variety of military weapons systems. In addition, it is doubtful whether the future constabulary officer can get all of his essential professional experiences within the military establishment. He will probably require duty in civilian agencies, at home and abroad, or with military agencies engaged in civilian enterprises, such as the Corps of Engineers who are working on technical assistance to underdeveloped countries.

Rotation through a wide range of military assignments is compatible with a greater degree of geographical specialization. In order for the military manager of the future to operate effectively in foreign areas, many years of experience—perhaps ten to fifteen years—are required. With the development of air transport, a counterpart of the old regimental system seems feasible by which an officer can rotate periodically from continental duty to overseas duty in the same area. Overseas duty would permit him to ac cumulate geographical and language expertise, while his career development would be influenced and molded by his continental assignments.

Such a career is fully compatible with a second career after the completion of military service. Under these circumstances, even the contemporary rates of officer resignation would not be considered unduly high, if they were not concentrated among those with the most superior talents. Rotation out of the military establishment, like professional mobility in civilian life, becomes a common feature of organization life and, in fact, assists in integrating the profession with the larger society.

Fourth, the military profession, because it has broadened its re-cruitment from a narrow, specialized, relatively high-status social base to a broader lower status and a more socially representative one, has conformed to the requirements of a political democracy. Even if the military profession increases the percentage of sons of officers in its ranks—as there is every reason to believe it will— there is little likelihood that the profession will become predomi-nately self-recruited On the contrary, in order to meet its personnel needs, the military will continue to expand the social base of its recruitment by relying more heavily on enlisted personnel as sources of officer personnel.

Because of the greater heterogeneity of officer recruits, social background emerges as progressively less important than profes-sionai experiences and personal alliances in fashioning the outlook of the military elite. But this does not mean that social background is of no consequence, for it still plays an important part in the com-plex issues of career motivation. The armed forces must continue tc tap those social groups most likely to predispose young men toward a public service and a military career. Sons of military officers enter the military with an outlook appropriate for perpetuating military traditions and the heroic ideal. The military profession will continue

to recruit heavily from more rural areas—although geographic concentration in the South has declined—since from this background
personal inclination for a military career persists, and the military
remains a significant avenue of social mobility.

Since there are no valid psychological instruments for selecting
military leaders, social background from a military family or a
rural setting are still meaningful criteria. Moreover, as the importance of social pedigree declines as a criterion of recruitment,
the academies have resisted, when possible, the application of purely
academic criteria as the basis of selection.[3] The social basis of
recruitment is likely to continue to operate to select persons with a
conservative orientation toward life styles and human nature. The
organizational milieu of the military profession is likely to re-
enforce such belief patterns. But, in the broadest terms, the internal
indoctrination system, rather than social origins, will determine the
political orientations of the military profession.

Therefore, the fifth problem for the military profession centers
on the increased importance of these indoctrination procedures. For
the constabulary force, the officer must be given a candid and
realistic education about political matters. But it would be in error
to assume that contemporary political education in the armed
forces serves all the needs of a political democracy. Since 1945, the
increase in advanced political-military education has been impressive, particularly because of the military's efforts to draw on civilian
resources. But this system has had a strong built-in tendency to
produce conformity to a service point of view. Masland and
Radway conclude that, despite the broadened consequences, ". . .
most military schools remain service-oriented and in this respect
the intangibles—the traditions, slogans and unwritten customs—
are of more significance than the formal programs."[4]

Much of the study of politico-military affairs deals with the
most general policy issues in international affairs, and, in this sense,
it provides an indispensible general education. Higher military
education, as well as actual military experience, press the military
professional to become more rational, that is, he becomes more
interested in the relationship between military means and political
objectives. But this is not an unmixed advantage. The professional
officer may come to exaggerate his competence in judging alternative political goals. His new knowledge may increase his profes-

sional frustration, unless it sufficiently emphasizes the limits on violence in influencing international relations. All evidence indicates that both absolutists and pragmatists—in varying degree—over-emphasize the potentials of force. The realistic study of international relations involves an appreciation of the limits of violence. Military education does not continually focus on these issues, as it relates both to nuclear and limited conventional warfare. Paradoxically, military education does not emphasize the potentialities of unconventional warfare and political warfare, since these are at the periphery of professionalization.

There is little in the curriculum to prepare the officer for the realities of participating in the management of politico-military affairs. While the case study and war game approaches give the officer a direct understanding and "feel" for the logistics and organizational apparatus that must be "moved" for military operations, there is no equivalent training for the political dimensions of international relations. The military establishment, especially the ground forces, operates a variety of special schools, dealing with military government, psychological warfare, and strategic intelligence, which are relevant, but which have as their student body staff specialists, rather than future members of the military elite. No arrangement exists for giving selected officers an integrated training in politico-military administration.

Moreover, military education at all levels fails to give the officer a full understanding of the realities of practical politics as it operates in domestic affairs. Because it is constrained in exploring the strength and weakness of the democratic political process, military education does not necessarily develop realism and respect for the system. Its content is still dominated by moralistic exhortations regarding ideal goals. Equally important, military education has little interest in discussing the standards that should govern the behavior of officers vis-à-vis civilian appointees and Congress. There is little emphasis on the complex problems of maintaining administrative neutrality.

Finally, the constabulary concept would be facilitated by an effective unification of the military and organization of the military establishment along more functional lines. The present military organization does not permit adequate appraisal of the relative allocation of resources on the various tasks of strategic deterrence, versus limited warfare, versus the management of international security affairs. But in developing unification, each service faces a different set of problems in moving toward the constabulary concept. The Air Force, in particular, as constituted at the end of the 1950–60 decade, was confronted with the deepest crisis. Its organization was dominated by heroic leaders, who had risen to the top by accumulating managerial skill. The imbalance in the future will come from the larger concentration of military technologists who will rise to the very top. The training of future military managers for the Air Force remains a most problematic issue. In adapting themselves to future requirements, both the Army and the Navy will be confronted with the same issue, but not to the same extent.

Military Intellectuals

IN THE MILITARY PROFESSION, as in any profession, self-criticism is an essential prerequisite in effecting change. But if it is to be more than self-castigation, self-criticism must have significant intellectual content. Intellectual ferment very often means stimulation from "the outside," even though the "outsider" may be found within the profession. The rise of the military manager has meant that greater effort has been exerted among officers to keep abreast of intellectual currents outside the profession. Ironically, the military profession seems to be vulnerable to new fashions in intellectual life, even before they have been submitted to adequate scrutiny.

Although military leaders do not think of themselves as intellectuals, their approach toward intellectual activity is a curious mixture. The military profession, because it emphasizes education and schooling, has a formal respect for intellectual achievement. The military manager must be prepared to make use of intellectual accomplishments, because he is so concerned with producing scientific solutions to complex administrative and organizational problems. Since the destructive capacities of weapons have virtually eliminated trial and error, military commanders are required to do their military planning more effectively. In such a setting, the products of intellectual efforts are deeply respected, to the measure of their practical worth.

Moreover, the educated man is seen as having an intrinsic merit as well. The military leader believes that the research scientist ana university professor is a dedicated public servant like himself, and, as such, is immune to the excesses of sheer commercial pursuits. The military stand in respect for those men in civilian society who devote their lives to intellectual pursuits, although there are impoi- tant service differences. Of the services, the Navy displays the least respect for intellectuals—civilian or military.

Negativism toward intellectual pursuits is rooted partially in the fear that unguided intellectualism produces irresponsibility. Clearly, action, and responsibility for one's action, are more valued than reflection in any organization where combat is the basic goal. Thus, despite its propensity to introduce technological change, the mili- tary establishment remains resistant to sudden innovations or bril- liant insights which might cause doubt and temporary paralysis. Among professional soldiers, anti-intellectualism can also express itself in an uncritical veneration of the military treatises of the past which, with almost metaphysical reverence, are taken as permanent contributions to military doctrine. Another manifestation of anti- intellectualism is the reduction of complex problems to technical formulations. Ideas are judged as practical or impractical after there has been a staff study by men who can exaggerate the power of their "generalist" thinking.

In describing intellectual pursuits among officers, the intellec- tual officer can be distinguished from the military intellectual. The intellectual officer is the soldier who brings an intellectual dimen- sion to his job. His intellectual quality is held in check by the needs of the profession. He sees himself primarily as a soldier, and his intellectuality is part of his belief that he is a whole man.

The military intellectual is a markedly different type. Although he is a professional soldier, his attachments and identifications are primarily with intellectuals and with intellectual activities. He would have no trouble shifting from military to university life, for his orientations are essentially scholarly. He is generally denied, or unequipped, for the highest command posts, as would be the case with intellectuals in civilian society. His position is essentially ad- visory, but, in the military setting, the advisory post is institutional- ized and accepted.

Both the Army and Navy point with pride to a past succession of military thinkers and theoreticians. More often than not, these men were recognized for their achievements long after the fact. Up until World War II, they served mainly as self-appointed critics, usually located at the military academies or the war colleges. They had relatively limited contact with civilian intellectual life, for the problems of conducting war or the role of violence in international relations were not the central concerns of university professors. As the source of their analytic approach, military intellectuals drew heavily upon history, but their outlook was derived essentially from the engineering sciences.

In the Army the first figure of distinction was Dennis H. Mahan, father of Alfred T. Mahan, the naval theoretician and ideologist. The elder Mahan served for many years before the Civil War as professor of engineering at West Point. Steeped in Napoleonic military law, he viewed engineering as a crucial component of military strategy, so much so that he insisted that his title be elaborated to that of professor of engineering and the art of war. Among his students were commanding generals on both sides of the Civil War. His conception of military operations as a complex engineering undertaking supplied the intellectual background for the emergence of the military manager. The line of intellectual succession in the Army included such names as Emory Upton, Charles W. Larned, Tasker H. Bliss, and John McCauley Palmer, each of whom was preoccupied with the organizational problems of converting the ground forces from a collection of regiments into a large-scale military establishment. In varying degrees, they saw themselves as concerned not only with administration and command, but as simultaneously contributing to a military doctrine and operational code which would embody American values. In retrospect, their contributions appear pragmatic, mainly professional, and relatively devoid of political content.

Alfred T. Mahan became the leading naval intellectual, and rose to prominence during Spanish-American War period. Although Mahan was concerned with professional and strategic problems, he was more patently a publicist and ideologist. Mahan's ideas represented a mixture of Christian doctrine, social Darwinism, and nationalism. Although he led an intolerable existence as naval officer, he became the foremost champion of naval power in support of national expansion

Between World War I and World War II no military intellectuals rose to professional or public eminence.[5] Since 1945, the intellectual ferment within the military profession has been continuous. Military intellectuals have emerged as a distinct and visible type. Their training, their activities, and their tasks are differen from those of the older military intellectuals, however, for intellec tual activity within the military has become organized.

First, the traditional intellectual isolation of the military prc fession from university life has broken down. One of the major task of the contemporary military intellectual is to maintain contact outside the military establishment. This task is complicated becaus the universities have lagged in their efforts to integrate the stud, of military affairs. Whereas the medical and legal professions fin their direct counterparts in the university community, the militar does not.

Secondly, intellectual life within the military is no longer th work of self-appointed spokesmen, but, rather, is carried on by trained professionals. In both civilian and military life, intellectua activities have become more and more group and staff activities This involves sending the brightest and most articulate military officers to civilian universities for advanced professional training. As a result, the services have a small cadre of their own Ph.D. intellectuals.

Thirdly, a shift has been under way from engineering as a center of intellectual ferment toward the social sciences, and particularly toward the study of international relations. This shift reflects a change from a concern with the purely "hardware" aspects of the military establishment toward an interest in the broader political implications of military affairs.

The relevance of social science as a basis for the military intellectual remains problematic. Social science can be a tool of detached intellectual inquiry, or it can be merely a device for supporting existing policies. In any organization as large and complex as the military establishment, social science is assured a measure of acceptance as ῾ managerial device, for personnel selec tion, for intelligence researcı, for internal management. But the aspirations of military intellectuals are beyond these housekeeping tasks. They are concerned with applying social science to the strategy of national security.

The most ambitious claims of general social science are put forth in the name of game theory as the basis of a general theory for managing international conflict. Game theory was originally devised as a form of mathematics, different from traditional theories of probability, which found its most fruitful application in the area of economics. The essential idea in mathematical game theory is that, by taking into consideration our own reactions to our opponent's response to our moves, we can evolve a strategy designed to make him involuntarily choose a course of action favorable to us. Such a theoretical framework seems most appropriate for international relations.

But a social science theory of international relations based upon game theory appears to be an unfulfilled promise, for it has not produced hypotheses and understanding beyond common sense.[6] The point has been reached where the drive for a general theory of international relations and a general theory of conflict resolution has become a rigid act of faith and ideology, rather than a problem-solving effort.[7] There is reason to believe that the relevance of social science for the military intellectual rests with its contribution to understanding the specific consequences of force (and other agents of social change) in molding behavior; that is, in helping to clarify the relations of means to ends in a variety of concrete settings.

The ability of the military intellectual to use social science hinges upon organizational arrangements, because intellectual activity has become a complicated group activity. On the one hand, the military intellectual requires detachment from immediate policy questions in order to produce new ideas and new solutions. On the other hand, he requires access to the military elite in a staff capacity if his endeavors are to be realistic and if they are to be brought to bear on the professional life of the military establishment. Attempts to utilize the social sciences for strategic issues in the military establishment have not been conspicuously successful, in part because of an inability to achieve a proper balance between detachment and involvement.[8] Some of the most conspicuous efforts have been tied too closely to immediate operational problems. At the war colleges, including the National War College, advanced research groups have been established to draw upon developments in the social sciences. These enterprises have not been considered highly successful, partly because expectations were too great and partly because the armed forces have been reluctant to underwrite sufficient long-term support. Nor have efforts to utilize social science by means of semi-independent research groups, under military sponsorship, been profoundly successful, except in the field of economics, where these enterprises have been effectively linked with both the military establishment and the most competent university-based social scientists. The efforts of the military intellectual will remain hampered until the university community develops a more organized and more sustained concern with the social science study of military and national security affairs

Control of Frustration

THE EVOLUTION of the constabulary concept is obviously more than an intellectual accomplishment—military or civilian. In a pluralistic society, the future of the military profession is not a military responsibility exclusively, but rests on the vitality of civilian political leadership. The constabulary force concept is designed both to insure the professional competency of the military and to prevent the growth of a disruptive sense of frustration. To this end, the following requirements must be met by authorities: one, to limit military goals to feasible and attainable objectives; two, to assist in the formulation of military doctrine, so that it becomes a more unified expression of national political objectives, three, to maintain a sense of professional self-esteem in the military; and four, to develop new devices for the exercise of democratic political control

With regard to the first requirement, from 1945 to 1960 the American military were not confronted with prolonged limited warfare and policing assignments which might have produced pervasive frustration, although there has been an accumulation of considerable professional discontent. In this respect, United States experience has paralleled that of Great Britain, in contrast to that of France. During the post-war period, the British forces demonstrated considerable resourcefulness in developing a constabulary concept to deal with their policing missions. As a result, they have contributed to the political stability of the members of the British Commonwealth and associated states. In part, the British forces have been able to draw on their colonial traditions, which sensitized them to the tasks of political warfare. Nevertheless, their experiences in Kenya and Cyprus were painful. The intervention at Suez, with inadequate resources, internal mismanagement, and conflicting and unclear objectives strained the British armed forces to its professional limits. But, in the end, political solutions have saved the British Army from undertakings which would have been profoundly disruptive of its professional ethic. By contrast, French political direction assigned its military such tasks that professional frustration and direct involvement in domestic politics were the most likely outcomes.

In Korea, the United States armed forces were tested to the utmost in limited warfare and, in the end, performed effectively. This is not to overlook the sense of discontent generated among many officers which has been nourished by military budgets which they believe are inadequate for limited warfare responsibilities. In the absence of colonial possessions, the direct tasks of policing politically unstable areas seem more limited, if not more manageable, for the United States, although commitments in the Far East present potential areas of involvement. Alliance politics may, of course, force the United States into policing actions in other areas of the world, particularly in Africa, where the United States has guaranteed, for example, the security of Liberia.

In the future the major source of potential professional frustration will center around the management of strategic nuclear deterrence. Since many responsible officers are committed to an absolutist doctrine, they still seek to perpetuate notions of military superiority in strategic weapons. An added dimension is the effort of military technologists to emphasize that biological and chemical weapons can restore the "initiative" and "superiority" of the United States. Although the idea of extensive disarmament is likely to remain illusive, important segments of the military establishment are reluctant to take the steps that are required to inhibit the arms race. The de facto, or the negotiated, suspension of massive nuclear tests within the earth's atmosphere is increasingly likely, either because they are no longer technically necessary, or because of both the political liabilities and radiological hazards they create. Some measure of limited arms control in very specified geographic areas also appears likely. Resistance to disarmament schemes among pro fessional officers, especially of the absolutist persuasion, is not mainly an expression of career interests, although this operates. It is an expression of a belief that in such negotiations the United States is likely to come out "second best."

In part, arms control constitutes a constabulary task, and the operational code of the military must be adapted to these requirements. The assumptions of the original Baruch-Lillienthal proposals that peacetime nuclear production and arms control be joined together were unrelated to the realistic tasks of international relations. Implicitly, these proposals assumed that the policing function could not attract the requisite human resources to be effective and creative. But the detection and control of radiation became scientific problems for radiologists and other health scientists. For the constabulary force, too, policing the suspension of nuclear tests and arms control is a positive function. It will require a division of labor between civilian and military personnel; and it will also require a division of labor between the United States, the Soviet Union, and the United Nations. In fact, these new tasks will involve the expertise of the military technologist, the military manager, and even the heroic leader—for there is much that is heroic in the assumption that these systems can be effective. Stated in other terms, civilian leaders, in order to prevent a sense of professional frustration, must make clear the new responsibilities that will accrue to the military in an inhibited arms race.

The second goal cannot be accomplished unless there is less divergence in the operational codes of the competing factions in the military establishment. There is every reason to believe that a more unified code will emerge because of the realities and pressures of international relations. The actuality of direct negotiations with the Soviet Union may force the absolutists to modify their goals; the pragmatists will learn of the narrow limits within which their recommendations can be implemented. Since the actuality of general nuclear war is remote, the question of the military operational code has real meaning in the day-to-day conduct of "international security affairs" particularly in strengthening mutual security alliances and in communicating protective military intentions.

The pressure of the differing military doctrines has operated as a form of countervailing power. During the decade 1950–60, while the American military posture became more absolutist, public criticism by pragmatic military leaders was extensive, and not without real effect. However, if these political activities of the military served national interests, they did not necessarily contribute to the strengthening of civilian control. In the next decade the pressure from the military is more likely to oppose pragmatic trends in civilian political leadership. To strengthen the civil service concept of anonymity, discretion, and subservience to political direction does not deprive the military of an active policy-recommending role.

By the same token, the effectiveness of the constabulary concept, during a period of active diplomacy, does not depend on ill-conceived and exaggerated "psychological warfare." The growing sense of frustration which leads the military to a search for a comprehensive ideology also contributes to the belief that the professional soldier should be a self-appointed publicist.[9] The military establishment must have an active public information role—both domestic and foreign. To remain completely silent is to invite confusion. However, the constabulary concept, especially as it relates to strategic deterrence, rests on a self-conception of the older naval tradition of the "silent service."

Three, the maintenance of self-esteem in the military profession, requires that civilian leadership be constantly aware of the conditions of employment in the military. The constabulary force obviously requires an adequate standard of living and a style of life appropriate to its tasks. Uninhibited criticism of this style of life by political leaders is deeply resented. A feeling of injustice similarly arises when the profession feels that the basic terms of its contractual relations with the government have been violated, as some have come to believe since passage of the 1958 legislation on retirement pay, which discriminates between retired officers on the basis of the arbitrary criteria of date of retirement. Because the military career has become the first step in a two-step career, greater concern with the mechanics of transfer is likely to emerge. Officers enter private industry, in part, because Congress has passed the Dual Compensation Act which deprives the officer of his pension if he enters government service after retirement. Since many officers wish to continue a public service career, university-based programs for retraining officers for educational administration, teaching and social welfare services appear as likely alternatives.

However, the self-esteem of the military will require a clearer public image of the constabulary concept. It is not enough for the civilian population to recognize its dependence on the military profession. It must recognize the worth and meaningfulness of the professional career, since such recognition is an essential component of the self-esteem of the soldier. To some extent, the worth of the military profession has been historically rooted in the importance of its non-military functions. In the past its exploration and engineering activities have enhanced its self-esteem and given it an alternative role in civilian society. Exploration has been broadened to include outerspace and undersea activities of almost boundless scope. The military engineer can become part of the international technical assistance and military assistance programs. The constabulary force concept is also compatible with a social education and social welfare function at home for the conservation of human and natural resources.

On the basis of a professional redefinition, toward the constabulary concept, new devices of civilian control become feasible. Foremost would be a congressional review of the adequacy of its own procedure of legislative oversight. In the executive branch changes would center around a stronger notion of a permanent higher civil service, and a system of longer tenure for political appointees seems in order. But the formulation by both Congress and the executive branch of acceptable limits for pressure group activities and domestic public information activities of the armed forces is not unimportant. Bold experimentation in the political education of the officer corps s also required. It is impossible to isolate the professional soldier from domestic political life, and it is undesirable to leave the tasks of political education completely to the professionals themselves, even though they have been highly responsible in this assignment. The goal of political education is to develop a commitment to the democratic system and an understanding of how it works. Even though this task must rest within the profession itself, it is possible to conceive of a bipartisan contribution by the political parties.

The political control of the military cannot be separated from the control of the activities of the Central Intelligence Agency, especially since Congress has avoided any such supervision. In 1959 a report of the Senate Foreign Relations Committee, concerning the views of retired senior foreign service officers, included the following statement: "It is true that there is little accurate information available, but every senior office of the Foreign Service has heard something of C.I.A.'s subversive efforts in foreign countries and probably most of them have some authentic information of this nature in some particular case. Unfortunately, most of these activities, if not all of them, seem to have resulted to the disadvantage of the United States and at times in terrible failure."

Ultimately, political control of the military profession hinges on the answer to the question why do officers fight. In a feudal society political control is civilian control only because there is an identity of person and interest between aristocratic groups and military leaders. The officer fights because he feels that he is issuing the orders. Under totalitarian control, the officer fights because he has no alternative. As they emerge into power, totalitarian political leaders make temporary alliances with military leaders, but, finally, they destroy the autonomy of the military profession.

Political democracies assume that officers can be effectively motivated by professional ethics alone. The officer fights because of his career commitment. The strain on democratic forms under prolonged international tension raises the possibility of the garrison state under which the military, in coalition with demagogic civilian leaders, wield unprecedented amounts of political and administrative power. In the garrison state the officer fights for national survival and glory.

But the constabulary force is designed to be compatible with the traditional goals of democratic political control. The constabulary officer performs his duties, which include fighting, because he is a professional with a sense of self-esteem and moral worth. Civilian society permits him to maintain his code of honor and encourages him to develop his professional skill. He is amenable to civilian political control because he recognizes that civilians appreciate and understand the tasks and responsibilities of the constabulary force. He is integrated into civilian society because he shares its common values. To deny or destroy the difference between the military and the civilian cannot produce genuine similarity, but runs the risk of creating new forms of tension and unanticipated militarism.

Notes

1. When they have intervened in domestic civil disorders, federal troops have encountered little opposition, except for the Pullman strike. In the past, the presence of a limited number of troops, for there were usually no more than a limited number available, has been sufficient to restore order and prevent further disturbance. By contrast, General MacArthur engaged in a relatively large-scale operation when 500 troops were used, with more than 1000 held in reserve, in order to evict the 8,000 bonus marchers on Washington, D.C. during the administration of President Herbert Hoover. The cavalry led the way, followed by tanks, machine-gunners, and infantry. The troops wore gas masks, and in a few minutes tear gas completely cleared the "Fort," where the bonus army lived in makeshift huts. Apparently, the Army had been requested to move into the troubled area without firearms, but the military authorities decided that if soldiers were to be involved, they would use guns, not sticks. However, this episode stands in contrast to the typical behavior of the Army in civil disorders. When properly trained, equipped, and commanded, it has sought to limit the display and use of force. See Reichley, M. S. "Federal Military Intervention in Civil Disturbances." Unpublished Ph.D. dissertation, Georgetown University, 1939.

2. Despite the growth of reporting and control devices, it is the infrequent real tests which lay bare the state of the military establishment. The small scale landing in Lebanon in 1958, undertaken under most favorable condition: was considered by observers to have been a defective military operation, aside from its political dimensions. See, in particular, Baldwin, Hanson, "Concern Over Defense." *New York Times*, 1958, p. 14. Such disclosures constitute the basis for fundamental civilian review of the adequacy and organization of constabulary forces, although, in actuality, this particular instance was not used either by Congress or by executive leadership.

3. In February 1959, the United States Naval Academy announced that it was changing its system of selecting midshipmen who entered by the reserve channels of non-congressional appointment and examination. While, in the past, the results from entrance examinations were the only determining factor for these candidates, thereafter, school records, leadership potentials, and recommendations from principals and others would be considered. (*New York Times*, February 11, 1959.)

4. Masland, John W. & Radway, Laurence I., *Soldiers and Scholars*. Princeton: Princeton University Press, 1957.

5. One noteworthy figure was Colonel Herman Beukema, who taught social science at West Point and anticipated post-World War II intellectual trends.

6. See, in particular, Shelling, Thomas C., *Toward a General Theory of Conflict Applicable to International Relations*. Publication No. 1648. Santa Monica: Rand Corporation, March 19, 1959.

7. Much of game theory, and other general theories of international relations, makes it possible for the analyst to think about international relations without constantly returning to the content of the real world. See Guetzkow, Harold, "Limits and Potentialities of Inter-Nation Relations Through Complex Organizations." International Relations Conference, Northwestern University, 1959. The task of social science is not simply to produce theories, but to in-

crease the understanding that might come from a theory. The purpose of
social science is to enhance the rationality of political leadership, but it is
clear that this purpose is not necessarily achieved by developing theories which
assume that international relations are guided by rationality.

8. See Janowitz, Morris, *Sociology and the Military Establishment*. New
York: Russell Sage Foundation, 1959.

9. A naval commander, without previous political-military experience,
served on the United States truce team at the Israeli-Arab border. Instead of
maintaining detached discretion, shortly thereafter he wrote a book in which
he issued a bitter attack on the Israeli government, although such an outburst
by a truce officer could hardly contribute to the constabulary image of the
United States armed forces. See Hutchison, Commander E. H., *Violent
Truce: A Military Observer Looks at the Arab-Israeli Conflict, 1951–1955*.
New York: Devin-Adair, 1956.

A rear admiral, annoyed with the impasse of the activities of the Joint
Military Armistice Commission in Korea, sought to throw the "spotlight on
Communist tactics," by inviting United States Embassy and service wives to
observe the proceedings, although it is difficult to infer what objectives were
involved. (*New York Times*, January 22, 1959.)

Methodological Appendix

IN ADDITION to the historical, documentary, biographical, and autobiographical sources, three systematic sources of primary data were employed in the course of this research. First, a historical sample of over 760 generals and admirals was developed for the purpose of analyzing trends in social background and professional careers. Second, a reanalysis was undertaken of the questionnaires administered to a sample of staff officers on duty in the Pentagon. These data were collected by Professors John W. Masland and Laurence I. Radway of Dartmouth College in connection with their study of officer education.* Third, 113 officers were intensively interviewed about their career motives and ideology.

    1. *Historical Sample.* The years 1910, 1920, 1935, and 1950 were selected as appropriate for analyzing the changing social composition and skill of United States military leadership, because the basic features of the professional officer corps stand out in sharp relief in periods between armed conflicts. The number of general and flag officers on active duty included in this historical sample, and the lowest ranks included, were as follows:

	1910	1920	1935	1950	Total
U.S. Army	14 (Brig. Gen.)	51 (Brig. Gen.)	64 (Brig. Gen.†)	166 (Maj. Gen.†)	295
U.S. Navy	29 (Rear Adm.)	67 (Rear Adm.)	61 (Rear Adm.†)	204 (Rear Adm.†)	361
U.S. Air Force				105 (Maj. Gen †)	105
	43	118	125	475	761

†Includes temporary rank.

    * Masland, John W., & Radway, Laurence I., *Soldiers and Scholar.* Princeton: Princeton University Press, 1957.

For the contemporary period, in order to get adequate data on social background, a short questionnaire was mailed to each member of the sample under the auspices of the Institute of Public Administration, University of Michigan. Three follow-up letters reduced the nonrespondents to a minimum; and the information supplied by the questionnaires was amplified by checking with published biographical sources. For the historical sample, an extensive search was made in available biographical dictionaries, *Who's Who*, and military publications. By means of a mass of correspondence with surviving relatives, and on the basis of information supplied by Professor C. S. Brown, State Teachers College, Buffalo, who, in the course of his study of Army generals[*] had contacted local historical sources, almost total coverage was possible, except for the 1910 members of the naval sample.

Material on professional career lines was supplied by official sources and by an examination of the Annual Registers of the United States Army, Navy, and Air Force.

The following classification system for analyzing the background characteristics and career lines of the 761 officers was used. It is reproduced here in order to facilitate comparative research on other military leadership groups, as well as on other segments of the American elite.

Code for Military Elite Study

1–4. *Identification Numbers*

5. *Service*
     Army Navy Air Force

6. *Sample Period*
      1910 1935
      1920 1950

7. *Rank in Sample Period*
      Captain, or lower   Lt., or lower
      Major   Lt. Commander
      Lt. Colonel   Commander
      Colonel   Captain
      Brig. General   Rear Admiral
      Major General   Vice Admiral
      Lt. General   Admiral
      General   Admiral of the Navy
      General of the Army

[*] Brown, C. S. "The Social Attitudes of American Generals, 1898–1940." Unpublished doctoral dissertation, University of Wisconsin, 1951.

8.   *Rank in 1950*
9.   *Rank in 1935*
10.   *Rank in 1920*
11.   *Rank in 1910*

12–13. *Date of Birth*

14.   *Place of Birth* (Double Punch if military installation)
      Outside the United States
      Pacific (California, Oregon, Washington)
      Mountain (New Mexico, Arizona, Colorado, Utah, Nevada, Idaho, Wyoming, Montana)
      West North Central (N. Dakota, S. Dakota, Minnesota, Iowa, Nebraska, Kansas, Missouri)
      East South Central (Mississippi, Alabama, Tennessee, Kentucky)
      East North Central (Illinois, Indiana, Ohio, Michigan, Wisconsin)
      South Atlantic (Florida, Georgia, S. Carolina, N. Carolina, Virginia, West Virginia, Maryland, Delaware, Washington, D.C.)
      Middle Atlantic (Pennsylvania, New York, New Jersey)
      West South Central (Oklahoma, Arkansas, Texas, Louisiana)
      New England (Maine, Vermont, New Hampshire, Mass., Conn., Rhode Island)
      Military installation
      Not ascertained

15.   *Size of Place of Birth at Time of Birth*

Rural	Urban commercial
Small town	Army or Navy installation
Urban industrial	Not ascertained

16–17. *Religion*
      Protestant—no denomination specified

Unitarian	Evangelical and Reformed
Episcopalian	Mormon
Jewish	Disciples of Christ
Presbyterian	Non-avowed
Congregationalist	Latter Day Saints
Baptist	Universalist
Christian Scientist	Christian Church
Methodist	Christian-not specified
Roman Catholic	Not ascertained
Lutheran	

18.   *Service Career Interruptions*
      Service career not interrupted by civilian occupations
      Service career interrupted by civilian occupations

19–20. *Father's Occupation*
      Professional, technical, and kindred workers
         No data
         Engineer
         Lawyer or judge

Physician or surgeon
Teacher or minister
Other professional, technical, and kindred workers

Managers, officials, and proprietors
Small commercial or industrial businessman (small business earned less than $10,000 per year)
Large commercial or industrial businessman (large business earned more than $10,000 per year)
Manager or official
High-ranked civil servant
Low-ranked civil servant
Politician

Clerical and sales workers
Bookkeepers
Sales workers
Other clerical and kindred workers

Skilled workers and foremen
Self-employed artisans and craftsmen
Foremen
Craftsmen and kindred workers

Unskilled workers
Truckdrivers, taxicab drivers, chauffeurs, bus drivers, operators and kindred workers

Farm owners
Farm owners

Farm laborers
Farm laborers

Military officers
General grade
Field grade
Company grade
Enlisted man

21. *Social Class Standing*

Upper class
Upper middle class
Lower middle class

Upper lower class
Lower lower class
Not ascertained

22. *Family Military vs. Non-Military Background*
Respondent's family has a military background or history (father was a military officer)
Respondent's family doesn't have a military background or history.

23–24. *Occupation of Wife's Father*

25. *Educational Institution*
West Point or Naval Academy
Private military academy plus selected state military university
State college or university
Private college or university
Business college

Didn't graduate
Not ascertained

26. *Type of Education*

B.A.
B.S. or B.E.
M.A.
M.S.
L.D.
LL.B.

Ph.D.
M.D. or D.D.S.
D.S. or D.E.
Didn't receive degree
Not ascertained

27. *Type of Commission*

West Point or Naval Academy
Reserve Officer's Training Corps
Officer's Candidate School

Civilian military academy
Line commission or enlisted man
Not ascertained

28. *Class Standing at West Point*

High class standing (in upper one fourth)
Average class standing (below upper one fourth, and above lower one fourth)
Low class standing (in lower one fourth)
Not ascertained
Didn't attend

29. *Number of Years Expired between First Commission and Commission as Temporary Brigadier General or Equivalent Navy Rank*

18–21
22–25
26–29
30–33

34–37
38–and over
Not ascertained

30–31. *Major Branch of Service*

Infantry
Artillery
Cavalry
Medical
Signal (Communications)
Armored
Air-borne
Engineers (Army and Air Force)
Air Corps
Line Officer (Navy)
Logistics
Engineer (Navy)

Intelligence
Ordnance
Quartermaster Corps
Dental Corps
Chaplain
Inspector General
Command Pilot
Operations
Special Service
Personnel Procurement
Judge Advocate General
Not ascertained

32. *War College*

Army
Navy
Air Force

National War College
Didn't attend

33. *Staff and Command School*

Army
Navy

Air Force
Didn't attend

34. *World War 1 Service*
  Army
    Troop commander—combat
      service
    Troop commander—no combat
      service
    Staff officer, divisional level
    Higher staff officer
    Technical specialist

  Air Force
    Combat flyer or test pilot
    Pilot—no combat

  Served in Army—troop com-
    mander
  Staff officer (Army)
  Technical specialist

  Navy
    Sea duty—combat type
    Sea duty—non-combat
    Staff officer
    Higher staff officer
    Technical specialist
    Too young
    Not ascertained

35. *Special Weapons Service*
    Pilot and aircraft research
    Tanks
    Paratroopers
    Submarines and anti-sub-
      marine warfare
    Strategic specialist
    Chemical warfare and explosives

  Amphibious techniques
  Atom bomb and guided missile
    research
  Bombing techniques
  Engineering specialist
  None, or not ascertained

36. *Instructional Career*
    Taught at the Army, Navy, o
      Air Force military academy
    Taught at war college or Na
      tional War College
    Taught at staff and command
      school
    Taught at private military acad-

  emy or state college with
    ROTC
  Taught at specialized service
    schools
  No instructional career
  No perpetuation
  Not ascertained

37. *Specialized Assignment Preparatory to Major Command*
    Intelligence
    Military attache
    Congressional liaison and public
      relations
    Liaison with foreign armies
    Special operations

  Military government
  Military historian
  Military assistant
  No specialized assignmen
  Not ascertained

38. *First Responsible Staff Assignment*
    In five years or less
    Pre-1939 general

  Neither

39. *Military Function*
    Technical specialist (ordnance,
      supply, signal, etc.)
    Technical specialist (medical,
      chaplain, lawyer)

  Operational commander
  Staff officer
  Strategic commander
  Not ascertained

40. *Political Activities*
    Ran for Congress or major po-   Ran for lesser political office
      litical office   Didn't run for office
    Political publicist   Not ascertained

41. *Geographical Area of Affiliation*
    Southerner by birth   Non-southerner
    Southern by appointment   Southerner by education
    Southerner by marriage   Not ascertained

42. *Languages*
    German   Chinese
    French   None
    Spanish   Not ascertained
    Japanese

43. *Post-Military Occupation*
    Cabinet-level appointment   Educator (civilian)
    Ambassadorial level   Engineer
    Top civil servant   None
    Major business post   Lower civil servant
    Important business post   Not ascertained
    Educator (military)

44. *Perpetuation of Military Traditions*
    Married into military   No perpetuatio.
    Male children are officers   Not ascertained
    Female children married military
      personnel

45. *Type of Career*
    Unconventional   : cascripoa
    Routine

46. *Nucleus vs. Cadre*
    Nucleus   Cadre

Pentagon Staff Officer Questionnaire. In July 1954 Professors John Masland and Laurence I. Radway, by means of an extensive self-administered questionnaire, collected a variety of data on military education of the armed forces from a sample of officers assigned to the Office of the Secretary of Defense, the Joint Staff, and each of the three services

The questionnaire was administered to officers of the following organizations:

Office of the Secretary of Defense: Offices of International Security Affairs, Manpower and Personnel, Supply and Logistics

Joint Staff: Joint Strategic Plans Group, Joint Logistics Plans Group, Joint Intelligence Group

Department of the Army: G-3 Plans Division G-4 Logistics Plans Division, G-4 Foreign Aid Division

Department of the Navy: Strategic Plans Division, Politico-Military Policy Division, Pan-American and Military Assistance Division, Aviation Plans Division, Logistics Plans Division

Department of the Air Force: War Plans and Policy Divisions in the Directorate of Plans, Logistics Plans Division, and Office of the Assistant for Mutual Security.

In all but one of these organizations at least 80 per cent of the officers on duty completed the questionnaire.

For this study, 576 questionnaires by Army, Navy, and Air Force officers could be utilized for purposes of reanalysis. In addition to the quantitative data collected in response to specific questions, officers who filled out this questionnaire were encouraged to respond to the following question: "In the formulation of national security policy, military and civilian authorities sometimes find themselves taking different positions. How does this happen?" The answers to this question supplied a revealing body of material on the professional military officer's thinking about civil-military relations.

3. *Intensive Interviews:* In the summer of 1958 a sample of future military leaders, consisting of 113 officers on duty in the three service headquarters, were interviewed intensively. The distribution as among the three services was as follows: Army, 54; Navy, 32; and Air Force, 27. The rank distribution was mainly colonels and brigadier generals, since these were the officers who within ten years would be members of the future military cadres. While in no sense can a sample of this size be considered representative, it was selected to reflect the attitudes of officers in the various crucial and important upper-staff echelons.

Contact was made with these officers by means of the public information and public relations staff sections of the three services. In each case, the interviewer described the objectives of the research and its sponsorship. No effort was made to establish rapport on the basis of simulated warmth or friendliness. Instead, rapport was developed on the basis of the relevance of the questions, and the ability of the interviewer to effectively probe their implications. A wide variety of subjects was covered, including occupational choice factors, satisfactions and dissatisfactions with the military career, career commitments, attitudes toward military discipline, conceptions of military leadership and management, retirement plans, and a number of questions on military strategy. Although the interviewer was equipped with a standardized list of questions, these questions only supplied general guide lines for intensive interviewing.

Table 31

Officer Personnel Tabulated According to Years of Active Federal Military Service June 30, 1958*
(Excludes Officer Candidates and Reserves on Active Duty for Training)

Completed Years of Service	Department of Defense Officers	Army Officers		Navy Officers		Marine Corps Officers		Air Force Officers	
		Regular	Non-Reg.	USN	USNR	Regular	Non-Reg.	Regular	Non-Reg.
0	22,843	1,318	11,283	207	2,557	219	351	229	6,679
1	25,373	1,516	6,096	1,586	5,187	260	861	564	9,303
2	20,341	1,318	1,856	1,397	5,153	330	1,038	837	8,362
3	14,830	1,278	1,811	908	3,260	254	977	1,221	5,121
4	11,487	1,163	1,622	992	1,069	263	509	1,518	4,351
5	12,055	1,147	1,485	1,402	1,781	403	701	1,622	3,514
6	10,489	1,039	1,280	1,372	1,700	370	291	1,460	2,977
7	11,644	1,241	1,692	1,289	824	496	245	2,320	3,537
8	7,269	1,028	1,099	810	402	252	98	1,306	2,274
9	10,716	1,101	2,186	933	657	323	71	1,874	3,571
10	14,139	1,158	2,588	1,192	888	346	87	2,886	4,994
11	13,755	1,255	3,541	885	728	321	43	2,627	4,353
12	12,726	1,665	4,006	1,064	443	290	39	2,134	3,085
13	11,881	1,502	3,898	1,294	379	326	30	1,924	2,523
14	14,348	1,606	4,201	1,971	413	304	26	2,688	3,139
15	25,633	2,742	5,520	5,604	589	1,184	106	5,354	5,534
16	23,707	2,944	4,677	3,994	299	1,434	89	5,567	4,703
17	24,425	4,010	6,423	3,839	143	1,003	22	4,680	4,305
18	10,300	1,808	2,286	1,983	68	535	8	1,304	1,788
19	5,680	881	1,026	1,704	46	430	21	849	723
20	4,210	568	331	1,733	15	361	7	615	580
21	3,474	460	281	1,423	8	290	8	527	477
22	3,276	440	262	1,544	1	275	4	398	352
23	1,981	296	102	996	1	212	10	206	158
24	1,738	237	84	918	1	146	8	195	149
25	1,184	218	70	603		69	1	134	99
26	1,166	172	38	733		60	3	102	58
27	1,068	176	39	632		71		84	67
28	1,030	162	29	615		78	1	87	58
29	812	122	18	487		59	1	96	29
30	1,451	308	5	837		97	4	156	45
Total	326,031	34,881	69,835	44,947	26,613	11,081	5,660	46,116	86,898
Average Years Service	10.64	12.54	9.88	15.22	4.83	14.04	4.72	12.99	8.60

* Source: Office of Assistant Secretary of Defense (M P&R), "1959 Survey of Military Retirement and Retired Pay." Unpublished Tables, June 1959

Table 32

Sources of Commissioned Officers, 1957*

Army	Number	Per cent
United States Military Academy	406	2.0
ROTC (regular commission)	681	3.3
ROTC (reserve commission)	12,987	63.6
Officer Candidate School	626	3.1
Other (medical, legal, etc.)	5,715	28.0
Total	20,415	(100)

Navy	Number	Per cent
United States Naval Academy	572	4.4
NROTC regular	1,209	9.4
NROTC contract	1,110	8.6
Naval air cadet	1,401	10.5
Enlisted men integrated into officer corps	2,698	20.9
Officer Candidate School	3,758	29.1
Direct commission (including medical)	2,169	16.8
Total	12,917	(100)

Air Force	Number	Per cent
Service academies	341	2.7
ROTC (regular commission)	222	1.7
ROTC (reserve commission)	6,179	48.0
Air cadet	1,583	12.3
Officer Candidate School	1,187	9.2
Other (including medical)	3,369	26.1
Total	12,881	(100)

* Source: Lyons, Gene M., & Masland, John W., *Education and Military Leadership: A Study of the ROTC*, Princeton: Princeton University Press, 1959, pp. 246–47.

Acknowledgments

IN ORDER to explore the problems entailed in a comparative study of the military profession and civil-military relations, a conference was held during the initial phases of this study at the University of Michigan, under the auspices of the Institute of Public Administration. I am indebted to the participants for their critical review of my working paper on which this book has been based "The Professional Soldier and Political Power: A Theoretical Orientation and Selected Hypotheses," (Bureau of Government, Institute of Public Administration, 1953). Those in attendance included: Maury Feld, Harvard University; Samuel Huntington, Columbia University; Kurt Lang, Queens College; Richard E. LeBlond, Jr., Temple University; Elizabeth Marvick, Los Angeles; and Louis Nemzer, Ohio State University.

Collection of the life history and interview data was made possible by a grant-in-aid from the National Security Policy Research Committee of the Social Science Research Council. The study was written during my tenure as a Fellow of the Center for Advanced Study in the Behavioral Sciences, 1958-59.

I had the extensive assistance of a number of persons in assembling data and producing the final manuscript: Walter Boland, University of Michigan, was active in the intensive interviewing of military leaders; Professor C. S. Brown, Buffalo State Teachers College, placed the military biographical data he had collected at my disposal; at the Center for Advanced Study in the Behavioral Sciences, Robert Scott prepared the statistical tables, and Miriam Gallaher undertook the editorial work. I wish particularly to acknowledge the assistance of Professor John Masland, Provost,

Dartmouth College, who granted me complete access to the questionnaire data collected in connection with the study prepared by himself and Laurence Radway on military education. (*Soldiers and Scholars*. Princeton: Princeton University Press, 1957.)

The efforts of my colleagues to read and review this manuscript were prodigious and indispensable. Carl Auerbach, Albert Biderman, Harry Eckstein, Heinz Eulau, Maury Feld, Roger Hilsman, Samuel Huntington, Kasper Naegele, and Edward Shils each brought to bear his special talents.

M. J.

Ann Arbor, Michigan
October 15, 1959

List of Tables

Index

Byroade, Henry C., 393

Campbell, Donald, 41, 52
Cantril, Hadley, 255
Caplow, Theodore, 149
Carlson, Evans S., 251, 256
Carlson, Sten, 102
Carr-Saunders, A. M., 16
Carter, William H., 256
Cash, James, 79, 101
Chafee, Adna R., 222, 232
Chennault, Claire Lee, 74, 84, 102, 113, 124, 195
Child, Marquis, 157, 172
Christie, Richard, 52, 148
Churchill, Winston, 172
Clark, Colin, 246
Clark, Mark, 71, 72, 75, 161, 172, 187, 299, 321, 390, 394
Clark, Maurine, 187, 195, 212
Clay, Lucius, 161, 375
Codman, Charles R., 269, 279
Colcough, Oswald C., 381
Colgrove, Kenneth, 272, 279
Collins, J. Lawton, 126, 297, 313
Connolly, Richard L., 381
Cook, Orval, 376
Cooke, Alistair, 413
Coulter, John B., 381
Couzzens, James Gould, 5
Cowley, Malcolm, 5, 16
Craig, Malin, 171
Croffut, W. A., 278
Croker, George W., 394
Crommelin, John, 389
Crossman, Richard H. S., 279
Crozier, William, 45, 256

Daugherty, William, 343
Davidson, Garrison H., 17, 195, 211
Davis, Arthur K., 52, 151, 171
Davis, George W., 152
Dean, William F., 381
Demeter, Karl, 23, 36, 101
Dern, George H., 296

Deutsch, Karl, 344
Devers, Jacob, 161, 297
Deweerd, H. A., 171
Dewey, George, 158
Dexter, Lewis, 357
Dinerstein, R. S., 329, 344
Donovan, Robert J., 312, 321
Doolittle, James, 44, 154, 375, 383
Douglas, Paul, 358, 376, 413
Drum, Hugh, 295
Dulles, Allen, 380
Dulles, John Foster, 315, 320, 332
Dupuy, Richard E., 74, 148, 170

Eaker, Ira C., 376
Eddleman, Clyde, 314, 315
Eichelberger, Robert L., 84, 02, 161, 295
Eisenhower, Dwight, 154, 156, 157, 159, 274, 287, 288, 297–299, 311, 313, 316, 317, 321, 332, 369
Eisenstadt, S. N., 102
Ekirch, Arthur A., Jr., 232, 256
Elias, Norbert, 37
Embry, Basil, 320

Fainsod, Merle, 272
Fairfield, William S., 394
Fellers, Bonner F., 295, 390
Felt, Harry D., 320
Fischer, G. H., 256
Fiske, Bradley, 158
Flanagan, John, 146
Fleming, Philip, 256, 393
Foster, Paul Frederick, 379
Fox, Alonzo P., 315
Fox, T. R., 16
Frazier, E. Franklin, 138, 149
Freeman, Felton D., 52

Gallup, George, 227
Gannon, Robert, 387
Ganoe, William, 212
Garthoff, Raymond L. 257, 278, 330, 344

Morris Janowitz (1919–1988)

After graduating from New York University, Janowitz went to work for the Department of Justice Special War Policies Unit. In 1943, he entered the U.S. Army as a private attached to the Office of Strategic Services (OSS). In 1945, he received a field commission as a 2d Lieutenant as a result of his valuable work in psychological warfare. He earned his PhD in sociology from the University of Chicago in 1948 with a study examining how serving with black soldiers influenced the attitudes of white enlisted men. In that same year he and Edward A. Shils, a wartime colleague, published "Cohesion and Disintegration in the Wehrmacht in World War II" in *Public Opinion Quarterly*. The article broke new ground in understanding why soldiers fight.

Janowitz taught at the University of Michigan in the 1950s. In 1958 Janowitz and William E. Daugherty compiled *A Psychological Warfare Casebook*, a foundational text for the armed forces. From 1960 until retirement he taught at the University of Chicago, and also edited the extensive Heritage of Sociology series. He was honored by the army and air force for his service as a civilian.

He founded the Inter-University Seminar on the Armed Forces and Society, bringing together scholars from inside and outside the military, to improve research. The IUS remains a vital force in civil-military relations and scholarship today, publishing the journal *Armed Forces & Society*. Janowitz's publications include *Dynamics of Prejudice* (with Bruno Bettelheim, 1950), *The Community Press in an Urban Setting* (1967), *Institution Building in Urban Education* (1969), *Social Control of the Welfare State* (1976), *The Last Half-Century* (1978), *Mobility, Subjective Deprivation and Ethnic Hostility* (1980), and *The Reconstruction of Patriotism* (1983).

Bibliography of Publications of Inter-University Seminar on Armed Forces and Society

Books and Monographs

Morris Janowitz, *Sociology and the Military Establishment*, New York: Russell Sage Foundation, 1959.

Morris Janowitz, *The Professional Soldier*, Glencoe: The Free Press, 1960; second edition with new prologue, 1971.

Morris Janowitz (ed.), *The New Military*, New York: Russell Sage Foundation, 1964. (Contributors: Biderman, Feld, Grusky, Lang, Lissak, Little, Lovell, Seaton, Simon, Zald.)

Morris Janowitz, *The Military in the Political Development of New Nations*, Chicago: University of Chicago Press, 1964.

Morris Janowitz with Roger Little, *Sociology and the Military Establishment* (Revised Edition), New York: Russell Sage Foundation, 1965.

Kurt Lang, "Military Sociology: A Trend Report and Bibliography," *Current Sociology*, Vol. 13, No. 1 (1965), pp. 1–55.

Samuel M. Meyers and Albert D. Biderman (eds.), *Mass Behavior in Battle and Captivity; The Communist Soldier in the Korean War*, Research Studies directed by William C. Bradbury, Chicago: University of Chicago Press, 1968. (Contributors: Bradbury, Kirkpatrick, Meyers, Uliassi.)

Jacques van Doorn (ed.), *Armed Forces and Society*, The Hague: Mouton, 1968. (Contributors: Participants of the Working Group on Armed Forces and Society at the Sixth World Congress of Sociology, Evian, France, September, 1966.)

Henry Bienen (ed.), *The Military Intervenes*, New York: Russell Sage Foundation, 1968.

Gary L. Wamsley, *Selective Service and a Changing America*, Columbus: Charles E. Merrill Co., 1968.

Roger W. Little (ed.), *Selective Service in American Society*, New York: Russell Sage Foundation, 1969. (Contributors: Davis and Dolbeare, Katenbrink, Little, Marmion, Moskos, Roff, Wamsley.)

Jacques van Doorn (ed.), *Military Professions and Military Re-*

gimes, The Hague: Mouton, 1969. (Contributors: Participants of the London Conference on Armed Forces and Society, 1967.)

Henry Bienen, *The Military and Political Development*, New York: Atherton, 1968.

Charles C. Moskos, Jr., *The American Enlisted Man*, New York: Russell Sage Foundation, 1970.

Roger W. Little (ed.), *A Handbook of Military Institutions*, Sage Series on Armed Forces and Society, Beverly Hills: Sage Publications, 1971.

Charles C. Moskos, Jr., *Public Opinion and the Military Establishment*, Sage Research Progress Series on War, Revolution and Peacekeeping, Beverly Hills: Sage Publications, 1971.

Robin Luckman, *The Nigerian Military: A Sociological Analysis of Authority and Revolt, 1960–67*, New York: Cambridge University Press, 1971.

Morris Janowitz and Jacques van Doorn, *On Military Regimes*, Vol. I; *On Military Regimes*, Vol. II, Rotterdam: University of Rotterdam Press, 1971. (Contributors: Participants of the Working Group on Armed Forces and Society at the Seventh World Congress of Sociology, Varna, 1972).

Kurt Lang, *Military Institutions and the Sociology of War: A Review of the Literature with Annotated Bibliography*, Beverly Hills: Sage Publications, 1972.

Bengt Abrahamson, *Military Professionalization and Political Power*, Beverly Hills: Sage Publications, 1972.

Sam C. Sarkesian (ed.), *The Military-Industrial Complex: A Reassessment*, Sage Research Progress Series on War, Revolution and Peacekeeping, Vol. II, Beverly Hills: Sage Publications, 1972.

Philippe C. Schmitter (ed.), *Military Rule in Latin America: Functions, Consequences, and Perspectives*, Beverly Hills: Sage Publications, Inc., 1973.

John P. Lovell and Philip Kronenberg (eds.), *New Civil-Military Relations*, New Brunswick: Transactions Books, 1973.

James Clotfelter, *The Military in American Politics*, New York: Harper and Row, 1973.

Catherine McArdle Kelleher (ed.), *Civil-Military Systems: A Comparative Analysis*, Sage Research Progress Series on War, Revolution and Peacekeeping, Vol. IV, Beverly Hills: Sage Publications, 1974.

Zeb B. Bradford and Frederic J. Brown, *The United States Army in Transition*, Beverly Hills: Sage Publications, 1974.

Morris Janowitz, "Toward a Redefinition of Military Strategy in International Relations," *World Politics*, July 1974, pp. 473–508